Teaching for Intelligence I: A Collection of Ar ticles

edited by
Barbara Z. Presseisen

SkyLight
PROFESSIONAL DEVELOPMENT
Arlington Heights, Illinois

Teaching for Intelligence I: A Collection of Articles

Published by SkyLight Professional Development
2626 S. Clearbrook Dr., Arlington Heights, IL 60005-5310
Phone 800-348-4474, 847-290-6600
Fax 847-290-6609
info@skylightedu.com
http://www.skylightedu.com

Senior Vice President, Product Development: Robin Fogarty
Director, Product Development: Ela Aktay
Acquisitions Editor: Jean Ward
Editor: Barb Lightner
Cover Designer and Illustrator: David Stockman
Book Designers/Formatters: Christina Georgi, Donna Ramirez
Proofreader: Ann Wilson
Indexer: Candice Cummins Sunseri
Production Supervisor: Bob Crump

ISBN 1-57517-152-X
LCCCN: 98-61805

2400B-V
Item number 1718

ZYXWVUTSRQPONMLKJIHGFEDCB
06 05 04 03 02 01 00 99   15 14 13 12 11 10 9 8 7 6 5 4 3 2

ontents

Introduction

Teaching for Intelligence

T he 1998 Teaching for Intelligence Conference represents an important milestone in American education and international dialogue for at least two reasons. First, it focuses on key speakers whose works constitute major ideas about pedagogy and achievement that have been developed throughout the twentieth century. Many of the writers in the first section of this volume and various contributors in the following three sections are researchers and theorists who have grappled with the central tenets of teaching for intelligence and now report on their most significant findings.

Secondly, the presenters at this international conference have collectively examined the output of fifteen years of school reform in the United States and now ask, from one advocated approach, whether significant answers have been generated that can guide future education and practice and make a difference in students' lives wherever they live. On both counts, this collection of perspectives documents positive responses and provides extensive details that suggest viable next steps for the advancement of both American and global schooling.

The first section of this volume underlines what teaching for intelligence actually means: emphasizing the *intent* that students and teachers need to value inquiry, critical thinking, problem posing, and problem solving. From Sizer's praise of the skeptical mind to Greene's faith in rich conversation and dialogue, the objective of students actively engaged in thought and knowledge generation is the foremost goal of teaching and learning. Cognitive scientists such as Sternberg and Gardner emphasize *process* as well as *content*, and open the door to questions about methodology and the pursuit of *depth of meaning* in instruction. They raise the issues of who is the learner and under what conditions can teachers actually instruct for intelligence development. In the second and third sections of this volume, writers such as Rosenshine, Darling-Hammond, Barell, and Fogarty provide responses to these queries and report on empirical research findings that show that teaching for intelligence indeed does work.

The papers in this collection challenge educators to go back to the beginning of the current reform period and ask how teaching for intelligence has made a difference to the issues raised by *A Nation at Risk* (1983) or *Academic Preparation for College: What Students Need to Know and Be Able to Do* (1983). In the first case, writers in this volume suggest American schools have failed to serve their constituencies well because the goal to have all students learn to be intelligent has not really been pursued. Every student can learn and, given appropriate conditions for learning, can succeed academically in terms of his or her potential. But merely covering curriculum is not sufficient as the question of academic preparation is faced. The curriculum must be *accessible* to the learner. Whether it is in reading or mathematics or the wisdom of sound moral choices, according to Strickland, Gardner, Ginsburg, and Sternberg, teaching for intelligence can enable learners to master the skills and cognitive operations that underlie all the "frames of mind" necessary for every thinker's lifelong learning. The critical dimensions taught by experience in studying the arts, as Eisner suggests, or sound mechanisms of learning that increase one's knowledge base, as Rosenshine proposes, can transfer to other forms of decision making and help the young learner face new and varied issues that arise in a complex, fast-changing world.

One important educational development is particularly highlighted in this unique volume. We actually have learned a great deal about classroom instruction for intelligence in these valuable fifteen years. From understanding the requisites of a thinking classroom, to appreciating the importance of teacher support and setting up university partnerships, to learning from research about gifted and talented students, the years of American educational reform have not been an idle period. Writers such as Cooper, Levine, Renzulli, and Ben-Hur cite many successes in practical, instructional implementations of getting students to think. Their point is that we should be continually following up these studies and seeing that their results are promoted to others. The significance of past research and the need to continue its momentum are important outcomes in the collection of studies included in the 1998 conference. Although the documents speak for themselves, we need to see that their message is shared.

Last, but hardly least, the needs of special students were carefully addressed by several key contributors to the conference. The fourth section of this volume underlines how crucial teaching for intelligence is for children from poor, depressed, and immigrant backgrounds. These are children who are school-dependent for learning higher-order thinking skills. Whether it is Kozol or Comer describing the desperate conditions of children with such needs, it is also important to know that here, too, there are successes to report. The requisites of a *community* of learning are well known in a post-Vygotsky world. Child-centered environments, places that nurture thoughtfulness and focus on appropriate development and experience, can make all the difference in a child's ultimate ability and skill. The challenge is to provide such caring environments for all youngsters in need.

What does the 1998 Teaching for Intelligence Conference ultimately tell American education? It maintains that such teaching holds great promise for *all* America's learners. It advises us to study more carefully where we have been educationally over these past fifteen years. Beyond current schooling's narrow focus on IQs, standardized test scores, and minimal curriculum requirements, there is a vast world of thought, inquiry, wisdom, and beauty ready to help educate children. Open this volume and see what a treasure we have—pedagogical knowledge about *teaching for intelligence.*

Section 1

The Need for Intelligence in Schooling

F or centuries, there have been numerous philosophers and educational theorists who have called for "intelligence" in schooling. In America, such advocacy has sometimes clashed with demands for practical knowledge and empirical application. During periods of reform, however, researchers and educational leaders become more energized about intelligent teaching because they see policies and practices in place that actually run counter to this long-held approach. They also see the potential and promise of bringing intelligence development to the center of American schools.

This initial section reveals many of the essential arguments embedded in the need for intelligence in schooling. They have emerged over the last half century of educational research and represent philosophical, psychological, and sociological underpinnings of theory about pedagogy and achievement. Whether it is Sizer's informed skepticism or Goodlad's intended learning, these writers call for the development of an inquiring mind and the cultivation of critical skill. Above all, these experienced educators say, habits of thoughtfulness need to be accessible to all students so that as learners they become part of a stimulating, sensory environment—the surround of Goodlad's study. Such belongingness in a learning community, like citizenship in the Republic, is key to upholding the basic ideals of democracy and capitalism.

The contents or subjects of schooling are also entwined with their intelligent pursuit. Teaching thinking has long been associated with learning the disciplines of knowledge, but classroom educators are cautioned not to strive for mere "coverage" of academic content. Gardner and Greene both emphasize the importance of *depth of meaning* in the student's developing mastery. Intelligent education requires more than the mere transmission of knowledge from one generation to another; rather, the active use of information calls for instruction that creates uncommon experience, that forges new relationships, that sometimes raises uncomfortable issues and innovative challenges. Greene, in particular, emphasizes the importance of rich dialogue in learning, of conversation amidst new experience, so as to weave intricate nuances of thought into a creative, human act. The school of intelligent thinking must be a cauldron of invention and, down deep, the advocates of teaching for intelligence believe it is important to be avid humanists as well.

Among the supporters of intelligent education, the cognitive scientists question what the abilities that constitute intelligent behavior are. Gardner's multiple "frames of mind" are held in high repute and, to Goodlad, are only a starting point of a more fully defined education. Sternberg acknowledges that teaching *for* intelligence, based in constantly growing memory, involves building analytic, creative, and practical skill, as he has long advocated in his triarchic theory. Sternberg also calls for a new understanding of wisdom, an educated person's power to judge rightly and, ultimately, to select a sound course of action. Sternberg's approach emphasizes tacit knowing; the learner needs to become sensitive to what is not openly expressed, to what may only be implied and silently understood. It is in this sensitivity that intuition comes to play an important role in more complex thinking. It is in this sensitivity that values of the larger community can come to mediate the thought and reasoning generated by "book knowledge." Teaching for intelligence, with a goal to develop wisdom, can thus influence the moral base of society and, at the same time, strive for the achievement of the common good. In teaching for intelligence, then, Sternberg seeks to develop a new model of a balanced, *wise* education. He pushes the blueprint on teaching for intelligence forward into the realm of social, emotional, and ethical behavior.

It seems apparent that the larger landscape of teaching for intelligence is drawn in the writings of this initial section. This is not an easily mastered body of readings, but it is rich in ideas and represents many years of research and thought about productive teaching and lifelong learning. These selections also raise many of the issues that others will address in later entries: the role of questioning in the interplay between teacher and student, the rare understandings built by study of the various arts, the interdisciplinary relationships among several academic contents, and the special needs of certain groups and particular kinds of learners. Yet, these thoughtful studies speak in one voice about the importance of teaching for intelligence. In a world where communication grows so rapidly that how teaching occurs is altered daily, these major educational thinkers underscore that why it is important that we teach at all has not changed for centuries.

On the Habit of Informed Skepticism

by Theodore R. Sizer

L anguage tells us much about an age, including our own. It serves us always to listen to ourselves, testing the words we use, sensing what lies behind them. Words matter.

I recently received an invitation to a conference in Washington. Its focus was on what the conference announcement described as the "alignment of standards" for children, their schools, and their teachers. The conference invitation stated how vital standards were to improving education, yet how difficult they were to use effectively in practice because of their sheer number and complexity. The invitation called the alignment of standards one of the most essential and crucial issues facing educators today. This conference was to help to bring order to what was assumed to be a chaotic and thus incompetent educational system.

I know that the term *standards* is today's hottest educational catchword. Usually it is preceded by adjectives such as "rigorous," "tough," and "world class" (whatever that means). Apparently the simple word *standards* is not enough. It has to wear a hair shirt. Its presence in this conference announcement was expected. The discussion of "standards" draws participants.

However, for me, the most interesting word in the announcement was *alignment*. While there was no apparent challenge in the conference description to the emerging lists of "standards"—that is, of their substance or their political and educational legitimacy or exactly how they might function as a "vital way to improve education"—a need was expressed to gather all of the standards together and to string them into a usable and persuasive parade. A uniform set of national standards to drive reform, not only in the schools but in

From a paper based on a presentation at the Fourth International Teaching for Intelligence Conference, April 23, 1998, New York, NY. © 1998 by Theodore R. Sizer. Reprinted with permission.

the teacher education and related communities, would thereby emerge. Americans would then have a describable, predictable, and measurable American educational system. All the pieces of the complex educational structure would be, to a substantial degree, substantively united, a sweeping "One Best System" of education, one engineered in the name of high American standards.

> **The ambition as well as the arrogance of this conference was stunning.**

The ambition as well as the arrogance of this conference was stunning.

I turned from reading this announcement to the Sunday newspapers, and especially to the Commentary section. I caught up on the Inter-American conference in Chile. We in this country revel in the fact that most Latin American and the Caribbean countries today have capitalist economic systems and democratic forms of government. I read here again what I have read often in the newspapers over the last decade: *The American way is now and inexorably the world's way.*

The key words that generally describe this American way are *democracy* and *capitalism.* Behind these two words are two fundamental ideas: *The people decide. Free and competitive markets count.*

A wise nation prepares its youth well for such a world. Wise educators, I wonder, must look carefully at the intellectual essence of democracy and capitalism. What makes these globally triumphant enterprises tick?

What makes them tick is best expressed in demanding *questions.* Democracy and capitalism are necessarily supple enterprises, ones that give substantial freedom to individuals and prominence and riches to those individuals who use that freedom in effective ways. It is questions that count, with informed answers forthcoming. *What is that? Why is it so? So what? What if?* The answers to such questions draw their legitimacy from the respectful but insistent probing of *what is* in order to discover *what might be.*

For example, digital computing was crafted out of new questions asked of old realities in mathematics and physics. New ways of effective management arose from a challenge to the deeply entrenched factory system. Unexpected interweaving of the arts led to powerful forms of expression, and the interweaving at first deeply unsettled and still unsettles the traditional arts community. All emerged from smart people asking new sorts of questions, questions that the established order might understandably have found to be cheeky, not part of the anointed system, indeed, downright disorderly. They led to inventions, and the inventions demonstrably worked, at least in the view of enough serious people to sustain their existence. There was a competitive and free market and the people decided.

Democracy and capitalism depend on hard knowledge, on the disciplines of the past. However, their essence derives from their experiment with and beyond existing knowledge and practice, experiment that arises from powerful questions—and hardly from carefully "aligned" amassings of conventional wisdom.

I often puzzle about the extraordinary gap between the politics of establishment educational reform and the politics of reform in other fields. In education we are betting on a strategy of centralizing the control over what is taught and upon what basis that learning is assessed: nationally aligned goals and objectives. The people charged with that centralization are largely unelected and represent the existing power groups in American education. These are devoted and decent people, surely, but they are rarely considered entrepreneurs in the best capitalist sense.

In education policy, there is limited attention paid to research on the process of learning, especially if that research suggests substantial change in the ways that formal education is defined and "delivered" or if the needed change is likely to cost substantial amounts of money. There is but a tiny investment by government and the private sector in educational research and, especially, development. The existing ways of defining schooling remain—to any noticeable official extent—largely unchallenged.

We seem to be pushing the safe, conventional reform vessels, even as there is sweeping evidence both that they work poorly and that the tests and mandates being imposed correlate little with desired behaviors. There is no "market" out there to remedy these weak arguments; the control and now the "aligned" standards and assessment remain closely controlled and centralized.

There are many historical and political reasons for this astonishing lack of boldness. What is particularly interesting is how these sorts of policies run absolutely counter to the critical ideas that inform the much-applauded American way, the basic ideas behind democracy and capitalism.

Compounding the irony is the oft-heard and patronizing argument that centralized control is necessary to protect the poor, as though there were not equally effective and more democratic mechanisms available to accomplish that end.

Further, many argue that our schools today are too diverse, that standards suffer. Yes, student intellectual performance by any definition is low, but that is not inevitably to say that the means to raise performance is the introduction of centralized standards and assessments. Indeed, there is a wealth of evidence that the miserable showing of many students arises not from details found in a curriculum guide or a testing booklet but from much deeper, more profound causes.

Finally, as today's conference illustrates, there is at hand a provocative body of research in cognitive science that raises deep questions about the accepted ways or means of teaching and assessment.

My request today is for us who are concerned about the intelligence of the people—the aggregated wit, knowledge, conviction, and grit of the American population—to recognize the lack of connection between most contemporary education policy and the widely applauded character of democracy and capitalism.

A wise society is peopled by more than the merely adroit, the useful but conforming spinners of the familiar. It depends on people who are in the habit of asking questions that break new ground. Further, in an age when communications technology provides the society's "teachers"—the spin meisters of the advertising world—with unprecedented and sustained access into the lives of communities and families, the habitual questioner—the informed skeptic—becomes ever more important.

The young person must be taught to say: What is the evidence? How might that task be done better, more effectively, and at less cost? What is really behind this message? What is for sale? Do I like it or not, and why? Is this all a lie, or is what I am told a truth of some sort?

The constructive questioner is necessarily informed and, thus, difficult to gull. The effective questioner wraps his or her questions around disciplined knowledge, indeed, disciplined knowledge emerges from incessant questioning, both of past scholarship and that of the present. A wise society will invest in intellectually competent citizens who persist in asking why, who, what, and, especially, what if—in thoughtful, *informed* ways.

An interest in questions comes at birth. The *why* questions abound, as many an exasperated parent will testify. That curiosity must be seized, with all the nuisance it causes. It must not be crushed, however disrupting it may be.

Nurturing a questing mind can make schooling, especially secondary schooling, a complicated task for teachers. A good question is rarely disposed of quickly. It takes time to form. It must be challenged, massaged, played with. It can rarely be rushed.

A good question . . . must be challenged, massaged, played with. It can rarely be rushed.

The Holocaust is a topic that very often provokes deep questions. Usually it is recounted in but a few paragraphs in a textbook, usually situated chronologically at the end of World War Two when U.S. troops "liberated" the camps.

Kids will ask, How can people do that to other people? The Nazis were people like us who had been to school. Nazis went to church. What did they think when they engaged in this barbarism? How could they justify it as fair? What about all the Germans who were not Nazis? Did they know? If not, why not? How not? How can one know that these German citizens actually *knew*?

As the discussion typically deepens, and, as the details of the Holocaust emerge in young minds, some student will ask, Do we have a Holocaust today that *we* do not "see"? Cambodia's Killing Fields and the Rwanda genocide usually come up. Are they similar to what happened to European Jews? Someone raises the matter of American slavery. Is that *our* Holocaust? Does it continue today? Is there a Holocaust in our midst? The discussion will explode.

Most teachers must acknowledge the issue and then, however reluctantly, move on. There is too much in the conventional history curriculum to "cover." There are the tests on all this coverage to prepare for. Deep questions take too much time to answer. There are not hours for extensive reading on a complex topic, especially one that diverges from the syllabus, even if the class is captured by it. There is no expectation for or discipline with intense discussion. And the teacher's other section of U.S. history may not raise the same sort of questions. The two sections must be kept on the same schedule. I-the-teacher, shouldering responsibility for 150 students, cannot be expected to do two "preps" for the "same" eleventh grade social studies classes.

Further, there is no right answer to all those questions. I remark to the class, How can I tell if you kids know this stuff? And a cheeky kid will surely ask, What does it *mean* to know this "stuff" and just how and on what basis will you "test" us?

The habit of questioning is both the heart of democracy and capitalism and the heart of demanding pedagogy. *Why, why, why, why? What if? How do you know? What is the evidence? How sound is the evidence?* People's energies flow from questions. Questions capture the attention of people of all ages. Vibrant collective government and the exercise of informed free choice depend on it. However, conventional schooling, systematized in exquisite detail, usually trivializes it. If schools do not value this habit, what is the cost to the culture?

The habit of informed skepticism is the necessary habit of a vital democracy and creative capitalism. Generations of young people schooled to parrot other people's answers to other people's questions will not be the seed bed for a good society.

Educators and political leaders themselves must ask deep and troubling questions about our own system of public schools, questioning even the meaning of that too-readily-accepted word *system.* They must inform themselves deeply about learning, about why people try to learn, about intelligence, the expression of informed ideas. Simply, they must open their eyes to the possibility that there are very different ways to educate America's young than merely making traditional notions about learning and schooling more systematic and "aligned."

That is, we adults must practice the habit of informed skepticism about all that we do in schooling. It is a worthy habit. Let us exercise it, boldly.

Let me go back to the ideas of democracy and capitalism, and the words behind them: *The people decide. Free and competitive markets count.*

If applied to education, what might this mean?

If one assumes—as I assume—that, beyond the rudiments of linguistic and mathematical literacy, reasonable people can and should disagree about the substance and standard of a serious education, then families must have a choice among schools for their children.

"Choice" has a long history in America, but it is enjoyed almost entirely by those in upper-income levels. People choose a town with schools they trust or a private school. Realtors tell us that the "quality of the schools" is a major criterion governing a move. If choice among schools is undeniably good for rich folks it should be for poor folks as well. *Let the people decide which school among many they want their child to attend.*

What, then, is the role of government?

To insist on tested evidence of each student's mastery of basic literacy and numeracy skills and on continued effort in some acceptable setting for learning beyond that.

To provide adequate financial support for those settings to which students are admitted by lottery and which serve no special interest in violation of the Constitution, this most likely by means of a system whereby the money follows the child.

To make available funds in excess of the basic per-child support for children with special needs or from highly stressed or dysfunctional families.

To promote the creation of schools in underserved areas.

To make available evidence and examples of good practice and to support research and development to create such examples.

To support financially the recruitment and preparation of each generation of new teachers and administrators.

To insist upon "transparency." All schools should be required to report fully and publicly, on an annual and comprehensive basis, on their programs and the performance of their students.

To have the power to shut down schools that either lie about their offerings and performance or that demonstrably hurt children.

These ideas will not be popular in many quarters. Many will say they spell the end of public education. The opposite will be the truth. American public education today is profoundly segregated by social class, is inequitably funded, has massive and repeatedly reported shortcomings, and is in the effective control of a very small number of people, many of them unelected. If anything, that control is being extended . . . witness calls for "alignment."

Many Americans will be terrified to try something so new. And yet, there are indications that a grassroots movement in such a direction is already underway. Home schooling, while yet involving but a small group of children, is reportedly the fastest growing reform effort in the country. The demand for charter schools and their equivalents is heard in every state. "Upstart" schools within many public systems are struggling into existence, usually in the teeth of top-down regulation. There is constructive restlessness in communities across this country.

Most telling, however, is the unwillingness of governments to put financial muscle behind their calls for reform. As always, Americans should attend carefully to what their governments *do* and pay only skeptical attention to what their governments *say*. For a quarter century we have had national political posturing, much of it studded with self-righteous and apocalyptic rhetoric. However, there has been no serious and sustained outpouring of funds to make significant reform possible.

Sputnik got a man on the moon. The 1983 *Nation at Risk* report began low-cost standards setting and assessment schemes, a sea of studies and reports, a plethora of name calling and little sustained attention to the central problems facing the country's children. The signal here is clear—government itself has deep doubts about the existing system. If it did not, it would have acted decisively as it has in other areas of national life.

In 1974, David Tyack, one of America's most respected historians of education, published a history of American urban education. Tyack's final words, written a quarter century ago, still ring true:

> "Old reforms need to be reformed anew, for today many lack confidence in the familiar patterns of power and authority that developed at the turn of the century. Substantial segments of this society no longer believe in centralism as an effective response to human needs, no longer trust an enlightened paternalism of elites and experts, no longer accept the inevitability or justice of the distribution of power and wealth along existing class and racial lines. To create urban schools which really teach students, which reflect the pluralism of the society, which serve the quest for social justice—this is a task which will take persistent imagination, wisdom, and will."[1]

The intelligence of the American people requires an end to careful and highly controlled tinkering with the old system and a scary leap into something that promises to be better. We must turn to our "persistent imagination, wisdom, and will." Democracy, much less capitalism, cannot survive without them.

America must prepare its students well to be informed skeptics. America must itself become an informed skeptic about its system of schooling—and act accordingly.

NOTE

1.   David B. Tyack, *The One Best System: A History of American Urban Education* (Cambridge: Harvard University Press, 1974), p. 291. Tyack and his Stanford colleague Larry Cuban recently published, also with Harvard University Press, a further critique of school reform: *Tinkering Toward Utopia: A Century of Public School Reform* (1995).

Narratives of the Educative Surround

by John I. Goodlad

E DUCATION VIS-À-VIS TEACHING

Seeking to tidy my mind somewhat regarding the work I'm in, I find it helpful to distinguish sharply between education and teaching. Education is of the self: partaken by the self; driven by the self. Education is not a commodity that can be given or taken away by somebody else. Yet it is not context-free. What the self is at any given time is the consequence of personal, evolving interactions with the surround.[1] There is no such thing as an autonomous self.[2]

One's education is both deliberate and serendipitous—that is, both sought for and *not* sought for. When one appears to have developed a measure of expertise without benefit of tutoring or some form of schooling, we say that she or he is self-taught. This, for me, is not helpful. Education *is* self-teaching: a process of preparing for and making choices—some deliberately, some not—that determine one's view of selected elements of the surround and, indeed, the whole of it. "Self-teaching" becomes a sloppy, redundant synonym for "education" and carries with it the assumption that "teaching" also is a synonym for "education." Such leads to the misleading, conventional equating of education and schooling and all sorts of consequential mischief.

Teaching, quite unlike education, is a process external to the self that the self assimilates, interprets, or ignores. We think of teaching as deliberate, but much of it is not; it is just there. The self is as likely to fix on the unintended as on the intended in sorting through the ubiquitous teaching of the daily surround. Definitions of education

From a paper based on a presentation at the Fourth International Teaching for Intelligence Conference, April 24, 1998, New York, NY. A portion of this article was published as "Schools for All Seasons" in *Phi Delta Kappan*, May 1998, pp. 670–671. © 1998 by John I. Goodlad. Reprinted with permission.

that exhort the deliberate cultivation of desired sensibilities and sensitivities are, more accurately, exhortations to the mission of teaching and schooling. When teaching becomes deliberate and takes on a mission, it becomes a moral act, with all the dilemmas associated with such.[3]

> **The nearer the threat of doom, promise of redemption, expectation of gratification, or utopia envisioned, the more impactful the teaching.**

The most troubling phenomenon of teaching is the unpredictability, particularly in the moral consequences, of the interactions between self and surround. And one of the greatest errors in seeking attribution regarding the effects of teaching is looking only to the self for reasons and explanations for what occurs in the individual. The individual self cannot be held responsible for arranging all the contingencies of the educative surround.

The whole of one's surround is teacher—for better or for worse. The self is free to ignore or relate to, wittingly or unwittingly, anything in the ecosystem of which it is a part. The connections and interpretations shape individual values, beliefs, and dispositions. What is not in or encountered in the surround may stunt or deprive the development of certain dispositions—once again, for better or for worse. In a cosmic sense, what is not part of this whole teaches, too; the self is denied some of both the good and the bad.

DIVERSITY IN THE NARRATIVES OF TEACHING

The crowing of roosters soars clearly above the quiet of education, intensifying as dawn comes to the cathedrals of humankind. Their sounds are soon lost, however, to the rising decibels of teaching—that cacophony of telling, pleading, questioning, showing, promising, praising, condemning that courses through the streets and marketplaces.[4] We are all teachers, our lessons tied to narratives of incentives and consequences. The nearer the threat of doom, promise of redemption, expectation of gratification, or utopia envisioned, the more impactful the teaching. The more ubiquitous the message, the less likely the promulgation and hearing of dissenting alternatives.

Over the centuries, several major narratives have dominated the human conversation: the narratives of salvation and everlasting life, of sectarian superiority, of gender privilege, of war and peace, of absolutism and relativism, of economic utility, of consumption and conservation. The struggle for dominance of ideology and belief has rarely been resolved on the basis of self-evident truth. Rather, it has been resolved on the basis of power in the political and physical combat arenas. After triumphing over his opposition, the despot's first actions are to exercise control over as much of the teaching cacophony as possible. The invention of the printing press and its rapidly expanding use changed the balance of power by ensuring that the local priest and soothsayer were not the only people with the book and the word. Superior invention and skill in the use of gunpowder reversed the economic fortunes of nations, superimposed new languages over the old, and converted to treason religious teachings previously unquestioned.

We are all born with the potential to develop a multiplicity of intelligences that together constitute the whole of intelligence.[5] Although interrelated and intercontributory to this whole, each proceeds on its own trajectory. There is no assurance that an environment rich in musical contingencies will produce musical intelligence, but such increases the probability. Then, as parents massage these contingencies, and music-addicted peers fill up the social surround, the education of musical intelligence in the self is more likely to blossom. There is no guarantee, however, that some other narrative will not prevail, perhaps turning one's attention more to the development of mathematical intelligence. Very often—not just rarely—it is a serendipitous encounter that triggers attention. The road to deliberate manipulation of the environment to foster in others an envisioned intelligence is marked by both successes and abysmal failures.

The combination of profound belief in the narrative and unpredictability of success in teaching it is potentially explosive. Nowhere is this more evident than in the history of what arguably has been the most powerful and influential narrative genre: religion. Probe deeply and one finds an astonishing convergence of basic principles in the world's major religions, especially in regard to tolerance and love. It turns out, however, that these tenets of faith are not sufficiently grounded in the believers to risk the transcendence of love from sect to sect. And so the divine idiom is suspended for recourse to the terrestrial ground of the battlefield. The burnings and beheadings in the name of God and Allah are legion.

We see this two-headed model of contradiction today in every aerie of the human habitat. The concept of "family values" is so appealing to interpretation that it has become a tool of political manipulation. Yet, parental abuse is the leading cause of children's injury and death. The narrative of empathy for the poor and home-less always is at odds with the narrative of the poor as lazy underclass, conjuring up a host of negative connotations. We know the educative power of modeling the narrative of kinesthetic intelligence but employ the pedagogical shortcut of resorting to linguistic teaching— "do as I say, not as I do." Observation tells us that the virtue of loy-alty to clients, employees, and friends always is at risk to the appeal of self-serving narratives.

The competition for teaching time and space is as old as civiliza-tion. Rarely have the dominant narratives been comprehensive in encompassing the human condition. Few have been evolutionary in the sense of benefiting from use so as to reach more people. Most narratives have been advanced to benefit those most in command of rhetorical place and space. It should come as no surprise, then, that advancing the readiness of technological place and space to accom-modate those with the resources of command became a narrative in its own right ready to serve any narrative, regardless of message. Today, communications is our most encompassing and ubiquitous industry, essential to the fortunes and accompanying power of other industries. The word of the warlord has been replaced by the corpo-rate word. That Bill Gates said it carries more weight than what Bill Gates said. But what Bill Gates said is incorporated into the lexicon of the narrative of economic utility anyway. The old power game is sustained and intensified; those controlling the medium control the messages that massage the populace.[6]

History argues that the less widely distributed the power, the less diverse the educative ecosystem of the surround; the less diverse this ecosystem, the less diverse the cultivation of intelligences; the less diverse the cultivation of intelligences, the fewer the narratives of possibilities and human sustainability; the fewer these narratives, the less the chances of survival. History provides an array of examples: the "ethnic cleansing" of jihad, the monopolies of cartels,[7] the subju-gation of means to ends, the sacrifice of serendipity to narrowly focused purpose and assumed certainty, the divine mandate to con-trol or master. The teaching of history is powerfully persuasive: our survival depends in large part on learning to let things be, on devel-oping the ecological intelligence to know when we must be leavers and not mere victims of our passion for taking.[8]

But even as these words and thoughts take shape in my mind, I am awed by the complexity of what, on the surface, appears so obvious, necessary, and simple: We must take care of one another and the habitat of which we are a part. Two profound complications surface immediately. First, although the rhetoric of goodwill toward all takes up a sizable chunk of airtime, especially on nostalgic ceremonial occasions, other narratives, often appealing to divisiveness and personal aggrandizement, compete for time, attention, and acceptance. What are the chances for a narrative of moral principle to be heard? Second, surely not all opinions, customs, choices, and dispositions are equally good. How does the moral principle become pervasive without the annihilation of those deeply committed to other narratives?

> **The word of the warlord has been replaced by the corporate word.**

Through education, of course. But this is asking a great deal of a process that is invisible, never fully harnessed, personal, unpredictable, hardly ever linear, and heavily influenced by the narratives of the ecological surround. These narratives are not neutral and they are rarely for the common good. We depend largely on the rule of law to sustain the common good. Yet, when we refer to education as intended learning, the rhetoric is of the common good and soon turns to schools. Our assumption appears to be that we cannot expect much of the educating we need from what transpires in the daily marketplace and so we must count on the schools. My, what a burden to lay upon them!

NARRATIVES FOR SCHOOLS

Schools are political entities charged with carrying out teaching functions directed to deliberate student outcomes. These outcomes are determined through a political process by which an array of interests purported to be in the common good compete for attention and, ultimately, supremacy in the ends and means of the schools.

Given the principles enunciated in the founding of the American Republic, we would assume that the process of setting the purposes for the deliberate teachings of the schools would be one of reaffirming the mission of developing democratic character in the young: an understanding and appreciation of liberal democracy and efficacy in upholding "a political system marked not only by free and fair elections, but also by the rule of law, a separation of powers, and the protection of basic liberties of speech, assembly, religion, and property."[9] In addition to these attributes of political citizenship, one might anticipate also the moral dispositions of fairness, equality, justice, freedom, caring, community, and relatedness.[10] We literally endorse, then, the symbiotics of both personal and community health and well-being: civility and civitas, respectively.

> **But when you set preparation for this fray as the mission of our schools, you know not what you do.**

Given these liberal political and social democratic principles and concepts as the solid backdrop—the rhetorical fabric—of our discourse, we might also assume that all other persuasions would be granted only very tentative status, until discarded or incorporated into the design of this fabric. We might also assume that the school need pay little heed to the surrounding cacophony of interests and ideologies competing for attention while being steadfastly guided by the educative narrative, and would go about its business of developing democratic character in the young. As in the past, a new subject might be added or an old one given a more prominent place in the curriculum in recognition of changes in the balance of expectations for effective citizenship. Hence, today, greater attention to ecology and technology might well be appropriate. But the mission of schooling would remain stable.

Not so. A major complaint of today's school-based educators is that there is no clear, agreed-upon mission for schooling; it changes after election time. But these changes provide no greater clarity and stability than existed before. The narrative of developing democratic character in the young enjoys no premier status among the diverse expectations of the marketplace. Further, there is no deep-grained professional ethos that grounds the educator in a teaching ethic of educational responsibility to the pupil, an ethic sufficient to transcend these expectations. There is little in the paltry professional education of the teacher and the administrator even to suggest the possibility of such an ethic.[11] The empty cliché, "all children can learn," provides as little guidance as a street sign lying in a field, torn from its moorings by a windstorm.

What a marketing opportunity! With an unassailable mission for schools largely unattended and little advocated, no alternatives with a solid constituency, and the gates into teaching loosely latched to admit a polyglot of school stewards lacking a common core of resolve and belief, the economic juggernaut that once regarded schools as off-limits simply expands the marketplace. The narrative of economic utility takes over.

The narrative's appeal is straightforward and highly utilitarian: "Addressing the young," Neil Postman writes, "it offers a covenant of sorts with them: If you will pay attention in school, and do your homework, and score well on tests and behave yourself, you will be rewarded with a well-paying job when you are done." Postman continues: "Its driving idea is that the purpose of schooling is to prepare children for competent entry into the economic life of a community. It follows from this that any school not designed to further this end is seen as a frill or an ornament—which is to say, the waste of valuable time."[12]

It is this twisting and narrowing of school purpose that threatens development of the full, individual self and heightens the diabolical nature of this narrative of economic utility. There is nothing new or obscure in the hope that our young people will do well and feel good about their lives in school and, when adults, find satisfying jobs. Connecting the two has been and continues to be a motivating ploy used by parents and teachers alike. Even Mortimer Adler, no advocate for supremacy of the economic imperative in the mission of schooling, included "preparation for earning a living" with "preparation for duties of citizenship" and "preparation for discharging everyone's moral obligation to lead a good life and make as much of one's self as possible" as one of the three objectives of public schooling in our society.[13] Currently, however, we see not just the covenant with children regarding the jobs they will have but a covenant to be the human capital for the high-value-added industries fighting on the economic battlefields of the future for domination over "computers and software, robotics, civilian aviation, synthetic materials, microelectronics, biotechnology, and telecommunications"—to cite Professor Theodore Hershberg.[14]

This may be the battlefield you enthusiastically covet for your children's children, Professor, but when it comes to mine and theirs, I'm a conscientious objector. Your grandchildren and mine will assuredly have that option. But when you set preparation for this fray as the mission of our schools, you know not what you do. You report answering queries about your earlier proposals for "radical school reform" with the response, "I don't have a clue."[15] This would be precisely the appropriate answer to questions about your proposed economic mission for schooling.

We should not be at all surprised or turned off by the business interest in the schools as a market and a machine tool for ratcheting up the economy. To expect otherwise would be akin to expecting squirrels to eschew the bird-feeder. And so my blood pressure rises only a little in response to the most crass exhortations of corporate leaders addressing educational conferences regarding the schools' responsibility to process student raw material for the nation's humanpower needs. My body language suggests a little tension when still one more politician stages the tired ploy of severely blasting the schools in the hope that this sorry picture will be remembered a few years from now when he makes claims for improvement as a result of the efficient, bottom-line, corporate practices he was successful in injecting into state legislation for the schools. And I squirm only a little when one more school board, boasting last year about increased expenditures for computers (with no check on the availability of appropriate software), complains this year about the rising costs of instruction.

No, it is the reverence of so many educators for the god of Technology, now risen from the ashes of all previous gods of Technology,[16] that rouses my passion. Technology has become a religion. It is a religion that has no moral affinity with the great religions of the world, all of which "affirm and reverence life; . . . believe in the freedom and integrity of the person; . . . urge the existential self to seek self-transcendence in organic union with mankind and with mystical or divine ground of the cosmos. . . ."[17]

We have been promised educational salvation before by hucksters of previous gods of Technology. "Education for the Air Age" and "Education for the Space Age" are two puffballs of promised school reform that come to mind. But these and others were only weakly driven by the narrative of economic utility and soon drifted off to rest inconspicuously in that graveyard of educational fantasies marked, "Whatever happened to the future?" We need a *Journal of Educational Autopsy* to remind us of the common characteristics of technologically related, hysterical follies of the past and their kinship with today's.

Educators have had before them for decades creative proposals regarding the seemingly limitless possibilities for enriching both the educative surround and classroom instruction through the very technologies now available. Seymour Papert, for one, likened the child's future computer to her present pencil, the shaft wired to a technologically driven educative universe, with which she could interact any hour of the day, any day of the week.[18] The computer, teamed with the human teachers, would simply make it easier for the school to achieve its ideal goal of maximizing the abilities of every child encompassed by its stewardship. Neither Papert nor the others of like vision had in mind a world only speculated where such a school mission would be replaced with goodness knows what. A handful of schools cautiously added a few computers to their arsenal of instructional aids and went about their usual business.

> **We have been promised educational salvation before by hucksters of previous gods of Technology.**

But, suddenly, Armageddon is just beyond the millennium. In the apocalyptic struggle to be waged, says the narrative, the implicit holiness of the god of Technology will triumph. Let us eschew the present and prepare for salvation in the glorious-to-come future. It comes to me as a surprise (as it most certainly would to all who know me well) that I am increasingly called upon to describe this future and what we must try to do in our schools to prepare their students for it. Unfortunately, I have yet to meet a person living in the future to turn to for a description of what it is like, how it feels to be there, and how to present myself to the then-incumbent god of Technology.

My life as a clairvoyant promises to be blessedly short. Unsought clients are monumentally disinterested in my answers to their questions. A recent group appeared to be about as nervous as those denizens of the woods who trembled at Chicken Little's dire predictions of the sky about to fall. Surrounded by the rhetoric of those most likely to profit from a technologically driven future and clothed in guilt by the words of those early-believing and early-using colleagues, they sought from me confirmation of what the work of tomorrow's schools and teachers would be.

I may not have removed the fear, but I certainly took away the fun of speculation when I asked about the present: How was technology now changing or removing the mission of their schools? There was silence; body language suggested some annoyance. The priorities of the school, I suggested, arise out of determining critical areas of educational need not being taken care of now by other institutions or not likely to be taken good care of elsewhere. Instead of endeavoring to hurtle to an assumed inevitable but unknown and, therefore, scary future, we began to enjoy the calm of contemplating what we should be about in a relatively known present.

A reliable way to be unprepared for the future is to prepare for one confidently perceived. Predictions are far too much extrapolations from the present. B. C. Crandall quotes Ludwig Wittgenstein: "When we think about the future of the world, we always have in mind its being at the place it would be if it continued to move as we see it moving now. We do not realize that it moves not in a straight line, but in a curve, and that its direction constantly changes."[19] Some charts of the future, like the navigational charts of centuries ago, provide the general contours but, like those used by the early navigators, are useless for guiding one through the rocks and shoals.

We know that the future major domains of frontier exploration will be outer space, the oceans' depths, and the human mind and that what we know now pales in the face of what is yet to be known. We also know that these will ensure trillion-dollar industries. Apple Computer, Inc., was one of the three sponsors of the first workshop on artificial life held in Los Alamos, New Mexico, in 1987; two years later, the Global Business Network was one of the sponsors of the first international conference on nanotechnology.[20]

> **The school best prepared for tomorrow is the school best geared to today.**

Hence, it follows that there will be jobs—good jobs—in these domains, but to make preparation for them the mission of our schools is folly. Nonetheless, the narrative of economic utility will be alive and well, dominating rhetorical space with claims regarding the virtues of technology, exhortations regarding the schools' responsibility for ensuring the necessary human raw materials, and ensuring that those who stand to profit most from venturing into the three major domains of exploration will be first to describe the wondrous benefits we will enjoy.

The more specific and exclusive we are about preparing the young for logical-mathematical-technological intelligence, for example, the less likely the future availability of the other intelligences. From a practical, economic perspective, it is dangerous to play god, be it the god of Technology or any other, and set for schools the development of precise abilities that never can be more than guesses. From a moral perspective, to hone the classroom environment so as to eschew those intelligences not deemed necessary to national economic welfare is a monstrous denial of the possibilities of the self. Whether we have in mind the best interests of the nation or of the individual, an ecumenical mission for the schools is the best guarantee of a present that will ensure the diversity of human understandings, talents, and traits essential to a durable tomorrow—a mission with many open windows and doors to admit serendipity.[21]

SCHOOLS FOR ALL SEASONS

The school best prepared for tomorrow is the school best geared to today. It is a school for all seasons, engaging all of its students in as many domains of human experience as it is able to encompass. It is a school so committed to its comprehensive mission of preparing the young to participate broadly in the human conversation a democratic society seeks to sustain that it is not diverted into the narrowing of focus that devotion to some specific narrative requires. This is not easy.

Creating and sustaining in schools programs that cultivate a wide range of human potential and simultaneously ensure availability of the full range of abilities and dispositions a robust democratic society requires is not easy because the supporting narrative is so weakly sustained in the surrounding environment. Research shows that parents want for their children a very broad range of educational goals. Nonetheless, they are taught by the rhetoric of politically driven school reform to settle for what they are told are reliable surrogates—test scores. Teachers, with somewhat different weightings of the components, also opt for a comprehensive set of personal, social, economic, and academic goals. And they, too, are told to pay close attention to test scores. Those classroom activities that stress the intrapersonal and interpersonal are quite commonly regarded, as Postman points out, as frill and ornament. Nonetheless, it is difficult to come up with a domain of intelligence other than the personal that is more significant to individual development and the common welfare—and less reflected in test scores.

The loss to the young of narrowing school focus extends beyond deprivation in the domains of intelligence left out of the environment in at least two significant ways. First, the several intelligences are part of a functioning whole; the emotional, for example, profoundly affects the academic. The latter suffers in an atmosphere insensitive to the emotional states of the learners. The timeworn emphasis on teaching the whole child has depths of meaning extending far beyond the platitudes so often attached to the concept.

The second loss is in the richness of pedagogy teaching in schools productively requires. The narrowing of school expectations to a limited array of outcomes readily tested tends to restrict teaching to relatively uniform procedures that simply leave out some modes of learning. For example, the range of teaching methods common to most kindergarten classrooms commonly is cut in half by the fourth grade, where stress on testing increases significantly.

Accompanying this dual narrowing of curricula and teaching, very often, is an intensification of teacher interest in finding "*the* method," an interest endlessly fed by an educational business conglomerate peddling instructional "how-to-do-its." One carrying considerable intellectual baggage has been particularly popular over the last two decades: brain science and its promise (not supported by neural scientists) of revolutionizing educational practice. In spite of the fact that "we do not know enough about brain development and neural function to link that understanding directly, in any meaningful, defensible way to instruction and educational practice,"[22] it has been the rare conference for teachers lacking an ardent speaker exhorting the specifics of developing both the left and right hemispheres of the brain in daily classroom activities.

One of the most serious concomitants of a narrow view of what constitutes human intelligence and the role of the school in its development is the continued failure of public policy to recognize the level of teacher education required to ensure a system of schooling essential to developing our citizenry as the wealth of the nation that far transcends mere economic functionality.

The necessary school for all seasons sustains a learning environment rich in sensory stimulation. One need not worry pedagogically about what stimulates the right side of the brain and what the left if the organizing centers selected by the teacher are broad in encompassing the kinesthetic, the aesthetic, the social, the linguistic, the mathematical, and so on. But arranging for such organizing centers is exceedingly demanding, and flies in the face of years of emphasizing the selection of relatively small, sharply focused organizing centers with individual subjects and specific grade levels in mind. The unit of selection designed to involve all in the class over a period of weeks, with accompanying teacher observation and diagnosis of individual learners, has largely disappeared in our schools, in part because of being associated in the public mind with "progressive education" and in part because such is highly demanding in the necessary pedagogy. Teacher education programs that sprinkle a few courses in methods of teaching outside of and in between the demands of general education and a major over four years of college simply do not suffice.

As a nation, we balk at ensuring for our teachers *both* the general and the professional education the fostering of intelligence in the young requires. It should come as no surprise that the best guarantee of a broadly encompassing intelligence is to be born into a stimulating sensory environment and subsequently to attend a school in a community sufficiently affluent to provide the richest array of instructional resources and to attract and retain the teachers most favored in their own education. And, of course, there is a high correlation between these two sets of favoring circumstances,[23] both little affected by proposals for school reform. Schools for all our children and all our seasons await the ultimate impact of narratives designed to provide, if not the favoring circumstances of birth, the favoring circumstances of richly textured educational environments guided by caring, competent, professional teachers. Meanwhile, let us not be seduced by narratives offering covenants to our children that prescribe and limit their futures.

NOTES

1. For a fascinating analysis of the social origins of the necessarily individual mental functioning of the self, see Sam Wineburg, "T. S. Eliot, Collaboration and the Quandaries of Assessment in a Rapidly Changing World," *Phi Delta Kappan,* September 1997, pp. 59–65.

2. The connectedness of the self to the surround is compellingly portrayed by Wendell Berry, *The Unsettling of America: Culture and Agriculture* (San Francisco: Sierra Club Books, 1977). See especially Chapter 7.

3. Gabriel Moran, *Showing How: The Act of Teaching* (Valley Forge, PA: Trinity Press International, 1997). See particularly Chapter 1.

4. The ubiquitous nature of this teaching is described by Lawrence A. Cremin, *Popular Education and Its Discontents* (New York: Harper & Row, 1990). Specifically, see p. viii for his introductory summary.

5. This paper is premised on the assumption that there are several different kinds of intelligence, and that the educative surround should embrace development of the full array. I rely significantly on the seminal work of Howard Gardner.

6. For groundbreaking insights into the medium as both the message and the massage, see Marshall McLuhan, *Understanding Media: The Extensions of Man* (New York: McGraw-Hill, 1964); and Marshall McLuhan and Quentin Fiore, *The Medium Is the Massage* (New York: Random House, 1967).

7. See Benjamin R. Barber, *Jihad vs. McWorld* (New York: Times Books, 1995) for two phenomena that threaten the world's future—religious fanaticism and global megacorporations.

8. See Daniel Quinn, *Ishmael* (New York: Bantam, 1992) for a fascinating description and analysis of the differences between the "takers" and the "leavers" in history.

9. Fareed Zakaria, "The Rise of Illiberal Democracy," *Foreign Affairs,* November/December 1997, p. 22.

10. John White, *Education and the Good Life: Autonomy, Altruism, and the National Curriculum* (New York: Teachers College Press, 1991).

11. See the findings in John I. Goodlad, *Teachers for Our Nation's Schools* (San Francisco: Jossey-Bass, 1990).

12. Neil Postman, *The End of Education* (New York: Vintage, 1996), pp. 27–28.

13. Mortimer J. Adler, *We Hold These Truths* (New York: Macmillan, 1987), p. 20.

14, 15. Theodore Hershberg, "The Case for New Standards," *Education Week,* December 10, 1997, p. 52.

16. I draw more heavily from Neil Postman here than my citations imply. On the worship of and disappointments from today's and earlier eras of technological innovation, see Edward Tenner, *Why Things Bite Back: Technology and the Revenge of Unintended Consequences* (New York: Knopf, 1996).

17. Warren W. Wagar, *The City of Man: Prophecies of a World Civilization in Twentieth-Century Thought* (Boston: Houghton Mifflin, 1967), p. 171. For further explication of commonalities in both divine and secular idioms of thought, see John I. Goodlad, *In Praise of Education* (New York: Teachers College Press, 1997), Chapter 2.

18. Seymour Papert, *Mindstorms* (New York: Basic Books, 1980).

19. B. C. Crandall, *Nanotechnology* (Cambridge, MA: MIT Press, 1996), p. 187.

20. Crandall, pp. 24 and 25.

21. Ted Gup writes of the sheer joy of finding treasures of thought not sought. See his "The End of Serendipity," *Education Week,* November 21, 1997, p. A52.

22. John T. Bruer, "Education and the Brain: A Bridge Too Far," *Educational Researcher,* November 1997, p. 4.

23. For a penetrating, data-based analysis, see Bruce J. Biddle, "Foolishness, Dangerous Nonsense, and Real Correlates of State Differences in Achievement," *Phi Delta Kappan,* September 1997, pp. 9–13.

Truth, Beauty, and Goodness: Education for All Human Beings

John Brockman interviews Howard Gardner

JB: How do you educate everybody?

Gardner: I want people at the end of their education to understand the world in ways that they couldn't have understood it before their education. In speaking of the world I mean the physical world, the biological world, the social world—their own world, their personal world as well as the broader social and cultural terrain. I believe that these are questions that every human being is interested in from a very young age. They're questions which kids ask all the time: who am I, where do I come from, what's this made out of, what's going to happen to me, why do people fight, why do they hate? Is there a higher power? Questions like that—they don't usually ask them in their words, they ask them in their play, in their stories, the myths they like to listen to and so on.

These are also the questions that historically have been looked at in religion, philosophy, science. While it's great for people to ask these questions on their own, and to make use of their own experience, it's crazy for people not to take advantage of the other attempts to answer those questions over the millennia. And the disciplines represent to me the most concerted efforts to provide answers to those questions. History tells us where we come from. Biology talks about what it means to be alive. Physics talks about the world of objects, alive or not.

It's important to emphasize the role of disciplines when you're talking about precollegiate education. Some people think the disciplines are irrelevant, and some people think all the interesting work is interdisciplinary so you can kind of jump right into that. I reject both

Adapted from "Truth, Beauty, and Goodness: Education for All Human Beings, John Brockman interviews Howard Gardner," which appeared on Edge Foundation's Third Culture web site (http://www.edge.org/3rd_culture/gardner/), September 24, 1997. Reprinted with permission of Howard Gardner.

of these claims. Disciplines are what separates us from the barbarians; I don't think you can do interdisciplinary work unless you've done disciplinary work.

The people who defend disciplines often go to the opposite extreme; there's a joke in my field which is—in elementary school we love the kids, in high school we love the disciplines, in college we love ourselves. I don't think disciplines ought to be loved for their own sake; they ought to be seen as the best way to answer questions that human beings are interested in. Therefore I see the purpose of education as helping people understand the best answers that cultures and societies have come up with to basic questions, what I would call essential questions. So at the end we can form our own personal answers to those questions, which will be based to a significant extent on how other people have approached them, and will at the same time allow us to make our own syntheses.

> We don't need to remember the capital of Montana because it is likely to be at our fingertips.

The word *understanding* is very important here because I would say the overwhelming part of what we do in schools has nothing to do with understanding. It has to do with memorizing material and feeding it back in the form of short-answer tests. Understanding for me, on the other hand, is taking something that you've learned, a skill, a bit of knowledge, a concept, and applying it appropriately in a new situation. We very rarely ask students to do that. The most interesting finding of cognitive science for education is that when we ask even the best students in the best schools to make use of the knowledge in a new situation, they don't typically know how to do it.

JB: Maybe the premise of schools should be how to take tests. I became very good at it—I'm not being ironic.

Gardner: What you're saying is more true than you may realize. By and large throughout history, schools have not known exactly what it is that they want to do, but those who fund and operate schools have known that they want to have people who are responsible, and show up, and can master a task. So over the years they have developed what we might call ersatzes. If you wanted to go to Harvard College a hundred years ago, you had to be able to read Latin, Greek and Hebrew. Nobody went out and did a job where they had to read Latin, Greek and Hebrew. Nowadays, it's mastering a certain amount of mathematics, even though almost nobody will be using that mathematics when they go on. They are hurdles which we set up to discover whether somebody has—the Yiddish word is *yechas,* the German word is *sitzfleisch*—to sit down and do something they don't really want to do.

Suddenly the notion of seeing whether people can memorize lots of stuff and can sit down and study becomes irrelevant. Because we can get computers and other kinds of instrumentation to do that for us. We don't need to remember the capital of Montana because it is likely to be at our fingertips. When I talk about being able to understand the discipline so that we can approach fundamental questions, I mean that we need to be able to train ways of thinking, so when new stuff comes along, people will be able to say, "Gee, I know how to approach that because of some ways of thinking that I've learned"; or if not, at least I have some recourse where I can go to figure out what to do. And this can be other people, or books, or some kind of training that you do yourself or with a simulation—there are many options.

The notion of coverage, of going through a bunch of disciplines, and learning facts and concepts, is assessed by schools all over the world. It's never been a very good idea, but now it's really irrelevant. I would throw away 95 percent of the coverage that we do; figure out really important questions and issues, and give people lots and lots of time to learn about how disciplined minds think about those issues, and then to practice those disciplines themselves.

JB: Let's get more concrete about your present initiatives.

Gardner: I'm a progressive in education—a follower of Dewey and people like that—but I want essentially to seize the initiative from the conservatives, who have dominated educational discussion in this country to its detriment. I'm selecting as my examples things which no conservative could possibly shake a fist at, but which would drive postmodernists nuts. Truth, beauty, and goodness. When I talk about truth, I'm talking about science but also folk knowledge; when I talk about beauty I'm talking about the arts, but it could be nature as well; when I'm talking about goodness and evil I'm talking about morality.

My specimen topic in truth is the theory of evolution; my topic in beauty is the music of Mozart; my topic in morality is the Holocaust. Getting even more specific than that: my example in evolution is Darwin's finches; within the music of Mozart my example is a trio in *The Marriage of Figaro*—it's the 13th performed set piece in the first act; and in the Holocaust, my example, the Wannsee Conference, is the place where the Nazis actually launched the Final Solution. These three things—the finches, the trio, and the Wannsee Conference—actually respond to questions that kids are interested in. (For example, why are there so many different kinds of birds on a little island?) They are what I call entry points to topics which are crucial if you want to think scientifically, historically or aesthetically. What I would do as a teacher would be to spend weeks, months, even years, really going into these things so that people will develop the habits of mind so they can think about topics like that.

If you asked me should people be studying physics, or chemistry or biology or geology in high school, I would say it doesn't make the slightest bit of difference. They should study some topics, of course, but the choice is wide open—I'm interested in depth, not breadth. I'm not talking about college education; I'm just taking on K to 12. What I want when kids get through a K to 12 education is for them to have a sense of what their society thinks is true, beautiful and good; false, ugly and evil; how to think about it and how to act on the basis of your thoughts.

JB: Where is the Howard Gardner of multiple intelligences in all of this? Isn't this what you're known for in education?

Gardner: There have been literally hundreds and perhaps thousands of applications of my ideas educationally, both in this country and in the world. I say that with as much mystification and embarrassment as pride, because I have had almost nothing to do with it; these are things other people have done. But one thing that struck me is how incredibly superficial most of the applications have been, and one obsessive thought that's stimulating me through this current work in education is this: I don't want to be part of the trivialization of education. What I'm arguing is that if you decide which things are important and which things are worth spending time on, like evolution and the music of Mozart, then you can approach such a topic in many different ways. Multiple intelligences can be useful in three quite interesting ways in dealing with important topics that are worth spending time on.

First of all, by providing what I call *entry points*. Any topic that's worth spending time on can be approached in many different ways. I, in fact, have seven different entry points which roughly relate to my intelligences, but that's neither here nor there.

Second of all, by providing powerful *analogies or metaphors* for what you're trying to understand. Again, we don't know if there are seven analogies for anything you want us to understand, but there is always more than one analogy or metaphor.

> **But one thing that struck me is how incredibly superficial most of the applications have been . . .**

Third of all, by providing what I call different *model languages* for understanding a concept. Let's take evolution. You can learn about evolution in ordinary language; you can learn about it through logical propositions; you can draw diagrams with the branching tree of evolution; you can do taxonomic classifications of various kinds of species. Many people (including experts) make the mistake of thinking that one of these languages is so to speak a privileged representation of a topic. I would say on the contrary that our understanding of a topic is rich to the extent that we have a number of different ways of representing it and we can go pretty readily from one representation to the other.

Here I become Howard Gardner the progressive. We need to take what we know about the different ways in which children think, the different ways in which people can make sense of the world, and really build that into the teaching of important topics. First of all, we reach more kids, because some kids learn from stories, some kids learn from works of art, some kids learn from hands-on kinds of things. We also give kids a sense of what it's like to be an expert, because experts will think about something in lots of different ways. If you can only think about a topic in one way, your understanding is tenuous at best.

JB: What will parents think of this?

Gardner: It's going to confuse some of them, because in a sense I'm trying to have the best of a progressive and traditional perspective. When we talk about the true, the beautiful and the good, that's very classical. Then you have multiple intelligences. I went on radio and talked about how you could teach the Civil War through dance. I received the most outraged correspondence from people on that topic, even though I just heard about a wonderful dance about the Holocaust that's really quite amazing, and powerful; and many of us understand the Spanish Civil War through Picasso's paintings or Andre Malraux's novels. So, it's really going to confuse people.

> **But there are only three or four basic disciplines that we should worry about before college.**

JB: Is this approach for everybody? Have you tried it out on local boards of inner-city public schools, for instance?

Gardner: I am not saying that everybody should study evolution, Mozart and the Holocaust. I'm saying that each educator needs to work in his or her culture to figure out what are the important truths and beauties and falsities and uglinesses and moralities, and to spend time with those. And in the sciences there are hundreds of them. And if you don't believe in the sciences, then there are hundreds of them in folk knowledge. But the important point is to spend a lot of time on something, rather than just superficially sampling a lot of things. People say, well, you've got to read 500 books before you get through high school—I say bull! You've got to read a small number of good books very carefully, and learn how to think about books. You have the rest of your life to read *Moby Dick,* or *Silas Marner* or *The Color Purple.*

At the "Gardner school," we're going to interest your son, Max Brockman, and my son, Benjamin Gardner, in these really interesting questions, which are human questions; what life's all about. Then you encounter these funny squiggles you've got to make sense out of—the literacies. Why? Because we can't read those books and listen to those works of art and understand those machines unless we pick up some of those literacies. But the literacies are not ends in themselves. President Clinton said we want to have every kid reading by third grade. I say, we know how to teach kids how to read; the problem is kids *don't* read. Literacies have to be a *means* to get to the disciplines. The disciplines are the handmaidens to help us come up with reasonable first answers to all these essential questions. We can't do it on our own. But there are only three or four basic disciplines that we should worry about before college. One, how to think scientifically. Most people in America still believe in astrology; they're clueless of how to make sense of an experiment. They don't know what a hypothesis is. Two, they need to know something about the history of their country, something about the background, maybe a little about the rest of the world too. But again people don't know how historically; they think the Punic Wars occurred about the same time as the Truman administration. They don't understand the ways in which we are like and unlike other cultures, other historical eras; they tend to think the past was all different and all bad, the present is all good, they think history is progress—they're filled with misconceptions. So you need to know something about history. Three, people need to know something about how to make sense of works of art, because those are treasures of the culture, and four, they have to know something about mathematics because it's the language of science, and they're going to be stuck if they don't know. The particular books they read, the particular science they learn, are completely irrelevant until you get to college. You're picking up some tools so you can enter into the conversations of the centuries on these and other important questions.

So what happens in this ideal school? Students have learned a lot about some very important topics that the culture cherishes. And they've secured some tools so if they want to know about something besides the things they've focused on, they can study it in college or read about it on their own; they've got the rest of life there.

How do we find out what they've learned? We ask them to issue performances of understanding. We give them materials that they haven't encountered before, and ask, how can you make sense of it? You studied the Holocaust? I'm going to tell you about Bosnia. Or about what happened in Armenia in the first world war. And I want you to talk about that, or write about it, or enact it—do a play about it. Help me understand what's going on and tell me in what ways Bosnia or Armenia is like what happened in Germany and in what ways it's different.

You've been studying evolution? I'm going to tell you something about virtual reality, if you're interested in that. I'm going to tell you about computers. Stretch. Use that knowledge in a new situation.

You've read and understood the George Eliot book? I'm going to give you a book by Jane Austen. I don't care which book it is, it's simply not relevant. And the students who get to go on scholarship to private universities are not the ones who can tell me when every battle occurred, or who can memorize every chemical formula. I'm going to admit those students who can show me how to think about issues in those areas. I'll give them a hundred choices. They have to perform their understanding on something which matters in the culture.

JB: What about resistance from people who are in the education industry—teachers, among others?

Gardner: For one thing, I'm calling on people to change what they do. For another, coverage is very comforting. One of the reasons why E. D. Hirsch is so popular is you can say, god, they knew 300 things last year, now they know 600. Now they know 300 things more. But I say facts are completely discipline-neutral. If you don't learn how to think and speak differently about things then you really haven't been schooled at all. You remember the old *$64,000 Question? Jeopardy* and the *$64,000 Question* form the American consciousness about what it is to know things. Other countries aren't much better, but international studies bear me out, that the kids in East Asia and Western Europe who do better in science and math are the ones who attend schools where they actually do more uncovering and less covering. They go more deeply into topics and they build up more habits of thinking; they don't worry about spending ten seconds on many different things.

In fact a lot of my ideas have been less confusing to people in other countries than they have been in the United States. Our education discourse is so primitive. If you compare, for example, writing about science in our newspapers to writing about education, writing about science has really improved over the last 20 years—if you read *Science Times* and the science pages of other papers, you learn something in areas where you are not an expert.

In writing about education, everything is about test scores, and every six months about some cute place where they're teaching kids something in the arts—but there's no cumulative knowledge there, there's no *Wall Street Journal* for people who are interested in education. Yet in the rest of the world nearly everybody realizes that education is what it's all about.

The irony is that in countries that are very resource-rich, like the United States, Argentina, maybe Russia to a certain extent, one is able to get away with an education system that has just been okay for a small percentage of the population, because there are so many resources. That's not going to be true forever. It's individuals who will be better at problem finding as well as problem solving who will be better at working together at groups, who'll be able to be very good at troubleshooting, who will be able to take these disciplines and bring them to bear in new areas. They're the ones that will be in power 50 years from now. While there's some aspects of our society which are very benevolent with reference to those things, our schools aren't one of them. Our schools are behind except for very few schools which the elite get the chance to send their kids to, but that's not where the future's going to be cast. What's going to happen to the 75 percent of our population that doesn't have high-quality education? That's the question.

> **If you don't learn how to think and speak differently about things then you really haven't been schooled at all.**

JB: How do you see these ideas playing out over the next years? Implications of this new book [*The Disciplined Mind,* by Howard Gardner, Simon and Schuster, 1999] in terms of what you might do with it, or other people might?

Gardner: I've already given part of the answer to this; these ideas will fall on more receptive ears in other parts of the world, where not only is education taken more seriously, but where it's possible to have a more unified kind of national conversation. We may not like the French system, but when they make a decision, it gets implemented very widely. There are many countries which no longer are part French colonies which still run their schools the way the French ran their schools 50 or a hundred years ago.

JB: We're too patchy for that.

Gardner: The interesting thing will be to see whether individuals who are traditionally oriented, whether scholars or lay people, and who like the goal of a traditional orientation, will be drawn to the notion of deep uncovering, rather than covering superficially, and of being very imaginative and flexible in how you present such a curriculum to a very diverse population. That's what the issue is going to hang on. It could be that it'll serve as a meeting ground for people who have hitherto thought they were at each other's necks—but it could also elicit a "plague on both your houses" reaction. The people who are more liberal/progressive will say, god, Gardner's really lost it, because he's talking about "pale stale males," whereas the people on the right will say, well, granted he wants to talk about some things that are worth talking about, but first of all there are thousands of other things that the kids have to know as well, and he won't tell us what they are, and second of all, what is all this nonsense about teaching things in different ways; there's one way to teach, the right way, and either the kids will learn it or it's too bad.

JB: You're right. People might think you're losing it.

Gardner: Maybe I am!

JB: It's a departure.

Gardner: I probably feel more of a personal commitment to this than anything else I've ever undertaken—it really comes from my soul. I have been deeply involved in school reform for at least 15 years. I've been very frustrated by the superficiality of the discussion, and by my perception that people don't really get down to the basic of what an ordinary citizen ought to be able to know so that he can cope with a world that's changing very quickly and is very confusing.

JB: Ideas like this don't have a prayer of getting adopted by a typical school board—but they certainly can seep into the culture, in a very almost clandestine way.

Gardner: It will take 50 years to see whether the ideas I've developed have impact. One of the things I've pushed very much is the idea of individual centered education. Up to now, everybody's taught the same thing, the same way, they're tested in the same way, if you do well fine, if not too bad—it's seen as being very fair. My argument, which contradicts any argument ever made in history, is it's the most unfair method in the world. It privileges one kind of mind, which I call the language-logic mind, or sometimes the Al Dershowitz mind (which I admire), this view that says, the more you're like that, the better you'll do, and the more rewards we'll give you, and the more you're different from that, tough *nuggies.* (A technical term in Cambridge—Ed. Note)

With the advent of the new technologies, individual-centered education is only a matter of time. People in 50 years will laugh at the notion that we thought everybody had to be taught the same thing in the same way. Already anything that's worth teaching we know dozens of ways of teaching it; we can make available technologically these things to any individual. Moreover, because we have smart machines, they can record what the child learned well, what he learned poorly, how he learned well, how he learned poorly; and make use of that knowledge. So that's an idea that I know is right.

> It's malpractice to expose kids to things for a week or two and go on to something else.

Understanding, that's a much bigger enchilada, so to speak. We've been content to see whether kids can sit on their duffs and do what they don't particularly want to do; that's been the operational definition of making it and that just isn't going to be enough any more. That might take a hundred years, so our grandchildren will know whether the world has become more receptive to an education-centered understanding.

The evidence that students are not understanding even what we're teaching them is legion now. It's malpractice to expose kids to things for a week or two and go on to something else. We know that doesn't work. In this arena, the work of Project Zero, where I've worked for over 30 years, both in multiple intelligences and in teaching understanding, is promising. That's exactly the right word to use. If I had to go to a congressional committee and make the best case I could give numbers, but that would be a best case rather than the most accurate description. It's promising; it's tough work, and because education is not a science, it's an art. It's very hard when something goes well to know why.

Everybody in this country, including me, who knows about education, admires Debbie Meier; the school that she founded is in New York City, Central Park East, secondary school and elementary school. Those are schools in very tough areas, East Harlem, and they really turn out kids who get through, go on to four-year colleges, and do decently. But nobody really understands whether it's one thing or two things or 20 things there—it's too hard to really figure out what the variables are—you can't do a controlled experiment.

The important thing for someone like me is to do no harm. For the first ten years of work in multiple intelligences I kept my mouth shut and let people do what they wanted to do, and then I finally came to the conclusion that that was a mistake, because some of the things people were doing were harmful. So I began to speak up about it, and I began to take a more active role. In Project Zero, we're actually studying schools around the country that claim to be doing well in cultivating the intelligences, and we are trying to separate the wheat from the chaff. And I assume the same sense of responsibility for these new ideas.

Art, Imagination, and School Renewal: Toward a Common Language

by Maxine Greene

Confronting the problem of a common language—accessible to diverse artists, teachers, members of communities, administrators—I recall the title of an Adrienne Rich collection called *The Dream of a Common Language* (1978). To think of it as a dream, of course, is to imagine it as something still out of reach, something sought for, something (at least for Rich) in some manner extraordinary. She wrote:

> But there come times—perhaps this is one of them—
> when we have to take ourselves more seriously or die;
> when we have to pull back from the incantations,
> rhythms we've moved to thoughtlessly,
> and disenthrall ourselves, bestow
> ourselves to silence, or a severer listening, cleansed
> of oratory, formulas, choruses, laments, static
> crowding of the wires (1978, 74–75).

No one, she said, who survives to speak a new language can avoid a cutting of the wires, a kind of "free fall." Surely we know what she meant. She was calling on us to break with bureaucratic talk, pious talk, media talk, with what John Dewey called the "crust of conventionalized and routine consciousness" (1954, 183). He was, as many of you know, always critical of fixities, of the routine, the thoughtless, the mechanical, and what he sometimes called the "anaesthetic," meaning the banal, the repetitive, the static. In *The Public and Its Problems* (1954), he pointed to the superficial plane on

From a paper based on a presentation at the Fourth International Teaching for Intelligence Conference, April 23, 1998, New York, NY. © 1998 by Maxine Greene. Reprinted with permission.

which so many people formed their opinions and made their judgments and went on to say that our lives reach a deeper level that only art can touch. It is, after all, one of the functions of art to break through that crust of "routine consciousness," to awaken us, I would say (along with Virginia Woolf and Albert Camus) and enhance our being in the world. "Common things," Dewey said, "a flower, a gleam of moonlight, the wing of a bird, not things rare and remote, are means with which the deeper levels of life are touched so that they spring up as desire and thought. Poetry, the drama, the novel, are proofs that the process of presentation is not insoluble. Artists have always been the real purveyors of the news, for it is not the outward happening in itself which is new, but the kindling by it of emotion, perception and appreciation" (1954, 183–184). Virginia Woolf called what he was trying to describe "moments of being" (1976, 71). Albert Camus wrote about the break with deadly routine, and how "one day the 'why' arises and everything begins in that weariness tinged with amazement. 'Begins'—this is important. Weariness comes at the end of the acts of a mechanical life, but at the same time it inaugurates the impulse of consciousness" (1955, 13). It is my view that encounters with certain art forms from either the creative or the appreciative point of view (I would hope from both) are what make such awakenings, such beginnings possible. And I believe that it is only after such awakenings, such moments of what have been called unconcealment, that young people as well as older people are enabled to see, feel, hear what Dewey called "the common things" that touch the deeper levels of life.

> It is in encounters with the arts, informed encounters, that their capacities are activated in ways traditionally ignored.

I want to believe that it is the release of imagination that makes these moments more likely and more frequent. In a book entitled *Imagination*, Mary Warnock links imagination to the belief that "there is more in our experience of the world than can possibly meet the unreflecting eye, that our experience is significant for us, and worth the attempt to understand it . . . this kind of belief may be referred to as the feeling of infinity" (1978, 202). Oddly or not, I associate that with what Adrienne Rich, in quite another mood, called a "free fall." Warnock goes on:

> It is a sense . . . that there is always *more* to experience, and *more in* what we experience than we can predict. Without some such sense,

even at the quite human level of there being something which deeply absorbs our interest, human life becomes perhaps not actually futile or pointless, but experienced as if it were. It becomes, that is to say, boring. In my opinion, it is the main purpose of education to give people the opportunity of not ever being, in this sense, bored; of not ever succumbing to a feeling of futility, or to the belief that they have come to the end of what is worth having. It may be that some people do not need education to save them from this; my claim is only that, if education has a justification, this salvation for those who do need it must be its justification (1978, 202–203).

I have looked into (yes, and read about) the dead and empty eyes of children who think they have nothing to hope for. Some, when asked what they want to be when they grow up, cannot respond, or they tell us (as I have heard in several schools) that all depends on whether they live that long. We have seen the ways in which poor children or neglected children or homeless children inscribe their pain when they are given crayons or pastels or pieces of chalk, and when their teachers or visiting artists give them clues about translating thoughts or feelings into objects or movements or shapes or sound. I think of the poetry young people are writing and what it can mean when they are moved (as I was) to explore the work of those called "real poets" for suggestions when it comes to rhythm and image and even (although they may not know the word) metaphor.

One of the significant changes in what many conceive of as dark times in the public schools seems to me a growing acknowledgment of the richness, the complexity, often the darkness of young people's experience. It is not so long ago that schoolchildren, for all the efforts of progressive educators, were thought of as empty vessels, there to be filled with officially sanctioned knowledge, if not (as in the case of Dickens' Mr. Gradgrind) "facts, Sissy, facts." Teachers, asked to keep their own journals, to come in touch with their own life stories, are far more likely to recognize that young people too can be seekers of meaning, makers of meaning. Many teachers have begun to view themselves as coaches, concerned for children's active sense-making, active learning. Much depends on their imaginations being aroused, on their feelings infusing their thinking, their perceptions grounding what they come to know and understand.

It is in encounters with the arts, informed encounters, that their capacities are activated in ways traditionally ignored. Their under-standing, like their interest in bringing paintings and dance perfor-mance and musical pieces and poems to life in their experience, surely is enriched by whatever experiences we can make available in exploring media, the materials with which artists work. It is not only that they are provided a means of expression and symbolization, an unexpected way of making imprints on the world. They are enabled to comprehend the efforts that must be exerted, the discipline that must be grasped, if what they perceive and feel and remember is to be given form, the form, the meaning to which others might respond.

I remember a young man, a teenager, who had learned to work with others to make video renderings of his neighborhood and his friends. One that I saw had to do with boys in Harlem talking about why they needed guns. The youngsters who had chosen to frame those boys, to capture that conversation, told us how learning the skills required had given them a sense of purpose, even as they freed them to look at other people's videos and even television programs with more critical understanding. They had discovered, among other things, that they had a right to interpret what they saw against their own lived experience. Not only did they seem to recognize what Mary Warnock (1978) said—that their experience held more than they might have predicted, that there were openings, spaces they might never have suspected—but the adventure (and it was an adventure), like the work required, gave them a feeling of dignity they had never known. Surely, many of us have seen the same kinds of awakenings in poetry workshops or when youngsters are coached in the writing of stories. We have seen it when studios, as it were, are opened in schools where painters can work with students and visual transformations are made part of the curriculum and part of their lives.

I am very aware, as we all are, of the enjoyment and excitement that can envelop a school when artists come to perform, after (if time and budget allow) involving students in the preparation, in the making of a dance, say, or a Shakespearean work, or a Gilbert and Sullivan piece. And I am aware of the pleasures of working with papier-mâché in homage, say, to Red Grooms, or of gathering to listen to Midori's violin when she visits a school. Like all of you, I hope we can keep alive the excitement, the pure pleasure, the break in routine arts in school bring with them. The breaking of the old lockstep scheduling, the surprise that is so much a part of involvement with art forms (at least those appropriate to different stages of development) cannot but lighten the atmosphere, even in the grim old buildings where so many young people are compelled to spend their days or (and I have seen this too) to hang out (once they check in) in the hallways or at the doors.

I have a recollection of going to one of those schools, a high school in the Bronx, and finding a group of boys on the steps in front of the door. One of them had written "school sucks" on the doors, and I stopped for a minute to stare, and am not sure of the expression on my face. One of the boys looked questioningly at me and, suddenly, free associating a bit mindlessly, I asked whether they had ever read *Catcher in the Rye* (Salinger 1957). And then I told them that in that book, Holden Caulfield, the young hero, had talked about cleaning all the dirty words off the walls of the school—and that I wondered how he would have handled that door. One of the boys scoffed and said that no one could wipe off all the walls in their school; the writing would only come back again. And then a small voice asked me what was this book I was talking about anyway. Suddenly, this elderly lady from downtown was sitting on the step telling them—and I must say I had a hushed and attentive audience for a while—about Holden Caulfield, particularly about the fantasy having to do with keeping children from falling off the cliff from the field of rye—into what I always thought of and think Holden thought of too—as the adult world. Perhaps you remember Holden misreading the Robert Burns poem. Instead of "If a body meet a body coming through the rye," he thought it was "If a body catch a body." Then he says, "Anyway, I keep picturing all these little kids playing some game in this big field of rye and all. Thousands of little kids, and nobody's around,— nobody big, I mean—except me. And I'm standing on the edge of some crazy cliff. What I have to do, I have to catch everybody if they start to go over the cliff—I mean if they're running and they don't look where they're going I have to come out from somewhere and *catch* them. That's all I'd do all day. I'd just be the catcher in the rye and all. I know it's crazy but that's the only thing I'd really like to be. I know it's crazy." His sister finally tells him, "Daddy's going to kill you." And Holden says, "I don't give a damn if he does" (Salinger 1957, 224–225). I am not sure if I remembered to tell my auditors that right after that Holden wants to "phone up this guy that was my English teacher" (Salinger 1957, 224–225), now teaching English at NYU.

> And then a small voice asked me what was this book I was talking about anyway.

I think the kids listened to me because they were bored, but also because I was opening a kind of door for them, a door through which they could look into an as/if world, a created world, but one that might (at least for the moment) make their world a little more intelligible. If I had had time, if I could have kept their attention and taken them with me, I would have told them about Huckleberry Finn and maybe Bartleby, the scrivener, and Gatsby (you may remember that Holden was crazy about *The Great Gatsby*—"Old Gatsby. Old sport. That killed me" [Salinger 1957, 183]). I would have liked to provoke them to match their stories against the stories of those who pursued stubbornly and hopelessly the American dream, who "preferred not to" in the end, or who, refusing to be all cramped up and have people try to "civilize them," lit out for the territory ahead—unaware that it was closed.

> Most of us involved in any way with the arts know very well the interrogative role they play or ought to play in life.

No, I do not believe I was offering any solution for them or any promise of sanctuary. I know, as most of you know, that it is not the function of art to offer answers, nor the function of teachers to come in with comfortable certainties. Novels, for me great plays (I keep thinking of *The Doll's House,* a year or two ago, of *The Chairs,* of *The Beauty Queen of Leonane,* even certain paintings—Franz Hals's, as John Berger has taught me, Rembrandt's, Cezanne's, van Gogh's, Monet's, Goya's, even—and I keep seeing that dark cloud over the city of Delft—Vermeer's), open question after question, that sharpen the questions, make me—as Rilke (1934) told his young poet to do— love the questions because they make me reach in so many directions, because they make me feel alive. And I believe, wrongly or rightly, that the kinds of questions that make me so uneasy, that make me feel so alive, so eager to keep on in the face of meaninglessness, are questions I share with other human beings, young ones included, once they are awakened, once they are helped to see. That suggests for me one of the sources of a common language—perhaps what Dewey meant when he talked about "deeper levels of life" (1954, 183).

In any case, most of us involved in any way with the arts know very well the interrogative role they play or ought to play in life, the power (according to Denis Donoghue [1983]) to defamiliarize the taken for granted, to shed a new light, sometimes a light of unwanted exposure on our lived lives. (I cannot thrust away a closing scene in the recent production of Ionescu's *The Chairs* when a fierce light suddenly is lit on the back of the stage, making members of the audience rear back and cover their eyes—and perhaps, breathing hard at the end, manage to say, "I see.") I appreciate Donoghue's reminding us that the arts may be useless in the sense they cannot cure toothaches, but in another way are momentous "because they provide for spaces in which we can live in total freedom. Think of it as a page. The main text is central, it is the text of need, of food and shelter, of daily preoccupations and jobs, keeping things going. This text is negotiated mostly by convention, routine, habit, duty; we have very little choice in it. So long as we are in this text, we merely coincide with our ordinary selves. If the entire page were taken with the text, we would have to live according to its conventional rhythms, even in our leisure hour, because they too are subject to conventions" (1983, 129).

Donoghue goes on to say that, for him, the arts are on the margins of most of our lives, the margin being the place for those feelings and intuitions that daily life doesn't have a place for and mostly seems to suppress. "Yet those," he writes, "who choose to live within the arts can make a space for themselves and fill it with intimations of freedom and presence" (1983, 129). The idea of making spaces for ourselves, experiencing ourselves in our tension and connectedness, and taking initiatives to move through those spaces seem to me to be of the first importance—for learning, for teaching, for feeling alive. As the philosopher Martin Heidegger said, things happen now and then beyond what is when an open place suddenly appears. There is a clearing, a lighting, a reaching beyond what we are sure we know.

There are, I must say, a number of people who are beginning to point out the relevance of social class to all of this. Not only is it still affirmed that our choices of what we choose to call "art" are still influenced by our Western traditions and by elitist conception of quality. Granted, we are allowing for multiculturalism; we recognize the significance of major artists like Toni Morrison, Alice Walker, Maya Angelou, August Wilson, Audre Lorde, Ralph Ellison, James Baldwin, as well as major thinkers like Cornel West, Henry Louis Gates, Patricia Williams. But we tend to forget, time and time again, that many of the questions we foster, many of the critiques that find expression, are not those raised by newcomers, immigrants, outsiders eager, above all, to join the mainstream and to assure not only requisite skills for their children but an acceptance of the prevailing value system as well. Talk of spaces and intuitions of freedom, talk of the unpredictable, while understandable, are not what many of such people want from schools. As we learn from African-American scholar and teacher Lisa Delpit and others, they want structure, they want a kind of humane process of socialization, they want recognition, they want technological training for their young, as they want security and the ability to survive. And a few of them are convinced that the freedom, the perceptive acuity, the consciousness of possibility we stress when we argue for the arts deserve a priority in the curricula of so-called reformed schools.

Seeking a common language, as we do, hoping for an emancipatory role for the several arts (when reflected upon, when made accessible), we still need to think of the multiple realities now represented in our cities and our schools. A while ago, with New York's centennial celebration, we were reminded of the rich fabrics of different art forms and different cultures, some of which we have (deliberately or not) ignored. There is the Korean tradition, there is the Puerto Rican tradition, there are the multiple Caribbean traditions—French, English, Creole. There are Arabic and other Middle Eastern traditions; today, there are Russian colonies, Haitian colonies.

Think of the challenge to those of us in search of a common language. Think, even more importantly, of classrooms where most of the students are still caught up in the symbol systems of cultures that do not view "art" as individual creation or a phenomenon depending for its realization on individual percipients' seeing or listening or constructing as meaningful.

Clifford Geertz, the anthropologist, writes about the gap most of us feel between the amount of talk about art that proceeds all around us and our ability to define or understand it. Because people perceive something important in the arts in general or in particular works, they talk or write about it endlessly. He writes that "we describe, analyze, compare, judge, classify; we erect theories about creativity, form, perception, social function; we characterize art as a language, a structure, a system, an act, a symbol, a pattern of feeling; we reach for scientific metaphors, spiritual ones, technological ones, political ones: and if all else fails, we string dark sayings together and hope someone will elucidate them for us" (1973, 95). Geertz views art in its multiple contexts as one of the several ways in which people participate in the general systems of symbolic forms we call cultures. Art, whatever its form, must be seen as part of the life of signs in a society, and Geertz asks his readers to move toward a consideration of them in their natural habitat—the "common world" in which we look, name, make things, and listen. "If there is a commonalty, it lies in the fact

that certain activities everywhere seem specifically designed to demonstrate that ideas are visible, audible, and tactile, that they can be
cast in forms where the senses and through
the senses, the emotions, can reflectively
address them. The variety of artistic expression stems from the variety of conceptions we
have about the way things are and is indeed
the same variety" (1973, 118–119). Signs,
Geertz says, are modes of thought as much as
they are modes of communication, and we
need still to concern ourselves with what they
tell us about the changing life around them—
life in its fullness and deficiency, in its wonder
and disillusionment, in its hopes and broken promises. They feed
into what Jerome Bruner (1986) describes as the mode of knowing
called story-telling; they orient us to the horizons and to the surrounding world.

> **Because people
> perceive something
> important in the arts
> in general or in
> particular works, they
> talk or write about it
> endlessly.**

In most of the cultures represented in today's classrooms, there
is relatively little interest in what reflective engagement with art forms
can mean when it comes to self-knowledge, to being in the world as a
conscious being who is in most ways induplicable. Children who
come from non-Western cultures are more than likely to conceive of
art as something incorporated into the textures of a shared social life,
if they think of the arts at all. The "margin" of which Donoghue
speaks, like the moments of freedom and presence, cannot have more
meaning for Islamic or Buddhist or Guyanian children than a description of art forms in terms of formal relationships. The more we
honor the traditions and expectations of such children and young
people, the more complex becomes the problem of arguing for the
arts in education. It may be that certain of their parents may view an
acknowledgment of individuality and point of view as an aspect of
the socialization process, but neither they nor their children are likely
to think of the Western view of aesthetic power as the authoritative
view. To visit an exhibition of Islamic or Byzantine art, to read novels
like *The God of Small Things, Lucy, Ceremony, Jasmine, A Pale View of
Hills,* or another post-colonial text is to recognize that the center has
shifted and that we can no longer refer to the same norms in arguing
for our conceptions of the artistic-aesthetic, or what represents, what
presents, what is beautiful, what moves us to aspire. Patrick
Chamoiseau, a writer from Martinique and the author of *Texaco*
(1997), wrote a small and revealing note at the start of an earlier book

called *School Days* (1994), which ought to also be taken into account as we seek a common language:

> Youngster,
> Of the West Indies, of French Guyana, of New Caledonia, of Reunion, of Mauritius, of Rodriques and other Mascarenes, of Corsica, of Brittany, of Normandy, of Alsace, of the Basque country, of Provence, of Africa, of the four corners of the Orient, of all national territories, of all far-flung dominions, of all outlying posts of empires or federations, you who have had to face a colonial school, yes, you who in other ways are still confronting one today, and you who will face this challenge tomorrow in some other guise: This voice of bitter laughter at the One and Only—a firmly centered voice challenging all centers, a voice beyond all home countries and peacefully diversal in opposition to the universal—is raised in your name.
> In Creole friendship,
> PC
> (Chamoiseau 1994, epigraph, n.p.)

As we search, it is that voice, I believe, that name to hold in mind.

There must be dialogue, particularly between teachers and artists, or so I believe. Democracy, Dewey (1916) told us, is a community in the making, and so, I would suggest, is a common language. If it ever solidified and became in some way absolute, it would begin resembling Chamoiseau's "One and Only" and give rise to the same bitter response. When I think of partnership, in any event, I do not think of institutions coming together. I think of individuals, live persons coming together. Again I turn to poetry, this time to a Muriel Rukeyser poem called "Effort at Speech Between Two People." Each verse begins with a variation "Speak to me. Take my hand. Where are you now?" (1992, 2). And this is the final verse:

> What are you now? If we could touch one another,
> If these our separate entities could come to grips,
> Clenched like a Chinese puzzle . . . yesterday
> I stood in a crowded street that was alive with people,
> And no one spoke a word, and the morning shone,
> Everyone silent, moving . . . Take my hand. Speak to me
> (Rukeyser 1992, 4).

Yes, I know partnerships have emerged and whom they are intended to include, as schools reach out to arts organizations that are willing to support and to sustain in the name of and hope for renewal or reform. At once, I know that collaboration and partnership can only be realized through personal encounters, which often begin where people are silent because they do not, at first, know what to say. It is not only that so many of the words are encapsulated in formulas, choruses, laments, as Adrienne Rich (1978) suggested. It is that, once we reach below the surface of spontaneity and entertainment, we discover contradictions, differences we never anticipated. What of the young, bathing in popular culture, defining the performances that make it to the screens as unquestionably art? What of the distances that still appear to yawn between theater (either Broadway this year or off-Broadway) and the films and concerts young people choose to attend, the videos they buy, the CDs in the countless disco stores? What of the teachers who still dread the "free fall," even as they dread the openings the unpredictable imagination makes possible? What of those teachers who teach to the test in order to insure predictability, the ones who need to measure in order to justify what they do? What of the teachers who have scarcely known the arts in the course of their lives, who think of them as frivolous, purely affective, at best, motivational? What of those who conceive standards as predefined, fixed to be imposed from above? What of those immersed in instrumental rationality, seeing themselves as molding the young, treating them as resources for the state, for the business community, for the new technology, not as existing persons in process, seeking their own ways?

Actually, there are at least three approaches to school reform in these times. There is one connected to "Goals 2000," centered on increasing general literacy for the sake of readying the new generation of a millennium governed by new technologies, linked by more and more complicated interests, respondent to free market ideologies. There is the one connected to the Christian Right, ostensibly preoccupied with virtue and character education, with abstinence, with chastity, with the family, with prayer in schools, with school choice, with campaigning against abortion and homosexuality. (I am reminded of Dewey again, writing about what he called "social pathology" in 1927, finding its symptoms in "idealization of long established, in a facile optimism assumes as a cloak, in riotous glorifications of things 'as they are,' in intimidation of all dissenters—ways which depress and dissipate through all the more effectual because they operate with subtle and unconscious persuasiveness" [Dewey 1954, 170].)

Then there is the reform that purportedly continues the progressive or the experiential tradition, stemming from Rousseau, Pestalozzi, Emerson, Froebel, Dewey, Bruner, Gardner, Duckworth, and others familiar to any of you in touch with that stream in American history running in the direction of personal liberation, awareness, and (in time) humane face-to-face community. Its watchwords today are active learning, critical questions, the construction of meanings, what Deborah Meier (1995) calls "the power of ideas." It involves efforts to release long silenced voices, to treat learners as situated persons speaking from their own locations as "who they are," to quote Hannah Arendt, "not what they are" (1958, 183). Collaborative learning, classroom communities, engagement with parents, outreach to neighborhoods, evolution by portfolio and exhibition, concern for the qualitative rather than the quantitative, a commitment to care and connectedness, as women's ways of knowing supplement and complement the autonomous rationality so long considered the source of standards as well as the goal of human development: all these mark many of the schools that see themselves involved in reform.

> We have to read the painting as well as the poem.

In the event of partnership between such schools and art organizations concerned for the health of children and as well for creative responses to their needs, the meaning of "art" and of "aesthetic experience" needs to be continually explored. It is not a matter of transforming teachers into artists or artists into public school teachers. Artists in the several domains themselves often reach for a common language, so that dancers may work in workshops with composers, poets with theater people, painters with musicians. In an atmosphere where dialogue is welcomed, teachers and artists may come together to articulate what they understand to be the meaning and ends in view of their distinctive projects. And they are distinctive. Teachers who reflect upon their projects (the projects by which they have defined themselves over the years) may think about their own thinking when it comes to devising situations in which young people are provoked to learn, and (often) to teach themselves. Artists, taking the initiative in an ongoing conversation, may consider the differences between teaching future practitioners of their own art forms and communicating to classroom teachers the languages of those art forms. The point in the classroom, as I see it, is to open spaces for the use of those languages to complement and extend what is understood through verbal and mathematical literacy. There are issues, however, having to do with how the concept of art is to be understood. (I can imagine, for instance, a dialogue generated by the play called *Art,* with all its hidden questions about representation, monochromatic paintings, price, elitism, and human friendship before and behind the painting on the wall. Or, thinking back to the play entitled *Six Degrees of Separation,* I can recall a mystery about a Kandinsky painting, which also can give rise to questions and to talk. And then there are the moral issues purportedly related to works of art in the debates surrounding the declining support for the National Arts Endowment. Teachers, too, might be involved in exploration of the Robert Mapplethorpe exhibitions, the performances of Karen Finley, the work of Robert Serrano. It may still be that dialogue among persons differently situated in the culture can advance the search for a common language.)

Nelson Goodman (1976), in the book *Languages of Art,* treats the arts as symbol systems that are invented, applied, transformed, and manipulated in a variety of ways—and that cannot be translated into one another. He makes what to me is a significant and relevant point when he challenges the notion that the aesthetic attitude is a kind of passive contemplation of the immediately given, uncontaminated by conceptualization, isolated from echoes of the past. He views it entirely differently (and compares old views of the disinterested and passive aesthetic attitude with gazing at a poem on a printed page without reading it). He goes on:

> I have held, on the contrary, that we have to read the painting as well as the poem, and that aesthetic experience is dynamic rather than static. It involves making delicate discrimination and discerning subtle relationships, identifying symbol systems and characters within these systems and that these characters denote and exemplify, interpreting works and reorganizing the world in terms of works and works in terms of the world. Much of our experience and many of our skills are brought to bear and may be transformed by the encounter. The aesthetic 'attitude' is restless, searching, testing—is less attitude than action: creation and recreation (1976, 242).

Not everyone will share Goodman's philosophy nor be willing to understand the different arts in terms of symbol systems or languages. Nonetheless, there is something in this paragraph suggesting active transaction between human beings and the world that brings it close to the spirit of what we think of as school reform. When I ponder the problem of a common language, words like *interpreting* and *reorganizing* and *restless, searching, testing* seem somehow essential to it and essential to our thinking about art.

It happens that Goodman is impatient with judgments of merit and with too much concentration of the question of excellence, which leads to distortion of aesthetic inquiry, he believes.

> To say that a work of art is good or even to say how good it is does not after all provide much information, does not tell us whether the work is evocative, robust, vibrant or exquisitely designed, and still less what are its alien specific qualities of color, shape, or sound . . . judging the excellence of works of art or the goodness of people is not the best way of understanding them (1976, 261).

Holding that in mind, I would suggest that the standards we affirm ought not to be imposed from without; they ought to be in some manner emergent as people work together, trying to discover how they ought to work together, reaching somehow beyond themselves with a sense of oughtness—a desire to appear before others as the best they can possibly be.

Surely, the common language we work toward can be infused—should be infused—with a sense of what both process and product ought to be. Quantification, the habitual ways of determining merit, the preoccupation with the measurable and the predictable: all must be cast aside as we concern ourselves with action and new beginnings, with imagination opening windows, allowing visions of what is not yet. I choose to conclude with an evocation of Toni Morrison's Nobel address. She was thinking primarily of literature, but what she says applies, I think, to the several arts and certainly to the dream we are nurturing with so many others, "the dream of a common language."

> Be it grand or slender, burrowing, blasting or refusing to sanctify; whether it laugh out loud or is a cry without an alphabet, the choice word or the chosen silence, unmolested language surges toward knowledge, not its destruction. But who does not know of literature banned because it is interrogative; discredited because it is critical; erased because alternate? And how many are outraged by the thought of a self-ravaged tongue? Word-work is sublime because it is generative; it makes meaning that secures our difference, our human difference—the way in which we are like no other life. We die. That may be the meaning of life. But we *do* language. That may be the measure of our lives (1994, 21–22).

We can dream and we can yearn and we can act. And we can say, as Muriel Rukeyser did in still another poem, "Something again is beginning to be born. A dance is dancing in me" (1992, 154).

REFERENCES

Arendt, Hannah. *The Human Condition.* Chicago: University of Chicago Press, 1958.

Bruner, Jerome. *Actual Minds, Possible Worlds.* Cambridge, MA: Harvard University Press, 1986.

Camus, Albert. *The Myth of Sisyphus and Other Essays.* New York: Alfred A. Knopf, 1955.

Chamoiseau, Patrick. *School Days.* Lincoln: University of Nebraska Press, 1994.

————. *Texaco.* New York: Pantheon Books, 1997.

Delpit, Lisa. *Other People's Children.* New York: The New Press, 1996.

Dewey, John. *Democracy and Education.* New York: Macmillan Company, 1916.

————. *The Public and Its Problems.* Athens, OH: Swallow Press, 1954. First published in 1927.

Donoghue, Denis. *The Arts Without Mystery.* Boston, MA: Little Brown and Company, 1983.

Geertz, Clifford. *Local Knowledge.* New York: Basic Books, 1973.

Goodman, Nelson. *Languages of Art.* Indianapolis, IN: Hachett Publishing Company, 1976.

Heidegger, Martin. *Poetry, Language, and Thought.* New York: Harper and Row Publishers, 1971.

Meier, Deborah. *The Power of Their Ideas.* Boston, MA: Beacon Press, 1995.

Morrison, Toni. *Nobel Lecture.* New York: Alfred A. Knopf, 1994.

Rich, Adrienne. *The Dream of a Common Language: Poems 1974–1978.* New York: W. W. Norton and Company, 1978.

Rilke, Rainer M. *Letters to a Young Poet.* New York: W. W. Norton and Company, 1934.

Rukeyser, Muriel. "Effort at Speech Between Two People," in *Out of Silence,* by Muriel Rukeseyer. Evanston, IL: Northwestern University Press, 1992. "Effort at Speech Between Two People" first published in *Theory of Flight,* 1935.

————. "Recovering," in *Out of Silence,* by Muriel Rukeseyer. Evanston, IL: Northwestern University Press, 1992.

Salinger, J. D. *Catcher in the Rye.* New York: Grosset and Dunlap, 1957.

Warnock, Mary. *Imagination.* Berkeley: University of California Press, 1978.

Woolf, Virginia. *Moments of Being: Unpublished Autobiographical Writings.* New York: Harcourt Brace Jovanovich, 1976.

Schools Should Nurture Wisdom

by Robert J. Sternberg

L uis Alberto Machado, formerly Minister for the Development of Intelligence in Venezuela, hypothesized that the road to peace and prosperity in a society could be found in the development of the intelligence of its citizens (Machado 1980). He put his money— or at least some of his country's money—where his mouth was and oversaw the development of more than a dozen programs to develop the intelligence of Venezuelan children. At least some of these projects succeeded (e.g., Herrnstein, Nickerson, de Sanches, and Swets 1986). But Machado's political party lost the next election, and with the loss of the election came the loss of most of the programs for developing intelligence. So Machado's hypothesis was never adequately tested in Venezuela.

Curiously, the hypothesis has been tested on a worldwide scale for several generations without anyone's being aware of it. The upshot is that Machado was well meaning, but wrong.

Flynn (1987) has pointed out that in the United States and in more than a dozen other countries for which records have been available, IQs have been rising roughly at a rate of 18 points per generation (thirty years). This increase has been going on for at least several generations (see also Neisser 1998).

Given that IQs have been rising, what does our world have to show for it? Judging by the amount and seriousness and sheer scale of global conflict, perhaps not much. There has been no apparent corresponding increase in peace and, in many countries, prosperity has not done so well either. Certainly there is no reason to believe that increasing IQs have improved people's relations with each other.

In the United States, the increase in IQs has been accompanied by another trend: increasing use of standardized test scores to determine people's place in society. Herrnstein and Murray (1994) suggested that our society is creating what they referred to as a "cognitive elite"—a socioeconomic upper class dominated by people of high cognitive ability. For whatever one may think of their other arguments, it is easy to accept this one. Universities heavily weigh standardized test scores for admissions, both at the college and graduate levels. It is difficult to gain admission to prestigious institutions without high test scores. Moreover, surveys such as that of *U.S. News and World Report,* which rank undergraduate and graduate programs using, in part, standardized test scores, place increasing pressure on institutions to weigh those scores heavily in admission. Institutions want to rank highly in the ratings and one road to high rankings is the admission of students with high test scores. It is easier for an institution to raise its test scores than to raise, say, faculty productivity or visibility in research.

> **Education is seen more as an access route than as an end in itself . . .**

So with IQs going up and IQ-related abilities counting more and more for success in the society, one can only conclude that the IQ-like abilities of those at the top of the socioeconomic spectrum are higher than ever before—even higher than would be predicted merely by the Flynn effect, because IQs have become more important for gaining access to premium jobs. But again, the rise in IQs among the socioeconomic elite does not seem to have created a happier or more harmonious society, and one only has to read the daily newspapers to see the poor uses to which high IQ can be put.

Simultaneously with the rise in IQ and in its importance has been another trend observed by Labaree (1997). This trend is the increasing use of education as a means of credentialing rather than of learning. Education is seen more as an access route than as an end in itself, and parents and children alike scramble for admission of the children to elite colleges not so much to obtain the best possible education but to obtain the best possible job later on. The result is that the IQs of both parents and children are directed not so much toward enhancing their learning and thinking as toward obtaining through education the best possible credentials for individual socioeconomic advancement. Education is seen not so much as a means of helping society but of helping one obtain the best that society has to offer socially, economically, and culturally.

This trend is likely to be amplified by the individualistic norms of U.S. society. When societies are ranked on an individualism-collectivism scale, U.S. society typically comes out right at the top in terms of individualism (Hofstede 1980). People learn how to live on their own, succeed on their own, and watch out for themselves. Few developed societies invest as little in helping the elderly, the poor, and the ill as does U.S. society. In short, we turn the increase in IQ not toward collective advantage but toward individual advantage. Although there is nothing wrong with such a trend, per se, it is driving us toward the tragedy of the commons, the situation in which people's looking out so well individually for themselves results in their collective loss. The tragedy can be understood hypothetically in terms of cows grazing on a common green. As each cow obtains more grass, the total available grass decreases. In our society, the total available resources are being sucked up in the service of those who can use their cognitive abilities and skills to maximize their own gains. What are these cognitive abilities and skills and how are they nurtured?

WHAT SKILLS DO SCHOOLS CURRENTLY NURTURE?

What skills do schools currently value and therefore nurture? Several, perhaps.

Memory

Memory is probably essential to all other higher level cognitive skills. For example, one cannot analyze, create, or apply knowledge without first having the knowledge to analyze, create, or use. But memory for an impressive knowledge base seems like a beginning rather than an end, as illustrated by "walking encyclopedias" who seem not to be able to use effectively much of what they know. Even people with less impressive knowledge bases often seem to be stuck with inert knowledge that they are unable to use. Many teachers and professors encounter students who get A's in courses but seem to be unable to use their knowledge in research projects or other types of applications of their knowledge.

Our research suggests that schools probably overemphasize the development and use of memory-based learning. We have found, for example, that students whom we taught in a way that matches their triarchic (analytical, creative, and practical) pattern of abilities learn more and perform better than do children simply taught for memory

(Sternberg, Ferrari, Clinkenbeard, and Grigorenko 1996; Sternberg, Grigorenko, Ferrari, and Clinkenbeard, in press). We have also found that children taught triarchically outperform children taught for memory, even on memory-based tests of achievement (Sternberg, Torff, and Grigorenko 1998a, 1998b).

Cognitive psychologists, like teachers in school, seem to devote a great share of their attention to memory, but one may wonder whether they, like the teachers, are not seduced by the greater ease of studying and assessing memory than of studying and assessing other cognitive phenomena, such as creativity or wisdom. There is, of course, a large body of evidence suggesting the importance of a large and well-organized knowledge base for expertise (Chi, Glaser, and Farr 1988; Ericsson 1996; Ericsson and Smith 1991). But such knowledge seems more to be a necessary than a sufficient condition for expertise (Sternberg 1996). Great thinkers like Descartes, Picasso, Mozart, Dante, Einstein, and Pasteur were clearly knowledgeable, but it seems implausible that it was their knowledge, per se, that led to their amazing expert contributions. So perhaps these abilities are not enough.

Analytical Abilities

Analytical abilities are the kinds of abilities most frequently measured by conventional tests of abilities (Sternberg 1997b). Clearly they are important for school success, in that scores on such tests are predictive of grades in school as well as other scholastic criteria (Jensen 1998). At the same time, one cannot help but wonder whether what distinguishes highly creative leaders of a field from their less creative counterparts is what is measured by these tests. It also seems unlikely that world leaders who are viewed as wise (Nelson Mandela, perhaps, or Abraham Lincoln or Winston Churchill) and those viewed as unwise (Adolf Hitler, Joseph Stalin, or Mobutu Sese Seko) were distinguished cognitively primarily by IQ. As noted earlier, the rise in IQs over the generations has not been matched by any obvious increase in world peace or world order.

Herrnstein and Murray (1994) have argued for the importance of IQ-like analytical abilities in the attainment of one's place in the socioeconomic ladder of societal success, but as I have argued elsewhere (Sternberg 1995a), the correlation between IQ and societal success seems in large part a societal creation. By requiring high ability test scores, achievement test scores, or grades for access to the routes to societal success, a society takes a large step toward ensuring that only those who are at high levels on measures of analytical abilities will achieve success, whether or not these particular abilities are actually instrumental for success in the jobs for which they are required. Caste, race, and gender have also been used to create distinctions among groups in their attained socioeconomic levels, a procedure that also creates an artificial correlation between an individual attribute and attainments. The correlation is artificial in the sense that the predictor variable predicts largely or only because we force it to. So perhaps these abilities are not enough.

> ... seems unlikely that world leaders who are viewed as wise and those viewed as unwise were distinguished cognitively primarily by IQ.

Creative Abilities

Creative abilities are attractive as a set of abilities schools should develop and nurture, if only because they seem so important to success, at least in the complex and rapidly changing world in which we live (Sternberg and Lubart 1995). These abilities seem important in distinguishing major contributors from minor contributors to a field (Simonton 1994; see also essays in Sternberg 1988). Yet, even creative abilities are not enough.

According to Gardner (1993), many creative contributors are extremely hard on those around them, making life miserable for others. They also may make life miserable for themselves, as is clear from the lives of people like Mozart, van Gogh, and Hemingway. Worse is the problem, as illustrated by notorious individuals such as Joseph Mengele, of people who use their creativity toward the worst possible ends. Creativity is not enough either.

Practical Intelligence

Practical intelligence would seem to be a good candidate for something schools should value and nurture, perhaps more than they do. Research shows the relative independence of practical intelligence from academic intelligence (e.g., Ceci and Liker 1986; Nuñes 1994; Sternberg, Wagner, Williams, and Horvath 1995; see essays in Sternberg and Wagner 1986). Practical intelligence complements memory and academic intelligence in that it concerns not just what one knows but how one uses it in one's everyday life. Yet practical intelligence, too, even on top of everything else I have discussed, may not be enough.

For one thing, some of the most cunning business people and even world leaders use their practical intelligence to advance themselves and perhaps their close associates, at the same time leaving their businesses or countries (as in the case of Mobutu or Suharto or Abacha) close to or in bankruptcy. For another thing, some of these individuals not only look out for themselves and their families or close associates, but further use their wiles to destroy anyone who seems like the slightest threat, real or imagined. Perhaps, then, something more is needed.

Memory, analytical, creative, and practical skills are all important, but they are not enough. What else is there? One additional skill is wisdom.

WHAT IS WISDOM?

Wisdom can be defined as the "power of judging rightly and following the soundest course of action, based on knowledge, experience, understanding, etc." (*Webster's New World College Dictionary* 1997, 1533). Such a power would seem to be of vast importance in a world that at times seems bent on destroying itself. A more detailed review of some of the major approaches to wisdom can be found in Baltes (in preparation) or in Sternberg (1990, in press-a).

MAJOR APPROACHES TO UNDERSTANDING WISDOM

A number of psychologists have attempted to understand wisdom in different ways. The approaches underlying some of these attempts are summarized in Sternberg (1990a). The approaches might be classified as philosophical, implicit-theoretical, and developmental.

Philosophical approaches have been reviewed by Robinson (1990; see also Robinson 1989, with regard to the Aristotelian approach in particular, and Labouvie-Vief 1990, for a further review). Robinson notes that the study of wisdom has a history that long antedates psychological study, with the Platonic dialogues offering the first intensive analysis of the concept of wisdom. Robinson points out that, in these dialogues, there are three different senses of wisdom: wisdom as (a) *sophia,* which is found in those who seek a contemplative life in search of truth; (b) *phronesis,* which is the kind of practical wisdom shown by statesmen and legislators; and (c) *episteme,* which is found in those who understand things from a scientific point of view.

Implicit-theoretical approaches to wisdom have in common the search for an understanding of people's folk conceptions of what wisdom is. Thus, the goal is not to provide a "psychologically true" account of wisdom but rather an account that is true with respect to people's beliefs, whether these beliefs are right or wrong. Some of the earliest work of this kind was done by Clayton (1975, 1976, 1982; Clayton and Birren 1980), who multidimensionally scaled ratings of pairs of words potentially related to wisdom for three samples of adults differing in age (younger, middle-aged, older). In her earliest study (Clayton 1975), the terms that were scaled were ones such as *experienced, pragmatic, understanding,* and *knowledgeable.*

Holliday and Chandler (1986) also used an implicit-theories approach to understanding wisdom. Approximately 500 participants were studied across a series of experiments. The investigators were interested in determining whether the concept of wisdom could be understood as a prototype (Rosch 1975) or central concept. Principal-components analysis of one of their studies revealed five underlying factors: exceptional understanding, judgment and communication skills, general competence, interpersonal skills, and social unobtrusiveness.

Sternberg (1985b, 1990b) has reported a series of studies investigating implicit theories of wisdom. For wisdom, six components emerged from ratings of behaviors by college students: reasoning ability, sagacity, learning from ideas and environment, judgment, expeditious use of information, and perspicacity.

Explicit theories are constructions of (supposedly) expert theorists and researchers rather than of laypeople. In the study of wisdom, most explicit-theoretical approaches are based on constructs from the psychology of human development. The most extensive program of research has been that conducted by Baltes and his colleagues. For example, Baltes and Smith (1987, 1990) gave adult participants life-management problems, such as "A fourteen-year-old girl is pregnant. What should she, what should one, consider and do?" and "A fifteen-year-old girl wants to marry soon. What should she, what should one, consider and do?" Baltes and Smith tested a five-component model on participants' protocols in answering these and other questions. The five components in the model are (a) rich factual knowledge (general and specific knowledge about the conditions of life and its variations), (b) rich procedural knowledge (general and specific knowledge about strategies of judgment and advice concerning mat-

ters of life), (c) life-span contextualism (knowledge about the contexts of life and their temporal [developmental] relationships),
(d) relativism (knowledge about differences in values, goals, and priorities), and
(e) uncertainty (knowledge about the relative indeterminacy and unpredictability of life and ways to manage). An expert answer should reflect more of these components, whereas a novice answer should reflect fewer of them. The data were generally supportive of their model.

> Sometimes organizations actually suppress the acquisition of tacit knowledge.

Some theorists have viewed wisdom in terms of postformal-operational thinking, thereby viewing wisdom as extending beyond the Piagetian stages of intelligence (Piaget 1972). Wisdom thus might be a stage of thought beyond Piagetian formal operations. For example, some authors have argued that wise individuals are those who can think reflectively or dialectically, in the latter case with the individuals realizing that truth is not always absolute but rather evolves in an historical context of theses, antitheses, and syntheses (e.g., Basseches 1984; Kitchener 1983, 1986; Kitchener and Brenner 1990; Kitchener and Kitchener 1981; Labouvie-Vief 1980, 1982, 1990; Pascual-Leone 1990; Riegel 1973). Other theorists have viewed wisdom in terms of finding important problems to solve (Arlin 1990).

Although most developmental approaches to wisdom are onto-genetic, Csikszentmihalyi and Rathunde (1990) have taken a philo-genetic or evolutionary approach, arguing that constructs such as wisdom must have been selected for over time, at least in a cultural sense. They define wisdom as having three basic dimensions of meaning: (a) that of a cognitive process, or a particular way of obtaining and processing information; (b) that of a virtue, or socially valued pattern of behavior; and (c) that of a good, or a personally desirable state or condition.

A TACIT-KNOWLEDGE APPROACH TO UNDERSTANDING WISDOM

The Nature of Tacit Knowledge

The view of wisdom proposed here has at its core the notion of tacit knowledge (Polanyi 1976), which we have defined as action-oriented knowledge, typically acquired without direct help from others, that allows individuals to achieve goals they personally value (Sternberg,

Wagner, Williams, and Horvath 1995). Tacit knowledge has three main features: (a) it is procedural; (b) it is relevant to the attainment of goals people value; and (c) it typically is acquired with little help from others.

When we refer to tacit knowledge as being procedural, and as intimately related to action, we are viewing it as a form of "knowing how" rather than of "knowing that" (Ryle 1949). In our work, we view condition-action sequences (production systems) as a useful formalism for understanding the mental representation of tacit knowledge. For example, if one needs to deliver bad news to one's boss and if it is Monday morning and if the boss's golf game was rained out the day before and if the boss's staff seems to be "walking on eggshells," then it is better to wait until later to deliver the news. Note that tacit knowledge is always wedded to particular uses in particular situations or classes of situations.

Tacit knowledge also is practically useful. It is instrumental to the attainment of goals people value. Thus, people use this knowledge in order to achieve success in life, however they may define success. Abstract academic knowledge about procedures for solving problems with no relevance to life would not be viewed, in this perspective, as constituting tacit knowledge.

Finally, tacit knowledge typically is acquired without direct help from others. At best, others can guide one to acquire this knowledge. Often, environmental support for the acquisition of this knowledge is minimal, and sometimes organizations actually suppress the acquisition of tacit knowledge. For example, a school system might not want its teachers to know how high-level decisions are really made, as opposed to how they are supposed to be made. From a developmental standpoint, this view suggests that wisdom is not taught so much as indirectly acquired. One can provide the circumstances for the development of wisdom and case studies to help students develop wisdom, but one cannot teach particular courses of action that would be considered wise, regardless of circumstances. Indeed, tacit knowledge is wedded to contexts, so that the tacit knowledge that would apply in one context would not necessarily apply in another context. To help someone develop tacit knowledge, one would provide mediated learning experiences rather than direct instruction as to what to do when.

Measurement of Tacit Knowledge

In a series of studies (summarized in Sternberg, Wagner, and Okagaki 1993; Sternberg, Wagner, Williams and Horvath 1995), we have sought to develop assessments of tacit knowledge in real-world pursuits. The methodology for constructing assessments is rather complex (Horvath et al. 1996) but involves interviewing individuals for how they have handled critical situations on their jobs. We then extract the tacit knowledge implicit in these interviews. Assessments then are constructed that ask people to solve the kinds of problems they find in managing themselves, others, and tasks on the job. Each of these problems typically presents a scenario about a job-related problem along with possible options for dealing with that problem. Test takers are asked to evaluate the quality of the problems on a Likert scale. Their response profiles for all items then are typically scored against the averaged profile of a nominated expert group.

Tacit Knowledge as an Aspect of Practical Intelligence

We have argued that tacit knowledge is a key aspect of practical intelligence (Sternberg 1985b, 1997b; Sternberg and Wagner 1993; Sternberg, Wagner, and Okagaki 1993; Sternberg et al. 1995), or the ability to apply various kinds of information-processing components of intelligence to experience for the purposes of adaptation to, shaping of, and selection of environments. Practical intelligence requires a balance of adaptation, shaping, and selection, in that different kinds of environments and environmental situations require different kinds of responses.

In a series of studies (see review in Sternberg et al. 1995), we have shown that tacit knowledge tends to increase with experience on a job but that it is what one learns from the experience rather than the experience itself that seems to matter. Measures of tacit knowledge tend to be correlated with each other, both within and across measures for different occupations. Our measures of tacit knowledge also predict actual performance in jobs such as sales, management, and college teaching. Not only is this prediction statistically significant and fairly substantial in magnitude (with correlations typically at about the 0.3 level), but this prediction is largely independent of the prediction provided by conventional tests of academic intelligence. This is true within a fairly broad range of academic abilities (Eddy 1988). But the prediction is not always independent. In one study among Kenyan schoolchildren, we have actually found a significant negative correlation between tacit knowledge relevant to environmental adaptation (knowledge of natural herbal medicines believed to fight infections) and performance on measures of fluid and crystallized abilities (see Sternberg and Grigorenko 1997).

> ... it is what one learns from the experience rather than the experience itself that seems to matter.

THE BALANCE THEORY OF WISDOM

Several of the theories described above emphasize the importance of various kinds of integrations or balances in wisdom. At least three major kinds of balances have been proposed: among various kinds of thinking (e.g., Labouvie-Vief 1990), among various self systems, such as the cognitive, conative, and affective (e.g., Kramer 1990), and among various points of view (e.g., Kitchener and Brenner 1990). Baltes has also argued for the importance of balance (Baltes 1993, 1994, in preparation; Staudinger, Lopez, and Baltes 1997). The view presented here expands on but also differs from these kinds of notions in also providing for particular kinds of balance in wisdom.

Wisdom as Tacit Knowledge Balancing Interests

The definition of wisdom proposed here draws both upon the notion of tacit knowledge, as described above, and on the notion of balance (Sternberg, in press-a). Wisdom is thus viewed as a kind of practical intelligence, but not the kind that is applied simply to benefit oneself or some individual one cares about, for whatever reason. In particular, wisdom is defined as the application of tacit knowledge as mediated by values toward the achievement of a common good through a balance among (a) intrapersonal, (b) interpersonal, and (c) extrapersonal interests in order to achieve a balance among (a) adaptation to existing environments, (b) shaping of existing environments, and (c) selection of new environments as shown in Figure 1.

Thus, wisdom is a kind of practical intelligence in that it draws upon tacit knowledge, but it is not just a kind of practical intelligence. Wisdom is not just about maximizing one's own or someone else's self-interest, but about balancing of various self-interests (intrapersonal) with the interests of others (interpersonal) and of

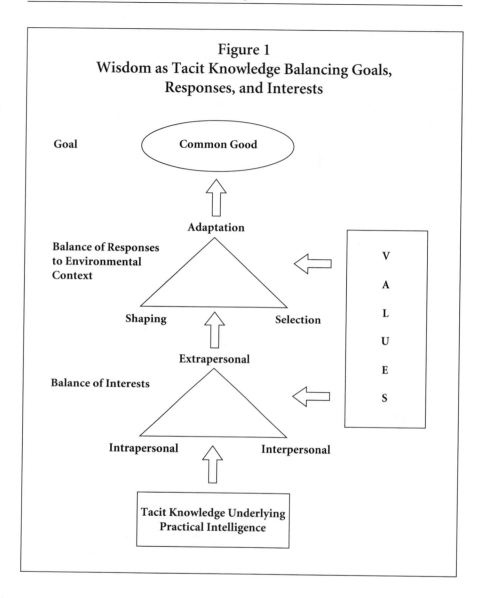

Figure 1
Wisdom as Tacit Knowledge Balancing Goals,
Responses, and Interests

other aspects of the context in which one lives (extrapersonal), such as one's city or country or environment or even God.

An implication of this view is that when one applies practical intelligence, one may deliberately seek outcomes that are good for oneself and bad for others. In wisdom, one certainly may seek good ends for oneself, but one also seeks common good outcomes for others. If one's motivations are to maximize certain people's interests and minimize other people's, wisdom is not involved. In wisdom, one seeks a common good, realizing that this common good may be better for some than for others. An evil genius may be academically intelligent; he may be practically intelligent; he cannot be wise.

> An evil genius may be academically intelligent; he may be practically intelligent; he cannot be wise.

I refer here to "interests," which are related to the multiple points of view that are a common feature of many theories of wisdom (as reviewed in Sternberg 1990a). Diverse interests encompass multiple points of view, and thus the use of the term "interests" is intended to include "points of view." Interests go beyond points of view, however, in that they include not only cognitive aspects of divergences but affective and motivational divergences as well. Sometimes differences in points of view derive not so much from differences in cognitions as from differences in motivations, as when teachers and boards of education have different ideas about how scarce budget dollars should be spent.

Problems requiring wisdom always involve at least some element of each of intrapersonal, interpersonal, and extrapersonal interests. For example, one might decide that it is wise to take a particular teaching position, a decision that seemingly involves only one person. But many people are typically affected by an individual's decision to take a job—significant others, children, perhaps parents and friends. And the decision always has to be made in the context of what the whole range of available options is. Similarly, a decision about whether to have an abortion requires wisdom because it involves not only oneself but the baby who would be born, others to whom one is close such as the father, and the rules and customs of the society.

As is true with all forms of practical intelligence (Sternberg 1985a, 1997b), wisdom involves a balancing not only of the three kinds of interests but also of three possible courses of action in response to this balancing: adaptation of oneself or others to existing environments; shaping of environments in order to render them more compatible with oneself or others; and selection of new environments. In adaptation, the individual tries to find ways to conform to the existing environment that forms his or her context. Sometimes adaptation is the best course of action under a given set of circumstances. But typically, one seeks a balance between adaptation and shaping, realizing that fit to an environment requires not only changing oneself but changing the environment as well. When an individual finds it impossible or at least implausible to attain such a fit, he or she may decide to select a new environment altogether, leaving, for example, a job, a community, a marriage, or whatever.

Wisdom manifests itself as a series of processes, which are typically cyclical and can occur in a variety of orders. These processes are related to what I have referred to as "metacomponents" of thought (Sternberg 1985a), including (a) recognizing the existence of a problem, (b) defining the nature of the problem, (c) representing information about the problem, (d) formulating a strategy for solving the problem, (e) allocating resources to the solution of a problem, (f) monitoring one's solution of the problem, and (g) evaluating feedback regarding that solution. In deciding about a teaching job, for example, one first has to see both taking the position and not taking it as viable options (problem recognition), then figure out exactly what taking or not taking the position would mean for oneself (defining the problem), then consider the costs and benefits to oneself and others of taking the position (representing information about the problem), and so forth.

The balance theory suggests that wisdom is at least partially domain specific in that tacit knowledge is acquired within a given context or set of contexts. It is typically acquired by selectively encoding new information that is relevant for one's purposes in learning about that context, selectively comparing this information to old information in order to see how the new fits with the old, and selectively combining pieces of information in order to make them fit together into an orderly whole (Sternberg, Wagner, and Okagaki 1993).

As noted above, however, our research has found significant correlations on scores of tacit knowledge across domains. For example, we have found that scores on tests of tacit knowledge for academic psychology and management correlate significantly (Wagner and Sternberg 1985), as do scores on tests of tacit knowledge for management and military leadership (Hedlund et al. 1998). Thus, although one's development of wisdom might be domain specific, the tacit knowledge one learns in one domain might well extend to other domains. At the same time, the wise individual necessarily would have to know the limits of his or her own tacit knowledge.

Wisdom may also correlate across domains, although such correlations have yet to be shown empirically.

Although tacit knowledge is acquired within a domain, it more typically applies to a field, following a distinction made by Csikszentmihalyi (1988, 1996). Csikszentmihalyi refers to the domain as the formal knowledge of a socially defined field. So, for example, knowing how to construct, conduct, or analyze the results of experiments would be knowledge important to the domain of experimental psychology. But knowing how to speak about the results persuasively, how to get the results published, or knowing how to turn the results into the next grant proposal would constitute knowledge of the field. Thus, academic intelligence would seem to apply primarily in the domain, practical intelligence and wisdom in the field. Because the field represents the social organization of the domain, it primarily is in the field that intrapersonal, interpersonal, and extrapersonal interactions take place.

Problems Measuring (and Not Measuring) Wisdom

If one looks at the kinds of problems that have been used to measure wisdom in empirical work, notably of Baltes and his colleagues, one can evaluate the degree to which they measure wisdom, at least according to this balance theory. A life-planning task (Baltes, Staudinger, Maercker, and Smith 1995) would be an excellent task for measuring wisdom because it involves one's own interests but inevitably must take into account the interests of others about whom one cares deeply as well as the context in which one lives and may live in the future. A task in which one must decide what to do when a good friend calls and says he or she wants to commit suicide (Staudinger and Baltes 1996) would also involve the interests of the other, one's own interest in getting involved and possibly failing to convince the person not to commit suicide, and also the difficulty of acting in the context of an unexpected telephone call. Similarly, counseling a fourteen-year-old girl who is pregnant or a sixteen-year-old boy who wants to marry soon (Baltes and Smith 1990) both involve balancing of the interests of the individuals to be counseled, the other people in their lives, and the costs of giving the wrong advice.

Perhaps the ideal problems for measuring wisdom, in light of the balance theory proposed here, are complex real-world dilemmas and especially conflict-resolution problems involving multiple competing interests and no clear resolution of how these interests can be reconciled (see, for example, Sternberg and Dobson 1987; Sternberg and Soriano 1984). For example, one might be asked to resolve a conflict between a board of education and teachers' unions. Given the relevance of such problems, it makes sense that Baltes and his colleagues (Smith, Staudinger, and Baltes 1994) would have found that clinical psychologists would do particularly well on wisdom-related tasks. Another group who might be expected to do well would be experienced mediators and other negotiators who have helped school boards and teachers' unions in conflict reach resolutions of their disagreements.

The tacit-knowledge approach to measurement described above might present a useful way of measuring wisdom. The exact problems would differ, however, from those we have used to measure practical intelligence. In particular, the problems would involve solutions that maximize not just one's own self-interest but a variety of intrapersonal, interpersonal, and extrapersonal interests. The stakes, therefore, would be higher and more complex because so many different interests would be involved. In our current work, we are using tacit-knowledge problems of these kinds to assess wisdom and its relation to other constructs.

In contrast to problems such as the ones we have suggested or the ones Baltes and his colleagues have used, typical problems found on conventional tests of intelligence, such as the Stanford-Binet (Thorndike, Hagen, and Sattler 1986) or the Wechsler (Wechsler 1991), measure wisdom minimally or not at all, according to the balance theory. There is no obvious similarity between these problems and the kinds of problems described above that would measure wisdom. Even when they measure thinking in a variety of domains, they typically do not involve judgments about intrapersonal, interpersonal, and extrapersonal interests for purposes of adapting to, shaping, and selecting environments. Similarly, there is little apparent similarity between problems measuring wisdom and those measuring creativity, whether from a psychometric point of view (e.g., Torrance 1974) or from a systems point of view (e.g., Sternberg and Lubart 1995). For example, wisdom-related problems seem remote either from finding unusual uses of a paper clip or from writing creative short stories, drawing creative pictures, or devising creative scientific experiments or explanations.

SOURCES OF DEVELOPMENTAL AND INDIVIDUAL DIFFERENCES IN WISDOM

The balance theory suggests a number of sources of developmental and individual differences in wisdom. In particular, there are two kinds of sources, those directly affecting the balance processes and those that are antecedent.

Individual and Developmental Differences Directly Affecting the Balance Processes

There are five such sources:

1. *Goals.* People may differ in terms of the extent to which they seek a common good, and thus in the extent to which they aim for the essential goal of wisdom.

2. *Balancing of responses to environmental contexts.* People may differ in their balance of responses to environmental contexts. Responses always reflect the interaction of the individual making the judgment and the environment, and people can interact with contexts in myriad ways.

3. *Balancing of interests.* People may balance interests in different ways.

4. *Tacit knowledge.* People bring different kinds and levels of tacit knowledge to judgmental situations, which are likely to affect their responses.

5. *Values.* People have different values mediating their utilization of tacit knowledge in the balancing of interests and responses.

These sources of differences produce variation in how wise people are and in how well they can apply their wisdom in different kinds of situations. To the extent that wisdom typically is associated with greater intellectual and even physical maturity, it is presumably because the development of tacit knowledge and of values is something that unfolds over the course of the life span and not just in childhood or even in early years of adulthood.

The above sources of individual differences pertain to the balancing processes. Other sources are antecedent to these processes.

Developmental and Individual Differences in Antecedent Variables

Antecedent variables leading to developmental and individual differences are those specified by my earlier theory (Sternberg 1990b). They include (a) knowledge, (b) analytical and creative as well as practical thinking (Sternberg 1997b), (c) a judicial thinking style (Sternberg 1997c), (d) personality variables, (e) motivation to think wisely, and (f) environmental variables.

Relations of Wisdom to Knowledge and to Analytical, Creative, and Practical Abilities

Wisdom is related to other psychological constructs but not identical to any of them.

First, wisdom requires knowledge, but the heart of wisdom is tacit, informal knowledge of the kind learned in the school of life, not the kind of explicit formal knowledge taught in schools. One could be a "walking encyclopedia" and show little or no wisdom because the knowledge one needs to be wise is not to be found in encyclopedias or even, generally, in the type of teaching found in most schools (with the possible exception of those that teach Socratically).

> High IQ has brought us a world on the brink of destruction with the power to finish itself off many times over.

Second, wisdom requires analytical thinking, but it is not the kind of analytical thinking typically emphasized in schools or measured on tests of academic abilities and achievements (discussed in Sternberg 1980). Rather, it is analysis of real-world dilemmas in which clean and neat abstractions often give way to messy and disorderly concrete interests. The kind of abstract analytical thinking that may lead to outstanding performance on a test such as the Raven Matrices, which presents figural reasoning items, will be of some but not much use in complex real-world dilemmas such as how to defuse the conflict between India and Pakistan.

Third, wise solutions are often creative ones, as King Solomon demonstrated in cleverly determining which of two women was truly the mother of a child. But the kind of crowd-defying, buy-low, sell-high attitude that leads to creative contributions does not in itself lead to wisdom (Sternberg 1995b). Creative people often tend toward extremes, although their later contributions may be more integrative (Gardner 1993). Creative thinking is often brash whereas wise thinking is balanced. This is not to say that the same people cannot be both creative and wise. It is to say, however, that the kinds of thinking required to be creative and wise are different and thus will not necessarily be found in the same person. Moreover, teaching people to think creatively (see, e.g., Sternberg and Williams 1996) will not teach them to think wisely.

Practical thinking is closer to wisdom than are analytical and creative thinking, but again, it is not the same. Wisdom is a particular kind of practical thinking. It is practical thinking that (a) balances competing intrapersonal, interpersonal, and extrapersonal interests, (b) balances adaptation to, shaping of, and selection of environments, in (c) the service of a common good. Thus, people can be good practical thinkers without being wise but they cannot be wise without being good practical thinkers. Good practical thinking is necessary but not sufficient for the manifestation of wisdom.

Wise thinking will not develop simply by teaching for other kinds of thinking. How might it be developed? And why is it so scarce?

IMPLICATIONS FOR EDUCATION

My speculation is that increases in intelligence—at least as measured by IQ—have not been matched by comparable increases in wisdom. Indeed, to the extent that our society has increasingly stressed the use of IQ to maximize one's own chances of admission to and success in the "cognitive elite" posited by Herrnstein and Murray (1994), increases in IQ may have been concomitant with decreases in wisdom. High IQ has brought us a world on the brink of destruction with the power to finish itself off many times over.

Wisdom might bring us a world that would seek instead to better itself and the conditions of all the people in it. At some level, we as a society have a choice. What do we wish to maximize through our schooling? Is it knowledge? Is it intelligence? Or is it wisdom? If it is wisdom, then we need to put our students on a much different course. We need to value not only how they use their outstanding individual abilities to maximize their attainments but how they use their individual abilities to maximize the attainments of others as well. We need, in short, to value wisdom.

What would education that valued wisdom look like?

First, students would be reading classic works of literature and philosophy (whether Western or otherwise) to learn and reflect upon the wisdom of the sages. The rush to dump classic works in favor of modern works would make sense only if the wisdom these modern works had to impart equaled or exceeded that of the classic works.

Second, students would be engaged in class discussions, projects, and essays that encouraged them to discuss the lessons they have learned from these works and how they can be applied to their own lives and the lives of others. A particular emphasis would be placed on the development of dialectical thinking. Such thinking, carried out over space, involves thinkers understanding significant problems from multiple points of view and understanding how others legitimately could conceive of things in a way that is quite different from one's own. Carried out over time, dialectical thinking involves thinkers understanding that ideas and the paradigms under which they fall evolve and keep evolving, not only from the past to the present, but from the present to the future (Hegel 1931; see also Sternberg, in press-b).

Third, students would need to study not only "truth," as we know it, but values. The idea would not be to force-feed a set of values but to encourage students reflectively to develop their own.

Fourth, such instruction would place an increased emphasis on critical, creative, and practical thinking in the service of good ends— ends that benefit not only the individual doing the thinking but others as well. All of these types of thinking would be valued, not just critical thinking.

Fifth, students would be encouraged to think about how almost everything they study might be used for better or worse ends and to realize that the ends to which knowledge are put *do* matter.

Finally, teachers would realize that the only way they could develop wisdom in their students would be to serve as role models of wisdom themselves. A role model of wisdom will, I believe, take a much more Socratic approach to teaching than teachers customarily do. Students often want large quantities of information spoon-fed or even force-fed to them. They then attempt to memorize this material for exams, only to forget it soon thereafter. In a wisdom-based approach to teaching, students will need to take a more active role in constructing their learning. But a wisdom-based approach is not, in my view, tantamount to a constructivist approach to learning. Students have not achieved or even come close to achieving wisdom when they merely have constructed their own learning. Rather, they must be able to not only construct knowledge from their own point of view but be able to construct and sometimes reconstruct knowledge from the point of view of others. Constructivism from only a single point of view can lead to egocentric rather than balanced understanding.

Lessons taught to emphasize wisdom would have a rather different character from lessons as they often are taught today. Consider the following examples.

First, social studies and especially history lessons would look very different. For example, high school American history books typically teach American history from only one point of view, that of the new Americans. Thus, Columbus is referred to as having "discovered" America, a ridiculous notion from the standpoint of the many occupants who already lived there when it was "discovered." The conquests of the southwest and the Alamo also are presented only from the point of view of the new settlers, not from the standpoint of, say, the Mexicans who lost roughly half their territory to the invaders. This kind of ethnocentric and frankly propagandistic teaching would have no place in a curriculum that sought to develop wisdom and an appreciation of the need to balance interests.

> **Lessons taught to emphasize wisdom would have a rather different character from lessons as they often are taught today.**

Second, science teaching would no longer be about facts presented as though they are the final word. Psychology, for example, is often presented as though it represents the end of a process of evolution of thought rather than one of many midpoints (Sternberg, in press-b). Students could scarcely realize from this kind of teaching that the paradigms of today, and thus the theories and findings that emanate from them, will eventually be superseded, much as the paradigms, theories, and findings of yesterday were replaced by those of today. Students further would need to learn that, contrary to the way many textbooks are written, the classical "scientific method" is largely a fantasy rather than a reality and scientists are as susceptible to fads as are members of other groups (Sternberg 1995a).

Third, teaching of literature would need to reflect a kind of balance that right now often is absent. Literature often is taught in terms of the standards and context of the contemporary U.S. scene. Characters often are judged in terms of our contemporary standards rather than in terms of the standards of the time and place in which the events took place. From the proposed standpoint, the study of literature must, to some extent, be done in the context of the study of history. The banning of books often reflects the application of certain contemporary standards to literature, standards of which an author from the past never could have been aware.

Fourth, foreign languages always would be taught in the cultural context in which they are embedded. I suggest that American students have so much more difficulty learning foreign languages than do children in much of Europe not because they lack the ability but because they lack the motivation. They do not see the need to learn another language whereas, say, a Flemish-speaking child in Belgium does. Americans would be better off, I suggest, if they made more of an attempt wisely to understand other cultures rather than just to expect people from other cultures to understand them. And learning the language of a culture is a key to understanding. Americans might be less quick to impose their cultural values on others if they understood others' cultural values. It also is interesting to speculate on why Esperanto, a language that was to provide a common medium of communication across cultures, has been a notable failure. I suggest it is because Esperanto is embedded in no culture at all. It is the language of no one.

> Many people will not see the value of teaching something that shows no promise of raising conventional test scores.

Culture cannot be taught, in the context of foreign-language learning, in the way it now often is—as an aside divorced from the actual learning of the language. It should be taught as an integral part of the language—as a primary context in which the language is embedded. The vituperative fights we see about bilingual education and about the use of Spanish in the United States or French in Canada are not just or even primarily fights about language. They are fights about culture, and they are fights in need of wise resolutions.

Finally, as implied throughout these examples, the curriculum needs to be far more integrated. Literature needs to be integrated with history, science with history and social-policy studies, foreign language with culture. Even within disciplines, far more integration is needed. Different approaches to psychology, for example, are often taught as competing when in fact they are totally compatible. Thus, biological, cognitive, developmental, social, and clinical psychology provide complementary viewpoints on human beings. They do not compete with each other as being the "right approach." The study of the brain is important, for example, but most of the insights about learning and memory that can be applied to instruction have come from behavioral and cognitive approaches, not from the biological approach. And some of the insights that have supposedly come from the biological approach—such as "left-brain" and "right-brain" learning—are based on ignorant or outdated caricatures of research in this area rather than on actual findings.

The road to this new approach is bound to be a rocky one. First, entrenched structures, whatever they may be, are difficult to change, and wisdom neither is taught in schools nor, in general, is it even discussed. Second, many people will not see the value of teaching something that shows no promise of raising conventional test scores. These scores, which formerly were predictors of more interesting criteria, have now become criteria, or ends in themselves. The society has lost track of why these scores ever mattered in the first place, and they have engendered the same kind of mindless competition we see in people who relentlessly compare their economic achievements with those of others. Third, wisdom is much more difficult to develop than is the kind of achievement that can be developed and then readily tested via multiple-choice tests. Finally, people who have gained influence and power in a society via one means are unlikely to want either to give up that power or to see a new criterion be established on which they do not rank as favorably. Thus, there is no easy path to wisdom. There never was and probably never will be.

Author Note: Preparation of this article was supported by a government grant under the Javits Act Program (Grant No. R206R50001) as administered by the Office of Educational Research and Improvement, U.S. Department of Education. Grantees undertaking such projects are encouraged to express freely their professional judgment. This article, therefore, does not necessarily represent the positions or the policies of the U.S. government, and no official endorsement should be inferred.

REFERENCES

Arlin, P. K. (1990). Wisdom: The art of problem finding. In R. J. Sternberg (Ed.), *Wisdom: Its nature, origins, and development* (pp. 230–243). New York: Cambridge University Press.

Baltes, P. B. (1993). The aging mind: Potential and limits. *The Gerontologist* 33: 580–594.

Baltes, P. B. (1994). *Wisdom.* Unpublished manuscript, Max-Planck-Institut für Bildungsforschung, Berlin.

Baltes, P. B. (in preparation). *Wisdom: The orchestration of mind and virtue.* Boston: Blackwell.

Baltes, P. B., and J. Smith. (1987, August). *Toward a psychology of wisdom and its ontogenesis.* Paper presented at the Ninety-Fifth Annual Convention of the American Psychological Association. New York City.

Baltes, P. B., and J. Smith. (1990). Toward a psychology of wisdom and its ontogenesis. In R. J. Sternberg (Ed.), *Wisdom: Its nature, origins, and development* (pp. 87–120). New York: Cambridge University Press.

Baltes, P. B., U. M. Staudinger, A. Maercker, and J. Smith. (1995). People nominated as wise: A comparative study of wisdom-related knowledge. *Psychology and Aging* 10: 155–166.

Basseches, J. (1984). *Dialectical thinking and adult development.* Norwood, NJ: Ablex.

Ceci, S. J., and J. Liker. (1986). Academic and nonacademic intelligence: An experimental separation. In R. J. Sternberg and R. K. Wagner (Eds.), *Practical intelligence: Nature and origins of competence in the everyday world* (pp. 119–142). New York: Cambridge University Press.

Chi, M. T. H., R. Glaser, and M. J. Farr. (Eds.). (1988). *The nature of expertise.* Hillsdale, NJ: Erlbaum.

Clayton, V. (1975). Erickson's theory of human development as it applies to the aged: Wisdom as contradictory cognition. *Human Development* 18: 119–128.

Clayton, V. (1976). *A multidimensional scaling analysis of the concept of wisdom.* Unpublished doctoral dissertation, University of Southern California.

Clayton, V. (1982). Wisdom and intelligence: The nature and function of knowledge in the later years. *International Journal of Aging and Development* 15: 315–321.

Clayton, V., and J. E. Birren. (1980). The development of wisdom across the lifespan: A reexamination of an ancient topic. In P. B. Baltes and O. G. Brim (Eds.), *Life-span development and behavior* (vol. 3, pp. 103–135). New York: Academic Press.

Csikszentmihalyi, M. (1988). Society, culture, and person: A systems view of creativity. In R. J. Sternberg (Ed.), *The nature of creativity* (pp. 325–339). New York: Cambridge University Press.

Csikszentmihalyi, M. (1996). *Creativity.* New York: HarperCollins.

Csikszentmihalyi, M., and K. Rathunde. (1990). The psychology of wisdom: An evolutionary interpretation. In R. J. Sternberg (Ed.), *Wisdom: Its nature, origins, and development* (pp. 25–51). New York: Cambridge University Press.

Eddy, A. S. (1988). *The relationship between the Tacit Knowledge Inventory for Managers and the Armed Services Vocational Aptitude Battery.* Unpublished master's thesis, St. Mary's University, San Antonio, TX.

Ericsson, K. A. (Ed). (1996). *The road to excellence.* Mahwah, NJ: Lawrence Erlbaum Associates.

Ericsson, K. A., and J. Smith. (Eds.). (1991). *Toward a general theory of expertise: Prospects and limits.* Cambridge, England: Cambridge University Press.

Flynn, J. R. (1987). Massive IQ gains in 14 nations. *Psychological Bulletin* 101: 171–191.

Gardner, H. (1993). *Creating minds.* New York: HarperCollins.

Hedlund, J., J. A. Horvath, G. B. Forsythe, S. Snook, W. M. Williams, M. Dennis, and R. J. Sternberg. (1998). *The acquisition of tacit knowledge for military leadership: Implications for training.* Manuscript in preparation.

Hegel, G. W. F. (1931). *The phenomenology of the mind* (2nd ed.). (J. D. Baillie, Trans.). London: Allen and Unwin. (Original work published 1807.)

Herrnstein, R. J., and C. Murray. (1994). *The bell curve.* New York: Free Press.

Herrnstein, R. J., R. S. Nickerson, M. de Sanches, and J. A. Swets. (1986). Teaching thinking skills. *American Psychologist* 41: 1279–1289.

Hofstede, G. (1980). *Culture's consequences: International differences in work-related values.* Thousand Oaks, CA: Sage.

Holliday, S. G., and M. J. Chandler. (1986). *Wisdom: Explorations in adult competence.* Basel, Switzerland: Karger.

Horvath, J. A., R. J. Sternberg, G. B. Forsythe, P. J. Sweeney, R. C. Bullis, W. M. Williams, and M. Dennis. (1996). *Tacit knowledge in military leadership: Supporting instrument development* (Technical Report 1042). Alexandria, VA: U.S. Army Research Institute for Behavioral and Social Sciences.

Jensen, A. R. (1998). *The g factor: The science of mental ability.* Westport, CT: Praeger.

Kitchener, K. S. (1983). Cognition, metacognition, and epistemic cognition: A three-level model of cognitive processing. *Human Development* 4: 222–232.

Kitchener, K. S. (1986). Formal reasoning in adults: A review and critique. In R. A. Mines and K. S. Kitchener (Eds.), *Adult cognitive development.* New York: Praeger.

Kitchener, K. S., and H. G. Brenner. (1990). Wisdom and reflective judgment: Knowing in the face of uncertainty. In R. J. Sternberg (Ed.), *Wisdom: Its nature, origins, and development* (pp. 212–229). New York: Cambridge University Press.

Kitchener, K. S., and R. F. Kitchener. (1981). The development of natural rationality: Can formal operations account for it? In J. Meacham and N. R. Santilli (Eds.), *Social development in youth: Structure and content.* Basel, Switzerland: Karger.

Kramer, D. A. (1990). Conceptualizing wisdom: The primacy of affect-cognition relations. In R. J. Sternberg (Ed.), *Wisdom: Its nature, origins, and development* (pp. 279–313). New York: Cambridge University Press.

Labaree, D. F. (1997). *How to succeed in school without really learning.* New Haven, CT: Yale University Press.

Labouvie-Vief, G. (1980). Beyond formal operations: Uses and limits of pure logic in life span development. *Human Development* 23: 141–161.

Labouvie-Vief, G. (1982). Dynamic development and mature autonomy. *Human Development* 25: 161–191.

Labouvie-Vief, G. (1990). Wisdom as integrated thought: Historical and developmental perspectives. In R. J. Sternberg (Ed.), *Wisdom: Its nature, origins, and development* (pp. 52–83). New York: Cambridge University Press.

Machado, L. A. (1980). *The right to be intelligent.* (M. C. Wheeler, Trans.). New York: Pergamon Press.

Neisser, U. (Ed.). (1998). *The rising curve.* Washington, DC: American Psychological Association.

Nuñes, T. (1994). Street intelligence. In R. J. Sternberg (Ed.), *Encyclopedia of human intelligence* (vol. 2, pp. 1045–1049). New York: Macmillan.

Pascual-Leone, J. (1990). An essay on wisdom: Toward organismic processes that make it possible. In R. J. Sternberg (Ed.), *Wisdom: Its nature, origins, and development* (pp. 244–278). New York: Cambridge University Press.

Piaget, J. (1972). *The psychology of intelligence.* Totowa, NJ: Littlefield-Adams.

Polanyi, M. (1976). Tacit knowledge. In M. Marx and F. Goodson (Eds.), *Theories in contemporary psychology* (pp. 330–344). New York: Macmillan.

Riegel, K. F. (1973). Dialectical operations: The final period of cognitive development. *Human Development* 16: 346–370.

Robinson, D. N. (1989). *Aristotle's psychology.* New York: Columbia University Press.

Robinson, D. N. (1990). Wisdom through the ages. In R. J. Sternberg (Ed.), *Wisdom: Its nature, origins, and development* (pp. 13–24). New York: Cambridge University Press.

Rosch, E. (1975). Cognitive representations of semantic categories. *Journal of Experimental Psychology: General* 104: 192–233.

Ryle, G. (1949). *The concept of mind.* London: Hutchinson.

Simonton, D. K. (1994). *Greatness: Who makes history and why?* New York: Guilford.

Smith, J., U. M. Staudinger, and P. B. Baltes. (1994). Occupational settings facilitating wisdom-related knowledge: The sample case of clinical psychologists. *Journal of Consulting and Clinical Psychology* 66: 989–999.

Staudinger, U. M., and P. B. Baltes. (1996). Interactive minds: A facilitative setting for wisdom-related performance? *Journal of Personality and Social Psychology* 71: 746–762.

Staudinger, U. M., D. F. Lopez, and P. B. Baltes. (1997). The psychometric location of wisdom-related performance: Intelligence, personality, and more? *Personality and Social Psychology Bulletin* 23: 1200–1214.

Sternberg, R. J. (1980). Sketch of a componential subtheory of human intelligence. *Behavioral and Brain Sciences* 3: 573–614.

Sternberg, R. J. (1985a). *Beyond IQ: A triarchic theory of human intelligence.* New York: Cambridge University Press.

Sternberg, R. J. (1985b). Implicit theories of intelligence, creativity, and wisdom. *Journal of Personality and Social Psychology* 49: 607–627.

Sternberg, R. J. (Ed.). (1988). *The nature of creativity: Contemporary psychological perspectives.* New York: Cambridge University Press.

Sternberg, R. J. (Ed.). (1990a). *Wisdom: Its nature, origins, and development.* New York: Cambridge University Press.

Sternberg, R. J. (1990b). Wisdom and its relations to intelligence and creativity. In R. J. Sternberg (Ed.), *Wisdom: Its nature, origins, and development* (pp. 142–159). New York: Cambridge University Press.

Sternberg, R. J. (1995a). For whom the bell curve tolls: A review of *The bell curve. Psychological Science* 6: 257–261.

Sternberg, R. J. (1995b). *In search of the human mind.* Orlando, FL: Harcourt Brace.

Sternberg, R. J. (1996). Costs of expertise. In K. A. Ericsson (Ed.), *The road to excellence* (pp. 347–354). Mahwah, NJ: Lawrence Erlbaum Associates.

Sternberg, R. J. (1997a). Fads in psychology: What we can do. *APA Monitor* 28, 7: 19.

Sternberg, R. J. (1997b). *Successful intelligence.* New York: Plume.

Sternberg, R. J. (1997c). *Thinking styles.* New York: Cambridge University Press.

Sternberg, R. J. (in press-a). A balance theory of wisdom. *Review of General Psychology.*

Sternberg, R. J. (in press-b). The dialectic as a tool for teaching psychology. *Teaching of Psychology.*

Sternberg, R. J., and D. M. Dobson. (1987). Resolving interpersonal conflicts: An analysis of stylistic consistency. *Journal of Personality and Social Psychology* 52: 794–812.

Sternberg, R. J., M. Ferrari, P. Clinkenbeard, and E. L. Grigorenko. (1996). Identification, instruction, and assessment of gifted children: A construct validation of a triarchic model. *Gifted Child Quarterly* 40: 129–137.

Sternberg, R. J., and E. L. Grigorenko. (1997). The cognitive costs of physical and mental ill-health: Applying the psychology of the developed world to the problems of the developing world. *Eye on Psi Chi* 2, 1: 20–27.

Sternberg, R. J., E. L. Grigorenko, M. Ferrari, and P. Clinkenbeard. (in press). A triarchic analysis of an aptitude interaction. *European Journal of Psychological Assessment.*

Sternberg, R. J., and T. I. Lubart. (1995). *Defying the crowd: Cultivating creativity in a culture of conformity.* New York: Free Press.

Sternberg, R. J., and L. J. Soriano. (1984). Styles of conflict resolution. *Journal of Personality and Social Psychology* 47: 115–126.

Sternberg, R. J., B. Torff, and E. L. Grigorenko. (1998a). Teaching for successful intelligence raises school achievement. *Phi Delta Kappan* 79: 667–669.

Sternberg, R. J., B. Torff, and E. L. Grigorenko. (1998b). Teaching triarchically improves school achievement. *Journal of Educational Psychology* 90: 374–384.

Sternberg, R. J., and R. K. Wagner. (Eds.). (1986). *Practical intelligence: Nature and origins of competence in the everyday world.* New York: Cambridge University Press.

Sternberg, R. J., and R. K. Wagner. (1993). The g-ocentric view of intelligence and job performance is wrong. *Current Directions in Psychological Science* 2: 1–5.

Sternberg, R. J., R. K. Wagner, and L. Okagaki. (1993). Practical intelligence: The nature and role of tacit knowledge in work and at school. In H. Reese and J. Puckett (Eds.), *Advances in lifespan development* (pp. 205–227). Hillsdale, NJ: Erlbaum.

Sternberg, R. J., R. K. Wagner, W. M. Williams, and J. A. Horvath. (1995). Testing common sense. *American Psychologist* 50: 912–927.

Sternberg, R. J., and W. M. Williams. (1996). *How to develop student creativity.* Alexandria, VA: Association for Supervision and Curriculum Development.

Thorndike, R. L., E. P. Hagen, and J. M. Sattler. (1986). *Stanford-Binet Intelligence Scale* (4th ed.). Itasca, IL: Riverside.

Torrance, E. P. (1974). *Torrance tests of creative thinking: Technical-norms manual.* Bensenville, IL: Scholastic Testing Services.

Wagner, R. K., and R. J. Sternberg. (1985). Practical intelligence in real-world pursuits: The role of tacit knowledge. *Journal of Personality and Social Psychology* 49: 436–458.

Webster's New World College Dictionary (3rd ed.). (1997). New York: Simon and Schuster.

Wechsler, D. (1991). *Wechsler Intelligence Scale for Children* (3rd ed.). San Antonio, TX: The Psychological Corporation.

Section 2

The Intelligent Learner

The meaning and concept of who is a learner are key concerns of teaching for intelligence. Many particular characteristics about learners are suggested in the second section of this volume. Writers come at the topic from various levels of teaching and with different assumptions in mind, but they all address many of the factors noted by the theorists in the first section.

Barell focuses on the significance of the inquisitiveness of students, on their inherent motivation to learn, and on the importance of the developing abilities required to ask good questions about whatever content is being studied. Darling-Hammond reminds us that teachers constantly need to be learners, too. Beyond the ability to ask important questions, she says, a teacher must raise for every student the issue of what makes learning accessible to the student's immediate skills for crafting knowledge. There is no one formula for who is a potentially successful learner, but there is no question that the teacher responsible for the educational program needs to take account of the individual learner's particular condition and background for becoming an inquiring student. What other insights about learners do the writers of this section uncover about the important concerns of being and becoming a serious thinker?

First, there seems to be a process to be mastered in learning to learn. According to the writers of this section, there are many paths that can be traveled in developing that process. Posing problems or asking meaningful questions are challenging tasks for the teacher and student alike. Darling-Hammond emphasizes the importance of language in the thinking classroom. While Eisner acknowledges that important cognitive functions may indeed include language development, he somewhat counters Darling-Hammond's position and suggests there is much more to be learned than a linguistic approach to the development of full, imaginative thought. Eisner stresses the essential role of learning the various arts in the developing cognitive curriculum. There are key discriminations in mastering aesthetic intelligence, and these critical means or standards provide a foundation, an enriched sense of the whole, of human experience. Eisner presents a conception of mind that encompasses perceptual as well as logical thought, that enables learners to deal with greater diversity in the world, and that fosters the development of complex patterns of interpretation. If we are to become true learners, he says, not mere mimics of others' knowledge, the arts provide essential tools of thoughtfulness. How troubling is the world of schooling, then, that cuts the arts from the school program as though they are frivolous contents.

Allington and Hill deal with the importance of reading ability as a cornerstone of developing intelligence in elementary school. Classrooms need to be rich environments that encourage reading, that provide many varied experiences in reading, and that enable students to master reading skills with confidence and fluency. While both writers underline the inherent educability of every youngster to read the language he or she speaks, they both are keen to point out that learners need to have access to an environment that engages their interest and commands their attention. Their assumptions are not that far off from Eisner's estimate of the classroom of the arts. Hill emphasizes the significance of the role of inference in learning to read, as well as the importance of writing at the same time one is mastering the complex abilities of decoding text. Young, developing readers, he says, are learning to construct their own linguistic intelligence, as they master the highly constrained operations of cultural as well as verbal significance. Because such constructive acts demand that young readers actively seek out unchartered nuances of meaning, Hill takes a negative position on a national fourth grade assessment that will test the learners' abilities at a most critical time of development. Learning to read needs to be as positively challenging as learning to think, he suggests. Intelligence, and its myriad ways of developing, underlies both capabilities. On assessment concerns, Hill has a great deal in common with Feuerstein-based theorists who are represented in the last section of this volume. Dynamic ways to assess young learners may hold promise where traditional, standardized measures do not.

Burke raises questions about the role of the professional teacher as both a mentor and a lifelong learner. She calls upon teachers to take seriously the task of reflecting on their everyday practice, of documenting experience in regular journals or long-term portfolios. As self-study is an important aspect of assessment in general, self-reflection for teachers becomes an important aspect of the process applied. Indeed, such meta-analysis ought to provide a base for determining more extensive professional development plans. Borrowing from staff development literature, Moye sees transfer as the pedagogical factor that links teachers' professional growth to issues of larger school reform. The dynamic transformation of the teacher-learner fuels a whole process of educational change, she says, within regenerating learning communities. As teachers grow professionally, they will develop the potential for new options in their classrooms and programs.

Schools are living systems. This section raises the continuous development of both learning teachers and learning students as the *raison d'être* of education itself. Looking inside the system, the first focus has been on the key actors and the dramatic parts they play. The next challenge is to examine the pedagogical act itself, to look at instruction under a magnifying glass. That is the substance of the next section of this book.

Teacher Learning That Supports Student Learning

by Linda Darling-Hammond

Today's schools face enormous challenges. In response to an increasingly complex society and a rapidly changing, technology-based economy, schools are being asked to educate the most diverse student body in our history to higher academic standards than ever before. This task is one that cannot be "teacher-proofed" through management systems, testing mandates, or curriculum packages. At its root, achieving high levels of student understanding requires immensely skillful teaching—and schools that are organized to support teachers' continuous learning.

What do teachers need to know to teach all students according to today's standards? What kinds of preservice training and ongoing professional development will make teacher success more likely?

WHAT TEACHERS NEED TO KNOW

First, teachers need to understand subject matter deeply and flexibly, so that they can help students create useful cognitive maps, relate ideas to one another, and address misconceptions. Teachers need to see how ideas connect across fields and to everyday life. This kind of understanding provides a foundation for pedagogical content knowledge (Shulman 1987), which enables teachers to make ideas accessible to others. The audience is also key: A skillful teacher figures out what students know and believe about a topic and how learners are likely to "hook into" new ideas.

From *Educational Leadership*, February 1998, pp. 6–11. © 1998 by the Association for Supervision and Curriculum Development. All rights reserved. Reprinted with permission.

Interpreting learners' statements and actions and shaping productive experiences for them require knowledge of child and adolescent development and an understanding of how to support growth in various domains—cognitive, social, physical, and emotional. Teaching in ways that connect with students also requires an understanding of differences that may arise from culture, family experiences, developed intelligences, and approaches to learning. Teachers need to be able to inquire sensitively, listen carefully, and look thoughtfully at student work, as well as to structure situations in which students write and talk about their experiences. This builds a foundation of pedagogical learner knowledge (Grimmett and MacKinnon 1992). Motivating students requires an understanding of what individual students believe about themselves, what they care about, and what tasks are likely to give them enough success to encourage them to work hard to learn.

> **Teachers need to know about collaboration—how to structure interactions among students so that more powerful shared learning can occur . . .**

Teachers need several kinds of knowledge about learning. Teachers need to think about what it means to learn different kinds of material for different purposes and how to decide which kinds of learning are most necessary in different contexts. Teachers must be able to use different teaching strategies to accomplish various goals and many means for evaluating students' knowledge and assessing students' approaches to learning. Teachers must be able to identify the strengths of different learners while addressing their weaknesses. In addition, all teachers need tools to work with students who have specific learning disabilities or needs. And because language is the gateway to learning, teachers must understand how students acquire language, so that they can build language skills and create accessible learning experiences.

Teachers need to know about curriculum resources and technologies to connect their students with sources of information and knowledge that allow them to explore ideas, acquire and synthesize information, and frame and solve problems. And teachers need to know about collaboration—how to structure interactions among students so that more powerful shared learning can occur, how to collaborate with other teachers, and how to work with parents to learn more about their children and to shape supportive experiences at school and home.

Finally, teachers need to be able to analyze and reflect on their practice, to assess the effects of their teaching, and to refine and improve their instruction. They must continuously evaluate what students are thinking and understanding and reshape their plans to take account of what they've discovered.

NEW STRATEGIES FOR TEACHER LEARNING

Acquiring this sophisticated knowledge and developing a practice that is different from what teachers themselves experienced as students requires learning opportunities for teachers that are more powerful than simply reading and talking about new pedagogical ideas (Ball and Cohen, in press). Teachers learn best by studying, doing, and reflecting; by collaborating with other teachers; by looking closely at students and their work; and by sharing what they see.

This kind of learning cannot occur in college classrooms divorced from practice or in school classrooms divorced from knowledge about how to interpret practice. Good settings for teacher learning—in both colleges of education and schools—provide lots of opportunities for research and inquiry, for trying and testing, for talking about and evaluating the results of learning and teaching. The "rub between theory and practice" (Miller and Silvernail 1994) occurs most productively when questions arise in the context of real students and work in progress, and where research and disciplined inquiry are also at hand.

Better settings for such learning are appearing. More than 300 schools of education in the United States have created programs that extend beyond the traditional four-year bachelor's degree program, providing both education and subject-matter coursework that is integrated with clinical training in schools. Some are one- or two-year graduate programs for recent graduates or midcareer recruits. Others are five-year models for prospective teachers who enter teacher education as undergraduates. In either case, the fifth year allows students to focus exclusively on the task of preparing to teach, with yearlong, school-based internships linked to coursework on learning and teaching. Studies have found that graduates of these extended programs are more satisfied with their preparation, and their colleagues, principals, and cooperating teachers view them as better prepared. Extended program graduates are as effective with students as are much more experienced teachers and are much more likely to enter and stay in teaching than their peers prepared in traditional four-year programs (Andrew and Schwab 1995, Denton and Peters 1988, Shin 1994).

Many of these programs have joined with local school districts to create Professional Development Schools. Like teaching hospitals, these schools aim to provide sites for state-of-the-art practice that are organized to support the training of new professionals, extend the professional development of veteran teachers, and sponsor collaborative research and inquiry. Both university and school faculty plan and teach in these programs. Beginning teachers get a more coherent learning experience when they are organized in teams with these faculty and with one another. Senior teachers deepen their knowledge by serving as mentors, adjunct faculty, co-researchers, and teacher leaders. Thus, these schools can help create the rub between theory and practice, while creating more professional roles for teachers and constructing knowledge that is more useful for both practice and ongoing theory building (Darling-Hammond 1994).

These new programs typically engage prospective teachers in studying research and conducting their own inquiries through cases, action research, and structured reflections about practice. They envision the professional teacher as one who learns from teaching rather than as one who has finished learning how to teach, and the job of teacher education as developing the capacity to inquire systematically and sensitively into the nature of learning and the effects of teaching. This is like the approach to knowledge production John Dewey (1929) sought—one that empowers teachers with greater understanding of complex situations rather than seeking to control them with simplistic formulas or cookie-cutter routines.

If teachers investigate the effects of their teaching on students' learning, and if they read about what others have learned, they become sensitive to variation and more aware of what works for what purposes in what situations. Training in inquiry also helps teachers learn how to look at the world from multiple perspectives and to use this knowledge to reach diverse learners. As Lisa Delpit (1995) notes,

> We all interpret behaviors, information, and situations through our own cultural lenses; these lenses operate involuntarily, below the level of conscious awareness, making it seem that our own view is simply "the way it is" (p. 151).

Teachers concerned with democratic education must develop an awareness of their perspectives and how these can be enlarged to avoid a "communicentric bias" (Gordon et al. 1990) that limits understanding of students as well as of different areas of study.

These goals suggest a new relationship between research and practice. For most of this century, policymakers sought knowledge to aid in the remote control of teaching—generalizable dictums that could shape teaching via texts, curriculum packages, and teacher manuals. When these proved inadequate, teachers were left with the knowledge they'd managed to accumulate on their own. By contrast, the kind of learning found in rich professional development settings has several key features (Ball and Cohen, in press):

> They envision the professional teacher as one who learns from teaching rather than as one who has finished learning how to teach.

• It is centered around the critical activities of teaching and learning—planning lessons, evaluating student work, developing curriculum—rather than in abstractions and generalities;
• It grows from investigations of practice through cases, questions, analysis, and criticism; and
• It is built on substantial professional discourse that fosters analysis and communication about practices and values in ways that build colleagueship and standards of practice.

These elements need to be part of a seamless process of professional learning that begins in preservice education, continues through the early years of induction, and extends through years of developing accomplished practice. This approach is common elsewhere around the world and in a growing number of schools in the United States.

PROFESSIONAL LEARNING IN PRACTICE

Countries like Germany, Belgium, and Luxembourg have long required two to three years of graduate-level study for prospective teachers on top of an undergraduate degree in the subject(s) to be taught. Education courses include the study of child development and learning, pedagogy, and teaching methods, plus an intensively supervised internship in a school affiliated with the university. In 1989 both France and Japan undertook major teacher education reforms to extend both university- and school-based training. In

France, all candidates now complete a graduate program in newly created University Institutes for the Preparation of Teachers that are connected to nearby schools. In Japan and Chinese Taipei, new teachers complete a year-long supervised internship with a reduced teaching load that allows for mentoring and additional study. By Japanese law, first-year teachers receive at least 20 days of inservice training and 60 days of professional development. Master teachers are released from their classrooms to advise and counsel them. In both Japan and China, new teachers watch other teachers at length, discuss problems of practice, present and critique demonstration lessons, and, with groups of colleagues, imagine and act out how students might respond to certain presentations of material. In their study of mathematics teaching in Japan, Taiwan, and the United States, Stigler and Stevenson (1991) note:

> [One of the] reasons Asian class lessons are so well crafted is that there is a very systematic effort to pass on the accumulated wisdom of teaching practice to each new generation of teachers and to keep perfecting that practice by providing teachers the opportunities to continually learn from each other (p. 46).

Because schools in other countries provide for this kind of regular collegial exchange, teachers share knowledge and refine their practice throughout their careers.

Without these supports, learning to teach well is extremely difficult. Most U.S. teachers start their careers in disadvantaged schools where turnover is highest, are assigned the most educationally needy students whom no one else wants to teach, are given the most demanding teaching loads with the greatest number of extra duties, and receive few curriculum materials and no mentoring. After this hazing, many leave. Others learn merely to cope rather than to teach well. After entry, teachers are expected to know everything they will need for a career, or to learn through workshops mostly on their own, with few structured opportunities to observe and analyze teaching with others. As one high school teacher who has spent 25 years in the classroom once told me: "I have taught 20,000 classes; I have been 'evaluated' 30 times; but I have never seen another teacher teach." With this degree of isolation common, is it any wonder that shared knowledge and standards of practice are so difficult to forge?

Some school districts have begun to create new models of induction and ongoing professional development for teachers and principals. These feature mentoring for beginners and veterans; peer observation and coaching; local study groups and networks for specific subject matter areas; teacher academies that provide ongoing seminars and courses of study tied to practice; and school-university partnerships that sponsor collaborative research, inter-school visitations, and learning opportunities developed in response to teachers' and principals' felt needs.

For example, at Wells Junior High, a Professional Development School working with the University of Southern Maine,

> The whole notion of staff development was turned on its head. The emphasis shifted from outside consultants to in-house experts. Collaborative learning groups replaced the traditional lecture/demonstration format. Problem posing and problem solving supplanted the recipes and prescriptions for effective schools that teachers had heard for years and never managed to implement.
>
> "Using the knowledge" became the starting point for developing a new view of staff development. . . . [Allocated workshop days] were used for teachers' review of research and for critical discussion and reflection. On one such day teachers spent two hours individually reading research about grouping. During another day, they worked in cooperative groups to share their perceptions on the research they had read. On yet another day, the staff met to engage in the process of consensus building with the goal of reaching a decision about grouping practices in the school (Miller and Silvernail 1994, pp. 30, 31).

Similarly, at Fairdale High School in Louisville, Kentucky, teachers' research coupled with shared decision making produced major changes:

> As part of a self-study, 10 teachers followed 10 children through a school day. When it was over, teachers said things like, "It was boring," or, "You know, this isn't a very humane place to be." Teachers read and began to trade articles from the *Kappan, Educational Leadership,* and *Education Week.* . . . Even before participative management was initiated at Fairdale, the teachers started changing things. . . . "Make no mistake about it," [the principal] said, "We are building a professional culture" (Kerchner 1993, p. 9).

In other schools, teachers have organized their learning around the development of standards and assessments of student work, evaluating both student learning and the effectiveness of their own teaching in the process. The result is a greater appreciation for what matters and what works, as well as what needs to change to promote student success.

Professional development strategies that succeed in improving teaching share several features (Darling-Hammond and McLaughlin 1995). They tend to be:

- experiential, engaging teachers in concrete tasks of teaching, assessment, and observation that illuminate the processes of learning and development;
- grounded in participants' questions, inquiry, and experimentation as well as professionwide research;
- collaborative, involving a sharing of knowledge among educators;
- connected to and derived from teachers' work with their students as well as to examinations of subject matter and teaching methods;
- sustained and intensive, supported by modeling, coaching, and problem solving around specific problems of practice; and
- connected to other aspects of school change.

These approaches shift from old models of "teacher training" or "inservicing" to a model in which teachers confront research and theory directly, are regularly engaged in evaluating their practice, and use their colleagues for mutual assistance.

THE BENEFIT FOR STUDENTS

Growing evidence suggests that this kind of professional development not only makes teachers feel better about their practice, but it also reaps learning gains for students, especially in the kinds of more challenging learning that new standards demand (Darling-Hammond 1997, NFIE 1996). Creating a profession of teaching in which teachers have the opportunity for continual learning is the likeliest way to inspire greater achievement for children, especially those for whom education is the only pathway to survival and success.

Author's Note: This article draws in substantial part on the author's recently published book, *The Right to Learn* (San Francisco: Jossey-Bass, 1997).

REFERENCES

Andrew, M. D., and R. L. Schwab. (Fall 1995). "Has Reform in Teacher Education Influenced Teacher Performance? An Outcome Assessment of Graduates of Eleven Teacher Education Programs." *Action in Teacher Education* 17, 3: 43–53.

Ball, D., and D. Cohen. (in press). "Developing Practice, Developing Practitioners: Toward a Practice-based Theory of Professional Education." In *The Heart of the Matter: Teaching as the Learning Profession,* edited by L. Darling-Hammond and L. Sykes. San Francisco: Jossey-Bass.

Darling-Hammond, L. (1997). *Doing What Matters Most: Investing in Quality Teaching.* New York: The National Commission on Teaching and America's Future.

Darling-Hammond, L., and M. W. McLaughlin. (1995). "Policies That Support Professional Development in an Era of Reform." *Phi Delta Kappan* 76, 8: 597–604.

Darling-Hammond, L., ed. (1994). *Professional Development Schools: Schools for Developing a Profession.* New York: Teachers College Press.

Delpit, L. (1995). *Other People's Children: Cultural Conflict in the Classroom.* New York: New Press.

Denton, J. J., and W. H. Peters. (1988). "Program Assessment Report: Curriculum Evaluation of a Non-traditional Program for Certifying Teachers." Unpublished report. College Station: Texas A&M University.

Dewey, J. (1929). *The Sources of a Science of Education.* New York: Horace Liveright.

Gordon, E. W., F. Miller, and D. Rollock. (1990). "Coping with Communicentric Bias in Knowledge Production in the Social Sciences." *Educational Researcher* 19: 14–19.

Grimmett, P., and A. MacKinnon. (1992). "Craft Knowledge and the Education of Teachers." In *Review of Research in Education* 18, edited by G. Grant. Washington, D.C.: American Educational Research Association.

Kerchner, C. T. (1993). "Building the Airplane as It Rolls Down the Runway." *School Administrator* 50, 10: 8–15.

Miller, L., and D. L. Silvernail. (1994). "Wells Junior High School: Evolution of a Professional Development School." In *Professional Development Schools: Schools for Developing a Profession,* edited by L. Darling-Hammond. New York: Teachers College Press.

National Foundation for the Improvement of Education. (1996). *Teachers Take Charge of Their Learning: Transforming Professional Development for Student Success.* Washington, D.C.: Author.

Shin, H. (1994). "Estimating Future Teacher Supply: An Application of Survival Analysis." Paper presented at the annual meeting of the American Educational Research Association, New Orleans.

Shulman, L. (1987). "Knowledge and Teaching: Foundations of the New Reform." *Harvard Educational Review* 57, 1: 1–22.

Stigler, J. W., and H. W. Stevenson. (Spring 1991). "How Asian Teachers Polish Each Lesson to Perfection." *American Educator* 15, 1: 12–21, 43–47.

Did You Ask a Good Question Today?

by John Barell

O UR NATURAL CURIOSITIES
Have you ever wondered what goes on inside the head of a
baby, as physicist Freeman Dyson has? Or like psychologist
Nicholas Humphrey, have you ever asked yourself, "Why is music
such a pleasure?"[1]

Have you ever speculated about the size of the sun as it sets
upon the horizon where it always looks so much bigger than when
it's at the high noon position? But is it? My grandfather had fun asking me about this seeming incongruity when I was a child, leading me
to consider how the sun's rays might be affected by shining through
Earth's atmosphere.

We are always posing questions such as these and have since the
dawn of time when Homo sapiens first began to walk upright on east
African savannahs. We, as a species, wouldn't be here were it not for
the ability to use language and, with this incomparable tool, to communicate our sense of wonder at the natural world. As Ian Tattersall
noted, Homo sapiens came upon the world as a new creature, a new
concept far different from existing Neanderthals. We were able to use
language and to create symbols and artistic products, such as drawings in the caves at Lascaux and Venus figurines, and to bury our
dead with artifacts for an afterlife.[2]

I imagine Cro-Magnons asked themselves a lot of questions:
What is that brilliant orange ball that grows into the sky? What is
fire? How shall we capture that woolly creature and can we eat it?
Where shall we live? What happens when one of us no longer can
walk or talk? Where do we go?

From a paper based on a presentation at the Fourth International Teaching for
Intelligence Conference, April 24, 1998, New York, NY. © 1998 by John Barell.
Reprinted with permission.

Our development and our destiny are structured by questions such as these.

MEANING OF QUESTIONING

What does it mean, "to question"? It means an ability to think beyond what we see, touch, and hear with our senses. For example, to see the sunset and to imagine, to reason, to wonder, to speculate on what the sun might be composed of, to ask ourselves how it originated. To see the possibility of there being a creator of that heavenly body.

It means to recognize that we are confronted with a mystery, a puzzle. There is that bright yellow-orange object and every day it seems to rise above the horizon and move. What makes it go across the skies and then disappear?

Richard Feynman, a Nobel prize–winning physicist and member of the *Challenger* space shuttle disaster investigating committee, once noted that science flourishes within a free, democratic society where we have the freedom to doubt, to wonder:

> "I feel a responsibility to proclaim the value of this freedom and to teach that doubt is not to be feared, but that it is to be welcomed as the possibility of a new potential for human beings. If you know that you are not sure, you have a chance to improve the situation."[3]

SIGNIFICANCE OF QUESTIONING AND WONDERING

First, questioning represents our humanity. To ask a question reflects our human ability to think beyond the immediate present, to speculate beyond the concrete realities confronting us at this very moment. When we have doubts about governmental policies toward China, about the inflation rate, about our relationships with loved ones, we are challenging the status quo, questioning the realities we perceive. We are developing our potential for continuous intellectual, social, and emotional growth when we recognize incongruities and follow our curiosities.

Second, curiosity is a road to success. The best example of this comes from scientist Isidore I. Rabi. Someone once asked him, "Why did you become a scientist, rather than a doctor or lawyer or businessman, like other immigrant kids in your neighborhood?"[4]

Dr. Rabi's response is very revealing and instructive:

"My mother made me a scientist without ever intending it. Every other Jewish mother in Brooklyn would ask her child after school, 'So? Did you learn anything today?' But not my mother. She always asked me a different question. 'Izzy,' she would say, 'did you ask a good question today?' That difference—asking good questions—made me become a scientist."[5]

Without Izzy's mother encouraging him to follow up on his curiosities, perhaps he would not have gone on to graduate from MIT, to work on the Manhattan Project, or to conduct Nobel prize–winning research on the electron.

So, questioning is one road to becoming more fully the human beings we are capable of being.

A "GOOD QUESTION"

What do you suppose mother Rabi knew about such questions that she asked her son, Izzy, if he asked not just a question but a "good question"? She must have had some ideas in her mind about the characteristics of good questions and it's unfortunate that we cannot ask her, nor her son!

To gain some insight into what a good question might contain, let's consider a well-known example from another scientist, Albert Einstein. One of his questions as a young man was the following: "What would happen if I rode along a ray of light and looked back? What would I see?"[6]

This was an amazing question! As astronomer Carl Sagan observed, Einstein noted that "something strange happens at the speed of light. The more Einstein thought about such questions, the more troubling they became. Paradoxes seemed to emerge everywhere. . . ."[7]

This question led Einstein to determine that Newton's way was not the only way to see the universe. His special theory of relativity, proposed in 1905, changed the "glasses" through which we view the world of subatomic particles, outer space, and time travel. Einstein's imaginative curiosity was a good question because it challenged our underlying assumptions about the universe.

But you do not need to be an Einstein to pose a good question!

MOTHER AND THE EAGLE NEBULA

Recently I was showing my mother a spectacular picture of towering brownish and yellow images of hydrogen gas in the Eagle Nebula on the Hubble Space Telescope (HST) website. I was amazed that these towers of hydrogen gas some 7,300 light-years from Earth depicted stars in formation. When I told my mother this, she looked at the bright white images at the head of these towers of hydrogen, then looked at me and asked, "Well, how do they know that these are stars being created?"

I fumbled around for a few minutes talking about data gathering and she kept countering with, "How did astronomers figure this out before the launching and perfecting of the HST?" I couldn't answer fully. I had to seek out the university astronomer.

Had my mother asked a good question? Yes! She is just like the mother of Pulitzer prize–winning Annie Dillard, who used to ask her young daughter, "How do you know?" when Annie would make a claim about politics she had picked up around the neighborhood.[8] Both mothers wanted to know the sources of their children's information. They are challenging the credibility of our sources and our unquestioning acceptance of what we are told, in print, on the Internet, and in person.

Questioning involves, as philosopher John McPeck asserted, a "certain skepticism" about what we are told to do or believe.[9] When someone asserts that the dinosaurs died out because of a huge meteor falling onto what is now Latin America, we most certainly will pose a few questions about the evidence that supports this conclusion, what assumptions it might be based upon, and what we know about the biases or special interests of the source of the claim.

Good questions do all of the following:

• Reflect our genuine curiosities, our wonderings about mysteries, ambiguities, and puzzling situations we do not understand.

• May uncover assumptions, biases, sources of evidence, and the reliability of sources.

• Lead us to investigate, to inquire, to search for answers.

• Help us reflect on our ways of knowing.

WHY AREN'T WE MORE CURIOUS IN SCHOOLS?

Educational researcher J. T. Dillon conducted research on questioning in high school history classrooms where he found that during twenty-seven discussions in six schools students posed only eleven questions, most of which had to do with management of the classroom and lower levels of intellectual challenge! Ninety-nine percent of students asked nothing.[10] Why might this be so?

Recently *The New York Times* printed a story about the U.S. State Department's chief spokesperson James P. Rubin. When Secretary of State Madeline K. Albright was ambassador to the United Nations, she brought Rubin along to handle her public relations. In this position he was asked many, many questions about the United States's position on various conflicts. Occasionally, he responded in a fashion that might have had an effect on whether or not a particular reporter ever asked him a question again: "He was known to demean reporters for less prestigious news organizations with put-downs like, 'That question bespeaks incredible ignorance!'"[11]

. . . during twenty-seven discussions in six schools students posed only eleven questions . . .

Imagine how you would feel, as a reporter trying to get a story for a hometown paper about the United States's position vis-à-vis Bosnia, for example, and being slapped with that remark. How likely is it you would approach Mr. Rubin again, at least in a public forum?

Do you think these kinds of comments do anything to foster the kind of curiosity we are speaking about? Do you suppose such put-downs ever occur at home? In the school?

My own informal survey of students in a university genetics class suggested that students quite often encounter these kinds of remarks when they ask a question to resolve a doubt or difficulty they are having. Some professors responded to questions with comments such as "*I* ask the questions here!" "See me after class for that one," "Let's not bother with those kinds of speculations [in response to a student's what if question]. We have enough to do to figure out what the facts are," and "I'm not sure. Why don't you look it up?"

These kinds of responses, according to the students, led them to think, "Well, this guy's not interested in my thinking here! So I'll just shut up."

Our inabilities to create an invitational environment that encourages students to take risks and to adventure into the unknown with their questioning is undoubtedly one reason why students do not ask more questions in our classes.

WHAT CAN WE DO IN OUR CLASSROOMS?

Model Inquiry

If we want our students to become curious about the world, we need to model our own curiosities within an invitational environment.[12]

> If we want our students to become curious about the world, we need to model our own curiosities within an invitational environment.

We need to take situations from our own daily lives and to think aloud before our students, for example, relating how we confront the situation of getting into a jam with our laptop computers. We model our inquiry process and then invite participants to analyze our thoughts and feelings in these kinds of complex and challenging situations.

Another approach is to present the models of several of the nation's foremost scientists and researchers and their questions. For example, astronomer John Barrow posed this question to himself: "Is the universe a great mechanism, a great computation, a great symmetry, a great accident or a great thought?"[13]

Author Duncan Steel asked: "Why are most individuals and all human societies grossly underachieving their potentials?"[14]

The New York Times recently published an article on some of the nation's foremost intellectuals posing these questions for themselves, and their questions were posted on the Internet website organized by John Brockman, a literary agent and author. Brockman's question, "What is the question you are asking yourself [now]?"[15] might help us consider what we can learn from others who pose meaningful, good questions.

Make Questioning Part of Every Day's Lessons

One way of making inquiry a part of every classroom is to develop our students' abilities to pose meaningful questions about content. After modeling our own curiosities about, for example, why an author begins his short story with a specific line or paragraph, we encourage our students to develop their own questions about content. One easy way to do this is through a thinking journal.

Biology teacher Dorothy Lozauskas modeled inquiry for her students and then assigned them to develop questions from their own readings and lab experiments using a thinking journal. The students' questions would become the topics for discussion the following day.

She assisted her students' inquiry by suggesting lead-in statements such as "What I do not understand is . . ., I wonder why . . ., What I want to know is . . ., Suppose . . ., and What if ?. . . ."

These lead-in statements resulted in questions such as "In lab we are making models of molecules with different bonds, and have just made a butane molecule that has free bond rotation. Even though they have the capability of doing so, why would they? I wonder what the world would be like if there was no free bond rotation—really cold?"[16]

Peg Murray, a third-grade teacher, experimented with students posing their own questions about their immediate surroundings— "Why are school buses always yellow?"—and about science—"Why do sun flares shoot out into space?"[17]

Create Problem-Based Units That Focus on Inquiry

Problem-based learning is a way of organizing whole units of instruction around students' interest in figuring out complex phenomena.[18] If, for example, students are studying the Appalachian region, the nature of bacteria in public places, how to create a geometric patio adjacent to a house, or the issue of censorship in public education, they can engage in an inquiry process that facilitates their identifying the problematic situations worthy of investigation. Rather than having the teacher identify the problem, which is what is likely to occur most often, the students' questions can structure the inquiry if they use the following strategy:

K   What do we think we know about the subject?
W   What do we need and/or want to find out?
H   How will we go about finding answers?

Then after investigation:

L   What have we learned and how does it compare with our expectations?
A   How might we apply our findings to this subject, to other subjects, and to our lives?
Q   What are our questions now?

This process is designed to shift the balance of power and control within the classroom from the teacher toward the students so they can take more responsibility for their own learning.[19] Teachers are creating problem-based units for kindergarten through grade twelve that put students into situations requiring them to think productively and gain authentic assessment and feedback; for example, "You are members of the mayor's ecology team charged with investigating the status of the water supply in our town . . ."

Make Metacognitive Self-Questioning Part of the Learning Process

As educational researcher Barbara McCombs noted, self-reflection is one avenue toward enhancing students' self-direction, sense of efficacy, and "inherent motivation to learn."[20] Metacognitive reflections engage us in a process of planning, monitoring, and evaluating.[21] This process involves questioning ourselves in this fashion: What is my task and how do I intend to accomplish it? How well am I doing? How well do I think I have done? What might I do differently next time?

Sixth graders in Regina Kamlet's classroom reflected on their learnings in science and one student noted: "I work better when there is a task and I ask questions and make a plan . . ."[22]

CONCLUSION

When my grandfather asked me about the sun, he knew I probably hadn't thought about this incongruity. But he posed the questions because we both loved the game of it. Consequently, I grew up with a certain amount of curiosity about the world. Now, I realize that he was my model; he introduced me to a process of questioning that I now value more than any answers I might discover. As with problem solving, it may be that the process of inquiry is more important for brain development than any one answer.[23]

Monsignor Richard Mohan, prior of St. Patrick's Purgatory, a shrine in Station Island, Ireland, recently noted: "I don't go around with answers. I hear people's questions. It's far more important to have questions than answers. The people who have all the answers have stopped living."[24]

Yes.

NOTES

1. "In an On-Line Salon, Scientists Sit Back and Ponder: 'What Is the Question You Are Asking Yourself?'" *The New York Times,* December 30, 1997, p. F4.

2. Tattersall, Ian. 1998. *Becoming Human: Evolution and Human Uniqueness.* New York: Harcourt Brace and Co.

3. Feynman, Richard. 1998. *Thoughts of a Citizen Scientist.* Reading, MA: Addison-Wesley.

4, 5. Sheff, Donald. 1988, January 19. "Letters to the Editor," *The New York Times.*

6. Sagan, Carl. 1980. *Cosmos.* New York: Random House, p. 199.

7. Sagan, Carl. 1980. *Cosmos.* New York: Random House, p. 80.

8. Dillard, Annie. 1987. *An American Childhood.* New York: Harper and Row.

9. McPeck, John. 1981. *Critical Thinking and Education.* Oxford, England: Martin Robertson.

10. Dillon, J. T. 1988. *Questioning and Teaching: A Manual of Practice.* New York: Teachers College Press.

11. Henneberger, Melinda. 1998, January 10. "Albright Right-Hand Man Finds Spotlight's on Him," *The New York Times,* p. 1.

12. Barell, John. 1995. *Teaching for Thoughtfulness.* 2nd ed. White Plains, NY: Longman.

13, 14, 15. "In an On-Line Salon, Scientists Sit Back and Ponder: 'What Is the Question You Are Asking Yourself?'" *The New York Times,* December 30, 1997, p. F4.

16. Lozauskas, Dorothy, and John Barell. 1992, November. "Reflective Reading: A Journal for Inquiring Minds." *The Science Teacher,* 42–45.

17. Barell, John. 1992. *". . . Ever Wonder . . .?"* Columbus, OH: Zaner Bloser.

18. Barell, John. 1998. *Problem-Based Learning: An Inquiry Approach.* Arlington Heights, IL: SkyLight Training and Publishing.

19. McLaren, Peter. 1998. *Life in Schools: An Introduction to Critical Pedagogy in the Foundations of Education.* 3rd ed. New York: Addison Wesley Longman.

20. McCombs, Barbara. 1991. "Metacognition and Motivation for Higher Level Thinking." Paper presented at the annual meeting of the American Educational Research Association, Chicago.

21, 22. Barell, John. 1995. *Teaching for Thoughtfulness.* 2nd ed. New York: Longman, p. 267.

23. Jensen, Eric. 1998. *Teaching with the Brain in Mind.* Alexandria, VA: Association for Supervision and Curriculum Development.

24. Clarity, James. 1995, August 5. "Finding Faith the Hard Way: The Pluck of the Irish," *The New York Times,* p. A4.

The Misunderstood Role of the Arts in Human Development

by Elliot W. Eisner

Providing a decent place for the arts in our schools may be one of the most important first steps we can take to bring about genuine school reform, Mr. Eisner maintains.

I n America 2000 the American people are presented with a reform agenda for their schools in which the arts are virtually absent. Should they be? To provide an intelligent answer, one needs a concept of the arts and a view of the functions of education. What conception of the arts do people who shape education policy have? What image do they have of the aims of education? What kind of culture do they prize? What do they feel contributes to a life worth living? I believe that prevailing conceptions of the arts are based on a massive misunderstanding of the role of the arts in human development and education. This misunderstanding is rooted in ancient conceptions of mind, knowledge, and intelligence. Collectively, these conceptions impoverish the programs of schools and the education of the young.

Make no mistake, the curriculum we prescribe for schools and the time we allocate to subjects show children what adults believe is important for them to learn. There is no more telling indicator of the importance of the subjects students study than the amount of time allocated to them.[1] In American schools, the arts receive about two hours of instructional time per week at the elementary level and are generally not a required subject of study at the secondary level. The allocation of time to what we teach has other consequences as well. The amount of time allocated to a field of study influences the kinds of mental skills children have the opportunity to acquire.

Thus time represents both value and opportunity: value, because it indicates what is considered significant; opportunity, because the school can be thought of as a culture of opportunity. A culture in the biological sense is a place for growing things. Schools, too, are cultures. They are cultures for growing minds, and the direction this growth takes is influenced by the opportunities the school provides. These opportunities are defined by the school's program—its curriculum—and by the artistry with which teachers mediate that program. A school in which the arts are absent or poorly taught is unlikely to provide the genuine opportunities children need to use the arts in the service of their own development.

To speak of mind as developed or, even more pointedly, as grown may seem strange. Yet, in a basic sense, mind is a form of cultural achievement. We are born with brains, but our minds are made, and the shape they take is influenced by the culture in which that development occurs. For children, the school constitutes a primary culture for the development of mind. Therefore, decisions that are made about the school's priorities are also fundamental decisions about the kinds of minds children will have the opportunity to develop. Since our educational priorities are significantly influenced by our conceptions of mind, knowledge, and intelligence and since I believe that prevailing conceptions of the arts misconceive their primary features, I will briefly identify five widely held but fundamentally flawed beliefs about mind, knowledge, and intelligence that give direction to our schools. I will then describe what the arts can contribute to the educational development of the young.

1. *Human conceptual thinking requires the use of language.* Perhaps no belief shapes our understanding of cognition more than the conviction that language plays a necessary role in its operation. Indeed, thinking itself has sometimes been thought of as a kind of subvocalizing, a physical process that accompanies the chain of language activity that best represents the higher mental processes. Language and thought are inseparable.

There are many reasons why this belief will not stand scrutiny. First, to argue that language is a necessary condition for cognition is to conclude that children cannot think until they are able to speak. Yet anyone who has lived with a child knows firsthand how inquisitive a child can be before speech has developed and how intelligent such a child can be in solving problems: a child who cannot think cannot survive.

Second, language as we normally use it is a symbolic device, and symbolic devices that do not have referents do not symbolize. To symbolize, a symbol must be connected to a referent—that is, to an array of qualities one can experience, or that one has experienced, or that one has imagined. To speak meaningfully of baroque music—or of an oak tree or of a jet airplane—requires a conception of these objects and events, and these objects and

> **We are born with brains, but our minds are made.**

events exist as qualities in our experience prior to the labels we assign to them. Contrary to popular opinion, in the beginning there was the image. It is the image that gives meaning to the label. The information the image provides is a cognitive event.

2. *Sensory experience is low on the hierarchy of intellectual functioning.* The genesis of this belief can be found in Plato's ideas about the nature of human understanding. You will recall that, in the sixth book of *The Republic,* Socrates asks Glaucon to imagine a single, vertical line divided unequally into an upper and a lower segment. The longer upper half of the line represents the intelligible world; the bottom portion, the visible world. The intelligible world is grasped through rational procedures; the visible world, through perception. Rationality is high; perception is low. Plato's hierarchy was not diluted by the expansion of the Roman Empire. It is alive and well in the schools and universities of modern America.

But is it true that the perception of qualities is a low-level cognitive activity? When those qualities are complex and subtle, as they are in the arts, the perception of their relationships and nuances can be daunting. To put this matter in context, listen to Rudolf Arnheim:

> By "cognitive" I mean all mental operations involved in the receiving, storing, and processing of information: sensory perception, memory, thinking, learning. This use of the term conflicts with one to which many psychologists are accustomed and which excludes the activity of the senses from cognition. It reflects the distinction I am trying to eliminate; therefore I must extend the meaning of the terms "cognitive" and "cognition" to include perception. Similarly, I see no way of withholding the name of "thinking" from what goes on in perception. No thought processes seem to exist that cannot be found to operate, at least in principle, in perception. Visual perception is visual thinking.[2]

Ironically, indifference to the refinement of perception and inattention to the development of imagination have limited children's cognitive growth. Since no teacher has direct access to a child's mind, it is the child's ability to see the connections between the example the teacher uses, what the child already knows, and what the teacher hopes he or she will understand that makes the example instrumental to new meaning. In short, understanding depends on the child's ability to think by analogy and to grasp, often through metaphor, what needs to be understood. Poetry may indeed be closer to the most sophisticated forms of cognition than many people suspect.

3. *Intelligence requires the use of logic.* The importance of logic in the exercise of intelligence is clear *if* the form that is to be used to speak to the world is one in which the literal use of propositions is necessary. Mathematics and the sciences place a premium on a certain form of precision: literal statement. Logical consistency in such forms of representation is a condition for meaning. But to regard logic as a necessary condition for the exercise of intelligence is to restrict intelligence to those forms of representation that require its use.[3] The result of such a conception is to banish from the domain of intelligence those forms of representation whose meanings are not conveyed by and do not depend upon the use of logic. Poetry, for example, achieves meaning by employing language in ways that do not depend solely on logic; poetic meaning is often "extra-logical." The meanings conveyed by this extra-logical feature of poetry are what might better be thought of as the product of human rationality, and the same point pertains to the other arts.

Although rationality and logicality have been closely associated, rationality is a broader and more fundamental concept. Logic is one of the ways in which rationality is expressed, but it is not the only way. Individuals who manage human relationships well, those who draw or paint well, those who dance well, those who sing well—all do their thinking *within* the medium in which they work. Writing in 1934, John Dewey recognized that intelligence is usually regarded as the sole property of those whom we regard as intellectuals—especially, but not exclusively, in the academy. For those holding such a view, Dewey said:

> Any idea that ignores the necessary role of intelligence in the production of the works of art is based upon identification of thinking with use of one special kind of material, verbal signs and words. To think effectively in terms of relations of qualities is as severe a demand upon thought as to think in terms of symbols, verbal and mathematical. Indeed, since words are easily manipulated in mechanical ways, the

production of a work of genuine art probably demands more intelligence than does most of the so-called thinking that goes on among those who pride themselves on being "intellectuals."[4]

4. *Detachment and distance are necessary for true understanding.* Emotion has long been regarded as the enemy of reflective thought: the more we feel, the less we know. Now there certainly is a case to be made that such emotions as rage can radically influence one's perception and judgment. When running rampant, emotions can cloud vision, impair thought, and lead to trouble of all kinds.

But perception without feeling can do the same. Not to be able to feel, say, a human relationship is to miss what may very well be its most critical features. Not to be able to get a sense of history, not to be able to stand with Columbus on the deck of the *Santa Maria* and experience the pounding of the vessel by the relentless sea and the excitement of the first sighting of land is to miss—and perhaps even misunderstand—that aspect of history. And in failing to experience the emotion of such moments, we miss out on an aspect of life that has the potential to inform. Detachment and distance have their virtues, but they are limited resources for understanding, and any conception that assigns them dominion in cognition misconceives the ways in which understanding is fostered.

5. *Scientific method is the only legitimate way to generalize about the world.* The traditional, flawed conception of the arts claims that, when they are about anything, the arts are only about particulars: they yield no generalizations. Their virtues reside in delight rather than insight. They provide nothing that can reasonably be regarded as knowledge or understanding. Since the instrumental value of the products of science is considered greater than the delight derived from the arts (which in any case is usually thought to be merely a matter of personal taste), the value of the arts in comparison to the sciences is set low.

This conception of generalization defines much too narrowly the sources through which generalizations are actually made. The need to generalize is fundamental. Human beings generalized long before either science or statistics were invented. Generalizations are not only scientific and naturalistic; they also emerge from those intense forms of experience that we call the arts: concrete universals they are sometimes called.

Consider the paintings of Francis Bacon, Velásquez, or Picasso, or consider the novels of John Steinbeck or Cervantes. Even fiction—perhaps especially fiction—can help us grasp the meaning not only of Don Quixote, the particular man, but of what we all share with him as we tilt at our own windmills, struggling to overcome seemingly insurmountable obstacles.[5] Cervantes helps us understand such travails, and, because he succeeds so well, we come away from his work with a new view, a view that enables us to recognize and reflect on one of the important features of our own lives. Through his work, we are also able to recognize these features elsewhere.

> The last thing a modern teacher of the arts in America wants is a class full of standardized performances on a given task.

My argument thus far has focused on beliefs that have given direction to the educational enterprise. I have contended that the five beliefs I have described—that thought requires language, that sensory experience is a low-level function, that logic is necessary for intelligence, that detachment and distance foster understanding, and that science is the only legitimate way to generalize—create an intellectual climate that marginalizes the arts because what these beliefs celebrate seems to have little to do with what the arts provide. I will now focus on four contributions that I believe are central to all the arts. In doing so, I will not describe the specific contributions that each individual art makes to children of different ages. Instead, my aim is to identify the common, core contributions of the arts and their potential role in furthering the aims of education.

1. *Not all problems have single, correct answers.* One of the important lessons the arts teach is that solutions to problems can take many forms. This lesson from the arts would not be so important were it not for the fact that so much of what is taught in school teaches just the opposite lesson. Almost all of the basic skills taught in the primary grades teach children that there is only one correct answer to any question and only one correct solution to any problem. Spelling, arithmetic, writing, and even reading are pervaded by conventions and rules that, in effect, teach children to be good rule followers.

The arts teach a different lesson. They celebrate imagination, multiple perspectives, and the importance of personal interpretation.

The last thing a modern teacher of the arts in America wants is a class full of standardized performances on a given task. The last thing an English teacher wants are idiosyncratic interpretations of how words are spelled. This is as it should be. Creativity in spelling is no virtue. But when the curriculum as a whole is so heavily saturated with tasks and expectations that demand fealty to rule, opportunities to think in unique ways are diminished. When carried to an extreme, the school's program becomes intellectually debilitating.

2. *The form of a thing is part of its content.* We have a tendency in our schools to separate form from content. Form is regarded as the shape something takes, and content is the meaning something conveys. In notational systems, we can live with a such a dichotomy. In such systems, attention to form *as such* is largely irrelevant. For example, the number six can be symbolized in many ways, but its meaning is the same as long as one recognizes it as a six. The task is one of categorization. Early reading also emphasizes categorization. And when children learn to assign a form—say, a particular tree—to its category rather than to explore its distinctive features, perception is aborted. As Dewey pointed out, perception ceases when recognition begins. Assigning a label to an entity is an act of categorization, and when entities are assigned to categories, the exploration of their uniqueness stops.

The arts, however, teach the child that the grass is not simply green; it is lavender, grey, gold. And when it is green, its varieties are endless. Furthermore, in the arts and in much of life, the form something takes is very much a part of its content. In fact, what the content *is* often depends on the form it takes. The arts are prime examples of how this marriage of form and content is created and of the effect that it has on our experience.

I have made a special point here of emphasizing the function of the arts in human development. The arts are neglected resources and deserve attention in our schools. But I do not want to give the impression that at least some of the features that the arts possess are not also to be found in the sciences. The products of science have their own aesthetic features: the parsimony of theory, the beauty of conceptual models, the elegance of experiments, and the imagination and insight of interpretation. Indeed, the qualities for which a work of science is cherished are often related as much to its aesthetic appeal as to its explanatory power. A theory, after all, is a perspective about the way the world is. It is a way to secure a coherent view, and coherence is so important that we are often unwilling to give up the views we find attractive, despite contradictory evidence.

My point here is that, although my primary focus is on what may be called the fine arts, some of the features for which the arts are valued are also exhibited by the sciences. At the risk of oversimplifying the differences between the arts and the sciences, let me say that, in the context of creation, a work of science is a work of art.

3. *Having fixed objectives and pursuing clear-cut methods for achieving them are not always the most rational ways of dealing with the world.* There is a tendency in technologically oriented cultures to conceive of rationality as a method for tightly linking means and ends. To be rational, we tell children (and teachers), they must first formulate clear-cut objectives for their work, then use these objectives to define means for their achievement, and finally implement and evaluate the effectiveness and efficiency of the means for achieving the desired objectives.

Of course, there is a sense of sweet reason about such a procedure. Yet we often conceptualize and implement this process in mechanical ways: we give students goals for each lesson, we expect teachers to know exactly where they are headed, and we appraise classrooms and the quality of teaching on the basis of their achievement. We try to create a technology of management so that efficiency in learning and teaching is achieved and public accountability is provided. Our narrow conception of rationality is expressed in our incessant search for "what works": it supports the belief that there is, in fact, a single best way, that the main task of researchers is to find it, and that the primary obligation of teachers is to use it. The entire effort to standardize educational outcomes is premised on a conviction that efficient and effective systems can be designed that will take luck out of the educational process.

These beliefs not only affect the conditions of teaching, they also create a climate that affects what and how students learn. Moreover, these views are antithetical to what the arts teach. The arts teach that goals need to be flexible and that surprise counts; that chance, as Aristotle wisely remarked, is something that art loves; that being open to the unanticipated opportunities that inevitably emerge in the context of action increases insight; and that purposeful flexibility rather than rigid adherence to prior plans is more likely to yield something of value. No painter, writer, composer, or choreographer can foresee all the twists and turns that his or her work will take. The *work* of art—by which I now mean the *act* of creation—does not follow an unalterable schedule but is a journey that unfolds. The relationship of the maker to the work is not that of lecturer to listener, but a conversation between the worker and the work.

> **Life outside of school is seldom like school assignments—and hardly ever like a multiple-choice test.**

In the context of much of today's schooling, the lessons taught by the arts are much closer to what successful and intelligent corporations do and to what cognitive psychologists are discovering constitute the most sophisticated forms of thinking.[6] These recent psychological discoveries are lessons artists have long understood. What are these lessons? They are that solving complex problems requires attention to wholes, not simply to discrete parts; that most complex problems have no algorithmic solutions; that nuance counts; and that purposes and goals must remain flexible in order to exploit opportunities that one cannot foresee. These newly discovered cognitive virtues are taught in every genuine *work* of art. Yet, ironically, the arts are typically thought of as noncognitive.

What is even more ironic is that, while we say that the function of schooling is to prepare students for life, the problems of life tend not to have the fixed, single correct answers that characterize the problems students encounter in the academic areas of schooling. The problems of life are much more like the problems encountered in the arts. They are problems that seldom have a single correct solution; they are problems that are often subtle, occasionally ambiguous, and sometimes dilemma-like. One would think that schools that wanted to prepare students for life would employ tasks and problems similar to those found outside of schools. This is hardly the case. Life outside of school is seldom like school assignments—and hardly ever like a multiple-choice test.

4. *In addition to their expressive function, the arts perform another function of critical importance.* In all that I have said so far, I have emphasized the contributions that the arts make toward helping students recognize that problems are not restricted to those having single correct answers, that form and content interact, and that purposeful flexibility is a mark of fluid intelligence coping with the vicissitudes of the unpredictable. But I have neglected a contribution that is surely as important. That contribution hinges on a distinction between *expression* and *discovery*. In the arts, students learn that

some kinds of meaning may require the expressive forms that the arts make possible. In this sense, the arts expressively represent; they provide the forms through which insight and feeling can emerge in the public world. Indeed, humans invented the arts to serve expressive functions. For most people who have thought about the arts, this particular function is the one most commonly recognized.

Through the arts students can learn how to discover not only the possibilities the world offers but also their own possibilities.

But the arts also make discovery possible. Discovery occurs as students learn through adventures in the arts something of the possibilities of human experience. The journeys they take through the patterned sound we call music, through the visual forms we call painting, and through the metaphorical discourse we call poetry and literature are means through which students can discover their potential to respond. In other words, the arts can help students find their individual capacity to feel and imagine.

While such journeys are experienced through the arts, they can also be secured through the ordinary aspects of daily life when it is approached aesthetically. The world outside of art can become something to explore and relish: through the arts students can learn how to discover not only the possibilities the world offers but also their own possibilities. Expression and discovery are two major contributions the arts make to human development.

Just how are such discoveries made? As children learn to manipulate, manage, and monitor the nuances of voice, movement, and visual form, they discover the effects that their own fine-tuning achieves. As form is modulated, so too is feeling. As imagination is given permission to rise, children have the opportunity to enter worlds not tied to the literal, to the concrete, to the practical. Discovery emerges in the appreciation of qualities examined and images pursued. The arts, more than most fields, put a premium on such activities, and those activities can help students discover the special qualities of experience we call aesthetic.

Let me close by returning briefly to my initial claim that prevailing conceptions of the arts are based on a massive misunderstanding of their role in human development. This misconception is reflected in the narrow educational priorities of America 2000. In turn, these priorities are rooted in beliefs that regard mind as fixed rather than developed, that conceive of knowledge as the exclusive property of science, and that consider intelligence as limited to forms of abstract thought dependent on the use of logic. These narrow and misguided conceptions are not ivory tower theories without practical consequences. They influence our educational priorities, shape what we teach, and affect our children's lives. They result in schools that have an antiseptic environment that seldom provides even a nod to our sensuous, poetic, or imaginative sides.

I hope readers realize that my argument here is an optimistic one. What is pessimistic is a fixed view of mind, a conception of knowledge limited to what literal language can convey, and a view of intelligence constrained by the rules of logic. Human intellectual capacity is far wider. The realization of this capacity is surely more likely as we create a richer, more nurturant culture for our students. That culture, as I see it, ought to include significant opportunities for students to experience the arts and to learn to use them to create a life worth living. Indeed, providing a decent place for the arts in our schools may be one of the most important first steps we can take to bring about genuine school reform. Let's hope that, despite the priorities of America 2000, we have the courage and the wit to take it.

NOTES

1. Basil Bernstein, "On the Classification and Framing of Educational Knowledge," in Michael Young, ed., *Knowledge and Control* (London: Collier, Macmillan, 1971), pp. 47–69.

2. Rudolf Arnheim, *Visual Thinking* (Berkeley: University of California Press, 1969), pp. 13–14.

3. Elliot W. Eisner, *Cognition and Curriculum: A Basis for Deciding What to Teach* (New York: Longman, 1982).

4. John Dewey, *Art as Experience* (New York: Minton, Balch, 1934), p. 46.

5. Nelson Goodman, *Ways of Worldmaking* (Indianapolis: Hackett, 1978).

6. Lauren Resnick, *Toward the Thinking Curriculum, Current Cognitive Research* (Alexandria, Va: Association for Supervision and Curriculum Development, 1989); and James Greeno, "Perspectives on Thinking," *American Psychologist,* vol. 44, 1989, pp. 134–41.

What Really Matters in Teaching Children to Read

by Richard L. Allington

In every nation there are some children who find learning to read difficult regardless of the nature of the writing system, the assessment plan, the national wealth, or the organization of educational system (Elley, 1992). Even when offered good instruction, some children struggle mightily to become literate. Unfortunately, too many children struggle because they do not have access to sufficient instruction. But just how can sufficient instruction be characterized? In other words, what is it that really matters in designing and delivering instruction to children who find learning to read difficult?

After a century of research on reading instruction and on children who find learning to read difficult, there are only a few things of critical instructional importance that have been identified. Unfortunately, professional debates and discussions often ignore each of these important dimensions of effective instructional environments and interventions. However, it is important to identify and briefly explain what has mattered historically and what matters now in terms of classroom strategies, structures, and environments.

PROFESSIONAL BELIEFS MATTER

Since the study of reading difficulties began around the turn of the 20th century, three broad factors have been touted regularly as sources of reading difficulties. Each of these factors remains influential in school response to the problem of reading difficulties (Johnston & Allington, 1991).

The Intelligence Factor

First, limited intellectual abilities were viewed as a primary source of the difficulties. But then it was discovered that achievement on purported measures of intelligence and measures of reading achievement did not actually correlate all that well. In fact, terms were invented—hyperlexia and dyslexia—to explain aberrations, those children who read better or less well than was expected. But when educators believed intelligence, or the lack of it, was the source of difficulty, little was offered in the way of instructional interventions because some children were just never going to be readers due to limited intellectual capacity. Some children were just "slow learners" and not much could be expected of them. Thus, the "slow it down and make it concrete" instructional plan was widely implemented—virtually ensuring that some children developed only minimal levels of reading proficiency (Allington, 1991).

> Yet for too long our professional beliefs have literally resulted in educational efforts that produced children who remained largely illiterate.

The "Disadvantage" Factor

However, after noting the less than perfect correlation between measures of intellect and measures of reading, other explanations emerged. Probably the most popular was targeting "disadvantage"—both economic and educational—as a source of the difficulties (McGill-Franzen, 1987). This explanation got a boost from the research showing that many more poor children had difficulty learning to read. Thus, interventions were developed in the hopes of overcoming the disadvantages of poverty. But few of these programs actually seemed to much enhance the instruction children received and in some cases the older "slow it down" plan was continued with "disadvantaged" children. The result therefore, was that many of the "disadvantaged" children failed to develop into readers and writers even after participating in the compensatory education programs (Puma, Jones, Rock, & Fernandez, 1993). Some educators and researchers argued that schools just could not be expected to overcome the negative effects of growing up poor. But the "disadvantage" conceptualization shaped the sorts of instructional programs that were offered.

The Learning Disabilities Factor

A third, and more recently popularized belief about children who find learning to read difficult is that these children suffer a disability (McGill-Franzen, 1987). Usually this disability is characterized in terms of neurological damage or difference that makes perceptual or verbal learning exceedingly difficult, if not impossible. But evidence of a neurological basis for reading difficulties has been difficult to find. If children with such conditions exist they exist in incredibly small numbers, far too few to account for the range of difficulties now observed (Vellutino et al., 1996). Nonetheless, believing in a neurologically based disability meant some children could not be expected to learn to read and so little effective instruction was offered (Allington & McGill-Franzen, 1989). For instance, few individualized educational plans set annual goals for accelerated literacy development (an annual goal of 1.5 years growth per year, for instance) because the disability conceptualization suggested damaged or limited capacity for learning.

Current Professional Beliefs: Sufficiency of Instruction

Most recently, there has been a growing recognition that reading acquisition is relatively easy for some children and relatively difficulty—exceedingly difficult in a few cases—for other children. But only a very few children cannot, seemingly, acquire reading proficiency alongside their peers (Lyons, Pinnell, & DeFord, 1993; Slavin, Madden, Karweit, Dolan, & Wasik, 1993; Vellutino et al., 1996). This might be labeled the sufficiency of instruction conceptualization. Because children vary in the ease with which they acquire literacy and because they arrive at school with varied levels of literacy experience, we should expect that providing a standard instructional program would result in large discrepancies in achievement. Only when the instructional program offers varied levels of instructional intensity can we reasonably expect all children to develop reading proficiency—especially developing that proficiency on a schedule similar to peer development.

However, we must first believe virtually all children can become readers before we even begin to think about how to design instruction to ensure that this happens (Winfield, 1986; Zigmond, 1993). This belief leads us to design programs in which some children have access to larger amounts of higher quality and more intensive instruction.

Beliefs are important because they drive our thinking, our planning, and our actions (Allington, McGill-Franzen, & Schick, 1997). Yet for too long our professional beliefs have literally resulted in educational efforts that produced children who remained largely illiterate. Believing in the inherent educability of all children is a necessary first step in creating schools where all children become readers and writers.

CHILDREN NEED TO READ A LOT TO BECOME READERS

In addition to professional beliefs, it also matters how successful we are at creating instructional environments that foster wide reading by all children, but especially by those children who have found learning to read difficult. Unfortunately, an overwhelmingly consistent finding in the research is that children who find learning to read difficult often participate in educational programs that fail to foster much reading at all—these children do less guided reading with their teachers and less independent, voluntarily reading (Krashen, 1993).

Only occasionally are interventions purposefully designed to alter this situation (Morrow, 1992). More often the instruction for children who find learning to read difficult occupies them with skill games, practice dittos, and drills (Allington, 1983; Allington & McGill-Franzen, 1989). Too often, in some schools children who have difficulty with reading have literally no books in their desks that they can actually read or learn to read from. This occurs even though schools spend substantial additional funds on interventions intended to assist the struggling readers (Guice, Allington, Johnston, Baker, & Michelson, 1996).

The Importance of Instructional Environment

If children are going to engage in substantial amounts of reading, there seem to be at minimum two aspects of the instructional environment left that must be attended to. First, children need access to a large supply of books of appropriate difficulty, books that fit the Goldilocks principle (Fountas & Pinnell, 1996); they are not too hard, not too easy, but just right. This means books that they can read fluently while also understanding the story or information. This is not a new idea. For most of this century fitting children to books has been advocated and teachers have been taught to administer informal reading inventories and, more recently, to gather running records, in an attempt to ensure appropriate book placement. In some schools, unfortunately, there is little evidence that this feature of appropriate instruction is of much concern. For instance, we too often still find classrooms where all children are taught from the same book regardless of how well the book matches their level of literacy development. We find remedial and special education programs that offer little support to either children or classroom teachers in this regard (McGill-Franzen, 1994). Many programs exert little effort to ensure that struggling readers have easy access to a large supply of appropriate books. We find state educational policies that support the purchase of more skill and drill workbooks although classrooms have few, if any, books appropriate for the children having difficulty with reading acquisition and although school libraries remain underfunded, understaffed, and understocked.

> Research on effective instruction suggests that we have not yet found a way to package good teaching.

If we want to foster wider reading there is another feature of instructional environments that is important, but often overlooked. Children need access to books and stories that are interesting and engaging to them and they need the freedom to choose at least some of the books they read, especially if we are attempting to foster independent, voluntary reading. Again, however, too few efforts to help children who find learning to read difficult are focused on ensuring a supply of interesting and appropriately difficult books is readily available.

Often we hear talk of the need to motivate reluctant readers but perhaps we should think more about examining the environments we create more carefully rather than characterizing the lack of voluntary reading as a motivational problem located in children. We need to worry more about putting enticing, just-right books in children's hands and less about schemes that bribe children into taking home an uninteresting book that is too difficult.

CHILDREN NEED TO BE TAUGHT

Although there may be some natural readers, most children need good instruction and some need enormous amounts of personalized instruction if they are to become readers. Research on effective instruction suggests that we have not yet found a way to package good teaching. In study after study, it is the quality of the teacher, not variation in curriculum materials, that is identified as the critical factor in effective instruction (Bond & Dykstra, 1967; Knapp, 1995; Shanklin, 1990). That is not to say that materials are wholly unimportant, but that investing in teacher development has a better result than investing in curriculum materials. Good teachers, expert teachers, produce more readers than other teachers regardless of the curriculum materials used.

> Unfortunately, all too often we have designed extra-instructional programs in a one-size-fits-all scheme.

Good teachers know their students better and are more precise in targeting instructional needs (Johnston, 1997). Good teachers know more about literacy acquisition and use this expertise in planning instruction. They offer a more comprehensive sort of reading instruction with more attention to individual instructional needs (Pressley et al., 1996). These teachers create literacy-rich classrooms and teach strategies using explicit modeling. In other words, these teachers do not just assign work nor attempt to cover some segment of the curriculum material. Instead, these teachers teach actively and teach the useful strategies students need when they need them as opposed to following some predetermined schedule or pacing (Duffy, 1997). These teachers also push children to become more independent, more thoughtful readers.

Good teachers create classrooms where reading and writing activity fill large blocks of time. They develop effective decoding strategies, spelling strategies, and composing and comprehension activities, and they are constantly monitoring children's reading development and intervening when instruction is needed (Goatley, Brock, & Raphael, 1995).

But some children need more intensive instruction than a classroom teacher can provide. Some children will need additional small-group work and some can be expected to need tutorial assistance. Some children will need such help only for the short term, while others will need assistance for the long term. In other words, some children will need extra instruction this Wednesday after school, some will need a tutorial all next week, and some will need the added time that a summer school experience would provide for the remainder of their school career. Unfortunately, all too often we have designed extra-instructional programs in a one-size-fits-all scheme (Walmsley & Allington, 1995), in which everyone will receive three 30-minute small-group sessions every week all year, regardless of their real needs. Almost no one will participate in tutoring because educators have not devised a plan that makes short term tutoring available (even though such efforts are generally more successful than other efforts [Wasik & Slavin, 1993]).

Until we redesign school programs so that children have access to sufficient instruction—of whatever level of intensity and duration is needed—then we will have children who will struggle with reading acquisition when compared with their peers. The key to success is good teachers working within a flexible school framework that allows them to provide the instruction children need.

SCHOOLS WORK BETTER WHEN FAMILIES ARE PARTNERS

Good schools are more important to literacy development than are families (Snow, Barnes, Chandler, Goodman, & Hemphill, 1991), but the most successful schools have fostered and supported family involvement. It is schools that are charged with responsibility for developing reading proficiency, not families. Inviting family involvement, providing families with support in working with their children, and gaining the confidence of the families of children attending the school are all wonderfully important tasks to be undertaken after the school has ensured the adequacy of the school program.

Creating schools where children are neither rewarded nor penalized for their family status must be the first task of educators (Allington & Cunningham, 1996). Once effective school programs are in place—programs that provide children with access to sufficient high-quality instruction—then work on family support and involvement efforts can proceed. Interestingly, once good school programs are in place, family involvement often seems less a problem.

Developing strategies to support families should be the first order of business. For instance, schools might work to ensure all children have an adequate supply of appropriate books to take home in the evening or over the weekend. Extending this support further might involve opening the school library evenings, on weekends, and over the summer. In some schools this has been accomplished with no added costs by using flexible scheduling of library staff.

Many families simply do not have the discretionary funds to purchase books for a child's bedroom library. A recent study in California reported home supplies of appropriate books varied widely by community with the wealthiest homes reporting nearly 200 age-appropriate books and the less wealthy homes reporting one age-appropriate book available in every other household (Smith, Constantino, & Krashen, 1997). Often the local elementary school has the largest supply of children's books in the near vicinity and yet, that supply often is largely unavailable to the parents of children who own no books of their own. To address this problem, schools might develop sponsorships for book give-away programs so that every child receives a number of personal books each year. Schools also might invite parents of preschool age children to use the library.

Families can support school learning in other ways but many will need substantial guidance and support to help effectively. We need to understand that family literacy experiences differ across families and family ability to support school instruction also varies (Purcell-Gates, 1995). It often seems that schools would do better to make a greater effort to learn from families than to assume that families need to be taught or told what to do.

SO WHAT TO DO FIRST?

There are only a very few things that really matter in developing avid and proficient readers. A good beginning is a taking stock activity that attempts to evaluate reliably just how those things that really matter are addressed in your school. Do children who find learning to read difficult have easy access to appropriate and engaging books and stories? Has the instructional program been designed to offer children access to reading instruction of sufficient quality and intensity to accelerate their literacy development? Is the instruction exemplary and focused on developing independent, engaged readers?

Although there are only a few things that really matter, creating schools that work well for all children is not easy. Changing schools is hard work and it takes time, energy, and expertise. Individuals hold the key in those matters. It is up to you.

REFERENCES

Allington, R. L. (1983). The reading instruction provided readers of differing abilities. *The Elementary School Journal, 83,* 548–559.

Allington, R. L. (1991). The legacy of "slow it down and make it more concrete." In J. Zutell & S. McCormick (Eds.), *Learner factors/teacher factors: Issues in literacy research and instruction* (pp. 19–30). Chicago: National Reading Conference.

Allington, R. L., & Cunningham, P. M. (1996). *Schools that work: Where all children read and write.* New York: HarperCollins.

Allington, R. L., & McGill-Franzen, A. (1989). Different programs, indifferent instruction. In A. Gartner & D. Lipsky (Eds.), *Beyond separate education: Quality education for all* (pp. 75–98). Baltimore: Brookes.

Allington, R. L., McGill-Franzen, A., & Schick, R. (1997). How administrators understand learning difficulties: A qualitative analysis. *Remedial and Special Education, 18,* xx:xx.

Bond, G. L., & Dysktra, R. (1967). The cooperative research program in first-grade reading instruction. *Reading Research Quarterly, 2,* 5–142.

Duffy, G. G. (1997). Powerful models or powerful teachers? An argument for teacher-as-entrepreneur. In S. Stahl & D. Hayes (Eds.), *Instructional models in reading* (pp. 351–365). Hillsdale, NJ: Erlbaum.

Elley, W. B. (1992). *How in the world do students read? IEA study of reading literacy.* The Hague, Netherlands: International Association for the Evaluation of Educational Achievement.

Fountas, I. C., & Pinnell, G. S. (1996). *Guided reading: Good first teaching for all children.* Portsmouth, NH: Heinemann.

Goatley, V. J., Brock, C. H., & Raphael, T. E. (1995). Diverse learners participating in regular education "Book Clubs." *Reading Research Quarterly, 30,* 352–380.

Guice, S., Allington, R. L., Johnston, P., Baker, K., & Michelson, N. (1996). Access?: Books, children, and literature-based curriculum in schools. *The New Advocate, 9,* 197–207.

Johnston, P. A. (1997). *Knowing literacy.* York, ME: Stenhouse.

Johnston, P. A., & Allington, R. L. (1991). Remediation. In R. Barr, M. Kamil, P. Mosenthal, & P. D. Pearson (Eds.), *Handbook of reading research: Volume II* (pp. 984–1012). White Plains, NY: Longman.

Knapp, M. S. (1995). *Teaching for meaning in high-poverty classrooms.* New York: Teachers College Press.

Krashen, S. (1993). *The power of reading: Insights from the research.* Englewood, CO: Libraries Unlimited.

Lyons, C. A., Pinnell, G. S., & DeFord, D. E. (1993). *Partners in learning: Teachers and children in Reading Recovery.* New York: Teachers College Press.

McGill-Franzen, A. (1987). Failure to learn to read: Formulating a policy problem. *Reading Research Quarterly, 22,* 475–490.

McGill-Franzen, A. M. (1994). Is there accountability for learning and belief in children's potential? In E. H. Hiebert & B. M. Taylor (Eds.), *Getting reading right from the start: Effective early literacy interventions.* Boston: Allyn & Bacon.

Morrow, L. M. (1992). The impact of a literature-based program on literacy achievement, use of literature, and attitudes of children from minority backgrounds. *Reading Research Quarterly, 27,* 250–275.

Pressley, M., Wharton-McDonald, R., Ranking, J., Mistretta, J., Yokoi, L., Ettenberger, S. (1996). The nature of outstanding primary grade literacy instruction. In E. McIntyre & M. Pressley (Eds.), *Balanced instruction: Strategies and skills in whole language* (pp. 251–276). Norwood, MA: Christopher-Gordon.

Puma, M. J., Jones, C. C., Rock, D., & Fernandez, R. (1993). *Prospects: The congressionally mandated study of educational growth and opportunity—The interim report* (No. GPO 1993 0-354-886 QL3). Washington, DC: U.S. Department of Education.

Purcell-Gates, V. (1995). *Other people's words: The cycle of low literacy.* Cambridge, MA: Harvard University Press.

Shanklin, N. L. (1990). Improving the comprehension of at-risk readers: An ethnographic study of four Chapter 1 teachers, grades 4–6. *International Journal of Reading, Writing, and Learning Disabilities, 6,* 137–148.

Slavin, R. E., Madden, N. A., Karweit, B. L., Dolan, L. J., & Wasik, B. A. (1993). Success for All: A comprehensive approach to prevention and early intervention. In R. E. Slavin, B. L. Karweit, & B. A. Wasik (Eds.), *Preventing early school failure: Research, policy, & practice* (pp. 175–205). Boston: Allyn & Bacon.

Smith, C., Constantino, R., & Krashen, S. (1997). Differences in print environment: Children in Beverly Hills, Compton and Watts. *Emergency Librarian, 24,* 8–9.

Snow, C., Barnes, W., Chandler, J., Goodman, I. F., & Hemphill, L. (1991). *Unfulfilled expectations: Home and school influences on literacy.* Cambridge, MA: Harvard University Press.

Vellutino, F. R., Sipay, E. R., Small, S. G., Pratt, A., Chen, R., & Denckla, M. B. (1996). Cognitive profiles of difficult-to-remediate and readily remediated poor readers: Early intervention as a vehicle for distinguishing between cognitive and experiential deficits as basic causes of specific reading disability. *Journal of Educational Psychology, 88,* 601–638.

Walmsley, S. A., & Allington, R. L. (1995). Redefining and reforming instructional support programs for at-risk students. In R. L. Allington & S. A. Walmsley (Eds.), *No quick fix: Rethinking literacy programs in America's elementary schools* (pp. 19–41). New York: Teachers College Press; Newark, DE: International Reading Association.

Wasik, B. A., & Slavin, R. E. (1993). Preventing early reading failure with one-to-one tutoring: A review of five programs. *Reading Research Quarterly, 28,* 178–200.

Winfield, L. F. (1986). Teachers' beliefs toward academically at-risk students in inner urban schools. *Urban Review, 18,* 253–268.

Zigmond, N. (1993). Learning disabilities from an educational perspective. In G. R. Lyon, D. B. Gray, J. F. Kavanagh, & N. A. Krasgegor (Eds.), *Better understanding learning disabilities: New views from research & their implications for education & public policies* (pp. 229–250). Baltimore: Brookes.

A National Reading Test for Fourth Graders: A Missing Component in the Policy Debate

by Clifford Hill

INTRODUCTION
In the state of the union address in 1997, President Clinton stated the goal that every child in this country should be able "to read independently by the end of the third grade" (*The New York Times* 1997, A20). In order to reach this goal, he proposed that a reading test be developed at the national level for children in the fourth grade. The proposal was designed to provide national leadership in developing an appropriate test while preserving for states the choice of whether they would participate.

This proposal has led to an extended policy debate about a national reading test. Those who support the proposal claim that since reading is fundamental to successful performance both in school and in the larger society, our educational system must insure that children learn to read well at an early age. They also claim that a national test is needed to make sure that such learning takes place for all children. If children do not pass the test, they can be placed in a reading program designed to give them special help. The test thus has a basic diagnostic role to play: it can identify not only individual children who need help but also schools in which there is a disproportionate number of such children. Both individuals and institutions can be targeted for special help.

Those who oppose a national test make two different kinds of arguments. Some opponents draw on a politically based argument that a national test violates the basic principle that education should

From a paper based on a presentation at the Fourth International Teaching for Intelligence Conference, April 24, 1998, New York, NY. © 1998 by Clifford Hill. Reprinted with permission.

be controlled at the local level. Even though the administration's proposal reserves for states the choice of whether to participate, the fact remains that the test itself is being developed at the national level. Other opponents draw on an educationally based argument that a national test would have negative effects on classroom practice. Given the high stakes attached to such a test, teachers would be required to spend a good deal of classroom time on test-taking skills that have limited value in developing children's capacity for reading comprehension. Indeed, those who make this argument claim that such skills often run counter to the constructivist curricula being used in many programs of early childhood education.

> Teachers would be required to spend a good deal of classroom time on test-taking skills that have limited value . . .

This last argument is based on a rather negative assessment of reading tests for children. Those who make this argument, however, generally do not provide evidence for why they hold this view. Indeed, the policy debate on a national reading test has proceeded with virtually no attention to how reading tests actually work and how children respond to them. This neglect is symptomatic of a problem that inheres in educational policy debates: attention is generally focused on the broad consequences of a particular program or activity rather than on the program or activity itself. Although these consequences are important in a policy debate, they should be considered in the context of a substantive review of the particular program or activity under consideration. In the case of testing, such a review should consist of close attention not only to representative test material but also to test takers' responses to it.

During the past twenty years at Teachers College, Columbia University, doctoral students and I have conducted a number of reviews of reading tests. These reviews have been carried out in a framework initially developed by Hill and Larsen (1983) in a study of test material piloted for the *Gates-MacGinitie Reading Tests*. At the heart of the framework was Hymes's (1962) model for examining language in social context. This model, known as the ethnography of communication, has been used to investigate not only oral communication but also written communication in a range of settings.

In order to understand what goes on when children take reading tests, Hill and Larsen used a framework in which we investigated how a reading test reflects the interpretive norms of a larger tradition in which it is embedded. Within this framework, we also investigated the interpretive norms that children bring to the experience. We used a range of methods not only for understanding how a reading test functions as institutionalized text but also how children draw on their own ethnocultural norms of language, thought, and experience in responding to it.

This framework has been used to examine the reading component of prominent tests in this country: the *Descriptive Test of Language Skills* (Adames 1987; Bhasin 1990), the *Test of Adult Basic Education* (TABE) (Hill, Anderson, Watt, and Ray 1989; Hill and Parry 1988, 1989), and the *Scholastic Aptitude Test* (Sims-West 1996). It has also been used to examine the reading component of tests widely used in other countries: the *Test of English as a Foreign Language* (TOEFL) in Japan and Chile (Hill and Pike 1985) and in Taiwan (Lin 1993); the English component of the major entrance exam for universities in Japan (Ingulsrud 1988; Matsumoto 1997) and in Taiwan (Yuan 1997); and British-style tests based on the School Certificate, which have been exported to Nigeria (Parry 1986) and Zimbabwe (Allen 1988). A number of the studies conducted both in the United States and abroad were included in an edited volume that placed reading tests within a theoretical debate about the nature of literacy (Hill and Parry 1994).

During the 1990s, the framework has been used to examine the reading component of tests presented as communicatively oriented alternatives to the traditional genre (Chu 1993; Coyle 1992; Hayes and McCartney 1997; Hill 1992, 1995; Hill and Larsen 1992). These recent studies are particularly relevant to the policy debate about a national reading test for children, for they shed light on a claim that is often made by those who support such a test: namely, that recent testing practices have been able to overcome certain problems associated with the traditional genre.

In this article I use the framework developed by Hill and Larsen to analyze material that exemplifies both the traditional genre and the more recently developed communicative alternatives. I then address the policy questions under debate. Is it advisable to develop a national test of reading comprehension for children at the fourth-grade level? If it is, what kind of a test should be developed? To what degree should it represent the traditional genre as opposed to the communicative alternatives that more recently have been proposed?

If a national test is not advisable, what kinds of assessment models are appropriate in early childhood education? More particularly, how can these models be best used to insure that children learn to read well at an early age?

THE TRADITIONAL GENRE

In focusing on the traditional genre of reading tests for children, I present only one of the eighteen test units analyzed in Hill and Larsen (1999).

> The fawn looked at Alice with its large, gentle eyes. It didn't seem at all frightened. "Here, then! Here, then!" Alice said, as she held out her hand and tried to stroke it. It moved back a little and then stood looking at her again.

A. How did the fawn's eyes look?
     sad   gentle
     tired   frightened

B. What did Alice try to do to the fawn?
     help it   hug it
     pet it   hide it

Before presenting children's responses to this test material, I would like to first introduce a theoretical distinction that van Dijk and Kintsch (1983) make between *text base* and *situation model*. The text base of the above passage includes not only the overtly stated propositions (e.g., *Alice tried to stroke the fawn*) but also inferences directly entailed by them (e.g., *Alice did not manage to stroke the fawn*). The term *automated* can be used to refer to such inferences.

As children work with a text base, which is, after all, only a set of propositions, they construct a situation that these propositions seem to represent. This conversion of text into meaning is a complex process that necessarily involves inferences that go beyond the automated ones. As children read the above passage, for example, they construct, no matter how inchoately, a physical scene (presumably one where wild animals are free to roam about) in which a human being (presumably a young girl) interacts in a rather personal way with one of these animals (presumably one she has not met before). Even with a relatively short passage, inferences rapidly multiply as children convert words into a world.

Ideally, what is to be comprehended in a reading test is the passage itself, but in actual practice the situation model that children construct is influenced by material in the tasks, particularly the potential answers that are supplied, which can lead children to make inferences that would not necessarily occur to them if they were dealing with the passage alone. Hence the text base to be comprehended on a reading test is constituted by not simply the passage, but rather the passage and the tasks combined.

I would like to present two kinds of situation models that are often associated with the choice of a task distractor:

- a *normative situation model* based on inferencing motivated by the text, and
- a *quasi-normative situation model* based on inferencing invited by the text base.

Using the above test unit, I will illustrate how children make what can be called *motivated inferences* and *invited inferences* in constructing these two kinds of situation models.

When interviewing children,[1] Hill and Larsen (1999) discovered that certain of them, cued by the distractor *frightened* in task A, inferred that the fawn was, indeed, frightened. They used two mutually supporting propositions in the text base to motivate this inference:

sentence 2	*It didn't seem at all frightened.*
sentence 4 (1st part)	*It moved back a little.*

Certain children used the presence of *-n't seem* in sentence 2 as a cue that the fawn was actually frightened. As an eleven-year-old African-American girl put it, "It didn't look frightened but it was" (note her use of the word *look* in task A, which echoes *seem* from the passage).

Children's tendency to contrast the fawn's appearance with its actual state was reinforced by the information in sentence 4: *It moved back a little.* In explaining their choice of frightened, children often focused on this passage information (*i* stands for the interviewer and *c* for the child):

i   Why did you choose *frightened?*

c   The fawn must have been frightened because when she tried to stroke him, he moved back.

This information was also salient when children were asked to recall the passage. In fact, children often used a more dramatic verb to describe the fawn's movement, as illustrated by the use of *jumped back* by two African-American children:

> Then the fawn *jumped back* and looked at her.

> So Alice reached out her arm to pet him but the fawn *jumped back* startled.

In the second example, the child makes clear that she thinks the fawn was frightened by adding the word *startled*.[2] Other children actually used the word *frightened* in reporting the fawn's final movement:

> It backed up as if it were *frightened.*

The point can be raised that task A focuses not on how the fawn itself looked but rather how its eyes looked. Given this focus, the target response to this task is *gentle,* which requires readers only to recycle information from sentence 1:

> *The fawn looked at Alice with its large, gentle eyes.*

Certain children who selected *frightened* ignored this choice, since they assumed that there was no need to repeat information that had already been given. Certain children made the further assumption that the task focused on the final state of affairs rather than an earlier state. From their perspective, by the end of the passage evidence has accumulated that the fawn was frightened.

In explaining their choice of *frightened* for task A, certain children attempted to focus on how the fawn's eyes looked at the end of the story. Consider, for example, the response of an eleven-year-old African-American boy when he was asked, "Why did you pick *frightened* as the answer to the first question?"

> Because it says in the story when she tried to stroke it, it moved back and looked at her. His eyes were wide open so it must be frightened.

In his response, the boy initially focuses on the crucial textual information—*it moved back*—that justifies the inference that the fawn was frightened. But since task A is concerned with how the fawn's eyes looked, he goes on to state that its eyes were "wide open" (this child apparently viewed the fawn as on full alert because of its fear).

Let us now turn to task B and illustrate how the distractor *help it* can lead children to construct a quasi-normative situation model. In constructing such a situation model, children make an inference less directly motivated by the text base, which is why it is described as merely *invited* rather than *motivated*. Certain children took the presence of *try* in (B) as cueing a search for a response that would represent what Alice was "actually trying" to accomplish when she stroked the fawn. In effect, these children understood the task as embodying the following kind of question:[3]

> What was Alice trying to do for the fawn when she stroked it?

In response to this question, these children, stimulated by the distractor *help it,* made an invited inference: that is to say, they extended the text base by inferring that Alice was stroking the fawn in order to help it. Here is how a ten-year-old African-American boy responded when he was asked why he thought Alice was trying to help the fawn:

c   Because it says right here, here it is [he then reads from the passage, replacing stroke with help].

i   How do you know she tried to help it?

c   She tried to stick her hand out for her to reach it.

While reading what Alice said to the fawn (*Here then! Here then!*), he provided an extremely soothing intonation.

A number of African-American children thought that the fawn was hurt and thus needed Alice's help. Consider, for example, the following exchange:

i   Why do you think Alice was trying to help the fawn?

c   Because the fawn was hurt.

i   Does the story say that it was hurt?

c   No, but that's what I think.

When African-American children were asked to retell what they had read, certain of them mentioned that the fawn was hurt. Here are two such retellings, one quite brief and the other considerably expanded:

> A fawn got hurt and the girl is trying to help it. The fawn kind of ran away, got scared.

> Once upon a time Alice was walking through the forest and she saw a fawn. It was beautiful and she saw how gentle it was looking at her. So she went over there and walked to it and tried to pet it. Then the fawn

jerked back. She was wondering why did the fawn jerk back.[4] So she went over there and she went to get her friend. Her friends came. They all surrounded the fawn and then suddenly she got to it. And then she realized that the fawn had a broken leg.

In the second recall, the use of the formulaic *once upon a time* signals that this child wishes to produce a story of her own, not merely repeat what she has read; still she retains substantial detail from the passage, weaving it into a larger narrative that culminates with Alice's discovery that the fawn had a broken leg. At first glance, such a detail seems totally unrelated to what was in the passage. When one considers, however, that a fawn is a skittish animal that runs away when approached by a human being, it becomes more plausible to think that perhaps the fawn was hurt and thus was unable to run away.

The situation model that readers construct when they read is based not simply on the text base but also on their real-world knowledge. The ways in which these two interact can be extremely complex. A major limitation of reading tests is that they have no systematic way of taking account of this interaction (see Hill and Larsen 1999, for an extended discussion of this problem). With respect to this particular test unit, the use of real-world knowledge often worked against children, for if they knew what a fawn is, they were more likely to select *frightened* for task A. By way of contrast, children who thought the fawn was a domestic animal were less attracted to *frightened*. One child, for example, thought the fawn was a duck and talked about how Alice "stroked the fawn's feathers."

Both tasks set up a tension between what can be called an *acommunicative target response,* which either recycles information (task A) or defines a vocabulary item (task B), and a *communicative distractor,* which is based on either a motivated inference (task A) or an invited inference (task B). They also make the point that African-American children are more likely to select the communicative distractor, as evidenced by the results of the pilot testing conducted by the test makers (see figure 1). On the other test units in the corpus of test material, African-American children selected a communicative distractor more frequently than the European-American children did.[5]

Within the traditional genre of reading tests, the problematic kind of material that has been described is ultimately related to various constraints that test makers work with. To begin with, they must produce a test that takes less than an hour so that it will be easy to administer (and also to allow for children's limited attention span). In addition, they must ensure that different kinds of reading material are adequately represented. These two constraints lead to passages that are brief and decontextualized.

		African American	European American
Task A	acommunicative target response (gentle)	46%	64%
	communicative distractor (frightened)	25%	17%
Task B	acommunicative target response (pet it)	26%	52%
	communicative distractor (help it)	47%	30%

Figure 1

In constructing tasks, test makers must work with two further constraints. On the one hand, they must be able to defend the choice that they designate as the target response. This leads them to construct tasks that do not violate the text base (i.e., they must accord with information that is either directly stated or automatically entailed). On the other hand, they must construct tasks that have sufficient discriminatory power: a task does not make it onto the test unless it elicits a sufficient number of distractor responses. In order to construct genuinely attractive distractors, test makers are drawn to various kinds of inferences that the passage stimulates; as illustrated by the test unit on Alice and the fawn, distractors can be based on a motivated inference or an invited inference.

We can thus see how these various constraints conspire to produce a textual configuration that easily leads young children astray. When they encounter a brief and decontextualized passage, they tend to expand it in order to achieve a coherent world of meaning. Once that expansion is in place, they are primed to select a distractor that accords with this world, unless, of course, they have learned to carry out the highly constrained operations that lead to the target response. In effect, children are encouraged to suppress the very processes that constructivist theory presents as fundamental to reading.

COMMUNICATIVE ALTERNATIVES TO THE TRADITIONAL GENRE

Let us now examine representative material from tests that are described as presenting communicative alternatives to the traditional genre. The *Progressive Achievement Tests of Reading* (1993) were developed by the New Zealand Council for Educational Research. According to Hayes and McCartney (1997), various features are included that can be found on more recent tests for children:

- Brief introductions that provide a context for the passages
- Pictures that accompany the passages
- Passages based on authentic material
- Passages of greater length
- More tasks per passage

The following folktale was used on one of these tests. It was preceded by a picture of a pukeko,[6] a bird with a long neck, sticking its head in a dog's mouth.

> *Here is a little story about a dog and what happened when he was helped by a pukeko.*
>
> One day when a dog was having dinner, a sharp bone stuck in his throat. Not long after his meal, he began to feel a great pain. He spent a long time trying to get the bone out, but he could not. At last he went to a pukeko and said, "If you take this bone out of my throat, I will give you a reward for your work." So the silly pukeko put his long neck into the dog's mouth and pulled out the bone. Then he asked for his reward.
>
> The dog said, "You already have your reward. You should thank me for not biting off your head while it was down my throat."

1. When did the dog go to the pukeko?
   (A) At dinner time.   (C) A long time after his dinner.
   (B) As soon as he had   (D) The next day.
       finished his meal.

2. Why did the dog go to the pukeko?
   (A) To ask the pukeko to   (C) To ask the pukeko for
       help him.   his reward.
   (B) To get a bone for his   (D) To bite off the pukeko's
       dinner.   head.

3. After the pukeko had pulled out the bone, he wanted the dog to
   (A) run away.
   (B) give him something for his work.
   (C) let him go.
   (D) tell him how clever he was.

4. The pukeko was able to help because
   (A) his head was very big.
   (B) his neck was long.
   (C) he was hungry.
   (D) he liked bones.

5. This story is **mostly** about a
   (A) dog finding a bone.
   (B) dog with a sore stomach.
   (C) pukeko's reward.
   (D) foolish pukeko.

Despite the presence of the innovative features, the problems associated with the traditional genre of reading tests have not disappeared. The target response for task 5 is (C) *pukeko's reward,* which requires that children adopt a neutral stance toward the information that the folktale presents. Within task 5, the word *mostly* is placed in bold, which provides a clue that the test makers view *pukeko's reward* as accounting for more passage information than the other choices do.

Such neutral information processing is not easily maintained by children who become engaged with the folktale. Not only do they have difficulty viewing the pukeko as having received a reward, but for them the real point of the story is that the pukeko was foolish. Indeed, the pukeko is actually described as *silly* and so children who choose (D) *foolish pukeko* can be viewed as doing what test makers often call for—recycling information from the passage.

In a study conducted with seventeen Latino and African-American fourth graders in metropolitan New York, Hayes and McCartney (1997) discovered that only four of them managed to select the target response. Among the other thirteen children, twelve selected the distractor (D) *foolish pukeko.* Here is how an eleven-year-old Latino girl explained her choice:

i   Why did you choose (D)?

c   Because he put his neck inside the dog's mouth and that's nasty and that's foolish.

i   Why is it foolish?

c   Because a normal person—or whatever it is—wouldn't actually put his mouth or his head or anything else into the dog's mouth.

i   Okay.

c   'Cause it could be a trap.

i   What kind of trap?

c   He puts his head into the dog's mouth and the dog just bites it off.

Many of the other children also made the inference that the pukeko was foolish to stick its head into the dog's mouth. Such an inference is clearly motivated; indeed, the whole folktale seems to turn on this inference.

When Hayes and McCartney presented this folktale without the picture, children were still able to make sense out of the story, even though they did not know what a pukeko is. When children were asked to describe a pukeko, a number of them said that it was a giraffe. Realizing that a giraffe's head would be too big for a dog's mouth, they tended to come up with ingenious ways of resolving this problem. One child, for example, pictured the giraffe as a baby:

i   What do you think a pukeko is?

c   Like a little creature with a long neck like a round head with a strong jaw. It reminds me of a baby giraffe, like only 5 inches, that big [he demonstrates].

i   Why do you think that?

c   Because a giraffe has a long neck and a big head. They have a strong jaw and stuff like that and jut like a body.

A giraffe was also frequently present when children were presented with an additional task:

Write an ending to this story in which the pukeko manages to get something that is a real reward. You can either change what the dog did or add something new that shows the pukeko getting the kind of reward (s)he wants.

Figure 2 shows how an eleven-year-old Latino girl responded to this task:

Figure 2

"That's not a reward!" Pukeo said outraged.
"What is it then"? said the Dog.
"It's a privlige" said Pukeo.
"What do you want then?" asked the Dog.
"I want you to be my housekeeper for a week!" Puekeo said.
"Okay." said the dog.

Unfortunately, the researchers did not probe what this girl intended by using "privlige," but perhaps it had to do with her sense that the pukeko's life somehow constitutes an inalienable right.

In reviewing the test material from New Zealand, Hayes and McCartney (1997) recognized certain improvements that have been made in the test (e.g., the use of passages based on a complete text structure rather than an incomplete one). At the same time, they point out that the tasks still reflect the communicative/acommunicative tension documented in Hill and Larsen's study of the traditional genre. They thus remain skeptical about the claims that more communicatively oriented testing can resolve the problems associated with the traditional genre. Indeed, as Hill and Parry (1989) pointed out when comparing a communicatively oriented version of the TABE (1987) with an earlier version based on the traditional genre (1976), if a communicatively oriented passage is followed by a multiple-choice task such as those discussed above, it actually encourages the choice of a communicative distractor. As long as test makers work with the multiple-choice format, it is not clear how they will resolve the problems that are basic to the genre that has dominated reading tests in this century.[7]

It is for this reason that I do not support a national reading test for fourth graders. I believe that such a high stakes test would have detrimental effects upon children during early years of schooling. Just as they are struggling to develop control over the constructive processes basic to reading, they would be penalized for making use of them on the national test. This penalty would then lead teachers to develop classroom activities that train children to adopt an acommunicative stance toward what they read. In effect, children would be encouraged to suppress the constructive responses to text that are fundamental to their development as readers.

ALTERNATIVE ASSESSMENT: THE *PROGRESS PROFILE*

What, then, constitutes a viable alternative to a national test for children? I believe that a constructivist model of assessment is appropriate for children of this age. A number of such models are available in early childhood education, and here I briefly describe the *Progress Profile,* a model that teachers and I developed for use in the Newburgh School District (the model has been adapted and used in other school districts in metropolitan New York). This model has two major components:

- testlike activities
- documentation activities (i.e., portfolios and teacher records of home-school interactions)

Given the limited space of this article, I can here describe only the testlike activities that have to do with reading comprehension (see Hill 1992 and 1995, for a description of the model as a whole).

The term *testlike* is used to indicate certain activities that fall loosely within a testing paradigm but that do not meet its strictest conditions. Hill and Larsen (1992) have described these conditions in the following way:

(1) a single time frame of specified duration

(2) prescribed tasks presented in a stable form

(3) individual responses relatively independent of external resources

(4) evaluation of individual responses based on a preestablished scheme[8]

Here is a brief outline of how testlike activities in the *Progress Profile* alter these conditions:

(1) Children carry out activities in a single time frame, but it is not of a specified duration; they are allowed, within reason, to use as much time as they need (i.e., no attempt is made to use time as a way of showing how efficiently children can respond to tasks).

(2) Children do respond to prescribed tasks initially presented in a stable form; if an individual child does not understand a given task or is unable to perform it, the test giver—who is ordinarily the child's teacher—can provide additional information. In fact, the teacher is encouraged to do so. The *Progress Profile* has been influenced by the model of dynamic assessment developed by Feuerstein (1972, 1977, 1978), in which teaching and learning are allowed, indeed encouraged, within assessment activities; from Feuerstein's perspective, one of the goals of assessment is to determine how well a child can use relevant information in problem solving (the evaluation of a child's responses takes into account the specific information that a test giver provides).

(3) Although it is the individual child who responds to the activities, the use of external resources is encouraged; for example, in writing a response to what they have read, a child can use a dictionary (i.e., the basic principle is that children should be in a position to use resources they ordinarily use in carrying out a particular activity).

(4) All children's responses are evaluated, but a preestablished scheme that yields a numerical score is used only for responses to certain tasks (e.g., a comprehension question that calls for factual information); such a scheme is not used to evaluate responses that involve a certain amount of inherent variation (e.g., an extension of

a story). Such responses are, however, evaluated in other ways. In the case of a story extension, the teacher makes notes on the degree to which the extension is motivated by elements in the text base.

The testlike activities that assess reading comprehension are built around small books that have been especially prepared for the *Progress Profile.* Certain of these books are built around a multi-cultural collection of folktales, which includes a version of the folktale about the dog and the pukeko. In this version, collected among the Hausa people in West Africa, the animal is a *dila,* "jackal"[9] and the bird a *zal'be,* "stork." In adapting the tale for use in American education, the jackal was changed to the more familiar fox.

> One day a fox was eating a chicken when a sharp bone got stuck in his throat. As he began to call for help, he said, "I'll give a reward to any-one who can get this bone out of my throat." A stork came walking along and said, "I'll help you get that bone out." So the stork stuck his head in the fox's mouth and pulled it out.
>   The fox then turned around and started to walk away. The stork was surprised and so he asked, "Where's my reward?" The fox answered, "Here's your reward: you stuck your head in a fox's mouth and you're still alive."

After reading the story, the children engage in the following testlike activities.

Retelling the story
Can you tell me in your own words what you just read?

Factual tasks
Why did the fox need the stork's help?
What did the stork do to help the fox?

Inferential tasks
Why was the stork able to help the fox?
Do you think the stork got a real reward? Please explain your thinking.

Holistic tasks
Write an ending to this story in which the stork manages to get some-thing that (s)he thinks is a real reward. You can either change what the fox did or add something new that shows the stork getting the kind of reward (s)he wants.

Experiential tasks
Describe an experience in which you were disappointed by a reward

that you received. Try to explain why you and the other person differed in your thinking about a reward.

Here is how two children responded to the retelling task, which provides an effective foundation for the tasks that follow. The first retelling can be described as *performance style,* the second as *summary style.*

> The fox was eating a chicken and he started choking and yelling, "Help! Help! I'll give you a reward." And a stork came and helped him. The fox didn't give him a reward and . . . um . . . the stork yelled, "Where's my reward?" The fox said, "You're just lucky to be alive. I didn't bite your head off." (11-year-old African-American boy)

> The fox was eating and . . . um . . . he was eating something and a bone got stuck in his throat and after he finished eating it . . . he felt pain and then he went to the stork—I think it was—and the stork helped him with the bone and took it out. (10-year-old African-American girl)

One major benefit of the *Progress Profile* is that it allows for legitimate variation in how children respond to a task. Many children whose language development takes place primarily in oral culture draw on a more performance-oriented style as they retell a folktale. As was earlier illustrated, when children retell test material, they may use a familiar formula such as "once upon a time." Rather than penalizing children for adopting a performance style (which a testing paradigm does by requiring them to adopt an acommunicative stance), the *Progress Profile* simply records what kind of style a particular child uses (such information can be useful in the cumulative school record). It also records the degree to which children include basic plot elements in their retelling. When teachers listen to children's retelling of this particular tale, they provide appropriate checks and comments on a preestablished form. Figure 3 shows how this form was used to record the summary offered by the ten-year-old African-American girl. The test giver did not check the four story elements that have to do with the reward. She also included brief notes on distinctive aspects of the girl's retelling.

The tasks that follow the retelling are built around the model of comprehension developed by Bloom (1984). The first two kinds of tasks reflect the familiar distinction between literal and inferential comprehension. Rather than setting up a tension between the two— as multiple-choice tasks frequently do—the *Progress Profile* keeps

---

Figure 3

	Yes/No	Comments
Story Style		
Performance		
Summary	√	*Hesitant style; use of "I think it was"*
Story Elements		
Fox gets bone stuck in throat	√	*Chicken not mentioned*
Fox offers a reward for help	√	
Stork gets bone out		
Fox doesn't give reward		
Stork asks for reward		
Fox explains what reward is		

---

them separate. One of the inferential tasks asks children to explain their response. Such an explanation helps to determine the degree to which children use the text base in motivating their inference (this information is recorded along with the response itself).

Having responded to the factual and inferential tasks, children are then asked to respond holistically by extending the folktale in some way. The particular way in which children respond to this task often sheds a good deal of light on their understanding of the tale. An eleven-year-old African-American boy, for example, focused on the stork getting the reward before providing any help (he begins with direct speech expressing the stork's indignation).

> "That is not fair. I did you a favor and I don't get anything." The stork left. A couple of days later the fox got a bone stuck in his throat. He went back to the stork and asked for help. The stork said, "No." The fox begged and begged so the stork said, "If you give me my reward before I do anything, then I will do it." The fox gave him a reward and he got the bone out of his throat.

It is interesting that this child doesn't bother to specify what the reward is. It is as if the real point of his story is achieved once the fox agrees to give the reward in advance.

The final testlike activity requires children to make a connection between what they have read and their own experience. In responding to this particular folktale, children frequently activate a scenario in which if they get good grades, their parents give them an unwanted book. As one child put it, "They should at least give us something fun for all the hard work."

After children complete this set of comprehension tasks, they respond to a set of tasks that focus on literacy conventions: they are asked, for example, (1) to identify specific uses of punctuation such as capitalization or quotation marks and explain how they are being used; (2) to read aloud a short excerpt so that teachers can do a miscue analysis (Goodman 1976); and (3) to write down a short excerpt that is read aloud so that their knowledge of sound-spelling correspondences can be evaluated. Children's responses to these tasks are evaluated quantitatively according to a preexisting scheme, but it is one designed to take account of appropriate variation: for example, when children write down what they hear, they receive partial credit for any phonetically motivated spelling, even if it is not the correct one (e.g., speakers of African-American vernacular receive partial credit for "axed" in place of *asked*).

These tasks, though metalinguistic in nature, do not confuse children in the way that a metalinguistic operation does on a reading test (for example, in the test unit about Alice and the fawn, children understanding that task B is really concerned only with defining a vocabulary item). These tasks do not, for example, force children to carry out metalinguistic analyses as a means of responding to comprehension tasks. We have clearly separated these activities from the comprehension activities that precede them. Moreover, the direct manipulations of language structure that they call for are ones that children are accustomed to doing within normal classroom routines. Combining these two kinds of activities sends a valuable message to both teachers and children—comprehension is at the heart of literacy development but it must not preclude attention to language form.

In closing this article, I would like to discuss various benefits that accrue from the use of testlike activities within the *Progress Profile*. To begin with, there is the political benefit: the presence of testlike activities in the overall assessment model allowed us to avoid the use of standardized tests. When I first worked on a model of alternative assessment with teachers, the administrators of the school district insisted that we include a component that would yield numerical scores: if we did not meet this condition, they were not willing to discontinue the use of standardized tests. We agreed with this demand because we were glad to have some kind of leverage over the use of such tests; not only did we oppose them for the reasons set out in this article, but we had observed in other situations how their continued use undermines efforts to build alternative assessment: children, teachers, and administrators have difficulty in taking such assessment seriously when standardized tests continue to operate.

Apart from this political benefit, another major benefit has been the professional development of teachers. To begin with, as teachers work together to develop these activities, they have an opportunity to share their best practices with each other. They also have an opportunity to develop clinical knowledge and skills as they learn to analyze a child's retelling of a story, conduct a miscue analysis, or evaluate sound-spelling correspondences. Moreover, as teachers administer testlike activities, they have an opportunity to make careful observations that carry over into their daily interactions with individual children. It is as if these activities foster development of their capacity to make responsible judgments about children.

Finally, there has been the benefit to the children themselves. The close attention that they receive from their teacher can be a rewarding experience that increases their confidence and motivation. We have discovered that children look forward to these activities as an opportunity to show what they know and can do; the fact that the teacher is able to provide them with help insures that they walk away from these activities with a feeling of achievement. This feeling contrasts sharply with the fear and intimidation that reading tests often engender. Most importantly, these testlike activities nourish what is most important to develop in young readers—the constructive responses that enable them to take pleasure in text and use it to expand their knowledge about the world.

Author's Note: This article draws on research initially funded by the National Institute of Education under grant #G-78-0095. I gratefully acknowledge the generous support of the Institute. I also acknowledge the support of the U.S. Department of Education, Office of Educational Research and Improvement, National Institute on Student Achievement, Curriculum, and Assessment. The views expressed in this article do not necessarily reflect the position of the U.S. Department of Education.

I would also like to acknowledge the support of Eric Larsen, who has coauthored the volume, *Children and Reading Tests,* on which this article is based. He has suggested a number of improvements in this article. Over the years, his contributions to the research on testing and assessment at Teachers College, Columbia University have been substantial.

NOTES

1. In investigating children's responses to test material, Hill and Larsen conducted individual interviews. One feature of these interviews was asking children to recall what they had read. We attempted to use think-aloud protocols but found that children of this age were generally unable to meaningfully engage with such a task. When the United States Department of Education issued a request for proposals to develop a national reading test for fourth-grade children, it specified that the proposals should include a plan for using think-aloud protocols as a means of test development. Eliciting information about readers' interactions with prospective test material is vital but it is questionable whether think-aloud protocols are an appropriate means of eliciting such information from young children.

2. This child's recall also includes the use of the word *but,* which had been present in the original text—Lewis Carroll's *Through the Looking Glass*—from which this passage was excerpted (see Hill and Larsen 1999, for a discussion of how the presence of *but* in the original text strengthens the inference that the fawn was frightened; they also point out that in the original text this inference was strengthened by the use of *started back*—which phonetically echoes *startled*—to represent the fawn's movement). The test makers' revisions of Lewis Carroll's text were apparently designed to dampen down the sense that the fawn was frightened.

3. From the test makers' perspective, the word *try* in (B) was supposed to guide children to the point in the passage where it was used (i.e., *tried to stroke it*). They would then understand that they were simply to provide a synonym for the verb *stroke* (i.e., the target response is *pet it*).

4. The girl maintains the inverted word order of a question even when it is embedded as a complement: *She was wondering why did the fawn jerk back.* She is here using a widespread feature of African-American English that can be paralleled to distinctive patterning in West African languages (Hill 1991).

5. This pilot testing focused only on the ethnocultural contrast between African-American and European-American children in large urban areas such as Houston. Such a dichotomous contrast risks being misleading, given the transcultural experience that children undergo in a modern society. I am thus using this dichotomy with a certain caution.

6. This folktale was presumably adapted from Maori oral tradition, since it includes a bird bearing a Maori name.

7. It is for this reason that Wang and Hill (1997) have proposed the use of short-answer tasks on the national test of College English in the People's Republic of China. Since this test is annually taken by about 2,500,000 students, the use of short-answer tasks presents a formidable challenge in scoring. Through the use of artificial intelligence programs, however, such tasks can be scored if they are carefully designed (i.e., they must elicit a relatively stable target response that is lexically differentiated from answers that do not count as a target response).

8. In addition, the evaluation of the responses must receive institutional sanction. In order to prepare students for a test, a teacher may administer an activity that meets the first four conditions, but this activity does not count as a test, since the teacher's evaluation of student responses is not entered into any official record (for further discussion, see Hill and Larsen 1992).

9. Hausa speakers typically describe a *dila* as the *malamin daji,* "a clever teacher in the wild."

REFERENCES

Adames, J. A. (1987). *A study of the reading process of selected English as a second language college students.* Unpublished doctoral dissertation, Teachers College, Columbia University, New York.

Allen, K. (1988). *The development of a test of communicative competence for speakers of English as a second language in Zimbabwe.* Unpublished doctoral dissertation, Teachers College, Columbia University, New York.

Bhasin, J. (1990). *The demands of main idea tasks in reading comprehension tests and the strategic responses of bilingual poor comprehenders.* Unpublished doctoral dissertation, Teachers College, Columbia University, New York.

Bloom, B. (1984). *A taxonomy of educational objectives.* New York: Longman.

Chu, H. (1993). *Assessing Chinese kindergarten children in New York City.* Unpublished doctoral dissertation, Teachers College, Columbia University, New York.

Clinton, W. (1997, February 8). State of the Union Address. *The New York Times,* p. A20.

Coyle, M. (1992). *The New Jersey high school proficiency test in writing: A pragmatic face on an autonomous model.* Unpublished doctoral dissertation, Teachers College, Columbia University, New York.

Feuerstein, R. (1972). Cognitive assessment of the socioculturally deprived child and adolescent. In L. J. Cronbach and P. Drenth (Eds.), *Mental tests and cultural adaptation* (pp. 265–275). The Hague, The Netherlands: Mouton.

Feuerstein, R. (1977). Mediated learning experience: A theoretical basis for cognitive human modifiability during adolescence. In P. Mittler (Ed.), *Research to practice in mental retardation. Vol. II* (pp. 105–115). Baltimore: University Park Press.

Feuerstein, R. (1978). The ontogeny of learning. In M. Brazier (Ed.), *Brain mechanisms in memory and learning.* New York: Raven Press.

Goodman, K. (1976). Miscue analysis: Theory and reality in reading. In J. E. Merritt (Ed.), *New horizons in reading: Proceedings of the Fifth International Reading Association World Congress on Reading* (pp. 15–26). Newark, DE: International Reading Association.

Hayes, T., and N. McCartney. (1997). *Progressive achievement tests of reading.* Unpublished manuscript.

Hill. C. (1991). Recherches interlinguistiques en orientation spatiale. *Communications* 53: 171-207.

Hill, C. (1992). *Testing and assessment: An ecological approach.* Inaugural lecture for the Arthur I. Gates Chair in Language and Education, New York: Teachers College, Columbia University.

Hill, C. (1995). Testing and assessment: An applied linguistics perspective. *Educational Assessment* 2: 179-212.

Hill, C., L. Anderson, Y. Watt, and S. Ray. (1989). *Reading assessment in adult education: Local detail versus textual gestalt* (LC Report 89-2). New York: Teachers College, Columbia University, Literacy Center.

Hill, C., and E. Larsen. (1983). *What reading tests call for and what children do* (Final report for NIE Grant G-78-0095). Washington DC: National Institute of Education.

Hill, C., and E. Larsen. (1992). *Assessment in secondary education: A critical review of emerging practices.* Berkeley: University of California, National Center for Research in Vocational Education.

Hill, C., and E. Larsen. (1999). *Children and reading tests.* (In the series *Advances in Discourse Processes,* edited by R. C. Freedle.) Stamford, CT: Ablex Press.

Hill, C., and K. Parry. (1988). *Reading assessment: Autonomous and pragmatic models of literacy* (LC Report 88-2). New York: Teachers College, Columbia University, Literacy Center.

Hill, C., and K. Parry. (1989). Autonomous and pragmatic models of literacy: Reading assessment in adult education. *Linguistics and Education* 1: 233–283.

Hill, C., and K. Parry. (1992). The test at the gate: Models of literacy in reading assessment. *TESOL Quarterly* 26: 433–461.

Hill, C., and K. Parry. (1994). *From testing to assessment: English as an international language.* Harlow, UK: Longman.

Hill, C., and L. Pike. (1985). *A comparison of cloze substitutions in English texts by native speakers of English, Spanish, and Japanese.* Unpublished manuscript.

Ingulsrud, J. E. (1988). *Testing in Japan: A discourse analysis of reading comprehension items.* Unpublished doctoral dissertation, Teachers College, Columbia University, New York.

Lin, H. S. (1993). *A TOEFL coaching school in Taiwan.* Unpublished doctoral dissertation, Teachers College, Columbia University, New York.

Matsumoto, K. (1997). *The approach of coaching schools to the JFSAT.* Unpublished manuscript, Teachers College, Columbia University, New York.

Parry, K. (1986). *Readers in context: A study of northern Nigerian students and School Certificate texts.* Unpublished doctoral dissertation, Teachers College, Columbia University, New York.

Sims-West, N. E. (1996). *An investigation of gender differences on the Scholastic Aptitude Test of verbal ability.* Unpublished doctoral dissertation, Teachers College, Columbia University, New York.

van Dijk, T. A., and W. Kintsch. (1983). *Strategies of discourse comprehension.* New York: Academic Press.

Wang, H., and C. Hill. (1997). *The use of short-answer tasks in testing reading comprehension.* International Conference on College English Teaching, Beijing University, Beijing, China.

Yuan, Y. P. (1997). *Reader response to the Taiwan Joint College Entrance Examination: English Reading Section.* Unpublished doctoral dissertation, Teachers College, Columbia University, New York.

The Professional Growth Portfolio

by Kay Burke

> To be successful, restructuring must start with a few clear goals to be achieved. Clear goals do not ensure success because a lot can happen along the way, but without them, it seems unlikely that a school or district will emerge from the process [to school improvement] triumphantly (Ellis and Fouts 1994, 27).

The traditional staff development model of providing one-day inservices on current "hot" topics to all educators, despite their needs or interests, is changing. The staff development days are still scheduled, but usually their purpose is to establish an awareness of a new strategy such as performance rubrics or problem-based learning rather than to train teachers in how to implement the strategies. The new direction of professional development involves teams of teachers working together over a one- to two-year period to reach specific goals that will benefit their students.

Rather than the district determining what innovative instructional strategies will help all the students, teachers are becoming empowered to address specific goals within the scope of school or district goals to help improve the achievement of their students. These goals may differ depending upon the subject area, grade level, or needs of the students.

Adapted from *Designing Professional Portfolios for Change*, chapter 2, by Kay Burke. © 1997 by IRI/SkyLight Training and Publishing, Inc.

For example, increased achievement on the state literacy examination could be a school or district goal, but each cadre of teachers could take a different approach to achieving that goal. One team could explore using portfolios to monitor growth and development in literacy; another group could explore using the multiple intelligences to teach and assess literacy, and yet another group could introduce metacognitive strategies to help students self-evaluate their own reading and writing achievement. The ultimate goal is the same; however, the means to achieve that goal could differ depending on the interests of the teachers and the needs of their students. Glatthorn states, "All persons have the potential to grow, to change, to develop. The ultimate goal is self-directed professionals who can direct, manage, and evaluate their own professional development" (1996, 46). Educators who are empowered and engaged in determining their own goals and the means to achieve those goals will grow as professionals.

THE TEAM APPROACH

Teachers, like other professionals, perform more effectively—even exponentially—if they collaborate. Although collaboration represents a significant change in how most teachers work, it should become an expectation (Schmoker 1996, 7).

The new vision of professional development as described by Sparks and Hirsh (1997) involves the following:

- A clear, coherent strategic plan for each department, school, and district
- A school-focused approach
- A focus on student needs and learning outcomes (results driven)
- Multiple forms of job-embedded learning
- Teachers involved in study groups, action research, and joint planning

Teachers who in the past worked in almost "hermetically sealed classrooms" in isolation often welcome the support of colleagues who work together to achieve a common goal. The most effective professional development as described by Bernhardt (1994) involves cadres of educators working together, making decisions, analyzing and using data, planning curricula, monitoring student achievement, and evaluating the effectiveness of the new approaches.

McGreal (as cited in Brandt 1996) predicts the next generation of professional development will come from schools in which many things are done in teams. The same teams that are already established—grade-level teams, interdisciplinary teams, interdepartmental teams—decide to develop a professional growth plan for the team. The administrator can meet with the team members once or twice a year to get progress reports and to assist them in collecting data, providing resources, or securing substitutes so members can visit other classes or schools.

Groups of teachers engaged in problem solving create a strong and informal action research sense of group purpose. This environment enhances professional satisfaction and "encourages teachers to reflect on their practice and explore ways to improve it on an ongoing, rather than episodic basis. It is an environment in which it is safe to be candid and to take the risks inherent in trying out new ideas or unfamiliar practices" (McLaughlin and Yee 1988, 36). The team approach to professional growth also allows more opportunities for study groups and peer coaching, whereby members can observe each other, give feedback, cover each other's classes, discuss new ideas, implement innovative strategies, evaluate the effectiveness of their plan, assess their own growth and development, and set new goals.

SIX STEPS TO PROFESSIONAL GROWTH

Professional growth often begins with a district, school, or teacher goal that addresses the needs of the students. Despite the desire to address a plethora of goals, most schools and individuals achieve more success if they limit their efforts to one or two focused goals.

The following flowchart suggests a sequence of steps.

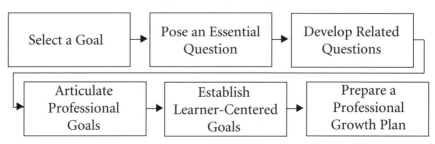

SELECT A GOAL RELATED TO STUDENT NEEDS

One of the first steps in the professional growth process is to review the strategic plan of the department, school, or district to determine goals that will help improve student academic achievement, student motivation, classroom climate, school management, or other goals deemed appropriate. For example, a school goal could be to help students become more critical problem solvers both academically and socially. Another goal could be to decrease school fights and discipline problems in order to ensure optimum conditions for learning. The most important guideline is that the goal relates to helping the students. A list of topics of professional growth, such as shown in figure 1, could help educators identify an area of concern or an area of potential growth within the context of their school goals.

POSE AN ESSENTIAL QUESTION

The next step in the process is to have each group pose an essential question the members hope to answer by studying the problem or implementing new strategies. The essential question should ask how studying and implementing a goal would help the students. Members of the cadres should brainstorm a list of potential questions that will eventually drive the professional growth plan. (See figure 2 for examples of essential questions.)

DEVELOP RELATED QUESTIONS

Once teams of educators have identified the essential research question that will drive their research, they also develop what Dietz (1993) calls "splinter questions" or questions that relate to the essential question. These related questions are intended to extend and elaborate additional information they want to learn about their topic. (See figure 3 for examples of developing related research questions.)

ARTICULATE PROFESSIONAL GOALS

Psychologist Mihalyi Csikszentmihalyi (1990) talks about the enjoyment people get from pursuing doable goals that they value. This connection of goals to happiness accounts for many people being as happy or happier at work than at leisure. Schmoker says goals drive us—"unfortunately, most schools do not make the connection

Professional Growth Topics

From the following topics, check two items in each category that you want to explore in depth. Talk to colleagues about how these topics or strategies could help the students.

Structural Formats

- ☐ Multiage Classroom
- ☐ Detracking
- ☐ Block Scheduling
- ☐ Year-Round School
- ☐ Team Teaching
- ☐ Grouping Practices
- ☐ Inclusion
- ☐ _____
- ☐ _____

Instructional Innovation

- ☐ Instructional Strategies
- ☐ Classroom Management
- ☐ Cooperative Learning Strategies
- ☐ Multiple Intelligences Theory
- ☐ Graphic Organizers
- ☐ Higher-Order Thinking Skills
- ☐ Technology
- ☐ Metacognition
- ☐ Transfer
- ☐ Teacher Expectation and Student Achievement (TESA)
- ☐ Mediated Learning
- ☐ _____
- ☐ _____

Curricular Possibilities

- ☐ Standards Development
- ☐ Thematic Teaching
- ☐ Curriculum Integration
- ☐ Case Studies
- ☐ Service Learning Projects
- ☐ Experiential Education
- ☐ Mentorship-Apprenticeship
- ☐ Problem-Based Learning
- ☐ Project-Based Learning
- ☐ School-to-Work Transition

- ☐ Performance Learning
- ☐ Curriculum Development
- ☐ Expeditionary Learning
- ☐ _____
- ☐ _____

Collegial Strategies

- ☐ Team Building
- ☐ Consensus Building
- ☐ Strategic Planning
- ☐ Team Teaching
- ☐ Curriculum Mapping
- ☐ Conflict Resolution
- ☐ Peer Mediation
- ☐ Parent Councils
- ☐ Peer Coaching
- ☐ Mentoring
- ☐ Action Research Teams
- ☐ Working with the Community
- ☐ _____
- ☐ _____

Evaluation Techniques

- ☐ Assessment of Standards
- ☐ Student Portfolios
- ☐ Teacher-Made Tests
- ☐ Authentic Performances
- ☐ Project Evaluations
- ☐ Standardized Tests
- ☐ Performance Rubrics
- ☐ Individual Evaluation Plans
- ☐ Professional Portfolios
- ☐ Report Card Revisions
- ☐ Communicating Results to Parents
- ☐ _____
- ☐ _____

Figure 1

Examples of Essential Questions

Elementary School

Multiple Intelligences: Would students' achievement scores on state tests improve if we plan and assess lessons using the multiple intelligences identified by Howard Gardner?

Cooperative Learning Strategies: Would students' behavior problems decrease if each teacher taught social skills explicitly in all grade levels?

Middle School

Problem-Based Learning: Would students' test scores in science and mathematics improve if we adopted a problem-based learning curriculum in our school?

Peer Mediation: Would the implementation of a peer mediation program in our school help reduce student detentions, suspensions, and expulsions?

High School

Block Scheduling: Would switching to a block scheduling format help improve our students' motivation to learn and their academic achievement?

Standardized Tests: Would students' standardized test scores improve if each teacher included a specific unit on test-taking strategies in their curriculum?

Figure 2

between goals, motivation, and improvement . . . without explicit learning goals, we are simply not set up and organized for improvement, for results. Only such goals will allow us to analyze, monitor, and adjust practice towards improvement" (1996, 18).

Educators need to articulate professional goals and learn more about teaching strategies and their content area in order to set meaningful learner-centered goals for their students. Educators also need to set a few specific goals and know their audience—in other words, who will benefit from the implementation of this plan?

Developing Related Research Questions

Question for a Team Member

Topic: Standardized Tests

Essential Research Question: Would students' standardized test scores improve if each teacher included a specific unit on test-taking strategies?

Related Questions:
1. What does the research say about coaching for standardized tests?
2. What programs on test-taking techniques are most effective?
3. Should we incorporate the test-taking strategies into the curriculum or teach a separate course as an elective?
4. How can we train our teachers in test-taking strategies?
5. How will we be able to evaluate the effectiveness of the coaching?

Question for the School

Topic: Block Scheduling

Essential Research Question: Would switching to a block scheduling format help improve our students' motivation to learn and their academic achievement?

Related Questions:
1. What does the research say about the effects of block scheduling?
2. What are the block scheduling options?
3. What training do our teachers need to teach in 70-minutes blocks?
4. Will students become more motivated to learn because they have more time for engagement?
5. Will students increase their academic achievement?

Figure 3

In addition, educators need to develop their own professional goals that will help them attain the goals for their students. Professional goals might include the following:

• Review the resources (literature, video, articles) about the topic or goal.

• Attend courses, workshops, and seminars related to the goal.

• Visit other teachers and schools who are implementing strategies or curriculum related to their goals.

ESTABLISH LEARNER-CENTERED GOALS

Even when schools establish goals, the goals tend to be too general. This unfortunate case of "general goals" creates a sense of "false clarity"—the erroneous belief that we understand and know how to work towards achieving the goal (Fullan 1991, 34–35).

The establishment of specific goals is crucial to improvement as noted by Rosenholtz:

• Specific goals convey a message directly to teachers that they are capable of improvement.
• Specific goals provide a basis for rational decision making, for ways to organize and execute their instruction.
• Specific goals enable teachers to gauge their success.
• Specific goals promote professional dialogue (as cited in Schmoker 1996, 23).

Glickman differentiates "innovations," which he criticizes, and objectives, which he advocates. The major difference between the two is that innovations like technology, cooperative learning, whole-language instruction, or interdisciplinary instruction can be considered successful by faculty members by the very fact that they are implemented. The results, however, should not be measured by the successful implementation of an innovation but by whether students learned. Glickman believes that the "litmus test for a good school is not its innovations but rather the solid, purposeful, enduring results it tries to obtain for its students" (as cited in Schmoker 1996, 25). When a faculty states that its goal is to integrate technology into their instruction, the emphasis is on what the teachers will *do* rather than what the students will *learn.* Implementing problem-based learning, authentic assessment, and brain-based learning may be considered innovative instruction, but what is the outcome of the implementation? What did the students learn? How did the new teaching strategies increase student achievement?

It is important, therefore, that educators look closely at their research questions and make sure the essential question and the related questions ask how the students will benefit. Even if the question relates to mentoring teachers or a structure such as block scheduling, educators must not ask how the school or the teachers will benefit, but instead how the students will gain from switching from traditional 50-minute periods to 70- to 90-minute blocks of time (see figure 4).

Goals Related to Professional Portfolios

Would mentoring beginning teachers have a positive impact on both teachers and students?

As a result of master teachers mentoring beginning teachers, the teachers being mentored will

- Develop more effective teaching strategies
- Implement more successful classroom management techniques
- Develop more collegial attitudes toward their colleagues
- Become more reflective about their teaching practices

As a result of the teachers being mentored, the students they teach will

- Increase their academic achievement
- Develop more cooperative social skills
- Spend more time on task with their learning
- Become more reflective about their learning

Would block scheduling change the way students learn?

As a result of moving to longer blocks of learning, students will learn to

- Work cooperatively to create long-term projects
- Construct a more in-depth understanding
- Reflect metacognitively on their learning
- Produce quality performances that meet the standards

Figure 4

. . . the last ten years should have taught us that establishing vague process or procedural goals in the absence of clear, concrete learning goals is foolish. Each undergirds the other. Learning goals give meaning to and act as a healthy check on the traditionally untethered tendency for public institutions to be satisfied with processes, regardless of outcome (Schmoker 1996, 27).

The next logical step in the professional growth process is to establish the specific learner goals that the person developing the plan hopes to achieve. The steps in developing learner-centered goals could be organized in many ways. The example in figure 5 shows how one team of teachers progressed from selecting a topic to formulating an essential question they wanted to investigate. The team

---

Goal Development Process

Name: _Patsy Saunders, Jim Smith, Frank Baker_   Date: _8/97_

Topic: _Classroom Management_

Essential Question:

Would students' behavior problems decrease if each teacher taught social skills explicitly during the year?

Related Questions:

1. *How much time should be spent teaching social skills?*
2. *What specific strategies should be used to teach the skills?*
3. *Should students' social skills be assessed?*
4. *How will we know our interventions worked?*
5. *Will social skills transfer outside the classrooms?*

Professional Goals:

To research information on classroom management and to talk to teachers who have mastered classroom management.

Goals:

As a result of teaching social skills explicitly, the students will
1. *Exhibit more on-task behavior*
2. *Demonstrate more positive behavior toward their peers*
3. *Decrease the number of "put-downs" (insults, sarcasm, jokes) to others*
4. *Accept their role assignments and contribute to the group efforts*
5. *Attend class more regularly because of their commitment to the group*
6. *Exhibit more positive social behaviors outside of class (lunchroom, recess, sporting events)*

Figure 5

brainstormed related questions that could also be addressed and then developed specific learner-centered goals to drive their research and provide the framework for their professional development plan.

PREPARE A PROFESSIONAL GROWTH PLAN

After educators have developed their learner goals, they often begin a professional growth plan that helps them focus on what they need to do to meet their goals. These plans vary from school to school and district to district but could include the items shown in figure 6.

The purpose of preparing a professional growth plan is to develop a framework that guides the process. It also provides the basis for dialogues between teachers and supervisors or teacher teams to see how well they are on target to meet their goals.

PROFESSIONAL DEVELOPMENT TIMELINES

Allowing educators to direct their own professional development allows for flexibility in scheduling and timelines. Most people prefer to set their own timelines depending upon their purpose and their individual goals. The timeline in figure 7 explains the essential steps and provides some suggested dates.

The professional growth process can be initiated anytime throughout the year; however, most districts have found that starting in late spring or early fall works best. If the process begins in the spring, teams could select their topics or goals and then have the

---

Professional Growth Plan Options

- ☐ Name
- ☐ Proposed Timeframe
- ☐ Topic of Interest or Concern
- ☐ Essential Question
- ☐ Related Questions
- ☐ Professional Goals
- ☐ Learner-Centered Goals
- ☐ Action Plan (Activities, Interventions, Timelines)
- ☐ Resources (Books, Videos, People)

- ☐ Team Members Involved
- ☐ Observations Planned
- ☐ Baseline Data (Diagnostic Information)
- ☐ Documentation for Portfolio
- ☐ Ways to Assess Effectiveness
- ☐ Checkpoints
- ☐ Conference Options
- ☐ Evaluation Options (Formal Performance Review)
- ☐ Goal Setting for Next Year

Figure 6

Timeline for Professional Development

PHASE ONE: **GOAL SETTING** *May–June*	• Select an area of concern • Pose an essential question • Develop related questions • Articulate professional goals • Establish specific learner-centered goals • Prepare professional growth plan
PHASE TWO: **RESEARCH** *June–August*	• Review the research • Review available resources • Attend workshops, courses, conferences related to goals
PHASE THREE: **DATA COLLECTION** *Sept.–March*	• Collect data (student work, surveys) • Meet with peers to discuss progress • Observe and be observed • Monitor progress toward goals
PHASE FOUR: **REFLECTION** *April*	• Select items for final portfolio • Write reflections on key artifacts • Organize final portfolio
PHASE FIVE: **CELEBRATION** *May*	• Reflect on process toward meeting goals • Engage in conference with peers • Exhibit at end-of-the-year celebration

Figure 7

summer to begin their professional reading and determine what courses or seminars to attend. Many groups meet once or twice during the summer to discuss their research or to "jigsaw" the readings or videos by asking each person to view one video or read one article and share their findings with the group. Since teachers often attend conferences or workshops or take graduate credit during the summer, they can select professional growth opportunities that relate to the topic they have selected.

Many educators feel more comfortable completing their preliminary research prior to the start of the school year. They have time during the summer to think about the type of baseline data they want to collect to measure where the students are at the beginning of the year. Another time to start the process is in the fall. The advantage of starting in the fall is that new teachers arrive and it's a logical time to form new teams and to determine what concerns or problems are important. Since each year's students are different, the problems may not emerge until several weeks into the new school year. The timeline would be adjusted according to when the research was initiated.

Many teams find they need more than one year to reach their goals; therefore, the professional development plan could be amended periodically to reflect progress toward meeting their goals.

Example

Figure 8 shows how a high school English teacher working with two colleagues developed her research questions, goals, and preliminary professional growth plan.

REVIEW OF THE PROCESS

Thus far in the professional growth process, educators have completed the following:

- Selected a focused goal related to their students.
- Posed an essential question related to that goal.
- Developed questions related to the goal.
- Articulated professional goals for themselves.
- Established three to five specific learner-centered goals.
- Prepared a professional growth plan to guide their investigation of the problem.

These six steps could be completed in an intensive one-day session or spread out in a series of three or four shorter sessions. In both cases, they are just the beginning of the journey. The rest of the journey includes regular meetings with peer groups to discuss research findings, conversations with peers to monitor progress, and most importantly, reflections on one's learnings.

Developing Research Questions

Name: *Kathy Brown*   Date: *August*

Topic: *Performance Rubrics*

Essential Question:
Can students develop rubrics to evaluate their work?

Related Questions:

1. *Will rubrics promote consistency in grading?*

2. *Will students generate criteria to evaluate their work?*

3. *How does traditional grading compare to rubrics?*

4. *Will students' work improve?*

5. *Will students evaluate their own work?*

Developing Goals

Name: *Kathy Brown*   Date: *August*

Essential Question:
Can students develop rubrics to evaluate their work?

Professional Goals

1. *Review research on performance assessment*
2. *Attend workshops and conferences*
3. *Visit teachers and schools using rubrics*

Learner-Centered Goals

As a result of introducing performance rubrics, students will:
1. *Determine criteria for all work*
2. *Create indicators of quality work*
3. *Develop rubrics to evaluate their work*

Professional Growth Plan
(Part One)

Name: *Kathy Brown*   Date: *August*

Topic selected: *Performance Rubrics*

Baseline Data:
Before using rubrics, I will ask students to evaluate one paper they wrote and one speech they gave (on video). I will collect the grades they give themselves and the grades I give them.

Action Plan (Intervention):
I will teach students how to create assessment criteria and indicators. We will create scoring rubrics for assessing their written and oral work.

Timeline:
September–April

Professional Growth Plan
(Part Two)

Name: *Kathy Brown*   Date: *September*

Topic selected: *Performance Rubrics*

Documentation of Study:
I plan to collect:

1. *Copies of students' self-evaluations done without rubrics*
2. *Grades students gave themselves on work and grades I gave them*
3. *Copies of rubrics we developed*
4. *Copies of students' self-evaluations using rubrics*

Methods of Evaluation:

1. *Compare students' grades and my grades prior to using rubrics (pre-test)*
2. *Compare students' grades and my grades after using rubrics (post-test)*

Observations:

1. *Peer observations by fellow English teachers*
2. *Informal observation by principal*

Figure 8

Other steps in the process could include

- Reviewing available resources (videos, books, people)
- Collecting diagnostic or baseline data on the students to find out where they are before implementing new instructional strategies
- Collaborative sharing and peer coaching among team members
- Documenting journey through a professional growth plan and portfolio
- Sharing reflections with colleagues
- Using rubrics for self-evaluation and assessment of goal attainment
- Conferencing with colleagues and supervisors about portfolios
- Celebrating successes by creating schoolwide exhibitions
- Sharing results and learnings with colleagues and students

A COMMUNITY OF LEARNERS

Darling-Hammond talks about the new reform that suggests greater regulation of teachers, "ensuring their competence through more rigorous preparation, certification, and selection—in exchange for the deregulation of teaching—fewer rules prescribing what is to be taught, when, and how" (1988, 59). She says, in essence, that all professionals make a bargain with society: "The profession guarantees the competence of members in exchange for the privilege of professional control over work structure and standards of practice" (1988, 59). Society has to trust teachers to make the right decisions before it gives up regulating education through legislative mandates.

Teachers can earn their professionalism by demonstrating their competence in professional growth plans, professional portfolios, study groups, journaling, mentoring, video analysis of their teaching, and exhibitions of their work. Regardless of what methods educators select for professional growth, portfolios can be used as the framework to help document their progress toward achieving their goals and growing as a professional. As Wolf states, "Portfolios can give teachers a purpose and framework for preserving and sharing their work, provide occasions for mentoring and collegial interactions, and stimulate teachers to reflect on their own work and on the act of teaching" (1991, 136).

Change is never easy. Educators need to believe that despite all the extra work involved, they will grow as professionals as a result of this process. They need to believe that the public will treat them as professionals and allow them to make instructional decisions that affect children. They need to believe that their students will benefit from this experience. They need to believe that professional development is a lifelong process and that they play the most critical role in all of public education. As Sykes states, "Teacher learning must be the heart of any effort to improve education in our society" (1996, 465).

REFERENCES

Bernhardt, V. L. (1994). *The school portfolio: A comprehensive framework for school improvement.* Princeton Junction, NJ: Eye on Education.

Brandt, R. (1996). On a new direction for teacher evaluation: A conversation with Tom McGreal. *Educational Leadership* 53, 6: 30–33.

Csikszentmihalyi, M. (1990). *Flow: The psychology of optimal experience.* New York: Harper Perennial.

Darling-Hammond, L. (1988). Policy and professionalism. In A. Lieberman (Ed.), *Building a professional culture in schools* (pp. 55–77). New York: Teachers College Press, Columbia University.

Dietz, M. E. (1993). Professional development portfolio: A site-based framework for professional development. San Ramon, CA: FRAMEWORKS.

Ellis, A. K., and J. T. Fouts. (1994). *Research on school restructuring.* Princeton Junction, NJ: Eye on Education.

Fullan, M. G. (with S. Stiegelbauer). (1991). *The new meaning of educational change.* New York: Teachers College Press, Columbia University.

Glatthorn, A. (1996). *The teacher's portfolio: Fostering and documenting professional development.* Rockport, MA: Proactive Publications.

McLaughlin, M. W., and S. M. Yee. (1988). School as a place to have a career. In A. Lieberman (Ed.), *Building a professional culture in schools* (pp. 23–44). New York: Teachers College Press, Columbia University.

Schmoker, M. (1996). *Results: The key to continuous school improvement.* Alexandria, VA: Association for Supervision and Curriculum Development.

Sparks, D., and S. Hirsh. (1997). *A new vision for staff development.* Oxford, OH: National Staff Development Council; and Alexandria, VA: Association for Supervision and Curriculum Development.

Sykes, G. (1996). Reform *of* and *as* professional development. *Phi Delta Kappan* 77, 7: 465–467.

Wolf, K. (1991). The schoolteacher's portfolio: Issues in design, implementation, and evaluation. *Phi Delta Kappan* 73, 2: 129–136.

Conditions That Support Transfer for Change

by Valerie Hastings Moye

T
HE MISSING LINK

The artist transfers color and form to canvas and creates an image that reflects what has been learned vicariously and through formal schooling. The builder transfers materials and learned skills to create a building that originally was envisioned through the architect's blueprint. The information highway was built upon a foundation of transferred electronic wizardry that conveys knowledge to all parts of our world. Even the story that the dancer portrays through movement is a product of transfer. We have come to expect transfer, "the carry over or generalization of learned response from one situation to another" (*Merriam-Webster's Collegiate Dictionary* 1980, 1231), as an essential process for changing and improving our world.

The construct of transfer has the greatest implications for educational leaders when related to educational reform initiatives. After all, the call for change in education has been widespread. In the past dozen years, Americans have "investigated and bemoaned the quality, the structure, and the purposes of their schools" (McLaughlin and Shepard with O'Day 1995, xi). Americans have united in the conviction that schools must improve what is taught, how it is taught, and the degree to which students learn what is taught. Fullan and Stiegelbauer linked reform initiatives to desired improvements by stating that the purpose of educational reform is "to help schools accomplish their goals more effectively by replacing some structures, programs, and/or practices with better ones" (1991, 15).

Adapted from *Conditions That Support Transfer for Change* by Valerie H. Moye. © 1997 by IRI/SkyLight Training and Publishing, Inc.

Despite sincere and well-intended efforts, educational reform has remained mostly an elusive goal. Since the turn of the century, numerous educational reforms have responded to widespread calls for change. But, as Cuban asked, "How can it be that so much school reform has taken place over the last century and yet so little has changed?" (1988, 341). Several studies of school reform efforts searched for possible answers to this question and revealed what has gone wrong with most school reform efforts. Huberman and Miles (1984) examined twelve case studies of large-scale school innovations and found that success was directly related to the amount and quality of assistance that was provided to those implementing the reform. The Rand Change Agent Study extensively examined projects that received federal funding and found that in many instances funding did not make a difference. However, this study found that successful projects were those that provided effective staff development that included "ongoing assistance, structures that promoted collegiality, concrete training and follow-through, and principal support and encouragement" (McLaughlin 1991, 79). Fullan (1990) agreed that successful reform is dependent on staff development. By considering transfer as the desired outcome of staff development, one can see how the question of transfer becomes an overarching theme that links professional growth to school reform.

> **Leaders who are serious about educational reforms must take into account the nature of teachers as adult learners.**

Staff development, "those processes that improve the job-related knowledge, skills, or attitudes of school employees" (Sparks and Loucks-Horsley 1990, 5), is crucial to increasing student achievement. Time has been devoted to staff development efforts; yet, sufficient evidence of transfer has eluded those who expect that staff development will lead to necessary changes in education. A recent survey of principals from eight school divisions in Virginia documented the premise that most staff development efforts do not transfer to classroom practices (Moye 1996). Slightly more than 85 percent of the surveyed principals reported that staff development effectively altered classroom practices only 50 percent or less of the time. This is not a good return on the investment of time that goes toward staff development initiatives. If staff development is critical to reforms that focus on increased student achievement, then clearly the issue of transfer is worthy of close scrutiny.

THE CHALLENGE

Major reform initiatives in America are concerned with improving the quality of education available to students throughout the United States. The proposed building blocks for improvement are high standards for student learning, high standards for teaching, high-quality teacher preparation and professional development, aggressive recruitment of able teachers, rewards for teacher knowledge and skill, and schools organized for student and teacher learning (National Commission on Teaching and America's Future 1996). Reform efforts that seek increased student achievement reflect the premise that the quality of student learning is directly related to the quality of teaching. The National Commission on Teaching and America's Future captured the crucial nature of this premise by stating, "Teaching quality will make the critical difference not only to the futures of individual children but to America's future as well" (1996, 6).

However, it is not enough to target staff development as a top priority for reform efforts. Leaders who are serious about educational reforms must take into account the nature of teachers as adult learners. All too often staff development does not lead to its ultimate goal—transfer or change in teachers' classroom practices. If leaders truly believe that all individuals can learn, they also must believe that it is possible to increase the likelihood that training will transfer to classroom practice. The challenge for leaders is to determine the conditions that scaffold the transfer of training to classroom practice and adopt practices that foster and support those conditions.

A CONCEPTUALIZATION OF FIVE CONDITIONS THAT FOSTER AND SUPPORT TRANSFER

What are the conditions that foster and support transfer? Research supports the premise that five conditions foster and support the transfer of training to classroom practice: (1) training content that is linked to student achievement, (2) the teacher's sense of efficacy, (3) a strong, positive school culture, (4) elements of effective training, and (5) coaching or follow-up. When these conditions are present, they form an interactive whole that constitutes effective staff development (see Figure 1).

The conceptualization of conditions that promote transfer begins with a focal point of training content that is linked to student achievement. This condition provides the unifying connection among the other four conditions. The centrality of this condition

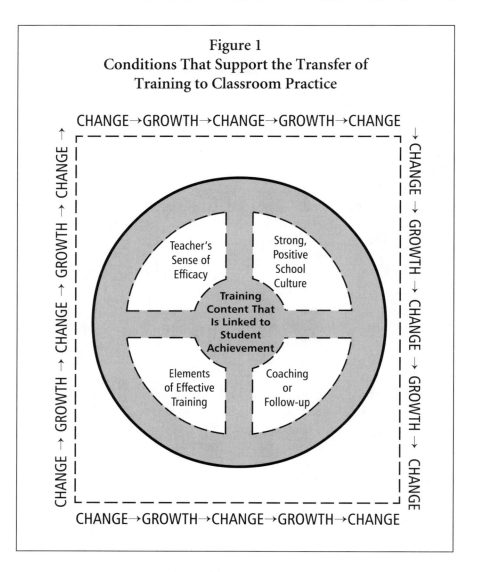

Figure 1
Conditions That Support the Transfer of
Training to Classroom Practice

communicates that staff development must be based on substantive content if it is to positively impact the teaching and learning process. Its primacy also indicates that the effects of teacher efficacy, a strong, positive school culture, training elements, and coaching will be realized only to the extent that the content of staff development is linked to student achievement. Training content that is linked to student achievement interacts with the other four conditions to (1) increase the success rate of teachers in improving student achievement and encourage a strong sense of teacher efficacy, (2) focus collaborative school efforts on increasing student achievement and shaping a strong school culture, (3) incorporate effective training design, and (4) provide coaching techniques that build collaborative relationships and render support to improvement efforts. A dynamic relationship exists among the five conditions. They are both interrelated and integrated. Leaders should consider the synergistic relationship among these five conditions in encouraging the transfer of training to classroom practice.

> **Leaders must nurture an environment in which teachers have opportunities to experience efficacy.**

IMPLICATIONS FOR SCHOOL LEADERS

School leaders have the power to promote learning communities in which student and staff growth are intertwined explicitly. Administrators can nurture teacher growth by relentlessly insisting on practices that support teachers' efforts to increase their repertoire of instructional skills and practices. In this endeavor, leaders can take concrete steps to promote the five conditions that support the transfer of staff development to student achievement.

First, school leaders can focus on training content that is known to increase student achievement. Thus, staff development initiatives need to reflect a careful analysis of student needs, concentrate on developing *research-based* skills and knowledge, and communicate to teachers *how* these skills and knowledge will increase student achievement. Moreover, strategies need to be taught in the context of content knowledge. The extent to which staff development content is linked to improved student achievement determines whether transfer takes place.

Second, leaders must nurture an environment in which teachers have opportunities to experience efficacy. One way this can be accomplished is by communicating an explicit link between staff development content and increased student achievement. Also, leaders should articulate a clear plan as to how support and follow-up will be provided during implementation of a new practice. The administrative support that leaders provide when teachers learn new skills can make a crucial difference in whether a teacher believes he or she is capable of learning and using a new strategy effectively. A teacher's belief in the ability to change is vital to his or her desire to persevere. Administrators also need to provide specific, consistent, and regular feedback concerning the impact of staff development on students and staff members. Such feedback reveals teachers' responsibilities in student learning and discloses the fruits of teachers' efforts. Administrative practices such as these highlight that training makes a difference in teacher *and* student learning. When teachers see that what *they* are doing makes a difference in student achievement, *they* experience a sense of efficacy that impacts future efforts.

A third way that leaders can encourage transfer is by establishing practices that foster the twelve cultural norms identified by Saphier and King (1985). Particular attention should be given to establishing administrative practices that promote these norms: (1) collegiality, (2) experimentation, (3) tangible support, (4) reaching out to the knowledge bases about teaching, and (5) honest, open communication. These five cultural norms are crucial for effective staff development and provide the framework upon which a strong, positive school culture can be built—the third condition that promotes transfer.

School leaders can sustain the fourth and fifth conditions by ensuring that the elements of effective training and coaching are implemented for all training endeavors and by providing the resources to support staffs' efforts. Personnel, material, and scheduling resources need to be considered. Also, school leaders need to ensure that specific goals are articulated and select coaching models that reflect the articulated goals.

Perhaps the most significant way that administrators can provide a discernible glimpse of the power these five conditions have in fostering transfer is by *demonstrating* a commitment to learning. Leaders must be willing to reveal their own desire to grow professionally *and* the explicit steps they are taking in that growth process. Leaders must *model* a willingness to try, evaluate, modify, and try again—the same behaviors required of teachers for transfer of training to classroom practice. As Dewey wrote, "The self is not ready-made but something in continuous formation through choice of action" (1916, 408). The extent to which all educators commit themselves to this ideal and the extent to which the five described conditions are manifested in our educational settings will determine the degree to which transfer among *all* learners will be realized.

BIBLIOGRAPHY

Cuban, Larry. "A Fundamental Puzzle of School Reform." *Phi Delta Kappan* 69 (1988): 341–344.

Dewey, John. *Democracy and Education.* New York: Macmillan, 1916.

Fullan, Michael G. "Staff Development, Innovation, and Instructional Development." In *Changing School Culture Through Staff Development,* edited by Bruce Joyce. Alexandria, VA: Association for Supervision and Curriculum Development, 1990.

Fullan, Michael G., and Suzanne Stiegelbauer. *The New Meaning of Educational Change.* New York: Teachers College Press, 1991.

Huberman, A. Michael, and Matthew B. Miles. *Innovation up Close.* New York: Plenum, 1984.

McLaughlin, M. W. "Enabling Professional Development: What Have We Learned?" In *Staff Development for Education in the '90s,* edited by Ann Lieberman and Lynne Miller. New York: Teachers College Press, 1991.

McLaughlin, M. W., and Lorrie A. Shepard, with Jennifer O'Day. *Improving Education Through Standards-Based Reform.* Stanford, CA: Stanford University, The National Academy of Education,1995.

Merriam-Webster's Collegiate Dictionary. Springfield, MA: G. and C. Merriam Company, 1980.

Moye, Valerie H. *Influencing Change Through Staff Development.* Manuscript submitted for publication, Williamsburg, VA: The College of William and Mary at Williamsburg, 1996.

National Commission on Teaching and America's Future. *What Matters Most: Teaching for America's Future.* New York: National Commission on Teaching and America's Future, 1996.

Saphier, Jon, and Matthew King. "Good Schools Grow in Strong Cultures." *Educational Leadership* 38 (1985): 66–77.

Sparks, Dennis, and Susan Loucks-Horsley. *Five Models of Staff Development for Teachers.* Oxford, OH: National Staff Development Council, 1990.

Section 3

Instruction for Intelligence

The general desire to teach for intelligence implies several corollaries worthy of consideration in order to turn the wish into reality. Spillane maintains that a staff that values intellect is a primary requisite for a school to embark on such instruction. A broad base of factual knowledge, embedded in a rich curriculum, is another primary ingredient, but *how* that program is presented and dealt with may be even more significant than content by itself. A teaching staff must provide opportunities for students *to use* the information that matters; and *how it is used,* say many writers, and the behavior or experience it leads to are the essential considerations of pedagogy in a thoughtful school.

The third section of this volume focuses on several major considerations about pedagogical implementation that have emerged over the past two or three decades, as researchers and practitioners have attempted to refine the appropriate teaching methods to deliver intelligent learning experience. There is no singular approach, it seems, that can guarantee intellectual success. There are some powerful tools that have been developed to serve the complex demands of a thoughtful pedagogy. They are described and research about them reviewed in several of the key writings in this section.

Fogarty underlines the role that knowledge about the teaching-learning process and the development of human intellectual potential has played in understanding the dynamics of a learning classroom. She cites many of the leading learning theorists of this century: Piaget, Vygotsky, Feuerstein, Gardner, Sternberg, Perkins, and a number of the contributors to this volume. She develops a list of key criteria for classroom success, from safe classroom climate to a balanced approach to varied assessments. Further, she suggests and describes many of the kinds of strategic applications by which it is possible to realize these key criteria. Bellanca focuses his discussion on teaching practices that have actually been proven effective; he asks educators to make a conscious choice of what teaching for intelligence actually *requires,* and he proposes that extraordinary steps must be taken not only to use traditional content but to create new content. Teaching for intelligence demands not only respect for the learner's ability to acquire information but stresses the need for both teachers and students to be competent in *generating knowledge.* Access to experiences to develop such a skill is the *sine qua non* of teaching for intelligence. The readings in this section show there is not a singular route to such an objective.

Rosenshine provides an excellent synopsis of the most recent research on cognitive processing, the means by which learners develop a well-connected body of accessible knowledge. His approach is primarily strategic, focused on the development of knowledge structures that are organized through carefully crafted relationships and gradually built-up patterns. The structural approach to pedagogy relies on a student's background knowledge being enriched and the frequent review, practice, and testing of developing concepts through an explicit learning process. The teacher's primary role is manager of that process, directly instructing the development of the algorithms and specific learning mechanisms required by the academic content. The master strategic instructor, according to Rosenshine, guides the learner in the process while, at the same time, he or she minimizes the occurrence of knowledge misconception. Rosenshine's explication of exemplary cognitive strategies is a catalogue of powerful, explicit tools that can serve every learner's developing intellectual competence.

Costa presents an alternative to the strictly strategic approach to becoming "intelligent." For him, teaching is concerned with building classroom experiences that *mediate* a child's continuous learning.

Teaching for intelligence is best accomplished by an indirect, facilitating pedagogy akin to Feuerstein's theory of cognitive modifiability and mediated learning experience. According to Costa, building such a dynamic, mediative classroom serves the teacher as well as students most productively. In intervening between the student or a group of students and the learning environment, the teacher struggles with determining the conditions that will engage and promote intellectual growth. In this interaction, the teacher defines, in extensive detail, the learning organization itself. Costa sees leadership of such a collaborative community as a kind of "environmental protection agency." He goes on to articulate what he calls the most important leverage points that must be accomplished by the instructor to make the intervention successful. These include clarification of goals and outcomes, establishment of trust, coaching, investing in various forms of leadership, valuing diversity, developing higher process-based curriculum, and focusing on continuous learning. A home for the mind, says Costa, resides in such a classroom environment—one that frees intellect, develops creative heuristics, and uses pedagogy as an enlivening art.

Interestingly, Strickland approaches classroom instruction in elementary school reading from both strategic and mediative considerations. The problem she attends to is how to differentiate instruction for the variations of student ability that every teacher confronts. The issue of *accessibility* is her key concern. Strickland warns that the most articulated algorithms for learners will not be operable if underlying student capabilities are not developed, and merely "covering the skills," like Sizer's concern for content coverage, is not a sufficient condition for "tapping into the intelligence of every learner." She begins by asking the common instructional questions: how to organize for instruction, what contents to teach and how, how to monitor progress, and how to reach low-achieving students. She replies with discussion about flexible groupings and how to plan for them productively; using national, and especially local, standards and benchmarks to determine classroom content and to plan activities in an integrated way; varying assessments to check student progress in alternative forms of reading performance; and, finally, attending to lesser able readers with many initiatives carried on within the mainstream classroom. Strickland blends solid and traditional techniques in a pedagogy that can grow to be innovative, always keeping in focus the issue of intellectual accessibility. Groups need to be flexible to relate to student needs in time; the independence of the reader must always be considered and maintained; appropriate challenge needs to be planned for in particular tasks; and consistent monitoring ought to provide data-based decision making for the teacher. Above all, she proposes that a teacher ought to initiate new learning gradually and carefully model the desired behaviors for key, clear communication. Strickland's teacher is not the fount of all wisdom, but he or she is a master at assessing a student's operable ability and providing for each learner's potential intellectual growth.

This section is concluded with two discussions about how the new pedagogy for intelligence development can become central to current reform in American education. Cooper and Levine are relatively optimistic, yet delineate issues that need to be carefully worked on if successful implementation is to be achieved. They remind practitioners of the need to make sure the basic intelligence paradigm is understood; then, leaders in this approach need to see that teaching for intelligence principles are adapted to the realities of classrooms, for teachers and for students. Further, Cooper and Levine say it is important to predict and overcome necessary obstacles, many of which are identifiable from existing research. Finally, they call for expanding the knowledge base of actual teaching thinking research. In that same vein, Levine and Levine present what they believe are key criteria for productive classroom intervention, and they indicate there are some promising models that have emerged from ongoing research conducted over the last two decades. These models need to be examined for what they can reveal about what successful implementation and practice require, and their results need to be shared.

Teaching for intelligence is not merely a hoped-for activity in the greater arena of cognitive instruction. This section presents *several* well-thought out approaches to such pedagogy with rich examples of what each methodology emphasizes. Actual practice suggests these approaches can be interrelated and that research on promising, current models needs to be pursued. Then, hopefully, the momentum for instructing for intelligence can continue to grow and influence actual school implementations.

Teaching for Intelligence: The Intellectual Life of Schools

by Robert R. Spillane

Teaching for intelligence" sounds like a wonderful thing. Who could be against it? But, as with any great-sounding concept, we need to be careful to define what we mean by it. Intelligence is the ability to understand and manipulate facts and ideas using language and mathematics. The existence of "general intelligence" is one of the most solidly established findings in psychology, as is the belief that intelligence can be assessed (although there is some dispute over the types of "IQ" tests that best measure it). But, contrary to common belief, general intelligence is not fixed, either in individuals or in groups. Worldwide average IQ, for instance, has been rising for several years. Also, there is substantial evidence that educational quality affects IQ levels.

The important question is how one improves the quality of education in a way that increases intelligence. In other words, once we have defined what it *is,* how do we teach for intelligence? There are no "new, improved" ways of doing this. Just as we do not yet have an intelligence pill, we also do not have a newly developed intelligence teaching method. Instead, we need to go back to some of the things that we have known for a long time.

One important element in a school that teaches for intelligence is a staff that values intellect. This means a staff that conveys to students the view that having information and being able to use it to make sense of new information is valuable and that academic disciplines like math, history, science, and language study are powerful tools for making sense of the world. Staff members who themselves value the life of the mind are invaluable for teaching for intelligence. They must, of course, also be able to convey this value to children, but teachers who are "great with children" but lack intellectual values are unlikely to do a great job teaching for intelligence.

A curriculum that teaches for intelligence must include a great deal of factual knowledge, beginning in the earliest years. This is especially true for students who do not receive background knowledge at home. A broad base of factual knowledge is critical to making sense of new information. If a student does not already know something about a subject, he or she cannot investigate the subject. If a teacher asks a student to comment on or research a topic that the student knows little about, the student will have little idea what questions to ask or what explanations make sense; he or she will be intellectually tied to people who *do* know—in most cases, teachers. Intelligence means intellectual independence, and only someone who is well informed is capable of such independence.

> ... teachers who are "great with children" but lack intellectual values are unlikely to do a great job teaching for intelligence.

A curriculum that teaches for intelligence must include opportunities to master language and mathematics. This mastery must include drills that help a student to achieve "automaticity," the ability to do many things (such as arithmetic and algebraic computation, spelling, and creation of grammatical sentences) automatically—without conscious thought. Without this automaticity, students will be forever counting on their fingers, struggling with the simplest algebraic equation, looking up spellings, and writing and rewriting the simplest sentences. They will have little time and energy for the complicated mathematical and linguistic expression required for intelligence. Building automaticity is critical and involves some degree of drill and practice.

A curriculum that teaches for intelligence must provide many opportunities for students to use what they have learned in order to investigate, understand, discuss, and comment on significant matters. No student should be asked to investigate or discuss matters about which he or she knows little, or to use math or language beyond the level the student has mastered. However, opportunities for investigation, discussion, and comment should be built into the curriculum as soon as the student has learned enough information and sufficiently mastered language and math to make the exercise authentic. By the end of high school, every student should have achieved sufficient knowledge, mastery, and practice in discussion and expression to respond, *intelligently,* to (for instance) an article in the *New York Times* on any subject.

A curriculum that teaches for intelligence must prepare students for the inevitable "interdisciplinary" nature of most issues in life. It should do this by helping students develop a strong understanding of the major academic disciplines. The student should understand how, for instance, the natural sciences differ from social science and humanities disciplines and how literary study differs from history. Only with this kind of understanding will students be able to evaluate claims and evidence from several disciplines to make judgments about complex issues. In general, "interdisciplinary" instruction should probably come in the early grades (when students cannot be expected to understand what an academic discipline is) and the later grades (after they have achieved that understanding).

Perhaps most of all, teaching for intelligence should be based on respect for students' abilities to acquire information, master math and language, and eventually to understand and intelligently comment on complex issues. With this respect, educators can provide the kind of systematic and intellectually serious instruction students need to be intelligent in the real world.

The Intelligence-Friendly Classroom: It Just Makes Sense

by Robin Fogarty

If we know that intelligence is emotional . . .
Then it just makes sense to use visceral hooks.
If we know that intelligence is nurturable . . .
Then it just makes sense to create rich environments.
If we know that intelligence is constructed . . .
Then it just makes sense to provide tools for the mind.
If we know that intelligence is developmental . . .
Then it just makes sense to move from novice to expert.
If we know that intelligence is experiential . . .
Then it just makes sense to challenge through doing.
If we know that intelligence is multiple . . .
Then it just makes sense to target many dimensions.
If we know that intelligence is modifiable . . .
Then it just makes sense to mediate learning.
If we know that intelligence is elusive . . .
Then it just makes sense to vary the measures.

I f we know these things and believe what we know to be true, then the intelligence-friendly classroom should be a given. It is as simple and logical as an "if . . . then" syllogism.

DEFINING INTELLIGENCE-FRIENDLY CLASSROOMS

Let's look more closely at the term *intelligence-friendly classroom* and see just what it means. An intelligence-friendly classroom is a classroom in which the teaching/learning process is governed by what is known about developing the intellectual potential of human beings.

Literally, intelligence-friendly means friendly to intelligence, which can be translated into friendly to the growth patterns of human intellect and friendly to the learner in fostering intelligent behavior for problem solving, decision making, and creative thinking. Figuratively, the intelligence-friendly classroom serves as a caring companion and mindful guide to the intellect of each and every child in it. Just as a friend in the real world furnishes certain kinds of support that are reliable, time-tested, and tried and true, so intelligence-friendly classrooms provide similar systems of support that foster the ongoing development of human intelligence potential.

In brief, intelligence-friendly classrooms are classrooms that celebrate the joy of the learner's emotional and intellectual world, not through rhetoric and repetition, but through richness and relationships. In this article, I'll take a closer look at these intelligence-friendly classrooms and investigate their theoretical underpinnings briefly and their practical implications in more depth.

THEORETICAL UNDERPINNINGS

Guidelines for the intelligence-friendly classroom are grounded in the works of the leading voices in the field. First, I offer a cursory examination of the various theories of intelligence and then suggest what each of them implies for the intelligence-friendly classroom.

• *Traditional theory of general intelligence.* Intelligence is inherited and unchanging.

• *Piaget's theory of developmental psychology.* Intelligence is developmentally constructed in the mind by the learner and moves from concrete to abstract stages of understanding.

• *Vygotsky's theory of social mediation.* Intelligence is a function of activity mediated through material tools, psychological tools, and other human beings.

• *Feuerstein's theory of structural cognitive modifiability.* Intelligence is a function of experience and can be changed through guided mediation.

• *Gardner's theory of multiple intelligences.* Intelligence is made up of eight realms of knowing (verbal, visual, mathematical, musical, bodily, interpersonal, intrapersonal, naturalistic) for solving problems and creating products valued in a culture.

• *Sternberg's successful intelligence.* Intelligence is triarchic, with analytic, creative, and practical components that need to be balanced.

- *Perkins's theory of learnable intelligence.* Intelligence is made up of neural, experiential, and reflective components that help us know our way around the good use of our minds.
- *Costa's theory of intelligent behaviors.* Intelligence is composed of acquired habits or states of mind that are evidenced in such behaviors as persistence, flexibility, decreased impulsiveness, enjoyment of thinking, and reflectiveness.
- *Goleman's theory of emotional intelligence.* Intelligence is both cognitive and emotional, with the emotional (self-awareness, self-regulation, motivation, empathy, and social skill) ruling over the cognitive.
- *Coles's theory of moral intelligence.* Intelligence is composed of cognitive, psychological or emotional, and moral realms.

IMPLICATIONS FOR APPLICATION

The intelligence-friendly classroom is an intricate and complex microcosm of nuance and activity that propels the teaching/learning process. The following eight guidelines, derived from the various theories of intelligence, have compelling implications for today's classroom. I explain each guideline briefly and offer a sampling of useful strategies. While some readers may find the suggestions familiar and already part of their current teaching repertoire, others may discover new ideas or, perhaps, novel ways to revisit an old idea with a fresh approach. Whatever the case, the guidelines serve as a bridge between theory and practice in the intelligence-friendly classroom.

1. *Set a safe emotional climate.* The intelligence-friendly classroom is a safe and caring place for all learners, regardless of race, color, creed, age, aptitude, or ability, to go about the business of learning. In setting a climate for thinking, risk-taking becomes the norm and learners understand that to learn is to make mistakes as well as to experience successes.

Specific strategies to use include the following: establishing classroom rules, being aware of verbal and nonverbal teaching behaviors (e.g., wait time), organizing diverse small-group work that feels "safe," tapping into the emotional and moral intelligences, setting up the room to facilitate student-to-student interactions as well as student-to-teacher interactions, and incorporating learner-centered structures (e.g., multiage groupings) that foster intelligence-friendly learning communities.

2. *Create a rich learning environment.* An enriched environment requires attention to the physical aspects of the intelligence-friendly classroom. The ideal classroom resembles a children's museum, in which students are repeatedly and implicitly invited to interact with the learning environment. In such a stimulus-rich setting, explorations, investigations, and inquiries are irresistible.

This enriched environment presents science equipment, art supplies, tools and workbenches, toys and building blocks, optical illusion posters, and an electronic circus of computers, telephones, and fax machines. The intelligence-friendly classroom has different mini-environments for quiet reflection, noisy projects, learning centers, and one-on-one tutorials. The sensory input—ranging from print-rich materials, music, and recordings to visually appealing bulletin boards and to signs, games, puzzles, and lab setups—provides an intriguing and engaging place for teaching for intelligence.

3. *Teach the mind-tools and skills of life.* Teaching the skills of life involves both mind and body "tools" that range from communication and social skills to the microskills of thinking and reflecting, to the technological skills needed for the Information Age, to the skills needed for solving algebraic equations or programming computers, and even to the skills needed to learn a craft or to participate in athletics.

More specifically, these skills might include critical thinking skills (e.g., prioritizing, comparing, and judging), creative thinking skills (e.g., inferring, predicting, and generalizing), social skills (e.g., communicating, teambuilding, leading, and resolving conflicts), technological skills (e.g., keyboarding, surfing the Net, and taking virtual field trips), visual skills (e.g., painting, sculpting, and drawing), skills in the performing arts (e.g., dancing, acting, and playing a musical instrument), and skills of the elite athlete (e.g., diving, skiing, and swimming).

4. *Develop the skillfulness of the learner.* The developmental path of skill training moves through fairly predictable stages: novice, advanced beginner, competent user, proficient user, expert. Inherent in this developmental arc is the understanding that skillfulness is achieved through mediation, practice, coaching, and rehearsal.

Skill development often occurs through formal teaching/learning structures, such as direct instruction models, that demonstrate the skill for students. Skills also are developed through independent readings and research and through the dialogue, discussion, and articulation of peer coaching, mentoring, and internships. Skill development can even happen with experiences in which the skill is embedded in application and in poised moments for achieving peak performances.

5. *Challenge through the experience of doing.* Learning is a function of experience and is shaped by internal processes that actually construct ideas in the mind, as well as by external processes of social interaction. In the intelligence-friendly classroom, a constructivist philosophy of education reigns. Active, experiential learning is the norm as the learner is invited to become an integral part of the teaching/learning process.

Specific strategies that abound in the constructivist classroom include hands-on learning with lots of manipulatives and lablike situations; small-group, cooperative tasks; the frequent use and unique application of graphic organizers (e.g., concept maps, attribute webs, flowcharts, and Venn diagrams); and authentic experiential curriculum models (e.g., problem-based learning, case studies, project and service learning, performance tasks, and the use of relevant overarching themes).

6. *Target multiple dimensions of intelligence.* The multiple intelligences (MI) approach taps into the unique profile of intelligences of each learner. The educational community embraces MI theory because it provides a natural framework for inspired practice. MI approaches to curriculum, instruction, and assessment target a full spectrum of teaching/learning strategies that encompass the many ways of knowing and of expressing what we know. The MI classroom is abuzz with activity as all eight of the intelligences are given fair time in the curriculum for authentic, relevant opportunities for development.

This does not mean that every lesson shows evidence of all eight intelligences but rather that the learning is structured in naturally integrated ways that call upon various intelligences. For example, while creating a school newspaper, students interview (interpersonal), write (verbal), design and lay out (visual), and critique (logical) as natural parts of the process.

7. *Transfer learning through reflection.* The reflective use of learning is the cornerstone of the intelligence-friendly classroom. It drives personal application and transfer of learning. It makes learning personal, purposeful, meaningful, and relevant and gives the brain reason to pay attention, understand, and remember. Reflection is

sometimes the missing piece in today's classroom puzzle, as the pacing of the school day often precludes time for reflection. Yet reflection, introspection, and mindfulness must accompany collaborations and discussions because the time for reflection is the time for internalizing the learning.

Specific strategies that enhance reflection include the use of reading-response journals in which the reader writes a personal, immediate response to what has been read; learning logs that record the learner's thoughts, comments, and questions prior to or following a learning experience; lab reports; personal diaries; sketchbooks; writer's notebooks; portfolios; partner dialogues and conversations with a mentor; mediation interventions; and metacognitive strategies of planning, monitoring, and evaluating through self-regulation.

8. *Balance assessment measures.* Human nature demands feedback. Whether that feedback is internally motivated or externally given, all of us who are intent on learning anxiously await the critique, the judgment. In the intelligence-friendly classroom, this critical phase of the learning process is integral to all other interactions. The feedback, analysis, and evaluation are ongoing as well as summative.

Assessment occurs by the traditional means of grades and rankings for required classwork, homework assignments, quizzes, criterion-referenced tests, and standardized tests. In addition, to provide the proper balance to the assessment process, both portfolio assessments (e.g., project portfolios, best-work portfolios, electronic portfolios, and videotape analyses) and performance assessments (e.g., speeches, presentations, plays, concerts, athletic performances, and lab experiments) occur.

A FINAL NOTE

In closing, let's circle back for a moment and revisit the title of this article: "The Intelligence-Friendly Classroom: It Just Makes Sense." Think about how I've described the intelligence-friendly classroom and how it matches or fails to match any preconceived notions you might have had as you began to read. Intelligence-friendly? What does that mean? What does that look like? Sound like? Did you learn in an intelligence-friendly classroom? Do you teach in one? Would you know one if you saw one?

Of course you would. The intelligence-friendly classroom is no enigma. It makes perfect sense. It draws on the many powers of intelligence of both the teacher and the learner. It is the teaching/learning process in all its glorious colors. It is the science of good, sound pedagogy coupled with the art of uniquely creative minds.

The intelligence-friendly classroom is part of the noble vision of schooling that led many of us into the field. It is the reason that we do what we do. It is about children, and it's about helping those children be as smart as they can be in every way they can be. The intelligence-friendly classroom just makes sense.

Teaching for Intelligence: In Search of Best Practices

by James Bellanca

Here are two statements from one teacher in the science department of a large, college-directed suburban high school.

> When I teach biology, my job is to cover the content. To get all the material required in our curriculum covered, I use two strategies. In class, I lecture or show films to get the material across. In the lab, I work through the lab book with the students. The labs correspond with the text chapters. I use pop quizzes, chapter tests, lab book grades, and a semester final to decide a student's grade for the semester.

*　*　*

> When I teach biology, my job is to interest students in the value of this science. This is much more than giving them information to spit back out on a test or quiz. I have to help them understand how all the information fits together and why it is important. I also have to help them get as excited about biology as I am. In class, I use a variety of methods. First, I teach them how to gather the right information from a variety of sources. These can include some lectures, some films, targeted reading from the text, or online resource materials. I also structure all-class and cooperative-group discussions so that they can relate the specific topics to the "big picture." Finally, I use the lab to engage them in applying the new information. I use the lab book as a start for the students to investigate applications outside the classroom. I use pop quizzes and tests to check what they know about the material. But

I also observe and grade how they do lab work, defend their findings, execute outside-of-class projects, contribute to the discussions, and complete the final exam. Unless I actively engage their minds in doing biology, I believe that I have shortchanged their opportunity to understand and to enjoy the subject.

These two views, expressed at different times, reveal changes in beliefs and practices that distinguish this teacher from most of the other biology teachers in the school. This teacher's new practices, developed from a study of Howard Gardner's theory of multiple intelligences, provide concrete examples of "teaching for intelligence."

In this teacher's science department, biology is usually taught as a body of information transferred from the text and each teacher's understanding of the subject to the students' heads. At set times, each student is expected to show the teacher how much was absorbed. Test scores document the amount of information recalled on each chapter test. Each day, the teacher enters the room, takes attendance, provides the day's lecture, and answers questions. On some days, the teacher precedes the lecture with a quiz or shows a video to illustrate a key topic. The students are expected to read the chapters, take notes in class, ask questions, follow the lab instructions, complete the workbook pages, and study for the unit tests. If students need assistance they can schedule an appointment with the teacher. The department chairperson explains that these have been accepted practices that have worked well in preparing students for college over the last forty years.

The department chair's claims, supplemented with the school's record of high test scores (its American College Testing Program scores have led the state for the last decade), seem to make the school a strong candidate for the "If it ain't broke, don't fix it" award. However, appearances often belie reality. In the same school we can find students who don't have high grades, high test scores, or a high motivation to achieve. When high standardized scores are the focus, it is difficult to switch attention to the needs of such students. It is even more difficult to argue how an intelligence-rich model of teaching and learning, which differs from the traditional information-centered model, might benefit the high achievers as well.

The most successful attempts to teach for intelligence replicate the second approach described by the biology teacher. To change one's practices as this teacher did, one must start with some basic assumptions.

1. *The traditional method is not wrong.* There are many high-achieving students who thrive with the traditional approach to teaching. However, the traditional method is inadequate for many students who are less achievement driven. If all students are to learn the curriculum, then all need the opportunity to be taught in ways that enrich their learning. This means that the teacher, when faced with less-motivated students, needs to develop a greater repertoire of methods. Best teaching practices that build on new theories of intelligence—such as Howard Gardner's theory of multiple intelligences, Robert Sternberg's theory of successful intelligence, Daniel Goleman's theory of emotional intelligence, or Reuven Feuerstein's theory of structural cognitive modifiability—provide rich opportunities for teachers who desire to teach for intelligence.

2. *Teaching is a strategic act of engagement.* The new theories of intelligence consider the active engagement of students' minds to be a prerequisite to learning. It follows from this concept that teachers and students will benefit when the teacher plans how best to ensure that all students are engaged. Such planning is facilitated when a teacher has a repertoire of proven engagement strategies and the skill to design lessons and units that integrate these strategies with the content so that each student "gets it."

3. *Changing how a teacher teaches takes more than conveying theoretical information.* The typical continuing education of teachers looks very much like traditional instruction in junior high and high school classrooms. Only the age of the students and the content differ. Theoretical talk dominates. Teachers as students hear about learning theories and research results. In some cases, they are given a few descriptions of best practices. If the professor or consultant has any recent classroom experience, the teacher/learners may receive a few practical tips on the side.

4. *Learning to change one's teaching style is as difficult as learning to change one's learning style.* Some teachers start the change process from an abstract, theoretical point of view. They want to study the underlying beliefs, the theory, and the research supporting ideas new to their experience. This approach helps them construct their own framework or "big picture." When they are comfortable with their new beliefs, they begin to test the practical tools that fit. Other teachers must start with a hands-on classroom test of a new method. These teachers will practice the method with their students and evaluate its effects. If the method works well, they look for other

similar methods and investigate the theoretical underpinnings. Between these two poles, there are a multitude of individual approaches to initiating change in classroom practice. In all cases, it is essential that the instructor honors the basic learning style of each individual by ensuring that all components of the intelligence-rich change models are included.

For teachers to change from using the more traditional, information-centered model of instruction, which may have dominated their own learning at least since junior high, their experiences in learning how to teach for intelligence need to balance the what, the why, and the how of the new models. The "what" includes descriptions of best practices followed by live or video demonstrations that model how to use these best practices in grade-specific contexts. The "why" includes investigations of the supporting research. The "how" provides mediated role-playing sessions with ample time for problem solving, reflection on application opportunities, collaborative planning for use, a structured assignment to implement the plan, and a collegial assessment of the application results. In this way, the teacher as reflective practitioner can resolve concerns through a low-risk experience that uses what research says about the proper conditions for adult learning transfer.[1]

> **Even the teacher most excited about the possibilities of a newly acquired practice needs the right school environment to sustain it.**

It is important to note that even the most carefully practiced classroom implementations of approaches new to the teacher/learner are in danger of falling by the wayside. When faced with the contrary, day-to-day classroom pressures that do not take into account the environmental conditions for effective transfer, teachers can abandon the less familiar and risky new practice for the safety and security of their usual approach. Even the teacher most excited about the possibilities of a newly acquired practice needs the right school environment to sustain it. At this point, it is most helpful for the principal, professional developer, or site mentor to step forward and apply research findings on best practice in professional development.

For example, we know that when the teacher/learner has time each week to interact with a peer support team, to share and to plan classroom-specific applications, to reflect on concerns about and problems with those applications, to gather student artifacts and other evidence for assessment, and to make needed adjustments, the targeted changes have an 80 percent chance of becoming regular practice. Without the support team, the chances of successful, long-term implementation can fall below 20 percent.[2] When a school principal encourages the attempts at new approaches and when colleagues respect these endeavors, the chance of long-term implementation increases.[3]

With built-in assessment strategies such as action research, portfolios, implementation checklists, and exhibitions, the focus changes from teacher/learners as acquirers of information to teachers as reflective practitioners who investigate how best practices in theory work for them in the classroom.[4]

When the conditions for change are honored, it is possible for teachers to make dramatic changes in how they teach. As was evident from the statements of the biology teacher quoted at the outset of this article, the changes benefit students as well as the teacher. Case studies of successful changes abound at each grade level. The following example, created by a first-grade teacher and inspired by Gardner's definition of intelligence as the ability to solve a significant problem or to produce a product, illustrates productive changes in classroom practice based on the application of a newly understood theory.

SCIENCE CURRICULUM CONTENT: SIMPLE MACHINES

The simple-machines project was based on the theory of multiple intelligences and integrated required language arts, mathematics, science, and social studies objectives into a single unit.

Instead of resorting to the text-based approach used in previous years, in which students were shown pictures of a machine with appropriate vocabulary words to memorize, the teacher assigned pairs of students (interpersonal) to create an invented animal that made use of several simple machines (mathematical/logical). After seeing a working example of each machine (e.g., a Lego plane to launch miniature racing cars), the class saw an example, made by the teacher, of a dinosaur that moved (visual/spatial). She pointed out how each simple machine was included and shared a rubric that identified how she would grade each project.

Next, the teacher provided ample supplies and led a whole-class brainstorming session to come up with ideas for the invented animals (interpersonal). Each pair selected its own idea and began the construction process. As the pairs worked, the teacher circulated among them to answer questions and to mediate understandings.

When all the projects were completed, each pair made a formal presentation (verbal/linguistic) to the class. As part of the presentation, the pair was asked to explain why and how they used each of the simple machines, which simple machines were most important in the project, how each partner contributed, and how each felt about the finished product (intrapersonal). The animals were labeled and set out for viewing by the other students and by parents on report card night.

The teacher graded the projects on the multiple dimensions she had outlined in her rubric:

- We used [X number of] machines.
- We helped each other.
- We each talked in the presentation.
- Our animal moved.
- We told which machines were most important.
- Our animal looked like an animal.

This example illustrates how beliefs about learning affect teaching practices. The realization that there is more to teaching than a sharing of information and a testing for recall springs from our ever-expanding understanding that intelligence is modifiable, multiple, and multifaceted. As new research provides us with new insights into how human minds work, we are assured that teaching for intelligence is a never-ending challenge as well as an infinite opportunity to help all children become active, engaged, and successful learners. As schools take advantage of the best practices in professional development, the change process ensures more success for teachers who seek to expand their repertoires with the best practices in teaching for intelligence.

NOTES

1.   Valerie Moye, *Conditions That Support Transfer* (Arlington Heights, Ill.: SkyLight Training and Publishing, Inc., 1997).

2.   Bruce Joyce and Beverly Showers, *Power in Staff Development* (Arlington, Va.: Association for Supervision and Curriculum Development, 1985).

3.   James Bellanca, *Professional Development for Change* (Arlington Heights, Ill.: SkyLight Training and Publishing, Inc., 1996).

4.   Richard Schmuck, *Practical Action Research for Change* (Arlington Heights, Ill.: SkyLight Training and Publishing, Inc., 1997).

Advances in Research on Instruction

by Barak Rosenshine

his article discusses what I regard as some of the most important instructional advancements of the last 30 years. These advancements came from three bodies of research: (a) research on cognitive processing; (b) research on teacher effects, that is, studies of teachers whose classes made the highest achievement gain compared to other classes; and (c) intervention studies in which students were taught cognitive strategies they could apply to their learning. Although I would not advocate converting these ideas into another evaluation form, I suggest that the ideas represented by this research can and should be used to discuss and improve instruction.

FINDINGS FROM RESEARCH ON COGNITIVE PROCESSING: THE IMPORTANCE OF WELL-CONNECTED KNOWLEDGE STRUCTURES

A major area of research, one with important implications for teaching, has been the research on cognitive processing—research on how information is stored and retrieved. This research has shown us the importance of helping students develop a well-connected body of accessible knowledge.

It is currently thought that the information in our long-term memory is stored in interconnected networks called *knowledge structures*. The size of these structures, the number of connections between pieces of knowledge, the strength of the connections, and the organization and richness of the relationships are all important for processing information and solving problems.

From *Issues in educating students with disabilities*, edited by J. H. W. Lloyd, E. J. Kameenui, and D. Chard (chapter 10, pp. 197–221), 1995. Mahwah, N.J.: Lawrence Erlbaum Associates. © 1995 by Lawrence Erlbaum Associates. Reprinted with permission.

It is easier to assimilate new information, and easier to use prior knowledge for problem solving, when one has more connections and interconnections, stronger ties between the connections, and a better organized knowledge structure. When the knowledge structure on a particular topic is large and well connected, new information is more readily acquired and prior knowledge is more readily available for use. Having a well-connected network means that any one piece of information can serve to help retrieve the entire pattern. Having strong connections and a richness of relationships enables one to retrieve more pieces of the pattern. When information is "meaningful" to students, they have more points in their knowledge structures to which they can attach new information. Education is a process of developing, enlarging, expanding, and refining our students' knowledge structures.

> When information is "meaningful" to students, they have more points in their knowledge structures to which they can attach new information.

Helping students to organize information into well-connected patterns has another advantage. When a pattern is unified, it only occupies a few bits in the working memory. Thus, having larger and better connected patterns frees up space in our working memory. This available space can be used for reflecting on new information and for problem solving. For example, when U.S. history is organized into well-connected patterns, these patterns occupy less space in the working memory and the learner has additional space in the working memory to use to consider, assimilate, and manipulate new information. A major difference between an expert and a novice is that the expert's knowledge structure has a larger number of knowledge items, the expert has more connections between the items, the links between the connections are stronger, and the structure is better organized. A novice, on the other hand, is unable to see these patterns, and often ignores them. This development of well-connected patterns and the concomitant freeing of space in the working memory is one of the hallmarks of an expert in a field.

To summarize, well-connected and elaborate knowledge structures are important because (a) they allow for easier retrieval of old material, (b) they permit more information to be carried in a single chunk, and (c) they facilitate the understanding and integration of new information.

There are three important instructional implications that follow from this research: (a) the need to help students develop background knowledge, (b) the importance of student processing, and (c) the importance of organizers.

Help Students Develop Their Background Knowledge

What can be done to help students develop well-connected bodies of knowledge? One important instructional procedure is providing for extensive reading, review, practice, and discussion. These activities serve to help students *increase* the number of pieces of information that are the long-term memory, *organize* those pieces, and *increase* the strength and number of these interconnections. The more one rehearses and reviews information, the stronger these interconnections become. Thus, the research of cognitive processing supports the need for a teacher to assist students by providing for extensive reading of a variety of materials, frequent review, testing, and discussion and application activities.

Provide for Student Processing

New material is stored in the long-term memory when one processes it. The quality of storage can depend on the "level of processing." For example, if we were told to read a passage and count the number of times the word "the" appeared, the quality of storage would not be as strong as if we read the same passage and focused on its meaning. Similarly, the quality of storage would be stronger if one summarized or compared the material in the passage rather than simply reading it.

Processing of new material takes place through a variety of activities such as rehearsal, review, comparing and contrasting, and drawing connections. Thus, the research on cognitive processing supports the importance of a teacher initiating activities that require students to process and apply new information. Such processing strengthens the knowledge network that the student is developing. Asking students to organize information, summarize information, or compare new material with prior material are all activities that require processing and should help students develop and strengthen their cognitive structures. In addition, Brown and Campione (1986) wrote:

> Understanding is more likely to occur when a child is required to explain, elaborate, or defend his position to others; the burden of explanation is often the push needed to make him or her evaluate, integrate, and elaborate knowledge in new ways. (p. 1061)

Other examples of such processing activities include asking students to do any of the following:

> Read a variety of materials extensively.
> Explain the new material to someone else.
> Write questions/answer questions.
> Develop knowledge maps.
> Write daily summaries.
> Apply the ideas to a new situation.
> Give a new example.
> Compare and contrast the new material to other material.
> Study for an exam.

All these activities are useful in helping students develop, organize, strengthen, and expand their knowledge structures.

Help Students Organize Their Knowledge

As has been noted, new information is organized into knowledge structures. Without these structures, new knowledge tends to be fragmented and not readily available for recall and use. However, students frequently lack these knowledge structures when they are learning new material. Without direction, students might develop a fragmented, incomplete, or erroneous knowledge structure. Therefore, the research suggests that it is important for teachers to help students organize the new material.

One way to do this is to provide students with "graphic organizers," that is, organizing structures for expository material. An outline is an example of such an organizer, concept maps are another example. These structures help students organize the elements of the new learning and such organization can serve to facilitate retrieval. In addition, having such organizers can enable the student to devote more working memory to the content.

Another approach is to teach students how to develop their own graphic organizers for new material. This process is facilitated by providing students with a variety of graphic organizer structures that they can use to construct their own graphic organizers. When teaching students to develop a graphic organizer, it is useful for the teacher to model the process and also provides models of thinking and thinking aloud as she or he constructs the maps.

In summary, the research on cognitive processing identified the importance of developing well-connected knowledge structures. Such structures might be developed by encouraging extensive reading and practice, student processing of new information, and helping students organize their new knowledge.

RESEARCH ON TEACHER EFFECTS

A second important body of research is the teacher effects studies. The teacher effects research represents a line of studies in which attempts were made to identify those teacher behaviors that were related to student achievement gain. The focus was on observing and recording classroom instruction and identifying those instructional procedures associated with the most successful and the least successful teachers.

> Having such organizers can enable the student to devote more working memory to the content.

In this research, the investigators first identified a number of instructional procedures to study. About 20 to 30 procedures would be selected, and these included a teacher's use of praise, a teacher's use of criticism, the number and type of questions that were asked, the quality of student answers, and the responses of a teacher to a student's answers. Then achievement tests were given to the students in 20 to 30 classrooms. After the achievement tests, the investigators observed the classrooms and recorded the frequency with which the teachers used instructional behaviors such as those mentioned earlier. After 3 to 6 months, a second achievement test was given to the same 20 to 30 classrooms.

After all the data were collected, the investigators used correlational statistics to specify the "adjusted gain" for each classroom. That is, the raw gain for each class, from pretest to posttest, was adjusted for the entry level of each classroom. In the final step, the investigators looked to instructional behaviors they had recorded for each class and correlated those behaviors with the measure of each class' adjusted achievement gain. Through the use of these procedures, the investigators were able to identify which instructional behaviors were associated or correlated with student achievement gain.

In many cases, these correctional results were tested in subsequent experimental studies in which one group of teachers were trained and helped to use these behaviors in their teaching and another group of teachers was told to continue their regular teaching. All the teachers were observed, and classes of all teachers were given achievement tests before the experiment began and at the end of the experiment. In most cases, students in the classes of the teachers who received the training had higher posttest achievement scores than those of students of teachers in the control classes.

Although a number of studies of this type were conducted by Barr (1948) and his associates, the modern era of this research began with the work of Medley and Mitzel (1959) and Flanders (1960). The largest number of teacher effects studies were conducted during the 1970s. The earliest studies were summarized by Rosenshine in 1971 and the studies that were conducted between 1973 and 1983 were summarized by Brophy and Good (1986) and by Rosenshine and Stevens (1986). The experimental studies have been summarized by Gage and Needles (1989).

I suggest that the teacher-effects era, between 1955 and 1980, was an impressive run of cumulative research. During this period, over 100 correlational and experimental studies were conducted using a common design and the different observation instruments shared many common instructional procedures, and it was cumulative: Researchers cited and built on the instructional findings of others.

Rosenshine and Stevens (1986) summarized this research and concluded that across a number of studies, when effective teachers taught well-structured skills and expository material, the teachers used the following procedures:

- Begin a lesson with a short review of previous learning.
- Begin a lesson with a short statement of goals.
- Present new material in small steps, providing for student practice after each step.
- Give clear and detailed instructions and explanations.
- Provide a high level of active practice for all students.
- Ask a large number of questions, check for student understanding, and obtain responses from all students.
- Guide students during initial practice.
- Provide systematic feedback and corrections.
- Provide explicit instruction and practice for seatwork exercises and, where necessary, monitor students during seatwork.

Rosenshine and Stevens (1986) further grouped these instructional procedures under six teaching "functions" as shown in Table 10.1. These teaching functions appear to be relevant today for teaching students skills that they can use to independently complete well-structured tasks.

Two findings from that research that are most relevant to teaching are (a) the importance of teaching in small steps and (b) the importance of guiding student practice. In addition, a third finding, the importance of extensive practice, is shared with the research on cognitive processing.

Present New Material in Small Steps

We learned, in the teacher-effects research, that the least effective teachers would present an entire lesson, and then pass out worksheets and tell students to work the problems. However, the most effective teachers taught new material in small steps. That is, they only presented small parts of new material a single time, and after presenting the material the teachers then guided students in practicing the material that was taught.

This procedure of teaching in small steps fits well with the findings from cognitive psychology on the limitations of our working memory. Our working memory, where we process information, is small. It can only handle five to seven bits of information at once; any additional information swamps it. The procedure of first teaching in small steps and then guiding student practice represents an appropriate way of dealing with the limitation of our small working memories.

Guide Student Practice

A second major finding from the teacher-effects literature was the importance of guided practice. The concept of guided practice was developed by Hunter (1982), and it first appeared in the teacher-effects literature in an experimental study by Good and Grouws (1979).

In the teacher-effects research we learned that it was not sufficient to present a lesson and then ask students to practice on their own. The least effective teachers—those teachers whose classes made the smallest gains—would present an entire lesson, and then pass out worksheets and tell the students to work the problems. When this happened, it was observed that many students were confused and made errors on the worksheets. One reason for these errors was the aforementioned limitation of the working memory. For many students, particularly those who had not learned the previous material well, the amount of material presented in the lesson was too large, and therefore swamped the working memory.

The most effective teachers—those teachers whose classes made the greatest gains—taught differently. First, as noted, the most effective teachers presented only some of the material at a time; that is,

---

Table 10.1
Functions for Teaching Well-Structured Tasks

1. **Review**

    Review homework.

    Review relevant previous learning.

    Review prerequisite skills and knowledge for the lesson.

2. **Presentation**

    State lesson goals or provide outline.

    Present new material in small steps.

    Model procedures.

    Provide positive and negative examples.

    Use clear language.

    Check for student understanding.

    Avoid digressions.

3. **Guided Practice**

    Spend more time on guided practice.

    High frequency of questions.

    All students respond and receive feedback.

    High success rate.

    Continue practice until students are fluent.

4. **Corrections and Feedback**

    Provide process feedback when answers are correct but hesitant.

    Provide sustaining feedback, clues, or reteaching when answers are incorrect.

    Reteach material when necessary.

5. **Independent Practice**

    Students receive overview and/or help during initial steps.

    Practice continues until students are automatic (where relevant).

    Teacher provides active supervision (where possible).

    Routines are used to provide help for slower students.

6. **Weekly and Monthly Reviews**

---

they taught in small steps. After presenting a small amount of material, these teachers then guided student practice. This guidance often consisted of the teacher working a few problems at the board and discussing the steps out loud. This instruction served as a model for the students. This guidance also included asking students to come to the board, work problems, and discuss their procedures. Through this process the students at their seats would see additional models.

The process of guiding practice also includes checking the answers of the entire class in order to see whether some students need additional instruction. Guided practice has also included asking students to work together, in pairs or in groups, to quiz and explain the material to each other. Guided practice may occur when a teacher questions and helps a class with their work before assigning independent practice.

Another reason for the importance of guided practice comes from the fact that we construct and reconstruct knowledge. We do not, we cannot, simply repeat what we hear word for word. Rather, we connect our understanding of the new information to our existing concepts or "schema" and we then construct a "gist" of what we have heard. However, when left on their own, many students make errors in the process of constructing this gist. These errors occur particularly when the information is new and the student does not have adequate or well-formed background knowledge. These constructions are not errors so much as attempts by the students to be logical in an area where their background knowledge is weak. These errors are so common that there is a literature on the development and correction of student misconceptions in science (Guzzetti, Snyder, & Glass, 1992). When students are left on their own, without the guidance of someone who understands the new area, there is a danger that they will develop misconceptions. Providing guided practice, after teaching small amounts of new material, and checking for student understanding, are ways to limit the development of misconceptions.

Guiding practice also fits the cognitive processing findings on the need to provide for student processing. Guided practice is the place where the students—working alone, with other students, or with the teacher—engage in the cognitive-processing activities of organizing, reviewing, rehearsing, summarizing, comparing, and contrasting. However, it is important that *all* students engage in these activities. The least effective teachers often asked a question, called on one student to answer, and then assumed that everyone had learned this point. In contrast, the most effective teachers attempted to check the understanding of *all* students and to provide for processing by *all* students.

In summary, the most effective teachers differed from the others in that they (a) presented smaller amounts of material at any time

and (b) guided student practice as students worked problems,
(c) provided for student processing of the new material, (d) checked
the understanding of all students, and (e) attempted to prevent students from developing misconceptions.

Provide for Extensive Practice

The most effective teachers also provided for extensive and successful
practice. As noted in the cognitive-processing research, students need
extensive practice in order to develop well-connected networks. The
most effective teachers made sure that such practice took place *after*
there has been sufficient guided practice, so that students were not
practicing errors and misconceptions.

THE TEACHING OF COGNITIVE STRATEGIES

The third, major instructional development in the last 30 years has
been the concept of cognitive strategies. Cognitive strategies are guiding procedures that students can use to help them complete less
structured tasks such as those in reading comprehension and writing.
The concept of cognitive strategies and the research on cognitive
strategies represent the third important advance in instruction.

There are some academic tasks that are "well structured." These
tasks can be broken down into a fixed sequence of subtasks and steps
that consistently lead to the same goal. The steps are concrete and
visible. There is a specific, predictable algorithm that can be followed,
one that enables students to obtain the same result each time they
perform the algorithmic operations. These well-structured tasks are
taught by teaching each step of the algorithm to students. The results
of the research on teacher effects are particularly relevant in helping
us learn how to teach students algorithms they can use to complete
well-structured tasks.

In contrast, reading comprehension, writing, and study skills are
examples of less structured tasks—tasks that cannot be broken down
into a fixed sequence of subtasks and steps that consistently and
unfailingly lead to the goal. Because these task are less structured and
difficult, they have also been called higher level tasks. These types of
tasks do not have the fixed sequence that is part of well-structured
tasks. One cannot develop algorithms that students can use to complete these tasks.

Until the late 1970s, students were seldom provided with any
help in completing less structured tasks. In a classic observational

study of reading-comprehension instruction, Durkin (1979) noted that of the 4,469 minutes she observed in reading instruction in grade 4, only 20 minutes were spent in comprehension instruction by the teacher. Durkin noted that teachers spent almost all of the instructional time *asking* students questions, but they spent little time *teaching students comprehension strategies* they could use to answer the questions. Duffy, Lanier, and Roehler (1980) noted a similar lack of comprehension instruction in elementary classrooms:

> There is little evidence of instruction of any kind. Teachers spend most of their time assigning activities, monitoring to be sure the pupils are on task, directing recitation sessions to assess how well children are doing and providing corrective feedback in response to pupil errors. Seldom does one observe teaching in which a teacher presents a skill, a strategy, or a process to pupils, shows them how to do it, provides assistance as they initiate attempts to perform the task and assures that they can be successful. (p. 4)

As a result of these astonishing findings, and as a result of emerging research on cognition and information processing, investigators began to develop and validate procedures that students might be taught to aid their reading comprehension. In the field of reading, the research consisted of developing and teaching students to use specific cognitive strategies that help them to perform higher level operations in reading. Other research focused on developing, teaching, and testing cognitive strategies that are specific to writing, mathematical problem solving, and science comprehension.

The research design usually consisted of the investigator locating or developing a cognitive strategy such as teaching students to generate questions about the material they have read. Then one group of students would be taught this strategy and would practice using this strategy; they would practice generating questions and answering other students' questions. Another group of similar students continued with their regular lessons. After a period of 4 to 20 weeks, both groups would take a comprehension test and the scores of the two groups were compared. This section focuses on the results of those intervention studies in which cognitive strategies were developed and taught.

Cognitive strategies are heuristics. A cognitive strategy is not a direct procedure; it is not an algorithm to be precisely followed. Rather, a cognitive strategy is a heuristic or guide that serves to support or facilitate the learner as she or he develops internal procedures that enable them to perform the higher level operations. Teaching students to generate questions about their reading is an example of a cognitive strategy. Generating questions does not directly lead, in a step-by-step manner, to comprehension. Rather, in the process of generating questions, students need to search the text and combine information, and these processes serve to help students comprehend what they read.

In the late 1970s, investigators began to teach students specific cognitive strategies such as question generation and summarization that could be applied to reading comprehension (Alvermann, 1981; Paris, Cross, & Lipson, 1984; Raphael & Pearson, 1985). Cognitive strategy procedures have also been developed and taught in mathematics problem solving (Schoenfeld, 1985), physics problem solving (Larkin & Reif, 1976), and in writing (Englert & Raphael, 1989; Scardamalia & Bereiter, 1985).

The concept of cognitive strategies represents at least two instructional advances. First, when teachers are faced with difficult areas they can now ask "What cognitive strategies might I develop that can help students complete these tasks?" The concept of cognitive strategies provides us with a general approach that can be applied to the teaching of higher order tasks in the content areas. Second, researchers have completed a large number of intervention studies in which students who were taught various cognitive strategies obtained significantly higher posttest scores than did students in the control groups. The cognitive strategies were taught in these studies and the procedures by which these cognitive strategies were taught can now be used as part of regular instruction. These intervention studies, in reading, writing, mathematics, and science, together with a description of the cognitive strategies and the instructional procedures that were used, have been assembled in an excellent volume by Pressley et al. (1995).

We can be proud of our progress as a profession. In place of Durkin's observation that there was little evidence of cognitive strategy instruction in reading, we now have a large number of intervention studies, studies that have been successful in providing instruction in cognitive strategies in a number of domains.

INSTRUCTIONAL ELEMENTS IN THE TEACHING OF COGNITIVE STRATEGIES

How have cognitive strategies been taught? This section attempts to identify and discuss the instructional elements that have been used to teach cognitive strategies. It is hoped that a knowledge of these elements might add to our knowledge of instruction and might be applied to the teaching of other cognitive strategies. Such information might serve as an aid that teachers can use to help teach cognitive strategies to their students.

Scaffolds

Cognitive strategies cannot be taught directly, as one teaches an algorithm. Rather, cognitive strategies are taught by providing students with a variety of support structures or *scaffolds* (Palincsar & Brown, 1984; Wood, Bruner, & Ross, 1976). Many of the instructional elements to be described here serve as scaffolds for the learner. A scaffold is a temporary support used to assist a learner during initial learning. This support is usually provided by the teacher to help students bridge the gap between current abilities and the goal. Examples of scaffolds include simplified problems, modeling of the procedures by the teacher, thinking aloud by the teacher as he or she solves the problem, prompts, suggestions, and guidance as students work problems. Scaffolds may also be tools, such as cue cards or checklists. A model of the completed task against which students can compare their work is another example of such support (Collins, Brown, & Newman, 1990; Palincsar & Brown, 1984). *Cognitive apprenticeship* (Collins et al., 1990) is a term for instructional process by which teachers provide and support students with scaffolds as the students develop cognitive strategies.

Scaffolds operate to reduce the complexities of the problems and break them down into manageable chunks that the child has a real chance of solving (Bickhard, 1992). "The metaphor of a scaffold captures the idea of an adjustable and temporary support that can be removed when no longer necessary" (Brown & Palincsar, 1989, p. 411). The scaffolds assist the learner in learning a cognitive process and are gradually withdrawn or faded as learners become more independent, although some students may continue to rely on scaffolds when they encounter particularly difficult problems.

Scaffolds can be applied to the teaching of all skills, but they are particularly useful, and often indispensable, for teaching higher level cognitive strategies. A number of investigators (Collins et al., 1990; Pressley et al., 1995; Rosenshine & Meister, 1995) have studied the intervention studies and identified instructional procedures that teachers might use to teach cognitive strategies. Through this process, 13 major instructional elements were identified. These are listed in Table 10.2.

TABLE 10.2
Instructional Elements Used in the Teaching of Cognitive Strategies

1. Provide procedural prompts specific to the strategy being taught.
2. Teach the cognitive strategy using small steps.
3. Provide models of appropriate responses.
4. Think aloud as choices are being made.
5. Anticipate potential difficulties.
6. Regulate the difficulty of the material.
7. Provide a cue card.
8. Guide student practice.
9. Provide feedback and corrections.
10. Provide and teach a checklist.
11. Provide independent practice.
12. Increase student responsibilities.
13. Assess student mastery.

The search of this literature, in which we looked for the instructional procedures that were used to teach cognitive strategies, led to the identification of scaffolds, such as cue cards, as well as the identification of other instructional procedures such as extensive independent practice. These elements are described and discussed in the following.

Provide Procedural Prompts or Facilitators
In these studies, the first step in teaching a cognitive strategy was the development of a *procedural prompt*. These procedural prompts (or procedural facilitators, a term used by Scardamalia & Bereiter, 1985) supply the students with specific procedures or suggestions that facilitate the completion of the task. Learners can temporarily rely on these hints and suggestions until they create their own internal structures. For example, the words "who," "what," "why," "where," "when," and "how" are procedural prompts that help students learn the cognitive strategy of asking questions about the material they have read. These prompts are concrete references on which students can rely for support as they learn to apply the cognitive strategy.

Another example of procedural prompts comes from a study by King (1990), where students were provided with and taught to use a list of question stems that served to help the students form questions about a particular passage:

How are _____ and _____ alike?
What is the main idea of _____?
What do you think would happen if _____?
What are the strengths and weakness of _____?
In what way is _____ related to _____?
How does _____ affect _____?
Compare _____ and _____ with regard to _____.
What do you think causes _____?
How does _____ tie in with what we have learned before?
Which one is the best _____ and why?
What are some possible solutions for the problem of _____?
Do you agree or disagree with this statement: _____?
   Support your answer.
What do I (you) still not understand about . . .? (p. 667)

Procedural prompts are scaffolds that are specific to the cognitive strategy. Procedural prompts have been used, successfully, in a variety of content areas. Prompts have been used to assist teaching the strategy of summarization (Alvermann, 1981; Baumann, 1984) and writing (Englert & Raphael, 1989; Scardamalia & Bereiter, 1985). Procedural prompts have also been used to assist college students to solve problems in physics (Hiller & Hungate, 1985; Larkin & Reif, 1976) and mathematical problem solving (Schoenfeld, 1985). Pressley et al. (1995) have compiled a summary of research on instruction in cognitive strategies in reading, writing, mathematics, vocabulary, and science, and in almost all of these studies, the student learning was mediated through the use of procedural prompts.

Procedural prompts are an important concept that might be applied to the teaching of a variety of cognitive strategies. Procedural prompts are discussed in more detail in a later section.

Teach the Cognitive Strategy Using Small Steps
An earlier idea that came from the teacher-effects literature, the importance of teaching new material in small steps, also appears in the research on teaching cognitive strategies. When teaching cognitive strategies, it is easier for the learner if cognitive strategy is taught in small steps because teaching too much of the cognitive strategy at once would swamp the working memory. This idea of teaching in small steps, therefore, has extensive support. It fits the research on cognitive processing on the limitations of the working memory, was derived from studying the classrooms of the teachers who obtained

the highest achievement gain, and was also an instructional procedure that was used in intervention studies to teach students cognitive strategies.

Provide Models of the Appropriate Responses

Modeling is particularly important when teaching cognitive strategies because we cannot specify all the steps in these strategies. Therefore, models provide an important scaffold for the learner. Almost all of the researchers in these studies provided models of how to use the procedural prompt they had selected or developed. Models, modeling, or both were used at three different places in these studies: (a) during initial instruction, before students practiced; (b) during practice; and (c) after practice. Each approach is discussed here.

Models During Initial Instruction. In some studies, the teacher began by modeling responses based on the procedural prompts. Nolte and Singer (1985), for example, provided students with questions based on elements of the story grammar (e.g., What action does the leading character initiate? What do you learn about the character from this action?). Then they began by modeling questions based on this story grammar. In other studies, students received models of questions based on the main idea and then practiced generating questions on their own (Andre & Anderson, 1978–1979; Dreher & Gambrell, 1985).

Models Given During Practice. Models were also provided *during* practice. Such modeling is part of reciprocal teaching (Palincsar, 1987; Palincsar & Brown, 1984). In reciprocal teaching, the teacher first models asking a question and the students answer. Then the teacher guides students as they develop their own questions, to be answered by one of their classmates, and the teacher provides additional models when the students have difficulty. Other studies also provided models during practice (Helfeldt & Lalik, 1976; Labercane & Battle, 1987; Manzo, 1969).

Models Given After Practice. In studies on question generation, teachers also provided models of questions for the students to view *after* they had written questions relevant to a paragraph or passage (Andre & Anderson, 1978–1979; Dreher & Gambrell, 1985). The intent of this model was to enable the students to compare their efforts with that of an expert (Collins, Brown, & Newman, 1990).

Think Aloud as Choices Are Being Made

Another scaffold, similar to modeling, is *thinking aloud,* that is, the vocalization of the internal thought processes one goes through when using the cognitive strategy. For example, when teaching students to generate questions, the teacher describes the thought processes that occur as a question word is selected and integrated with text information to form a question. A teacher might think aloud while summarizing a paragraph, illustrating the thought processes that occur as the topic of the passage is determined and then used to generate a summary sentence.

Anderson (1991) provided illustrations of thinking aloud for several cognitive strategies in reading:

> *For clarifying difficult statements or concepts:* I don't get this. It says that things that are dark look smaller. I know that a white dog looks smaller than a black elephant, so this rule must only work for things that are about the same size. Maybe black shoes would make your feet look smaller than white ones would.

> *For summarizing important information:* I'll summarize this part of the article. So far, it tells where the Spanish started in North America and what parts they explored. Since the title is "The Spanish in California," the part about California must be important. I'd sum up by saying that Spanish explorers from Mexico discovered California. They didn't stay in California, but lived in other parts of America. These are the most important ideas so far.

> *For thinking ahead:* So far this has told me that Columbus is poor, the trip will be expensive, and everyone's laughing at his plan. I'd predict that Columbus will have trouble getting the money he needs for his exploration.

As individual students accepted more responsibility in the completion of a task, they often modeled and thought aloud for their less capable classmates. Not only did student modeling and think alouds involve the students actively in the process, but it allowed the teacher to better assess student progress in the use of the strategy. Thinking aloud by the teacher and more capable students provided novice learners with a way to observe "expert thinking," which is usually hidden from the student. Indeed, identifying the hidden strategies of experts so that they can become available to learners has become a useful area of research (Collins et al., 1990).

"Thinking aloud" by the teacher while solving problems is an important scaffold that has been used when teaching students higher level cognitive strategies. Garcia and Pearson (1990) referred to this process as the teacher "sharing the reading secrets" (p. 4) by making them overt. Thinking aloud is also an important part of a cognitive apprenticeship model (Collins, Brown, & Newman, 1990). Thinking aloud was only described in one study, that of Richey (1985), who had "the teacher model the thinking involved in each step for finding the main idea" (p. 3).

Anticipate and Discuss Potential Difficulties
Another instructional scaffold found in these question-generation studies was anticipating the difficulties a student is likely to face. In some studies, the instructor anticipated common errors that students might make and spent time discussing these errors *before* the students made them. For example, in a study by Palincsar (1987) the teacher anticipated the inappropriate questions that students might generate. The students read a paragraph followed by three questions one might ask about the paragraph. The students were asked to look at each example and decide whether or not that question was about the most important information in the paragraph. In one choice, the children were shown a question that could not be answered by the information provided in the paragraph, and the students discussed why it was a poor question. In another choice, the students were shown a question that was too narrow, that focused only on a small detail, and the students discussed why it was a poor question. The students continued through the exercise discussing whether each question was too narrow, too broad, or appropriate.

Another example of anticipating problems occurred in the study by Cohen (1983) where the students were taught specific rules to discriminate (a) a question from a nonquestion and (b) a good question from a poor one:

A good question starts with a question word.
A good question can be answered by the story.
A good question asks about an important detail of the story.

Although only two studies discussed this scaffold of anticipating student difficulties (Cohen, 1983; Palincsar, 1987), this technique seems potentially useful and might be used for teaching other skills, strategies, and subject areas.

Regulate the Difficulty of the Material

Some of the investigators attempted to regulate the difficulty of the material. Some did this by having the students begin with simpler material and then gradually move to more complex materials. For example, when Palincsar (1987) taught students to generate questions, the teacher first modeled how to generate questions about a single *sentence.* This was followed by class practice. Next, the teacher modeled and provided practice on asking questions after reading a *paragraph.* Finally, the teacher modeled and then the class practiced generating questions after reading an entire *passage.*

Similarly, in studies by Andre and Anderson (1978–1979) and Dreher and Gambrell (1985) the students began with a single paragraph, then moved to a double paragraph, and from there to a 450-word passage. Another example comes from the study by Wong, Wong, Perry, and Sawatsky (1986). Here, students began by generating questions about a single, simple paragraph. When the students were successful at that task, they moved to single, complex paragraphs and, lastly, to 800-word selections from social studies texts.

In another study (Wong & Jones, 1982), the researchers regulated the difficulty of the task by *decreasing* the prompts. First, students worked with a paragraph using procedural prompts. After they were successful at that level, they were moved to a passage with prompts and finally to a passage *without* prompts.

Provide a Cue Card

Another scaffold was the provision of a cue card containing the procedural prompt, which might support a student during initial learning by reducing the strain on the working memory. With a cue card, students can put some of their limited short-term memory into the application of the strategy instead of having to use some short-term memory to store the procedural prompts. One example appeared in a study by Billingsley and Wildman (1984), who provided students with cue cards listing the signal words (e.g., who, what, why . . .) which could be used as prompts for generating questions. Singer and Donlan (1982) presented a chart listing the five elements of a story grammar that the students were taught to use as prompts for generating questions. Wong and Jones (1982) and Wong et al. (1986) gave each student a cue card that listed the steps in developing a question about the main idea. In all four of these studies, the investigators modeled the use of the cue card.

Cue cards were also used in studies where students were provided with generic questions. In these studies (Blaha, 1979; Wong et al., 1986) students were provided with cue cards listing specific questions to ask after they had read paragraphs and passages (e.g., "What's the most important sentence in this paragraph?"), and King (1990) provided students with question stems (e.g., How are _____ and _____ alike?; What is a new example of . . . ?).

Guide Student Practice

In many of these studies, the teacher guided the students during their initial practice. Typically, after the modeling, the teacher guided students during their initial practice. As they worked through the text, the teacher gave hints, reminders of the prompts, reminders of what was overlooked, and suggestions of how something could be improved (Cohen, 1983; Palincsar, 1987; Wong et al., 1986). This guided practice was often combined with the presentation, as in the study by Blaha (1979) where the teacher first taught a part of a strategy, then guided student practice in identifying and then applying the strategy, then taught the next part of the strategy, and then guided student practice. This type of guided practice is the same as the guided practice that emerged from the teacher effects research (Rosenshine & Stevens, 1986).

The reciprocal teaching setting is another example of guided practice. As noted earlier, in reciprocal teaching the teacher first models the cognitive process being taught and then provides cognitive support and coaching (scaffolding) for the students as they attempt the task. As the students become more proficient, the teacher fades the support and students provide support for each other. Reciprocal teaching is a way of modifying the guided practice so that students take a more active role, eventually assuming the role of coteacher.

A third form of guided practice occurred when students met in small groups of two to six, without the teacher, and practiced asking, revising, and correcting questions and provided support and feedback to each other (King, 1990; Nolte & Singer, 1985; Singer & Donlan, 1982). Such groupings allow for more support when revising questions and for more practice than can be obtained in a whole-class setting. Nolte and Singer (1985) applied the concept of diminishing support to the organization of groups. Here, students first spent 3 days working in groups of five or six, then 3 days working in pairs, and eventually working alone.

Provide Feedback and Corrections

Providing feedback and corrections to the students most likely occurred in all studies, but was explicitly mentioned in only a few. In these studies, there were three sources of feedback and corrections: the teacher, other students, and a computer.

Teacher feedback and corrections occurred during the guided practice as students attempted to generate questions. Feedback typically took the form of hints, questions, and suggestions. A second form of feedback—group feedback—was illustrated in the three studies by King (1990) and in a study by Richey (1985). In the King studies, after students had written their questions, they met in groups, posed questions to each other, and compared questions within each group. The third type of feedback—which was computer-based—occurred in the computer-based instructional format designed by MacGregor (1988). In this study, students asked the computer to provide a model of an appropriate question when they made an error.

Provide and Teach a Checklist

In some of the studies, students were taught to use another scaffold— a self-evaluation checklist. In a study by Davey and McBride (1986), a self-evaluation checklist was introduced in the fourth of five instructional sessions. The checklist listed the following questions:

How well did I identify important information?
How well did I link information together?
How well could I answer my questions?
Did my "think questions" use different language from the text?
Did I use good signal words? (p. 259)

Wong and Jones (1982) wrote that students in their study were furnished with the "criteria for a good question" (p. 235), although these criteria were not described in the report. In the three studies by King (1990), students were taught to ask themselves the question "What do I still not understand?" after they had generated and answered their questions.

There were differences between the studies with regard to when checklists were introduced into a lesson. Wong and Jones (1982) and King (1989, 1990, 1992) presented checklists during the presentation, whereas Davey and McBride (1986) presented them during the guided practice, and Richey (1985) presented them after initial practice.

Provide Independent Practice with New Examples

Independent practice refer to student practice in applying the cognitive strategy with diminishing help from the teacher and other students. One goal of independent practice is to develop automatic responding so the students no longer have to recall the strategy, and thus more of their limited working memory can be applied to the task. Another goal of independent practice is to achieve "unitization" of the strategy, that is, the blending of elements of the strategy into a unified whole. This unitization is usually the result of extensive practice—practice that helps students develop an automatic, unified approach. This extensive practice, and practice with a variety of material, also decontextualizes the learning. That is, the strategies become free of their original "bindings" and can now be applied easily and unconsciously to various situations (Collins et al., 1989).

Another purpose of independent practice is to facilitate transfer to other content areas. One hopes that the reading comprehension skills that are taught in one content area, such as social studies, might also be applied to other content areas, such as science. Such transfer might be facilitated if students receive guided practice in applying their skills to *different* content areas. For example, in a study by Dermody (1988) the last phase of the study involved application of cognitive strategy to a different content area than was used for the original instruction.

Increase Student Responsibilities

As students become more competent during guided practice and independent practice, the scaffolds are diminished and student responsibilities are increased. Thus, with greater competency, the teacher diminishes the use of models and prompts and other scaffolds, and diminishes the support offered by other students. In addition, the complexity and difficulty of the material is gradually increased. In reading, for example, one begins with well-organized, reader-friendly material and then increases the difficulty of the material. That way, students receive practice and support in applying their strategies to the more difficult material they can expect to encounter in their regular reading.

Assess Student Mastery

After guided practice and independent practice, some of the studies assessed whether students had achieved a mastery level, and provided for additional instruction when necessary. On the fifth and final day of instruction, Davey and McBride (1986) required students to generate three acceptable questions for each of three passages. Smith (1977) stated that student questions at the end of a story were compared to modeled questions, and reteaching took place when necessary. Wong et al. (1986) required that students achieve mastery in applying the self-questioning steps and students had to continue doing the exercises (sometimes daily for 2 months) until they achieved mastery. Unfortunately, the other studies cited in this review did not report the level of mastery students achieved in generating questions.

Fitting Things Together

How might the results from these three areas of research fit together? First, the research allows us to articulate a major goal of education: helping students develop well-organized knowledge structures. In well-developed structures, the parts are well organized, the pieces are well connected, and the bonds between the connections are strong.

We also know something about how to help students acquire these structures.

1. Present new material in small steps so that the working memory does not become overloaded.

2. Help students develop an organization for the new material.

3. Guide student practice by (a) supporting students during initial practice, and (b) providing for extensive student processing.

4. When teaching higher level tasks, support students by providing them with cognitive strategies.

5. Help students learn to use the cognitive strategies by providing them with procedural prompts and modeling the use of these procedural prompts.

6. Provide for extensive student practice.

SUMMARY

Thirty years ago, particularly with the publication of the first *Handbook of Research on Teaching* (Gage, 1963) and the investment of public and private funds into research, we began an extensive program of research and development in education. This chapter is an attempt to highlight some of the major results that have been obtained in the area of instruction, results which have relevance for today's teachers and students.

REFERENCES

Alvermann, D. E. (1981). The compensatory effect of graphic organizers on descriptive text. *Journal of Educational Research, 75,* 44–48.

Anderson, V. (1991, April). *Training teachers to foster active reading strategies in reading-disabled adolescents.* Paper presented at the annual meeting of the American Educational Research Association, Chicago.

Andre, M. D. A., & Anderson, T. H. (1978–1979). The development and evaluation of a self-questioning study technique. *Reading Research Quarterly, 14,* 605–623.

Barr, A. S. (1948). The measurement and prediction of teaching efficiency: A summary of the investigations. *Journal of Experimental Education, 16,* 203–283.

Baumann, J. F. (1984). The effectiveness of a direct instruction paradigm for teaching main idea comprehension. *Reading Research Quarterly, 20,* 93–115.

Bickhard, M. H. (1992). Scaffolding and self-scaffolding: Central aspects of development. In L. T. Winegar & J. Valsiner (Eds.), *Children's development within social context* (Vol. 2, pp. 33–52). Hillsdale, NJ: Lawrence Erlbaum Associates.

Billingsley, B. S., & Wildman, T. M. (1988). Question generation and reading comprehension. *Learning Disability Research, 4,* 36–44.

Blaha, B. A. (1979). *The effects of answering self-generated questions on reading.* Unpublished doctoral dissertation, Boston University School of Education.

Brophy, J., & Good, T. (1986). Teacher-effects results. In M. C. Wittrock (Ed.), *Handbook of research on teaching* (3rd ed., pp. 328–376). New York: Macmillan.

Brown, A. L., & Campione, J. C. (1986). Psychological theory and the study of learning disabilities. *American Psychologist, 41,* 1059–1068.

Brown, A. L., & Palincsar, A. S. (1989). Guided, cooperative learning and individual knowledge acquisition. In L. B. Resnick (Ed.), *Knowing, learning, and instruction: Essays in honor of Robert Glaser* (pp. 393–451). Hillsdale, NJ: Lawrence Erlbaum Associates.

Cohen, R. (1983). Students generate questions as an aid to reading comprehension. *Reading Teacher, 36,* 770–775.

Collins, A., Brown, J. S., & Newman, S. E. (1990). Cognitive apprenticeship: Teaching the crafts of reading, writing, and mathematics. In L. Resnick (Ed.), *Knowing, learning, and instruction: Essays in honor of Robert Glaser.* Hillsdale, NJ: Lawrence Erlbaum Associates.

Davey, B., & McBride, S. (1986). Effects of question-generation on reading comprehension. *Journal of Educational Psychology, 78,* 256–262.

Dermody, M. (1988). *Metacognitive strategies for development of reading comprehension for younger children.* Paper presented at the annual meeting of the American Association of Colleges for Teacher Education. New Orleans, February,

1988. (Louisiana State Department of Education, New Orleans Adolescent Hospital, New Orleans). ERIC ED 292070

Dreher, M. J., & Gambrell, L. B. (1985). Teaching children to use a self-questioning strategy for studying expository text. *Reading Improvement, 22,* 2–7.

Duffy, G., Lanier, J. E., & Roehler, L. R. (1980). *On the need to consider instructional practice when looking for instructional implications.* Paper presented at the Conference on Reading Expository Materials, Wisconsin Research and Development Center, University of Wisconsin–Madison.

Durkin, D. (1979). What classroom observations reveal about reading comprehension. *Reading Research Quarterly, 14,* 581–594.

Englert, C. S., & Raphael, T. E. (1989). Developing successful writers through cognitive strategy instruction. In J. Brophy (Ed.), *Advances in research on teaching, Vol. 1* (pp. 105–151). Greenwich, CT: JAI Press.

Flanders, N. A. (1960). *Teacher influence, pupil attitudes and achievement.* Minneapolis: University of Minnesota. (Also published under this title as FS 5.225:25040 U.S. Department of Education, U.S. Government Printing Office.)

Gage, N. L. (Ed.). (1963). *Handbook of research on teaching.* Chicago, IL: Rand McNally.

Gage, N. L., & Needles, M. C. (1989). Process-product research on teaching: A review of criticisms. *Elementary School Journal, 89,* 253–300.

Garcia, G. E., & Pearson, P. D. (1991). Modifying reading instruction to maximize its effectiveness for all students. In M. S. Knapp & P. M. Shields (Eds.), *Better strategies for the children of poverty: Alternatives to conventional wisdom.* Berkeley, CA: McCutchan. Also (Tech. Rep. #489). Champaign, IL: Center for the Study of Reading, University of Illinois.

Good, T., & Grouws, D. (1979). The Missouri teacher effectiveness program. *Journal of Educational Psychology, 71,* 355–362.

Guzzetti, B. J., Snyder, T. E., & Glass, G. V. (1992). Promoting conceptual change in science: Can texts be used effectively? *Journal of Reading, 35,* 642–649.

Helfeldt, J. P., & Lalik, R. (1976). Reciprocal student-teacher questioning. *Reading Teacher, 33,* 283–287.

Hiller, J. I., & Hungate, H. N. (1985). Implications for mathematics instruction of research on scientific problem solving. In E. A. Silver (Ed.), *Teaching and learning mathematical problem solving: Multiple research perspectives.* Hillsdale, NJ: Lawrence Erlbaum Associates.

Hunter, M. (1982). *Mastery teaching.* P.O. Box 514, El Segundo, CA: TIP Publications.

King, A. (1990). Enhancing peer interaction and learning in the classroom through reciprocal peer questioning. *American Educational Research Journal, 27,* 664–687.

Labercane, G., & Battle, J. (1987). Cognitive processing strategies, self-esteem, and reading comprehension of learning disabled students. *Journal of Special Education, 11,* 167–185.

Larkin, J. H., & Reif, F. (1976). Analysis and teaching of a general skill for studying scientific text. *Journal of Educational Psychology, 72,* 348–350.

Manzo, A. V. (1969). *Improving reading comprehension through reciprocal teaching.* Unpublished doctoral dissertation, Syracuse University.

Medley, D. M., & Mitzel, H. E. (1959). Some behavioral correlates of teacher effectiveness. *Journal of Educational Psychology, 50,* 239–246.

Nolte, R. Y., & Singer, H. (1985). Active comprehension: Teaching a process of reading comprehension and its effects on reading achievement. *The Reading Teacher, 39,* 24–31.

Palincsar, A. S. (1987, April). *Collaborating for collaborative learning of text comprehension.* Paper presented at the annual conference of the American Educational Research Association, Washington, DC.

Palincsar, A. S., & Brown, A. L. (1984). Reciprocal teaching of comprehension-fostering and comprehension-monitoring activities. *Cognition and Instruction, 2,* 117–175.

Paris, S. C., Cross, D. R., & Lipson, M. Y. (1984). Informed strategies for learning: A program to improve children's reading awareness and comprehension. *Journal of Educational Psychology, 76,* 1239–1252.

Pressley, M., Burkell, J., Cariglia-Bull, T., Lysynchuk, L., McGoldrick, J. A., Schneider, B., Symons, S., & Woloshyn, V. E. (1995). *Cognitive strategy instruction* (2nd ed.) Cambridge, MA: Brookline Books.

Raphael, T. E., & Pearson, P. D. (1985). Increasing student awareness of sources of information for answering questions. *American Educational Research Journal, 22,* 217–237.

Richey, P. (1985). The effects of instruction in main idea and question generation. *Reading Canada Lecture, 3,* 139–146.

Rosenshine, B. (1971). *Teaching behaviors and student achievement.* Slough, England: National Federation for Educational Research.

Rosenshine, B., & Meister, C. (1995). Scaffolds for teaching higher-order cognitive strategies. In A. C. Ornstein (Ed.), *Teaching: Theory into practice* (pp. 134–153). Boston: Allyn & Bacon.

Rosenshine, B., & Stevens, R. (1986). Teaching functions. In M. C. Wittrock (Ed.), *Handbook of research on teaching* (3rd ed., pp. 745–799). New York: Macmillan.

Scardamalia, M., & Bereiter, C. (1985). Fostering the development of self-regulation in children's knowledge processing. In S. F. Chipman, J. W. Segal, & R. Glaser (Eds.), *Thinking and learning skills: Research and open questions.* Hillsdale, NJ: Lawrence Erlbaum Associates.

Schoenfeld, A. H. (1985). *Mathematical problem solving.* New York: Academic Press.

Singer, H., & Donlan, D. (1982). Active comprehension: Problem-solving schema with question generation of complex short stories. *Reading Research Quarterly, 17,* 166–186.

Smith, N. J. (1977). *The effects of training teachers to teach students different reading ability levels to formulate three types of questions on reading comprehension and question generation ability.* Unpublished doctoral dissertation, University of Georgia.

Wong, B. Y. L., Wong, W., Perry, N., & Sawatsky, D. (1986). The efficacy of a self-questioning summarization strategy for use by underachievers and learning-disabled adolescents. *Learning Disability Focus, 2,* 20–35.

Wong, Y. L., & Jones, W. (1982). Increasing metacomprehension in learning disabled and normally achieving students through self-questioning training. *Learning Disability Quarterly, 5,* 228–239.

Wood, D. J., Bruner, J. S., & Ross, G. (1976). The role of tutoring in problem solving. *Journal of Child Psychology and Psychiatry, 17,* 89–100.

Mediative Environments: Creating Conditions for Intellectual Growth

by Arthur L. Costa

Many out-of-conscious factors influence teachers' thinking as they make daily decisions about curriculum and instruction. Their own culture, knowledge of content, their cognitive style, knowledge about their students, and their professional values and beliefs about education influence their judgments about when to teach what to whom. Jack Frymier, however, states:

> In the main, the bureaucratic structure of the workplace is more influential in determining what professionals do than are personal abilities, professional training or previous experience. Therefore, change efforts should focus on the structure of the workplace, not the teachers (1987, 10).

Frymier suggests that less obvious, but vastly more persuasive influences on teacher thought are the norms, culture, and culture of the school setting in which teachers work. Hidden, but powerful cues emanate from the school environment. These subtle cues signal the institutional value system that governs the operation of the organization (Saphier and King 1985).

Recent efforts to bring educational reform will prove futile unless the school environment signals the staff, the students, and the community that the development of the intellect and cooperative decision making are the school's basic values. While efforts to enhance the staff's instructional competencies, develop curriculum, and revise instructional materials and assessment procedures may be important components in the process of educational re-engineering,

From a paper based on a presentation at the Fourth International Teaching for Intelligence Conference, April 25, 1998, New York, NY. © 1998 by Arthur L. Costa. Reprinted with permission.

it also is crucial that the climate in which parents, teachers, and students make their decisions be aligned with these goals of development of intellectual potential. Teachers more likely will teach for thinking, creativity, and cooperation if they are in an intellectually stimulating, creative, and cooperative environment themselves.

EDUCATIONAL STRESSORS

Research by O. J. Harvey (1966) found that teaching is the second most stressful profession. Goodlad (1984), Rosenholtz (1989), Sarason (1991), Fullan (1993), and other authors have identified several sources of stress:

• Teachers may lack a sense of power and efficacy. They are often cast at the bottom of a hierarchy while the decisions about curriculum, staff development, assessment, instructional materials, and evaluation—decisions that affect them directly—are handed down from "above."

• Teachers feel isolated. Ours is probably the only profession that performs our most beautiful and creative craft behind closed doors. Contributing to this situation is the inadequate amount and inflexibility of time for teachers to reflect and meet, plan, observe, and talk with each other.

• The complex, creative, intelligent act of teaching is often reduced to a rubric, a simplistic formula, or a series of steps and competencies, the uniform performance of which naively connotes excellence and elegance in the art of teaching.

• The feedback of data about student achievement is for political, competitive, evaluative, or coercive purposes. It neither involves nor instructs the school staff members in reflecting on, evaluating, and improving their curriculum and instructional decisions.

• Educational innovations are often viewed as mere "tinkerings" with the instructional program. They are so frequent and limited in impact that frustrated teachers sometimes feel "this, too, shall pass." Instead of institutionalizing the change, deeply entrenched traditional practices and policies in the educational bureaucracy such as assessment, reporting, securing parent understanding and support, teacher evaluation, scheduling, school organization, and discipline procedures seldom are revised to be in harmony with the overall innovation.

The effects of excessive stress on cognition, creativity, and social interaction are well documented (MacLean 1978). In such barren, intellectually "polluted" school-climate conditions, some teachers understandably grow depressed. Teachers' vivid imaginations, altruism, creativity, and intellectual prowess soon succumb to the humdrum daily routines of unruly students, irrelevant curriculum, impersonal surroundings, and equally disillusioned coworkers. In such an environment, the likelihood that teachers would value the development of students' intellect and imagination would be marginal.

TOWARD AN ECOLOGY OF THE INTELLECT

The level of teachers' intellectual development has a direct relationship to student behavior and student performance. Higher-level intellectually functioning teachers produce higher-level intellectually functioning students (Sprinthall and Theis-Sprinthall 1983). Characteristic of these teachers is their ability to empathize, to symbolize experience, and to act in accordance with a disciplined commitment to human values. These teachers employ a greater range of instructional strategies, elicit more conceptual responses from students, and produce higher-achieving students who are more cooperative and involved in their work. Glickman (1985) concluded that successful teachers are thoughtful teachers and they stimulate their students to be thoughtful as well.

To achieve our educational outcome of developing students' intellectual capacities, educational leaders must redefine their role as mediators of schoolwide and community-wide conditions for continual learning and intellectual development. A mediator is one who deliberately intervenes between the individual or group and the environment with the intention of creating conditions that will engage and promote intellectual growth (Feuerstein et al. 1997). They design strategies for achieving their vision of a learning organization; they generate data as a means of assessing progress toward that vision; they constantly monitor the intellectual ecology of the school community to determine its contribution to or hindrance of intellectual growth. Their role is analogous to an "Environmental Protection Agency," monitoring and managing the environment to insure that intellectual growth, creativity, and cooperation are continually sustained and regenerated.

Systems analysts believe in "leverage points." These are places within a complex system where a small shift in one condition can produce big changes in the rest of the system. As mediators of the school's "intellectual ecology," the following seven leverage points are interventions that are intended to enhance continual intellectual growth and sustain the professional zest of the stakeholders in the educational enterprise. The intent is not to alleviate stress entirely. It is, however, intended to shift from *di*stress to *eu*stress ("eu" is taken from the word *euphoria*).

1. Clarifying Goals and Outcomes

Peter Senge (1990) states that leadership in a learning organization starts with the principle of "creative tension." He goes on to describe how creative tension emerges from seeing clearly where we want to be—the vision—and describing truthfully where we are now—our current reality. The gap between the two generates creative tension.

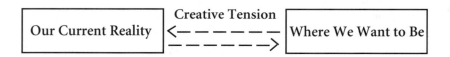

This principle of creative tension has long been recognized by leaders, such as when Martin Luther King Jr. proclaimed, "I have a dream. . . ." King believed that it was necessary to create a tension in society that will help us rise from the depths of prejudice and racism.

This tension, according to Senge (1990), can be resolved by raising current reality toward the vision. Effective leaders, therefore, stimulate intellectual growth by causing creative organizational tension. Leaders create for themselves and facilitate staff, students', and the community's visions of what could be, images of desired states, valued aspirations, outcomes, and scenarios of more appropriate futures.

Mission and vision statements, however, are not just exercises. They are employed continually as criteria for making decisions, developing policies, allocating resources, hiring staff, designing curriculum, disciplining, and lesson planning. A school's mission statement is given substance and value when it is systematically assessed. When our values are clear, the decisions we make are easy. What gives an organization integrity is how the staff members perceive the congruence between its policies, vision, and mission and its daily practices.

2. Building and Maintaining Trust and Collegiality

George Land and Beth Jarman (1992) believe that trust and the ability to work together toward a common vision are what fuel individuals to accomplish amazing results. Trust is a vital element in enhancing cognition. We know that higher level, complex and creative thinking closes down when trust is lacking in the environment or in the relationship with others. Teachers will be encouraged to inquire, speculate, construct meanings, experiment, self-evaluate, and self-prescribe when the leader manages a trusting environment. Building an atmosphere of trust is the leader's most important task.

Humans, as social beings, mature intellectually in reciprocal relationships. Collaboratively, individuals generate and discuss ideas, eliciting thinking that surpasses individual effort. Together and privately, they express different perspectives, agree and disagree, point out and resolve discrepancies, and weigh alternatives. Because people grow their intellect through this process, collegial interaction is a crucial factor in the intellectual ecology of the school.

The essence of building trust and collegiality is when people work together to better understand how to work together. People are more likely to engage and grow in higher-level, creative, and experimental thought when they are in a trusting, risk-taking, cooperative climate. Risk taking requires a nonjudgmental atmosphere where information can be shared without fear that it will be used for evaluative purposes.

Baker, Costa, and Shalit (1997) identify eight norms that may serve as standards that are understood, agreed upon, adopted, monitored, and assessed by each participant when working as a facilitating and contributing member of a group. They are the glue that enables school and community groups to engage in productive and satisfying discourse:

• *Pausing.* Taking turns is the ultimate in impulse control (Kotulak 1997). In a discourse, space is given for each person to talk. Time is allowed before responding to or asking a question. Such silent time allows for more complex thinking, enhances all forms of discourse, and produces better decision making. Pausing is the tool that facilitative group members use to respectfully listen to each other.

• *Paraphrasing.* Covey (1989) suggests we seek to understand before being understood. Paraphrasing lets others know that you are listening, that you understand or are trying to understand, and that you care.

• *Probing and Clarifying.* This is an effective inquiry skill to use when the speaker expresses vocabulary, uses a vague concept, or employs terminology that is not fully understood by the listener. The use of probing and clarifying is intended to help the listener better understand the speaker. In groups, probing and clarifying increase the clarity and precision of the group's thinking by clarifying understandings, terminology, and interpretations.

• *Putting Your Ideas On and Pulling Them Off the Table.* Groups are most productive when everyone shares their thoughts, dreams, mistakes, assumptions, and opinions. While group members offer ideas, opinions, information, and positions, they attempt to keep their suggestions relevant to the topic at hand. Because there are times when continuing to advocate a position might block the group's functioning, group members also volunteer to withdraw their ideas.

• *Paying Attention to Self and Others.* Meaningful dialogue is facilitated when each group member is sensitive to and conscious of the subtle cues inside themselves and within the group. Paying attention to learning styles, modalities, and beliefs when planning for, facilitating of, and participating in group meetings enhances group members' understanding of each other as they converse, discuss, deliberate, dialogue, and make decisions.

• *Presuming Positive Intentionality/Positive Presuppositions.* People operate on internal maps of their own reality and, therefore, we assume that they act with positive intentions. This assumption promotes and facilitates meaningful dialogue. Because our language contains overt and covert messages, deeper meanings may be misinterpreted. The subtle (and often not so subtle) way in which we embed presuppositions in our language can be hurtful or helpful to others. The deliberate use of positive presuppositions assumes and encourages positive actions (Costa and Garmston 1994).

• *Providing Data.* Groups exercising high levels of communicative competence act on information rather than hearsay, rumor, or speculation. Data serves as the energy sources for group action and learning. Seeking, generating, and gathering data from group members as well as a variety of other primary and secondary sources enhance individual and group decision making.

• *Pursuing a Balance Between Advocacy and Inquiry.* Advocating a position as well as inquiring into another's position assists the group to continue learning. Senge et al. (1994) suggest that balancing advocacy and inquiry is critical for an organization to perform in order to grow and learn.

Leaders encourage individuals and groups to monitor and assess their own use of these eight norms of collaboration. During and upon completion of meetings, group process observers provide feedback to the group about their performance of the norms. These data are discussed, the effects of their use on group effectiveness are illuminated, and strategies for individual and group improvement are planned (Costa and Kallick 1995).

3. Coaching

Coaching is one of the most powerful means to overcome the extreme isolation and intellectual depression of teachers. Coaching produces intellectual growth for a variety of reasons:

• *Coaching enhances instructional thought.* The act of teaching is, itself, an intellectual process. Jackson (1968) found that teachers make over 1,300 decisions a day. The behaviors observed in the classroom are artifacts of decisions that teachers make before, during, and after instruction (Shavelson 1976). The purpose of coaching, therefore, is to enhance the teacher's capacity to plan, monitor, and reflect upon his or her instructional decision making, perceptions, and the intellectual functions. Costa and Garmston (1994) cite that the intent of coaching is to modify teachers' capacities to modify themselves.

• *Humans who desire to continually improve their craft, seek and profit from being coached.* Skillful artists, athletes, musicians, dancers—such as Greg Louganis, Mikhail Baryshnikov, Kristi Yamaguchi, and Jackie Joyner-Kersey—never lose their need for coaching. Likewise, in education, to continually perfect their craft, teachers profit from coaching as well.

• *To work effectively as a member of a team requires coaching.* Welding together the individual efforts of team members into a well-organized and efficient unit requires the persistence and stamina of an expert coach. This concerted effort, however, does not "just happen." It takes someone—a conductor—who "knows the score" to provide the synergy. It takes time, persistence, practice, and coaching to develop a winning athletic team, a celebrated symphony orchestra, or a learning organization.

• *Few educational innovations achieve their full impact without a coaching component.* Joyce and Showers (1988) found that efforts to bring about changes in classroom practice are fruitless unless the teacher is coached in the use of the innovation. Only when the component of coaching was added was the innovation internalized, valued, and transferred to classroom use.

• *Coaching enhances the intellectual capacities of teachers, which, in turn, produces greater intellectual achievements in students.* The human intellect grows in reciprocity with others. Russian psycholinguist Lev Vygotsky (1978) suggests that intelligence grows in two ways. One is that intelligence develops through our own experience. And the other is that intelligence is shaped through reciprocity with others. Justifying reasons, resolving differences, active listening to another person's point of view, achieving consensus, and receiving feedback actually increase our intelligence.

Vygotsky's prospective provides a strong theoretical support for coaching as a means of intellectual growth. It is through social interaction that new concepts and intellectual behaviors are formed and grown. And, as was cited earlier, the teacher's level of intellectual development influences the students' level of intellectual development.

4. Investing Leadership in All

It was once thought that leadership was invested in a few individuals at the "top" of the organizational hierarchy and that the position of leadership was earned by position, credentials, or the number of academic degrees earned. In an intellectual ecology, however, all the players play all the roles. Leadership is a shared function: in meetings, in staff development activities, in action research, in networking different levels of the organization and, indeed, in classrooms as well (Garmston and Wellman 1997; Lambert 1998). Intellectual shifts result when the identities and roles of the participants in the educational process—students, teachers, administrators, and trustees—are redefined. Six major leadership roles include

• *Facilitating.* Conducting meetings for the purpose of shared decision making, planning, and/or problem solving.

- *Presenting.* Presenters teach groups to develop knowledge, skills, or attitudes that will be applied in the group members' work. Presenting requires clarity about outcomes, interactive teaching strategies, and ways to assess the effectiveness of the learning.
- *Coaching.* To coach is to convey a valued colleague from where he or she is to where he or she wants to be. Serving as a coach means mediating—not judging—a colleague's decisions, intellectual functions, and perceptions (Costa and Garmston 1994).
- *Consulting.* Consultants bring expertise to the relationship and an intention that their expertise be used by the other party. A consultant can be an information specialist who delivers technical knowledge (e.g., purchasing technology), an advocate for content who will influence the group based on his or her broader knowledge (e.g., adopting a curriculum), or an advocate for process (e.g., recommending an open rather than a closed meeting).
- *Networking.* Leaders pay attention to the flow and interchange of energy. Knowing one person's or group's needs and another's talents, information, and resources allows the networker to link people and groups together in mutually supportive relationships for the betterment of all.
- *Researching.* Meaning develops when individuals and groups generate, interpret, validate, and own the data that results from their decisions and actions. Researching creates a situation in which people learn with a higher degree of rigor. Experiences become learning experiences when they involve not only deliberate action but meaning-making through reflection on that action. Facilitative leaders support data-driven problem solving and solutions finding. By establishing such linkages, the data develop deeper importance and become a resource rather than a burden to be sidestepped (Costa and Kallick 1995).

5. Valuing Diversity

Human beings are made to be different. Diversity is the basis of biological survival. Each of us has a different genetic structure, unique facial features, a distinguishing thumb print, a distinctive signature, a diverse background of knowledge, experience, and culture, and a preferred way of gathering, processing, and expressing information and knowledge. We even have a singular frequency in which we vibrate (Leonard 1978). Leaders are sensitive to and capitalize on these differences to enhance intellectual growth.

Intellectually effective people seem able to "be at home" in multiple areas of functioning. They move flexibly from one style to another as the situation demands it. They have an uncanny ability to read contextual cues from the situation or the environment as to what is needed, then they draw forth from their vast repertoire those skills and capacities needed to function most effectively in any setting.

Organizational life might seem easier if all members of the learning community thought and acted in a similar fashion and remained in their own departments and grade levels. Limitations of time, isolation, and our obsession with the archaic compartmentalization of the disciplines and grades keep school staffs separated; thus, opportunities for teachers' intellectual growth are limited. Leaders realize that humans grow intellectually through resolving differences, achieving consensus, and stretching to accommodate dissonance. They realize there is a greater possibility for making connections, stimulating creativity, and growing the capacity for complex problem solving when such differences are bridged. (In some businesses, this is referred to as "skunkworks"—deliberately bringing together personnel from different departments, positions, and grade levels to make connections and find new and divergent ways to solve problems.)

Interdependent learning communities are built not by obscuring diversity but by valuing the friction those differences bring and resolving those differences in an atmosphere of trust and reciprocity. Therefore, leaders mediate appreciation for this diversity by deliberately bringing together people of different political and religious persuasions, cultures, genders, cognitive styles, belief systems, modality preferences, and intelligences. They structure groups composed of representatives from different schools, diverse departments, community groups, and grade levels to envision, describe learning outcomes, plan curriculum and staff development activities, and allocate resources.

6. Challenging Curriculum Models

Curriculum is like a cemetery. It is etched in stone, visited only on special occasions, filled with dead subjects, aligned in straight rows, and is a monument to the past. Furthermore, we keep putting more in and take nothing out!

Senge (1990) emphasizes a characteristic of the learning organization is that it challenges existing mental models. The leader, in an atmosphere of trust, challenges existing practices, assumptions, policies, and traditional ways of delivering curriculum. Intellectual growth is found in disequilibrium, not balance. It is out of chaos that order is built, that learning takes place, that new understandings are forged, that new connections are bridged, and that organizations function more consistently with their mission, vision, and goals.

We must finally admit that the process *is* the content. The core of our curriculum must focus on such processes as thinking, learning to learn, knowledge production, metacognition, transference of knowledge, decision making, creativity, group problem solving, and knowing how to behave when correct answers are not readily apparent. These *are* the subject matters of instruction. Content, selectively abandoned and judiciously selected because of its fecund contributions to the thinking/learning process, becomes merely the vehicle to carry the processes of learning. The focus is on learning *from* the objectives instead of learning *of* the objectives.

Since these process-oriented goals cannot be assessed using product-oriented assessment techniques, our existing evaluation paradigm must shift as well. Thus, assessment of students' thinking will focus on students becoming more conscious, more reflective, more efficient, more flexible, and more transferable (Costa and Kallick 1995; Costa and Liebmann 1997).

The leader continually challenges the organization's mental models about what learning is of most worth as students face an uncertain, technological, and global future (Costa and Garmston 1998).

7. Learning Continually

Experimentation implies that an atmosphere of choice, risk taking, and inquiry exists. Data are generated without fear that they will be used as a basis for evaluating success or failure. Creativity will more likely grow in a low-risk atmosphere. Frymier goes on to state:

> The solution is to empower teachers, to help them develop an internalized locus of control. Teachers and principals, supervisors and superintendents, boards of education and state legislators all must appreciate the possibilities of school improvement efforts that marshal the motivations and unleash the talents of those who work directly with children day after day (1987, 10).

For too long the process of assessment has been external to teachers' goal setting, curriculum, and instructional decision making.

School effectiveness, student achievement, and teachers' competence often have been determined by a narrow range of standardized student achievement test scores in a limited number of content areas: reading, math, and language acquisition. Rank-order test results have been published in newspapers; awards of excellence have been granted to schools that show the highest gains in scores.

In the process, teachers have become disenfranchised. Educators have had little say about what the test measured; what tests do measure often is irrelevant to the curriculum, and the results of testing disclose little about the adequacy of teachers' curriculum and instructional decisions. In many ways, the desire for measurable outcomes has signaled teachers that they are "incompetent" to assess student achievement. They, in effect, have been told they could not be trusted to collect evidence of students' growth and that the observations they made daily in the classroom were suspect and of little worth.

The accountability movement caused educators to search for "hard data" by which to assess their efforts. What teachers observed, by inference, therefore, was "soft data." The "hardest," most objective data available may be that collected by an *enlightened* teaching team that systematically and collectively gathers data over time in the real-life, day-to-day interactions and problem solving of the classroom. Conversely, the "softest," most suspect data may be that which is designed and collected by testing "experts" external to the school setting and ignorant of the school's mission, values, and goals, the community's culture and socioeconomics, and the classroom's mix of learning styles, teaching strategies, and group dynamics in which their tests are administered.

Leaders assist the teaching staff to design strategies for collecting data and to use the assessment data as feedback and a guide to informed and reflective practice. Staff members will need help in learning how to design feedback spirals, including multiple ways of gathering such data, establishing criteria for judgment, and working together to develop common understanding, reliability of observations, and reporting of results.

IN SUMMARY

Because learning to think, to cooperate, and to respect human uniqueness is best learned through imitation and emulation of significant others, leaders strive to model in their own behaviors those same qualities and behaviors that are desired in students and staff.

The development of thinking, individuality, and collegiality as goals of education is not just kid stuff. Education will achieve an intellectual focus when the school becomes an intellectually stimulating environment—a home for the mind for all who dwell there, when all the school's inhabitants realize that freeing human intellectual potential is the goal of education, when staff members strive to get better at it themselves, and when they use their energies to enhance the intelligent behaviors of others. Educational leaders serve as an "Environmental Protection Agency," constantly monitoring the intellectual ecology of the school. Their chief purpose is to insure that thinking, creativity, and collaboration will become neither endangered, nor worse, extinct.

REFERENCES

Baker, W., A. Costa, and S. Shalit. (1997). "The Norms of Collaboration: Attaining Communicative Competence." In A. Costa and R. Liebmann (Eds.), *The Process Centered School: Sustaining a Renaissance Community.* Thousand Oaks, CA: Corwin Press.

Costa, A., and R. Garmston. (1994). *Cognitive Coaching: A Foundation for the Renaissance School.* Norwood, MA: Christopher Gordon.

Costa, A., and R. Garmston. (1998, Spring). Maturing Outcomes. *Encounter: Education for Meaning and Social Justice.* Vol. 11, No. 1, pp. 10–18.

Costa, A., and B. Kallick. (1995). *Assessment in the Learning Organization: Shifting the Paradigm.* Alexandria, VA: Association for Supervision and Curriculum Development.

Costa, A., and R. Liebmann. (1997). *Process as Content: Envisioning a Renaissance Curriculum.* Thousand Oaks, CA: Corwin Press.

Covey, S. (1989). *The Seven Habits of Highly Effective People.* New York: Simon and Schuster.

Feuerstein, R., R. Feuerstein, and Y. Schur. (1997). "Process as Content in Education Particularly for Retarded Performers." In A. Costa and R. Liebmann (Eds.), *Supporting the Spirit of Learning: When Process Is Content.* Thousand Oaks, CA: Corwin Press.

Frymier, J. (1987, September). "Bureaucracy and the Neutering of Teachers." *Phi Delta Kappan,* p. 10.

Fullan, M. (1993). *Change Forces.* New York: Falmer.

Garmston, R., and B. Wellman. (1997). "Developing Adaptive Schools." In A. Costa and R. Liebmann (Eds.), *The Process Centered School: Sustaining a Renaissance Community.* Thousand Oaks, CA: Corwin Press.

Glickman, C. (1985). *Supervision of Instruction: A Developmental Approach.* Newton, MA: Allyn and Bacon.

Goodlad, John I. (1984). *A Place Called School: Prospects for the Future.* New York: McGraw-Hill.

Harvey, O. J. (1966). "System Structure, Flexibility and Creativity." In O. J. Harvey (Ed.), *Experience, Structure, and Adaptability.* New York: Springer.

Jackson, P. (1968). *Life in Classrooms.* New York: Holt Rinehart Winston.

Joyce, B., and B. Showers. (1988). *Student Achievement through Staff Development.* New York: Longmans.

Kotulak, R. (1997). *Inside the Brain: Revolutionary Discoveries of How the Mind Works.* Kansas City, MO: Andrews McMeel Publishing.

Lambert, L. (1998). *Building Leadership Capacity in Schools.* Alexandria, VA: Association for Supervision and Curriculum Development.

Land, G., and B. Jarman (1992). *Break-Point and Beyond: Mastering the Future Today.* New York: Harper.

Leonard, G. (1978). *The Silent Pulse: A Search for the Perfect Rhythm That Exists in Each of Us.* New York: Bantam Books.

MacLean, P. (1978). "A Mind of Three Minds: Educating the Triune Brain." In J. E. Chall and M. Mursky (Eds.), *Education and the Brain.* Chicago: University of Chicago Press.

Rosenholtz, S. (1989). *Teacher's Workplace: The Social Organization of Schools.* New York: Longman.

Saphier, J., and M. King. (1985, March). "Good Seeds Grow in Strong Cultures." *Educational Leadership,* pp. 67–74.

Sarason, S. (1991). *The Predictable Failure of Educational Reform.* San Francisco: Jossey-Bass.

Senge, P. (1990). *The Fifth Discipline.* New York: Doubleday.

Senge, P., R. Ross, B. Smith, C. Roberts, and A. Kleiner. (1994). *The Fifth Discipline Fieldbook.* New York: Doubleday.

Shavelson, R. (1976). "Teacher Decision Making." *The Psychology of Teaching Methods. 1976 Yearbook of the National Society for the Study Education. Part I.* Chicago: University of Chicago Press.

Sprinthall, R., and L. Theis-Sprinthall. (1983). "The Teacher as an Adult Learner: A Cognitive Developmental View." *Staff Development: 82nd Yearbook of the National Society for the Study of Education. Part II*. Chicago: University of Chicago Press.

Vygotsky, L. (1978). *Society of Mind*. Cambridge, MA: Harvard University Press.

Differentiating Instruction in the Classroom: Tapping into the Intelligence of *Every* Learner

by Dorothy S. Strickland

Sara glances around her room. She feels lucky to work in a district that is forward looking. She has a nice supply of children's literature, which keeps increasing each year. Her students' writing is everywhere, on the bulletin boards inside the classroom and in the corridors just outside. Their work can be read in the library corner and at the publishing table. Like most of the teachers in her school, Sara is gradually changing her instructional practices to reflect new knowledge about learning and teaching: she attempts to contextualize the teaching of skills for reading and writing and to integrate the teaching of all the language arts; she no longer swears by the three reading group format she used routinely for so many years; and she announces with pride that her students now do as much writing in a couple of months as they used to do in an entire year.

By all accounts, Sara and her colleagues are moving with confidence toward more holistic, literature-based instruction. Yet, they share a mixed bag of excitement and uneasiness. There is excitement about the learning that is taking place before their very eyes each day. But there is uneasiness about community concern over attention to the basics. Given the diversity of student abilities and backgrounds in her classroom, even successful teachers like Sara express anxiety over the district's call for uniform high standards. As

From a paper based on a presentation at the Fourth International Teaching for Intelligence Conference, April 24, 1998, New York, NY. © 1998 Dorothy S. Strickland. Reprinted with permission.

she prepares for the week ahead, Sara reflects on the issues she continues to find most challenging:

Organizing for instruction. "I know it's important to set high standards for everyone, yet I feel it's even more important to adjust the curriculum to meet individual needs. Too much of my teaching is geared to the whole group. But, it's hard to manage children doing different things at once. Flexible grouping is a real challenge."

"Covering" the skills. "In the past, I taught each skill and checked it off one by one. I suppose that could be called teaching to a uniform standard, but it only worked for some students. Now I try to go beyond merely covering the skills to vary the type and intensity of instruction to children's needs. More children are progressing, but I could sure use some help in making those decisions."

Monitoring progress. "With skill-by-skill teaching, I simply tested periodically to see who was 'getting it' and who was not and moved on to teach the next set of skills. Now, I see the need to continually assess and alter instruction. What I need are some manageable strategies for assessment."

Helping low-achieving students. "I worry about meeting the needs of my low-achieving students. I realize now where I let them down in the past. But I need help with managing materials and time. Also, I need teaching strategies that help these children get what they need within the framework of the regular day.

"In the elementary classroom, at least, treating everyone the same may not mean that everyone is treated fairly. The way I teach now really points up the diversity among my students. It has made differentiating instruction my biggest challenge."

Providing for individual differences is arguably one of the greatest challenges facing language arts teachers today. No doubt this has always been the case, but it has become even more evident as teachers move away from simply *delivering the curriculum* to focus on *making the curriculum accessible* to each and every student. Sara is like many teachers who have embraced some new ideas and experienced some success. She is more reflective about her teaching and more demanding of herself. Teachers like Sara, whether they are new to the profession or seasoned teachers in the midst of change, face new challenges as they attempt to think differently about their role in the classroom and about the reading and writing processes. According to Scharer (1992) and Pace (1992), most teachers find change difficult and anxiety producing. Support from peers and from the profession is important so that teachers know that they are not alone and that the self-questioning they do is in the tradition of reflective teaching.

The issues raised by teachers such as Sara are not the products of failure but the concerns of clear-thinking, reflective practitioners. Moreover, the questions they ask are major issues in language arts instruction today. Educators are attempting to meet public demands for setting high uniform standards for every student in settings where learner variability is inevitable and persistent. They know that setting standards alone does not make learning happen. Learning is highly dependent on effective classroom teaching that offers each child an equal chance to meet those standards. Ironically, this means less standardized teaching and more differentiation of approaches and strategies within a unified framework. This article addresses these issues and offers suggestions from the classrooms of informed and resourceful teachers engaged in the process of change.

> **Setting standards alone does not make learning happen.**

ORGANIZING FOR INSTRUCTION: FLEXIBLE GROUPING

One of the misconceptions that paralleled the advent of "whole language" was the notion that holistically oriented approaches were synonymous with whole-group instruction. Indeed, teachers were continually warned of the dangers of long-term, ability grouping—and rightly so. There is considerable research evidence to support these cautions (Allington 1983; Hiebert 1983; Pallas, Entwisle, Alexander, and Stluka 1994). Resistance to all ability-based instruction in the regular classroom is misguided, however, and often renders lower-achieving students with few opportunities for instruction tailored to their needs. Students who are progressing rapidly may also miss out on opportunities for special projects and the extension of ideas previously introduced to the entire class. Even when teachers attempt to provide frequent individual conferences in reading and writing, there are times when gathering a small group of students who have similar needs is the most effective and efficient way to provide extra support. As Roller so aptly stated: "We must remember that ability grouping and special pull-out programs arose as a solution to the real problem of variability in children's acquisition of literacy. To return to uniform instruction, uniform materials, and uniform expectations is unrealistic. Variability exists" (Roller 1996, 9).

Organizing instruction to account for variability offers students opportunities to work with others whose literacy development is most like theirs as well as those whose skills and abilities differ from theirs. Groups based on instructional needs are continually re-formed according to the results of ongoing evaluation and all children are exposed to a wide variety of heterogeneous grouping for a variety of purposes (Fountas and Pinnell 1996; Worthy and Hoffman 1996). Students receive regular, planned opportunities to learn through varied formats, including whole-group, small-group (including pairs), and one-to-one formats, heterogeneous and homogeneous groupings, and direct and indirect instruction. Although variety is emphasized, flexible grouping structures are highly predictable so that students and teachers have a sense of order and continuity.

> **Multilevel instruction acknowledges that children come to the classroom with varying backgrounds and abilities.**

One possible framework for use in planning for differentiated instruction starts with the assumption that there will be a large block of time designated for language arts each day. While this time is devoted to planned, systematic instruction in reading, writing (including spelling and grammar), and oral language, these skills are addressed throughout the day in all areas of the curriculum. Conversely, topics under study in subject areas such as science and social studies may provide the content through which the language arts are taught during the block of time designated for language arts. I have worked with teachers who had as little as 80 minutes specified for their language arts block and others who had as much as 120 minutes. The suggested format includes a whole-group segment for approximately 30 minutes, a brief planning time of 5 to 10 minutes, and a workshop segment for approximately 60 minutes. Following are some tips for planning.

Start by planning the whole-group activity. Consider each weekly plan as part of a larger unit of work or thematic focus, extending over several weeks' time. During the week under consideration, decide whether to work on a particular story or group of stories, a unit of poetry, or perhaps some informational material linked to the science curriculum. Decide what materials will be used: trade books, core literacy textbooks, content area materials, or collaboratively written charts. Plan lessons using a *whole-part-whole* framework (Strickland

1998). Start with *whole,* meaningful texts and encourage a variety of types of response. Focus on students' comprehension and construction of meaning. Follow this with explicit attention to specific textual features (the *parts* of written language) and conventions of print. Whole texts provide students with a purposeful basis for looking closely at parts of language. These may include specific phonics elements such as a sound-letter relationship, the use of quotation marks in dialogue, or interesting leads that authors use to grab and hold readers. After highlighting the parts through explicit instruction, reinforce the attention given them by returning to the original text or extending into other *whole* text activities.

Whole-group instruction usually ends with a follow-up assignment for the entire class. It is important that this task be *multilevel,* that is, all students should be able to approach it with a degree of success. Multilevel instruction acknowledges that children come to the classroom with varying backgrounds and abilities. It allows teachers to engage students in similar educational processes with the expectation that there will be variability in individual response. Thus, each child truly has an "equitable opportunity" to move forward toward meeting the curriculum performance standards. Writing assignments such as creating alternative texts (spin-offs based on works students have read and discussed) are examples of multilevel activities. They are a major departure from traditional seatwork activities, which usually are of the clone variety. That is, all children fill in the blanks, copy from the board, or answer a set of factual questions in which the goal is to have every student produce precisely the same product. Clone assignments keep children busy while the teacher works with small groups. But, because they are geared to the average student, they tend to frustrate struggling learners and offer little or no challenge to those who are progressing rapidly.

Use the planning time to make sure that everyone knows what is expected. Take a few minutes to discuss the who, what, where, and when of the workshop activities to follow whole-group instruction. Use name charts, lists, and other devices to help children ascertain who will work in small groups, who has a one-to-one conference with the teacher, whose turn it is to work with a buddy at the computer, which small group may go to the library, and so on. These procedures, as well as classroom routines related to conduct during activity time, need to be introduced gradually during the early part of the year and reinforced as the year proceeds. Each new routine or activity must be explained, demonstrated, and even rehearsed, where applicable, so that students may work as independently as possible.

Use the workshop for both teacher-assisted and independent activities. One useful way to think about the workshop segment is to envision it in terms of three smaller segments. Each child spends at least one segment to do the follow-up (to whole group) assignment already described. For some students, one segment is spent with the teacher in a small-group, direct instruction format in which the materials and instructional focus are tailored to meet group needs. These students will spend the remaining time at centers, doing research, working on projects, involved in buddy reading, having a one-to-one conference with the teacher, working in a reader response group, or doing any of the other various options that may be available. Some students may spend the two remaining segments involved in two or more of these activities. On occasion, three mixed-ability literature response groups might be operating simultaneously, with the teacher circulating among them. Establishing a clear pattern for these activities is extremely important and takes time. Response groups, in particular, need to be introduced in whole-group settings and then modeled by small groups with the remainder of the class observing. In this way, students will experience the process in advance and understand what is expected. My experience indicates that once the patterns are established, these classrooms run smoothly. And, in fact, teachers tell me there are fewer discipline problems because students have opportunities to work in a variety of ways rather than working entirely in whole-group, teacher-directed instruction.

"COVERING" THE SKILLS: ATTENDING TO THE PARTS AS WELL AS THE WHOLE

Providing for individual differences has always been an issue. In the past, however, the primary focus of teachers was given to moving students through a highly linear, skills-based curriculum. The teachers' responsibility was to present the material in a logical and sequential manner. The same scope and sequence was assumed to be suitable for everyone. Adjustments for individual differences focused primarily on the rate at which students moved through a given set of activities and materials. Today's effective teachers are attending to skills within a more purposeful framework. The difference occurs in how, when, and why they teach skills, as well as in the meaning they attach to skills (Dudley-Marling 1996).

Today's teachers are expected to take greater control over all the decisions involved in the instructional process. They are required to move beyond instruction that merely adjusts to students' rates of learning. At the very least, they must orchestrate a wide array of elements, including student achievement rates, teaching methods, and instructional materials. In order to be effective, they must pay close attention to the performance goals or benchmarks set by the school or district in which they teach. These generally are linked closely to statewide content and performance standards. Au, Carroll, and Scheu stressed the importance of local performance goals: "Because they generally are stated in more specific terms than national, state, and/or district standards, benchmarks help teachers and students understand the expectations at their grade level and work toward them" (Au, Carroll, and Scheu 1997, 293). Teachers are held accountable for the performance goals outlined for their grade level, however, they frequently are given considerable latitude in how they will go about addressing them. Curriculum supervisors have told us that most often they encourage teachers to think of performance goals in an integrated way. Teachers are cautioned against treating them in a linear manner by mindlessly moving through the list, treating each as an isolated objective, checking it off, and moving on to the next. Yatvin (1991) suggested that all teachers have at least an unconscious curriculum that dictates what is noticed that needs to be taught. Ideally, the district's stated curriculum should be the one that teachers draw upon as the basis for capitalizing on teachable moments and for assessing progress.

> **Teachers have at least an unconscious curriculum that dictates what is noticed that needs to be taught.**

Determining which skills and strategies will be taught involves (1) teacher familiarity with and attention to school and district-wide standards, (2) student learning opportunities that target the skills and strategies underlying those standards in a systematic and explicit manner within a holistic framework, (3) an abundance of student opportunities for meaningful application of skills and strategies through *planned* indirect instruction, (4) student accountability for what has been taught, (5) ongoing teacher monitoring of skills used in meaningful and purposeful situations, and (6) multilevel tasks and activities for student application of skills and for monitoring progress.

MONITORING PROGRESS: DOCUMENTATION IS NOT ENOUGH

Monitoring progress is at the heart of a successful program in which instruction is differentiated. Teachers who respect and respond to variability are constantly alert to individual needs and the implications for instruction. They use assessment to focus on students' strengths rather than just their weaknesses (National Center for Fair and Open Testing 1998). New forms of instruction in the language arts, such as literature response circles and cooperative learning groups, have created a need for new forms of assessment. "Conventional standardized tests, in which students can respond only in a multiple-choice format, cannot adequately assess students' learning of complex forms of reading and writing" (Au, Carroll, and Scheu 1997, 281). Students' progress must be documented on an ongoing basis, but merely documenting progress is not enough. The instructional decisions that are based on that documentation are what really count. Increasingly, teachers are integrating a system of ongoing, informal classroom assessment into their instructional programs. They have discovered that this type of documentation more truly reveals student needs as opposed to norm-referenced standardized tests or even teacher-developed paper-and-pencil tests alone (Calfee and Hiebert 1988). Viewed in this way, assessment is used to support better teaching and transform schooling rather than reify existing problems and inequalities (Darling-Hammond 1994).

> Teachers who respect and respond to variability are constantly alert to individual needs and the implications for instruction.

Students need to know that everything they do in the language arts class is important and that in one way or another it counts. Self-selected, independent reading and reader response groups sometimes are viewed by students as less important than a test or other types of written work: "After all, we choose the books ourselves" or "We're just talking about what we read." Teachers complain that these activities are difficult to monitor. They want simple but useful management systems for documenting student progress in a variety of areas.

By keeping the district's curriculum objectives in mind and offering students many opportunities to participate in activities of the type described under "covering skills," teachers can engage students in holistic, literature-based activities and still chart progress on targeted strategies over time. The information gathered can be analyzed in at least three ways: (1) progress of the individual learner in relationship to him- or herself, (2) progress of the individual learner in terms of the group, and (3) progress of the group as a whole. Each of these ways offers teachers insight into what skills need extra emphasis. Most important, teachers have a sense of where that emphasis should be placed: at the whole-group level, through small, needs-based groups, or through more personalized attention. Following are two examples of systems for monitoring literacy activities that many teachers find difficult to assess.

Monitoring reader response groups. Literature circles offer teachers an opportunity to use oral response to literature as a window into how children are thinking and responding to text (Roser and Martinez 1995). Strickland worked with several teachers to construct a method for evaluating the reading skills and strategies during such discussions (Strickland, Dillon, Funkhouser, Glick, and Rogers 1989). Peterson and Eeds (1990) also offered a system for monitoring students' preparation for and participation in literature study groups. A scheme for documenting discussion in these groups, which is based on both efforts, uses a response group assessment form that includes the date, the prompt or focus for the discussion, and the name of the students in the response group. During the discussion, the teacher makes comments next to each child's name regarding the following: (1) preparation for the discussion, (2) the quality of participation, (3) the application of knowledge about literary concepts (e.g., plot, theme, genre, characterization, etc.), and (4) the application of knowledge about aspects of reading comprehension (making predictions, getting the main idea, using supporting details, comparing and contrasting, etc.). Teachers may participate in the discussion or merely observe. The strategy has undergone several mutations as teachers attempted to keep the form as simple as possible without sacrificing the content they were after.

Keeping track of independent reading. Reader response journals are a major resource for helping students and teachers keep track of independent reading. Brief one-to-one conferences with children about their self-selected reading also go a long way to giving this kind of activity the stature it deserves as the most important practice for reading development (Greaney 1980; Anderson, Wilson, and Fielding 1988). In the past, too often only those children who finished their work early had time for independent reading. Enlightened about its importance, today's teachers are more apt to make independent reading, in and out of school, an integral part of their reading programs.

Teachers also are aware that this is an effective way to adjust materials to students' reading levels and interests. Children can, of course, keep their own records of their personal reading. However, the use of personalized conferences transforms the recordkeeping into a key time for documenting and monitoring progress. A three-ring binder with pages for each child provides a quick and easy method for recording information. Pages can be arranged alphabetically, according to each child's last name, for easy reference.

Conferences are scheduled for each child every one or two weeks and include the following:

Questions and discussion. Questions that can be asked about any book are useful to get the conversation started; for example, Well, how are you enjoying this book so far? How does this book compare with other books of this type? By this author? At times, the reader response journal may become the focus of the discussion.

Oral reading. After a brief discussion the child is asked to read a portion of the book aloud. The selection may be chosen by the teacher or prepared in advance by the student. Some teachers keep an audiocassette on hand for each child and record the oral reading or the entire conference. Over a year's time, each child has several such conferences recorded to place into a portfolio or to send home to parents as a gift.

Documentation. The teacher engages in a type of diagnostic recordkeeping in which information about the child's reading strategies, reading preferences, and ability to talk confidently about books is noted.

This very simple method of conducting individualized conferences fits easily into the framework for organization outlined. After several conferences, the written documentation may be grouped together and placed in students' portfolios as evidence of the amount, breadth, and overall proficiency of their independent reading.

HELPING LOW-ACHIEVING STUDENTS: TIME, MATERIALS, STRATEGIES

Addressing the needs of struggling readers and writers is one of the most perplexing problems teachers face. Low-achieving students need extra time, they need materials with which they can feel successful, and they need strategies that work for them. Attention to these learners within the regular classroom is important for several reasons.

Supplementary remedial programs such as Title I and "replacement" programs that substitute for regular in-class instruction have had mixed results over the years (Johnston, Allington, and Afflerback 1989). Some people argue that such programs cause classroom teachers to overrely on special help and neglect their responsibility for less able students. Others suggest that where these programs exist, instruction within and outside the classroom often is at odds with each other. Even when such programs are considered successful, most agree that they work best where there is a strong compatible instructional program in the student's regular classroom. The classroom will, no doubt, continue to be the mainstay of students' instructional performance. Therefore, regardless of the supplemental help offered, more attention needs to be given to incorporating the best prevention and intervention procedures into regular classroom instructional practice.

> **Addressing the needs of struggling readers and writers is one of the most perplexing problems teachers face.**

Many of the needs of these students have already been addressed: (1) classroom management that allows for flexible grouping gives low-achieving students more time in small groups and personalized instructional formats in which their needs can receive specific attention, (2) planned, independent reading activities that encourage children to select books that match their interests and reading abilities provide the kind of practice they need most, (3) multilevel activities help ensure that students who are struggling will engage in the same intellectual processes as other students with expectations that are challenging for them but also realistic, and, of course, (4) consistent monitoring of progress helps to inform instruction so that low-achieving students receive attention in those areas where they need help. Two types of activities that have a strong payoff for less able students are those in which teachers mediate to help make difficult texts, such as those in the content areas, more readable and strategies that engage children in a variety of rereading activities.

Making what they "must read" readable. Less able readers need specific instruction in the use of strategies for comprehending texts (Maria 1996; Dole, Valencia, Greer, and Wardrop 1991). Following are two activities that can help smooth the way for struggling readers and promote better access to key ideas for the better readers as well: (1) List potentially troublesome vocabulary words/concepts. Lead students in a discussion of the words and predicting what the selection might be about. Write their predictions on the board and periodically confirm or disconfirm them during the reading. (2) Read aloud the first paragraph or two after introducing a selection, as the students follow along. Have several children summarize what they learned or tell one new thing they learned from the passage you read. Students may volunteer their contributions individually or they may collaborate in pairs or groups and then share with the class. Continue, asking individual students to read aloud, as the others follow along. The oral reading should be preceded by opportunities for everyone to read the passage silently. After the oral reading make sure to include some of the struggling readers in summarizing or telling something new they learned. When appropriate, guide students to include some of the new vocabulary in their statements. Their statements should be listed on a chart to form a student-created summary of the selection. The chart then serves as a reduced version of the key ideas in the passage. It may be referred to and reread periodically as a review of the topic, both with the whole group and as a follow-up in small-group, teacher-directed activities with less able readers.

> Research suggests that the best readers read widely and often.

Rereading of familiar texts. Research suggests that the best readers read widely and often (Greaney 1980; Anderson, Wilson, and Fielding 1988). Fortunately, the very act of reading helps to build vocabulary and fluency and is the best way to apply developing skills. Unfortunately, research suggests that poor readers actually spend far less time actually engaged in reading than more able readers (Allington 1983). Rereading opportunities such as choral reading (students read orally together, usually with the teacher as lead reader), echo reading (students "echo" a fluent reader's rendition of a selection, one sentence at a time), read along (students read along silently while listening to a fluent reader read aloud or to a tape recording of the selection), partner reading (two students take turns rereading a selection aloud to one another), and reader's theater (students are assigned roles and reread the selection as a play) are especially helpful. Not only do less able readers and writers need more time involved in direct instruction, they need more time to independently apply what they have learned in situations in which they can experience enough success to self-monitor their own reading and writing behaviors.

CONCLUSION

To be effective, classroom teachers must juggle a myriad of factors simultaneously, and they must do it in a way that creates a positive learning environment for every child they teach. Legislators and administrators who offer policy initiatives calling for uniform standards and high expectations would do well to keep learner variability in mind, not as an excuse for poor performance but as a factor that must be addressed if every child is to succeed. Each day, many teachers demonstrate that this can be done. Many others need help through professional development in order to become more proficient. Recognizing the reality of learner variability and approaching it as a natural part of the instructional process can help students achieve. Rather than something to work around, correct, or complain about, learner variability becomes a factor that teachers and administrators know they have the ability to address. Providing quality instruction and support so that all children have the opportunity to learn is the best way to express belief in the notion that "all children can learn."

Sara reflects:

> "I have no intention of going backwards to the old ways. I realize that back then I concentrated more on teaching than on learning. It helps to know that the questions I am raising are shared by others. I am striving to make my teaching more skillful and strategic. It is the best hope I can give all my students to help them meet high expectations and standards. Each day I feel that I am growing in my understanding of the teaching/learning process—and my students are achieving. I have made a personal commitment to continue to reflect, rethink, and respond—but never to retreat."

REFERENCES

Allington, R. L. (1983). The reading instruction provided readers of differing reading abilities. *Elementary School Journal* 83: 548–559.

Anderson, R., P. T. Wilson, and L. Fielding. (1988). Growth in reading and how children spend their time outside of school. *Reading Research Quarterly* 23: 285–303.

Au, K., J. Carroll, and J. Scheu. (1997). *Balanced literacy instruction: A teacher's resource book.* Norwood, MA: Christopher-Gordon.

Calfee, R., and E. Hiebert. (1988). The teacher's role in using assessment to improve learning. In C. V. Bunderson (Ed.), *Assessment in the service of learning.* Princeton, NJ: Educational Testing Service.

Darling-Hammond, L. (1994). Performance-based assessment and educational equity. *Harvard Educational Review* 64: 5–30.

Dole, J. A., S. W. Valencia, E. A. Greer, and J. L. Wardrop. (1991). Effects of two types of prereading instruction on the comprehension of narrative and expository text. *Reading Research Quarterly* 26: 142–158.

Dudley-Marling, C. (1996). Explicit instruction within a whole language framework: Teaching struggling readers and writers. In E. McIntyre and M. Pressley (Eds.), *Balanced instruction: Strategies and skills in whole language.* Norwood, MA: Christopher-Gordon.

Fountas, I. C., and G. S. Pinnell. (1996). *Guided reading.* Portsmouth, NH: Heinemann.

Greaney, V. (1980). Factors related to amount and type of leisure-time reading. *Reading Research Quarterly* 15: 337–357.

Hiebert, E. H. (1983). An examination of ability grouping for reading instruction. *Reading Research Quarterly* 18: 231–255.

Johnston, P., R. Allington, and P. Afflerback. (1989). The congruence of classroom and remedial reading instruction. *Elementary School Journal* 85: 513–528.

Maria, K. (1996). Reading comprehension instruction for disabled readers. In Lillian R. Putnam (Ed.), *How to become a better teacher of reading.* Englewood Cliffs, NJ: Prentice Hall.

National Center for Fair and Open Testing (1998). Cambridge, MA: www.fairtest.org.

Pace, G. (1992). Stories of teacher-initiated change from traditional to whole language literacy instruction. *Elementary School Journal* 92: 461–476.

Pallas, A.M., D. R. Entwisle, K. L. Alexander, and M. F. Stluka. (1994). Ability-group effects: Instructional, social, or institutional? *Sociology of Education* 67: 27–46.

Peterson, R., and M. Eeds. (1990). *Grand conversations.* New York: Scholastic.

Roller, C. M. (1996). *Variability not disability.* Newark, DE: International Reading Association.

Roser, N., and M. Martinez. (Eds.). (1995). *Book talk and beyond: Children and teachers respond to literature.* Newark, DE: International Reading Association.

Scharer, P. L. (l992). Teachers in transition: An exploration of changes in teachers and classrooms during the implementation of literature-based reading instruction. *Research in the Teaching of English* 20: 408–443.

Strickland, D. S., R. M. Dillon, L. Funkhouser, M. Glick, and C. Rogers. (l989). Research currents: Classroom dialogue during literature response groups. *Language Arts* 66: 193–200.

Strickland, D. S. (1998). What's basic in reading instruction: Finding common ground. *Educational Leadership* 55: 7–10.

Worthy, J., and J. V. Hoffman. (1996). Critical questions. *The Reading Teacher* 49: 656–657.

Yatvin, J. (l991). *Developing a whole language program.* Newark, DE: International Reading Association.

Teaching for Intelligence: Parameters for Change

by Eric J. Cooper and Daniel U. Levine

I n the United States, emphasis on education reform for supporting social change has reached new heights through calls for change in the popular press, in educational journals, newsletters, and on the Internet. Yet, significant factors that will stall change reside in how reform is implemented, that is, the standards for what students know and need to know, how we implement professional development activities, and the ability of reformers to bridge the gap between policy and good implementation (Levine and Cooper 1991).

In many localities, school system leaders have called for teaching the basics—often forcing the district into implementing a curriculum that defines learning into separate pieces and the teaching of skills and knowledge taught independently of their context (Berryman and Bailey 1992). Yet, recent analyses cited in the popular press suggest the importance of teaching advanced thinking in the context of their subject matter and in conjunction with a new reality of the workplace, which indicates, for example, there is no difference in high school course-taking between a future engineer and an auto-trade journeyman (Barth 1997). The point is that all students will have to be taught advanced thinking.

How localities deal with implementation of change and the change process often decides the ability of a school system and community to remain competitive in the global economy and remain a viable place to live (White 1997). It is our contention that there are some general conclusions that are particularly pertinent for projects to improve students' performance in thinking and other higher-order skills. The general conclusions can be summarized as follows:

From a paper based on a presentation at the Fourth International Teaching for Intelligence Conference, April 22–25, 1998, New York, NY. © 1998 Eric J. Cooper and Daniel U. Levine. Reprinted with permission.

•   Successful innovations to improve instruction in thinking and other higher-order skills will generally have to be relatively large and complex.

•   If educators select a thinking-skills approach that utilizes specific teaching materials in order to enhance manageability for teachers or for other reasons, care should be taken to allow, encourage, and assist participating teachers to adapt the materials to the realities of their classrooms.

•   Whether or not the selected thinking-skills approach utilizes specific sets of teaching materials, project administrators should attempt to identify core components that require fidelity in implementation, and they should work with teachers to ensure that these components are stressed and implemented well.

•   Because thinking-skills approaches require large, complex, and difficult changes in the behaviors and attitudes of teachers and students, even more stress than usual should be placed on ensuring that innovations are manageable and implementable for teachers and that prerequisites and antecedents of successful implementation are firmly in place. Concern for manageability and prerequisites should include attention to such considerations as planning time, class size, change overload, amount of paperwork, adaptability in participating classrooms, compatibility with other demands, capacity for inspiring commitment, and large-scale staff development.

•   Predictable obstacles that should be addressed in advance include school realities that stress classroom order and passive learning, students' preferences for lower-order skills, student/teacher compromises that trade obedience for undemanding instruction, low-level learning scripts for low achievers, and teacher preferences for easy-to-teach lessons.

•   Projects to improve students' thinking are likely to be greatly hampered when student assessment focuses on low-level skills.

•   Successful implementation of approaches for improving thinking skills requires unusual stress on revising organizational and institutional arrangements and structures.

•   Initiation of effective projects for improving thinking skills is an imposing challenge not to be undertaken lightly (Levine and Cooper 1991, 388).[1]

A second overriding issue frequently addressed in research and analysis on the change process involves the extent to which initiative and decision making should emphasize "top-down" mandates or "bottom-up" participation. This issue is somewhat related to the fidelity/adaptation question, inasmuch as top-down approaches generally tend to emphasize fidelity to a mandate as compared to an adaptation emphasis that places relatively greater stress on widespread participation in determining the nature and details of implementation. And parallel to recent movement toward acceptance of the possibilities for faithful implementation of core components in a predetermined approach to innovation, research and analysis seem to be moving toward more stress on the importance and value of appropriate top-down initiative. During the 1970s and 1980s, many researchers and academic observers placed most of their emphasis on the need for teacher participation in initiating and guiding innovation, but during the 1990s, some research has shifted toward a more balanced conclusion.

Probably the best example of recent recognition of the role and possibilities of top-down leadership in bringing about successful change has been provided in longitudinal studies conducted by Miles (1983) and his colleagues. Miles summarized much of this research in an article in which he outlined the forces leading to "institutionalization" of innovation as follows:

> . . . high administrative commitment tends to lead to both administrative pressure on users to implement the innovation, along with administrative support, which often shows up in the form of assistance to users. Both the pressure and the assistance tend to lead to increased user effort. . . . the harder people worked at an innovation, the more committed they grew; that commitment was also fueled by increasing technical mastery of the innovation.
>
> Commitment and mastery both lead toward increasing stabilization of use . . . [which is] aided if administrators decide to mandate the innovation, which also naturally increases the percentage of use . . . [that in turn decisively encourages institutionalization] (Miles 1983, 18).

Emphasizing top-down action in bringing about change is not necessarily the same, of course, as de-emphasizing bottom-up participation. For one thing, the conclusions just quoted were concerned with institutionalization, not just initial mastery and implementation, and certainly Miles and his colleagues would be among the last researchers anywhere to ignore or play down the importance of teacher participation and commitment in designing and implementing innovation. In addition, their conclusions continue to emphasize the importance of "teacher-administrator harmony" and of "both teacher mastery/commitment and administrative action" (Miles

1983, 19). Nevertheless, their data and conclusions do provide an important balance to the work of some others who have tended to minimize the necessity for and possibilities of strong top-down mandates and action in carrying out innovation successfully.

Hall and Hord (1987) and Crandall, Eiseman, and Louis (1986) also have reviewed research related to the top-down/bottom-up issue and reached conclusions similar to those of Miles and his colleagues. Elaborating on some of the important considerations involved in devising and implementing innovations, Hall and Hord stressed that "mandates and decrees" are helpful in providing clear indications of priority, and Crandall, Eiseman, and Louis concluded that a strategy based on mandates by strong leaders "appears to require five elements: absence of debilitating conflict; an effective, debugged innovation; continuity of leadership; frequent reminders that successful and faithful implementation is important; and adequate resources and support" (Crandall, Eiseman, and Louis 1986, 40–41).

IMPLICATIONS FROM RESEARCH

The legacy of research from the 1980s is the conclusion that teachers must change their teaching practices in the direction of concentrating more time and effort on concept development, cognitive development, reasoning, thinking, higher-order comprehension skills, and advanced subject matter (Harris and Cooper 1985). A strong base of research linking cognitive development to prior knowledge in learning emerged in the late 1970s (Langer 1982). Those studies concluded that, particularly when reading is the learning mode, students with much prior knowledge and experience relevant to a subject have less difficulty learning new material and retain more than students with inadequate or incomplete prior knowledge and experience. Students need the benefit of teachers who know how to access prior knowledge that the students might not be aware of and that might help them with the material to be learned (Cooper and Sherk 1989).

Finding ways to help students relate what they already know to what is to be learned is often called preteaching or preparation. Research has suggested that teachers accomplish this in several ways. One way is by encouraging students to make predictions before a reading and/or learning task (Cooper and Sherk 1989). Predicting, based on the students' prior knowledge of the topic of a reading selection and on what students think the reading selection will be about, helps students to become aware of their knowledge base. It also helps them to focus closely upon how the text informs the reader (Cooper and Sherk 1989).

Another transportable practice is to allow students to examine the structure of textual material before detailed reading takes place. For example, if students can determine that they are going to read a narrative selection, then they can review their knowledge of the narrative structure (i.e., a narrative has a set-ting, characters, plot beginning, and is often structured in terms of organizational patterns in time/sequence and problem/solution). If the selection is an expository one, students can be alerted to look for signals that indicate a particular relationship of ideas (organiza-tional patterns such as cause-effect, compari-son-contrast, and/or problem-solution; and chronology or sequence). Teachers are in the best position to point out such distinctions to their students and to determine how best to utilize the text for problem solving and decision making (Cooper and Sherk 1989).

> **A strong base of research linking cognitive develop-ment to prior knowl-edge in learning emerged in the late 1970s.**

In considering the ideas generally introduced in this brief article, readers should keep in mind the likelihood that innovations to improve instruction and change in thinking and other higher-order skills (e.g., reflective, critical, and creative analysis in the translation and application of knowledge) generally have to be relatively large and complex. Given the urgency in responding on a wider scale to deepening gulfs between American haves and have-nots, we can not expect significant change to happen school by school, teacher by teacher. Many students are school dependent for learning advanced skills—yet teachers have not had the support to be prepared in the past to offer other effective instruction to enhance higher-order skills (e.g., MacGinitie and MacGinitie 1986), the knowledge base for teaching thinking is still relatively small and undeveloped in terms of classroom practices (Marzano et al. 1987), emphasizing higher-order skills constitutes a major change in many or most classrooms and schools (Goodlad 1984; Perkins 1995), and many students need close guidance and assistance (i.e., mediation) from highly skilled teachers (Marzano et al. 1987).

The general complexity and large magnitude of change involved in innovative projects to improve instruction in thinking was underlined in an analysis of teaching thinking skills prepared by Nickerson, Perkins, and Smith (1985). Although the authors first pointed out that thinking-skills approaches vary considerably with respect to considerations such as the amount of class time devoted to instruction, the specific skills addressed, and the amount of special training for teachers, they also emphasized the general conclusions that teachers of thinking need to be facilitators of knowledge, that students must explore and discover knowledge rather than passively absorb it, that many teachers resist approaches that do not yet offer a clear and definite technology, that assessment of thinking skills is still relatively primitive, and that significant time-on-task opportunity has to be available to students. They further concluded that implementation of any thinking-skills programs should make sure that tasks generally are intrinsically interesting to students, that objectives and exercises should be "calibrated" to "students' current level of knowledge and abilities," that reasons for students' success or failure should be explicitly addressed, that considerable feedback should be provided for students, and that practice should be provided in "a variety of problem contexts" (Nickerson, Perkins, and Smith 1985, 342–343)—no small job for any classroom teacher. If we are to recognize the importance of teaching advanced thinking for preparing students to go to institutions of higher education, to successfully compete in the workplace of the present and future, and to become lifelong learners, we will have to recognize that sustained and cohesive professional development is necessary to reach our goals. Nothing less than total commitment by all stakeholders in school communities, state departments of education, and the federal government to this end will work.

NOTE

1.   Levine, D. U., and E. J. Cooper. The change process and its implications in teaching thinking. In L. Idol and B. Jones (Eds.), *Educational values and cognitive instruction: Implications for reform.* 1991. Hillsdale, NJ: Lawrence Erlbaum Associates, p. 381. Reprinted with permission.

REFERENCES

Barth, P. (1997, November 26). Want to keep American jobs and avert class division? Try high school trip (A little physics goes a long way, too). *Education Week,* pp. 30–33.

Berryman, S. E., and T. R. Bailey. (1992). *The double helix of education and the economy.* New York: Teachers College Press.

Cooper, E. J., and J. Sherk. (1989). Addressing urban school reform: Issues and alliances. *Journal of Negro Education* 58, 3: 315–331.

Crandall, D. P., J. W. Eiseman, and K. S. Louis. (1986). Strategic planning issues that bear on the success of school improvement efforts. *Educational Administration Quarterly* 22, 3: 21–53.

Goodlad, J. I. (1984). *A place called school.* New York: McGraw-Hill.

Hall, G. E., and S. M. Hord. (1987). *Change in schools.* Albany: State University of New York Press.

Harris, T. L., and E. J. Cooper (1985). *Reading, thinking, and concept development.* New York: The College Board.

Langer, J. A. (1982). Facilitating text processing: The elaboration of prior knowledge. In J. A. Langer and M. Smith-Burke (Eds.), *Reader meets author/Bridging the gap.* Newark, DE: International Reading Association.

Levine, D. U., and E. J. Cooper. (1991). The change process and its implications in teaching thinking. In L. Idol and B. Jones (Eds.), *Educational values and cognitive instruction: Implications for reform.* Hillsdale, NJ: Lawrence Erlbaum Associates.

MacGinitie, W. H., and R. K. MacGinitie. (1986). Teaching students not to read. In S. DeCastell, A. Luke, and K. Egan (Eds.), *Literacy, society, and schooling.* Cambridge, England: Cambridge University Press.

Marzano, R. J., R. S. Brandt, C. S. Hughes, B. F. Jones, B. Z. Presseisen, S. C. Rankin, and C. Suhor. (1987). *Dimensions of thinking. A framework for curriculum and instruction.* Alexandria, VA: Association for Supervision and Curriculum Development.

Miles, M. B. (1983). Unraveling the mysteries of institutionalization. *Educational Leadership* 41, 2: 14–19.

Nickerson, R. S., D. N. Perkins, and E. E. Smith. (1985). *The teaching of thinking.* Hillsdale, NJ: Lawrence Erlbaum Associates.

Perkins, D. (1995). *Outsmarting IQ—The emerging science of learnable intelligence.* New York: Simon and Schuster.

White, K. A. (1997, November 26). Jobs will follow better schools, Miami-Dade leaders say. *Education Week,* p. 7.

Considerations in Introducing Instructional Interventions

by Daniel U. Levine and Rayna F. Levine

Many recent analyses have clarified issues involving successful implementation of approaches for bringing about significant improvement in the functioning of public schools. For example, Fullan and Miles (1992) examined the dangers inherent in introducing a large set of fragmented interventions. McKenzie (1995) provided useful material for analyzing and improving the effectiveness of site-based management teams in schools. Researchers participating in the Consortium for Policy Research in Education (1996) have identified central considerations in building capacity for school reform.

Our goal in this article is to contribute to this area of analysis by focusing on issues dealing with selection and implementation of instructional interventions that have a fighting chance to bring about substantial improvement in students' academic performance. We will consider aspects of selection implementation that involve

- neglect of critical prerequisites for successful implementation,
- selection of interventions low in "doability,"
- potential for mischievous misimplementation,
- lack of attention to predictable pitfalls, and
- downplaying of schoolwide and sociological perspectives.

NEGLECT OF CRITICAL PREREQUISITES

Researchers have identified a number of prerequisites required for success when implementing major instructional interventions. Using

From a paper based on a presentation at the Fourth International Teaching for Intelligence Conference, April 22, 1998, New York, NY. ©1998 Daniel U. Levine and Rayna F. Levine. Reprinted with permission.

varied terminology but usually focusing on similar basic concepts, they have identified requirements such as the following (Bullard and Taylor 1994; Levine and Cooper 1990; Levine and Lezotte 1990; Stringfield, Milsap, Scott, and Herman 1996):

• Massive staff development conducted primarily at participating school sites.

• Availability of one or more full- or largely full-time instructional specialists who provide classroom-level technical assistance to teachers.

• Regular monitoring to assess the workability and success of instructional arrangements at each stage of the implementation process.

We will not repeat the arguments and evidence that support the importance of these or other prerequisites for meaningful instructional reform. Instead, we will briefly review some of the reasons why critical prerequisites too often are ignored when planners design and proceed to implement ambitious change efforts.

Failure to recognize a prerequisite in the first place. Decision makers frequently seem unaware of the existence of a given prerequisite. Many reform plans, for example, assume that already overloaded principals somehow can find the time and possess the knowledge to help their teachers master difficult new instructional techniques and strategies. Similarly, reform plans too often assume that traditional staff development approaches involving occasional large-session workshops or short-term, superficial training for a few teacher leaders will result in sustained, meaningful change throughout a participating school.

Relatively high costs of prerequisites. Reform plans that include necessary prerequisites such as full-time instructional specialists in each school or ongoing, site-based staff development for entire faculties generally require considerable additional expenditures. In many cases, concentrating resources to fund these prerequisites to the extent necessary would limit reform efforts to only a few schools at a time. This approach risks allegations of favoritism or discrimination from constituents at other schools and thereby limits political support for the plan. It is easier to ignore expensive prerequisites and proceed "full speed ahead," particularly since decision makers receive accolades, publicity, and/or relief from criticism or state scrutiny when initiating large-scale plans that seek to reform entire systems. Failure will not be evident until a few years later, when administrators have already begun to implement other new, similarly underfunded "reforms."

A *"do something, do anything" mentality.* Tendencies to proceed with interventions that ignore prerequisites for successful change are exacerbated by perceptions that educational problems are too severe to allow for inaction or delay in bringing about systemwide improvement. Strong pressures from community groups, the school board, or high level business executives cause administrators to believe they are being urged to "do something, do anything." In our experience, it is astounding how quickly some administrators cave in to such pressures. Does a fully formed plan exist? Does that plan provide adequate resources and arrangements for staff development? Does it place unreasonably burdensome time demands and recordkeeping tasks on already overloaded teachers? No? No matter—going through the motions may satisfy critics at least temporarily, until the next reform effort replaces the current failed one a few years down the road.

> In our experience, it is astounding how quickly some administrators cave in to such pressures.

LOW DOABILITY INTERVENTIONS

Some interventions devised to improve students' performance are inherently more difficult to implement than others. This obvious truism frequently receives little or no explicit attention when deciding on an intervention or developing plans to implement it. For example, although the possible payoff from individualized, continuous-progress instruction potentially is greater than that from traditional mixtures of whole class and small group instruction, problems in implementing continuous-progress arrangements are so pervasive that they seldom have been addressed successfully in practice.

Similarly, although one of the potential benefits of heterogeneous grouping includes improved performance among low achieving students as well as important gains with respect to desegregation and school climate, productive heterogeneous grouping is extremely difficult to implement in most schools. This is true because typically it requires relatively small classes, well-trained and highly motivated teachers, and introduction of a range of new instructional strategies. Only in the past decade have advocates of heterogeneous grouping devoted much meaningful attention to school and classroom level challenges in delivering heterogeneous instruction effectively, and begun to identify practical strategies for doing so (Wheelock 1992).

Given the predictable problems encountered in implementing widely advocated reforms such as individualized instruction and heterogeneous grouping—not to mention performance assessments and portfolio-based accountability approaches, whole language, inclusion of students with disabilities in regular classes, interdisciplinary curricula emphasizing critical thinking, multiage grouping, and [insert your own favorite contemporary instructional reform approach], it would be prudent for decision makers to study research on the implementation requirements and demonstrated effectiveness of their proposed interventions. Perhaps they should use a "doability" index such as the following to summarize the results of their review:

1. Almost never works; hardly ever will
2. Works occasionally when very well implemented by an outstanding faculty
3. Works occasionally when very well implemented by a capable faculty
4. Usually works when very well implemented by an outstanding faculty
5. Usually works when very well implemented by a capable faculty
6. Almost always works given middling implementation by a mostly capable faculty (probably a null category).

Enhancing implementability. Some innovative approaches are basically nonimplementable in most situations because they are too complex to the point that they are counterproductive. Even though such approaches may incorporate excellent ideas that could improve student achievement, teachers cannot effectively implement highly complex approaches hour after hour, day after day, week after week. In some cases, educators can draw usefully on such approaches by radically simplifying them so they actually can be used in the typical classroom. Examples of potentially useful, but overly complex approaches include implementation of certain elaborate and highly prescribed models for teaching students in accordance with their distinctive learning styles, comprehensive use of cooperative learning arrangements, and planning and delivering all lessons in a specified sequence of steps.

Teachers in some districts have substantially improved instruction by drawing on approaches such as those listed above but, at the same time, explicitly simplifying their implementation. For example, educators in Johnson City, New York, have implemented mastery learning effectively, in part because they followed a relatively simple rule that corrective instruction for initial non-masters must be delivered in a mode different from the original lesson (Levine 1985). By way of contrast, teachers in many other districts have stumbled trying to continually utilize a variety of learning modes that presumably address each student's learning style. As this example shows, simpler is often better when simplification is done for the purpose of making a promising approach more implementable in real schools and classrooms.

INTERVENTIONS HIGH IN POTENTIAL FOR MISCHIEF

Proposals for major institutional reform also should be assessed according to their "Potential for Mischief Quotient" (PFMQ). Assessing proposed reforms in this way recognizes that some are much more susceptible than others to misimplementation. For example, mastery learning when well implemented may produce impressive gains in higher-order skills, but too many mastery learning implementations have involved superficial efforts to ensure that students acquire easily taught low-level skills (Levine 1985).

Another good example is apparent when one visits schools implementing so-called "whole language" approaches that stress the use of literature to teach reading. Frequently lacking comprehensive, ongoing training in how to help poor readers, and working virtually unsupervised and unmonitored, some teachers using this approach do little more than distribute materials and "let the children read." It is tempting for teachers to take this easy way out because their students appear to be functioning in accordance with expectations that they motor through lots of books. Other instructional and organizational approaches that are particularly high in PFMQ include

• Block scheduling in secondary schools, which depends to some extent on the presuppositions that teachers know how to meaningfully plan and deliver appropriate instructional activities using the expanded time, and that students can learn independently in extended blocks of time. In many schools, block scheduling is implemented without assessing or attending to problems involved in helping students who are unprepared or unmotivated to function meaningfully on their own or in small groups (Smith and McNelis 1996).

• Self-esteem improvement efforts that give little or no attention to learning strategies and skills. One reason why these approaches have high PFMQ is because they implicitly encourage users to disregard and postpone the hard work involved in actually bringing about achievement gains that might serve as a stable and potent basis for enhanced self-esteem. In turn, failure of such approaches to improve achievement enables detractors to more credibly go to an opposite extreme and ignore the importance of efforts to bolster students' self-esteem.

In this section, we have cited several superficially attractive ideas that sound as if they offer considerable potential for improving the quality of education. One of them—mastery learning—even has extensive research regarding its effectiveness when well implemented. Susceptible as they are to mischievous misinterpretation and misimplementation, they easily become faddish approaches likely to drop out of sight when the pendulum swings back toward their equally attractive-sounding opposites.

> ... they easily become faddish approaches likely to drop out of sight when the pendulum swings back toward their equally attractive-sounding opposites.

Approaches high in PFMQ share several characteristics. First, implementing them effectively requires more time, commitment, training, resources, and a great deal of hard work. At the same time, they lend themselves to a kind of quick and dirty implementation that appears to conform to the underlying model. Thus, busy teachers can discharge their responsibilities by implementing surface features while ignoring more challenging aspects. With mastery learning, for example, teachers may welcome the chance to teach and reteach small mechanical skills if doing so relieves (or is allowed to relieve) them of responsibility for developing students' mastery of higher-order skills.

Second, approaches that are high in PFMQ generally require significant additional resources to implement effectively, while their susceptibility to surface implementation allows planners to gloss over the fact that needed resources have not been provided. In schools with a substantial proportion of students who do not function well independently, for example, both whole language and block scheduling require relatively low ratios of staff-to-students so that faculty can provide appropriate individual help. In both cases, it is easy for administrators to point to activities and arrangements that theoretically indicate the approach is being implemented even though its fundamental presuppositions are violated in practice.

It is probably no accident that approaches high in PFMQ frequently have been promulgated under the banner of buzzwords or phrases popular during the time period they are most widely implemented—mastery learning in the 1980s and whole language in the early 1990s were yesterday's fads fated to be replaced by today's and then tomorrow's fads. Repetitive hyping in professional journals and newsletters of their promised benefits provided cover for administrators concerned more with responding to political pressures and the desire to be seen as "doing something" than with predictable probabilities that they will be mischievously misimplemented.

We would like to be able to discuss approaches that are very low in PFMQ, but when we limit our consideration to reforms substantial enough to have long-range impact on student performance, we cannot think of any. The best we can do is identify several that are relatively low in PFMQ. Among approaches we have encountered that can be placed in this category are

• The Higher Order Thinking Skills (HOTS) approach developed by Stanley Pogrow (1992, 1996) and his colleagues. Because HOTS can be implemented by one carefully selected and specially trained teacher or a small cadre of teachers and paraprofessionals, and because it provides participating instructors with detailed and concrete curricular and instructional materials to help them get started, it has produced positive outcomes in a majority of implementations. Even though HOTS involves "pulling" low achievers out of regular classrooms for supplementary instruction, it differs from most other compensatory education pullout arrangements (which usually are very high in PFMQ) in that it stresses active, engaged learning of meaningful material rather than low level, remedial instruction emphasizing mechanical skills.

• Assessment using the Degrees of Reading Power (DRP) test. Unlike other machine-scored tests designed to assess students' reading comprehension, the DRP was constructed to help teachers select materials that are appropriate for independent reading and for instruction aimed at improving the functional comprehension of a particular student or group of students. Since teachers are not given a set of scores indicating performance on subskills (e.g., identifying main idea), they are less likely to be diverted (or allowed to divert themselves) into introducing a long list of subskills that are of questionable value in improving reading comprehension (Sherk, n.d.).

LACK OF ATTENTION TO PREDICTABLE PITFALLS

We have noted that instructional and organizational reforms designed to improve student performance frequently fail in part because they neglect critical prerequisites for successful implementation, involve interventions that are highly complex, and/or inherently possess high potential for misimplementation. Besides attending to these general issues that should be considered in assessing any proposal for a sizable reform effort, planners also should recognize that particular interventions introduce their own unique pitfalls. For example:

• Some interventions require that unusually large amounts of assistance be provided to teachers. Expecting already overloaded building administrators to provide such help meaningfully on a day-to-day basis is a recipe for failure. The recent movement toward inclusion of exceptional education students into regular classrooms exemplifies this pitfall because it frequently assumes that teachers know how, have adequate time, and are able to differentiate instruction appropriately for a very diverse group of students who differ greatly in previous achievement. Failure to address this predictable pitfall all but guarantees that participating teachers either will try to ignore inclusion students as much as possible or will spend inordinate amounts of time and energy attending to their special needs to the detriment of other students.

• Mastery learning, as noted above, is particularly susceptible to mindless instruction emphasizing testing and reteaching of lower-order skills, and whole language approaches may easily morph into a version of laissez-faire nonteaching.

• Problems encountered in the operation of computer laboratories also tend to be highly predictable. Chief among these are tendencies to assign classes to a lab for only one or two periods per week—too little for meaningful learning but sufficient to squeeze in every class in the school. In elementary schools, educators frequently fail to coordinate instruction in the lab with regular classroom learning, especially where computer time is also teacher planning time. Too often the software available is little more than electronic worksheets. Students have little control over computer-generated activities and the small skill drills merely duplicate similar assignments in the classroom.

Such problems are highly predictable because they emerge directly from "natural" tendencies in the operation of schools. For example, the tendency to process all classes through the lab arises in part because it is easier to give every class equal time than to devise and defend flexible schedules that provide more time for some students than others as part of a larger school improvement plan. Since the problems are predictable, proactive administrators could take action early in the planning process to ensure that computer labs will be used productively to enhance student performance.

Somewhat comparable problems predictably arise in the implementation of after school programs often established either to help low achievers or provide expanded learning opportunities for students. If "natural" forces in program development and operation run their course, problems encountered are likely to include

- selection of teachers proceeds according to seniority, political influence, certification, or other criteria unrelated to suitability and motivation for working in the program,
- class sizes may be larger than reasonably should be accommodated given available resources, and
- planned activities constitute an uncoordinated hodgepodge that likely will have little or no discernible impact on student achievement.

Identifying and taking early action to avoid or solve predictable problems in implementing given innovations may be even more important than selecting interventions with relatively low potential for misimplementation. Even those that are relatively low in PFMQ frequently will not be successful unless likely problems are proactively identified and attended to, whereas even the most difficult and complex interventions sometimes are successful if their problematic aspects, such as massive staff development requirements, are adequately addressed. Over the years we have encountered a few schools that successfully implemented high PFMQ approaches, such as individualized instruction, mastery learning, and computer laboratories, respectively, usually because their leaders were able to work through problems that generally resulted in ineffective implementation at other locations. Based on such experience we believe that any approach can be successful somewhere if enough is done to anticipate and overcome difficulties that predictably will arise when attempts are made to implement it. Our problem is not with the isolated sites where innovations are successfully implemented; instead, our concern is the need to make school reform a reality across districts that are not now adequately serving all students.

DOWNPLAYING OF SCHOOLWIDE AND SOCIOLOGICAL PERSPECTIVES

Still another reason why instructional innovations are frequently ineffective is because they ignore sociological perspectives involving impacts on the school as a whole. Instead, interventions generally are assessed only in terms of psychological perspectives focused on individual students.

Inclusion policies provide instructive examples of innovations that have been assessed mostly on a psychological basis. In our experience, evaluators most often have examined effects on inclusion students placed in regular classrooms, but seldom have they provided meaningful data regarding classroom- or school-level outcomes. Slower pacing of instruction, increased frustration among teachers and administrators, lack of appropriate staffing, diversion of funds from other interventions and services, and similar potentially negative effects frequently are unexamined in determining whether inclusion programs in a given school or district are successful or unsuccessful.

Similarly, grade retention practices generally have been evaluated almost entirely in terms of effects on retained students, even though their major purpose and potential benefits frequently are schoolwide: to demonstrate to all students—not just those retained—that lack of effort and/or failure to meet specified standards will have serious consequences. Although information regarding unusually effective schools indicates that in at least some cases rigorous promotions policies have played an important part in effectuating high expectations (Levine and Lezotte 1990), we know little about how these policies were developed and implemented. To what extent do rigorous policies result in an initial spurt in retentions but then, if properly implemented, decline to relatively low levels? How can a faculty work cooperatively to implement a productive policy? These questions seldom have been investigated; all but a handful of the hundreds of studies dealing with retention have restricted their analyses to effects on students who have been retained.

CONCLUSION

Our major purpose in writing this article has been to delineate some of the questions that decision makers should consider in selecting among and proceeding with proposals for substantially improving the effectiveness of instruction in public schools. Among the most important of these questions are

- What are the critical prerequisites for successful implementation of a given intervention?
- How difficult is the intervention to implement, and what can be done to make it less complex so that it is implementable?
- How susceptible is the intervention to misimplementation?
- What pitfalls in implementation are most likely to be encountered, and what can be done to avoid them?

Ignoring or otherwise neglecting these and related questions and issues is likely to result in what some observers have referred to as "illusory" or "phantom" implementation or even, in more extreme cases, "reforms" that are delusional and hallucinatory (Levine and Lezotte 1990). Whether such interventions should be characterized as illusory or instead as delusionary, they seldom, if ever, will result in meaningful improvements in schools, classrooms, or student performance.

REFERENCES

Bullard, P., and B. O. Taylor. (1994). *Keepers of the Dream*. Chicago: Excelsior.

Consortium for Policy Research in Education. (1996). *Public Policy and School Reform*. Philadelphia: University of Pennsylvania Graduate School of Education.

Fullan, M., and M. M. Miles. (1992). "Getting Reform Right." *Phi Delta Kappan* 73, 10: 745–752.

Levine, D. U. (Ed.). (1985). *Improving Student Achievement Through Mastery Learning Programs*. San Francisco: Jossey-Bass.

Levine, D. U., and E. J. Cooper. (1990). "The Change Process and Its Implications in Teaching Thinking." In *Education Values and Cognitive Instruction,* edited by L. Idol and B. F. Jones. Hillside, NJ: Erlbaum.

Levine, D. U., and L. W. Lezotte. (1990). *Unusually Effective Schools.* Bloomington, IN: Phi Delta Kappa Center for Effective Schools.

McKenzie, J. (1995). *The Site-Based Decision-Making Guide for Practitioners,* at Internet site www.pacificrim.net/~McKenzie.

Pogrow, S. (1992). "What to Do About Chapter 1." *Phi Delta Kappan* 73, 8: 624–630.

Pogrow, S. (1996). "Reforming the Wannabe Reformers." *Phi Delta Kappan* 77, 10: 656–663.

Sherk, J. K. (n.d.). *DRP Materials Matching: Adjusting the System.* Kansas City, MO: University of Missouri at Kansas City.

Smith, D. L., and M. J. McNelis. (1996). *Status Report on Alternative Scheduling in Tennessee High Schools.* Memphis: University of Memphis.

Stringfield, S., M. A. Milsap, E. Scott, and R. Herman. (1996, April). "The Three Year Effects of Promising Programs on the Academic Achievement of Students Placed at Risk." Paper presented at the annual meeting of the American Educational Research Association, New York.

Wheelock, A. (1992). *Crossing the Tracks.* New York: New Press.

Special Concerns of Teaching for Intelligence

W hile teaching for intelligence is an educational position hard to disagree with, there is a realization, in this period of reform, that many groups of learners may not easily succeed in achieving the hoped-for objectives. Special concerns need to be examined relative to teaching the underserved, as well as the most fragile constituencies in schools, such as students in poverty, the learning challenged, the very young, and the unmotivated. Can past experience of working with talented and gifted students shed light on how to present accelerated learning to the most needy? These are topics addressed in the fourth section of this volume; they are drawn from both research and practical studies, much of which began when *A Nation at Risk* was initially published.

The world of poverty-stricken, drug-infested, restless students of the south Bronx is poignantly drawn by Kozol's sharp pen. It is a world devoid of intelligence, it seems; one weighed down by rotten luck, accumulated difficulties, and near hopelessness. Yet, Kozol returns regularly to this New York neighborhood, and with him comes the rare chance that something fundamental might change, that a real education might offer different possibilities to a child caught in this foul environment. According to Kozol, it is an investment many ought to be making and encouraging others to support.

Ginsburg challenges current educators to devise exciting and stimulating instruction for preschool students and, at the same time, to create developmentally appropriate educational activity for these three and four year olds. Working in the area of mathematics education, his research has found, even among poor, minority children, it is a myth that such learners have a short attention span and limited intellectual ability. When interested and motivated, these youngsters showed they can develop elegant strategies in mathematics operations. They were as curious and persistent as any preschoolers, and they particularly enjoyed social learning interactions developed by sensitive, caring teachers. Ginsburg presents an alternative scenario to Kozol's bleak, depressed neighborhood.

Interestingly, Ben-Hur reports on promising applications of Feuerstein's theory of cognitive modifiability and mediated learning experience; these examples seek to help the very students Kozol and Ginsburg write about. The mediating teacher, says Ben-Hur, intentionally intervenes in the learning process in order to help students develop clear meaning about the subject matter being instructed. A mediating teacher models appropriate thinking behaviors and through unique programs, such as Feuerstein's Instrumental Enrichment, provides key learning experiences that focus the student's attention and transform his or her essential understandings. The underprivileged student, often deprived of his or her own cultural awareness, needs to *learn how to learn*, which is essentially not a question of content but of developing systematic consciousness. It is a learning, these researchers maintain, that once mastered can transfer to different, parallel situations and build the child's overall cognitive intelligence. By raising the standard (not lowering it), by challenging the learner, by intervening and helping students develop their own tools of knowing, *every* youngster can come to realize they, too, can learn to think intelligently.

VanTassel-Baska seeks a program that can address needs of the most talented or gifted students and, at the same time, provide for multiple outcomes in cognitive, affective, aesthetic, and social areas. For the advanced learner, she suggests, the youngster's precocity especially in domain-specific contents must be honored, as well as his or her breadth of higher-order thinking skills and his or her ability to make interdisciplinary connections and systemic relationships. It would seem much collaboration is still required at Schools of Education and with Colleges of Liberal Arts and Sciences to even begin considering the research in this complex field. Unfortunately, as Van-

Tassel-Baska points out, only a few ventures have really been pursued to the point where they have yielded reliable, informative data.

One exception to the paucity of research on teaching for intelligence and actually delivering a promising program is the work of Renzulli, who presents his schoolwide enrichment model in this section. Originally an advocate of special education for the gifted and talented, Renzulli now proposes an application of what he learned from that earlier focus to promote "challenging and enjoyable high-end learning" across a full range of student populations, at different levels, and with varied demographics. Renzulli is practical; he considers how teachers must be supported while learning gradual change, and he is ever diligent about how to use precious time available for productive ends. What is most interesting about his relatively complex model is its unique way of dealing with the demands of the regular curriculum and, simultaneously, addressing the need to inspire and to be creative in providing for students' cognitive enrichment. Renzulli would modify use of the ever-present American textbook, so that time would be freed for the student to be challenged by an exciting, self-selected project in an area about which he or she is curious and motivated. The research findings on implementing Renzulli's model, at various sites across the country, make his contribution to this volume a rich resource in teaching for intelligence and for implementing innovations in real sites.

Finally, this section, and this volume, concludes with Comer's moving study of the climate and conditions needed to create an environment in which children—even the poorest and most neglected—can learn to think intelligently. His own personal story adds a touching view of nurturing and inspiration. His doubt about a false reliance on IQ scores makes one wonder how we determine what real quality is and how respect for learning actually develops. Comer stresses the importance of the *community* of knowing, of developing "no-fault" support for the learner in a child-centered school. He reports on the numerous schools that successfully implemented his Yale Child Study Center Model of schooling, emphasizing consensus and collaboration. Like his friend Feuerstein, Comer makes the world think differently about children. Given opportunity, guided by caring teachers, encouraged to learn to manage their own environment, every child from Alabama or south Bronx can learn and achieve at the highest level possible. Teaching for intelligence is the key to a whole new world of being. Every child deserves a chance to experience it.

Working with Kids Like Mario

by Jonathan Kozol

I've been working with kids like Mario one way or the other for most of my life. Started out back in 1964, thirty-four years ago, in the segregated public schools in Boston, and I have spent most of the decades since working with black and Hispanic kids, much of the past five years with children in New York, off and on in the south Bronx. In all, I have made about 200 visits up to the south Bronx to talk to children, mothers, fathers, teachers, and preachers who face challenges I couldn't have even dreamed of thirty years ago. I usually go up by the train. While you are here in New York you can take the same trip if you'd like. Number 6 train. Get on in front of Bloomingdale's, 57th Street and Lexington Avenue. One of the richest neighborhoods in the entire Western world. Get off fifteen minutes later on Brook Avenue in the south Bronx. Poorest section of the poorest congressional district in America. Also one of the physically sickest neighborhoods that I've been in in my entire life.

When I was writing *Amazing Grace,* doctors at the hospital told me nearly one fourth of all the young women who came into the hospital to have a baby tested positive for HIV. Imagine what that means. You visit kindergarten. I love to start the day visiting kindergarten when I'm up there because it is cheerful. It should be cheerful. If you know the numbers, you can't engage in phony boosterism and you can't be artificially optimistic. That's not good theology. You know the numbers, and you look at these little babies in front of you, and you are thinking to yourself, 1, 2, 3, 4, every fourth child may lose their mother to an early death and many will follow their mothers to the grave.

From a transcript of a presentation at the Fourth International Teaching for Intelligence Conference, April 25, 1998, New York, NY. © 1998 by Jonathan Kozol. Reprinted with permission.

Challenging Preschool Education: Meeting the Intellectual Needs of All Children[1]

by Herbert P. Ginsburg

T his article is about *challenging* preschool education—"challenging" in two senses. First, we need to question current conceptions of preschool education. They underestimate children and result in programs that fail to stimulate young children as much as they want and need to be stimulated in order to enjoy preschool and prepare for school (which in turn also needs to be made more exciting, stimulating, and enjoyable than it is now!). Second, we need to make preschool education, for all children, more challenging than it is now. We need to devise exciting, simulating, and, at the same time, developmentally appropriate preschool programs. In this article, I describe research showing that all preschoolers are capable of interesting mathematical thinking, want to engage in it, and enjoy doing so. This research suggests ways to create a mathematics education that is both "developmentally appropriate" for preschoolers and more stimulating and enjoyable than what they now receive.

WHAT SHOULD PRESCHOOL EDUCATION INVOLVE?

Across the United States, and indeed around the world, an increasingly large number of families—both two parent and one parent families—require child care because they either must or want to work. In New York City, for example, there are hundreds of private daycare centers and nursery schools, and the New York City Agency for Child Development (ACD) serves some 50,000 preschool children, most of them poor African-American and Latino children, in

From a paper based on a presentation at the Fourth International Teaching for Intelligence Conference, April 25, 1998, New York, NY. © 1998 by Herbert P. Ginsburg. Reprinted with permission.

various daycare and Head Start settings. New York State has introduced an initiative to mandate universal preschool education. All four- and five-year-olds in New York State now have the right (although not necessarily the opportunity) to attend a preschool. The public schools in many states are opening preschools and, in some cases, kindergartens for the first time.

As these demographic trends intensify, there is a great deal of ferment in early childhood education. Everyone of course agrees that we must provide preschoolers with safe care and we must enhance their physical, social, and emotional development. But many now recognize that although essential, these goals are not sufficient. Many early childhood educators and parents are grappling with the fundamental question of how we can improve *education* for the children in daycare and preschool, particularly four- and five-year-olds.

• States like Texas have undertaken the task of rethinking what preschool education ought to cover.

• The National Science Foundation and the U.S. Office of Education have funded new initiatives to develop mathematics and science curricula for preschool and kindergarten children.

• Programs like *Sesame Street, Blue's Clues,* and *Reading Rainbow* are planning to expand the intellectual content of their preschool offerings.

• Large textbook publishers are considering whether to produce preschool materials and what form they should take.

This article aims to contribute to the discussion of the nature, goals, and content of preschool education. I argue that we need to *educate* preschoolers in at least two ways: We must promote their current intellectual development and we must prepare them for schooling so that they can succeed in their academic work.

Further, we have a special responsibility to provide poor children and disadvantaged minority children with effective early education. Because they lack advantages and resources available to middle-class children, because they are at risk of school failure and of failing schools, because they are likely to be shortchanged when it comes to receiving a decent elementary school education, they need all the early preparation they can get.

Unfortunately, we have not done very well by these children. We generally provide very little financial support to early childhood programs. Daycare providers and preschool teachers receive little training, are poorly paid, and often must make do with minimal facilities and equipment. This is yet one more example of this country's shameful neglect of its children.

Further, the educational community has developed little in the way of interesting educational activities for preschoolers. Often, daycare providers perceive no alternative but to seat the children in front of the television or to impose on them dreadful workbooks for the purpose of teaching reading, writing, and arithmetic.

> ... aside from a few exclusive nursery schools, education receives low priority in most daycare and preschool settings.

Sad to say, it is a fact that aside from a few exclusive nursery schools, education receives low priority in most daycare and preschool settings. In most cases, adults do little to foster development of the mind beyond helping children to count and to recognize common shapes, and beyond reading books to children and teaching them to make the letters. These of course can be worthwhile activities, but as we shall see, they do not come close to responding to preschool children's cognitive needs.

Why this lack of attention to preschool *education?* One reason, I think, is that we have lacked both a clear understanding of young children's cognitive development and a coherent vision of the very nature and goals of early childhood education. The National Association for the Education of Young Children (Bredekamp and Copple 1997) correctly advises us to avoid rote drill in the preschool—also not a very good idea as the mainstay of education at the older grades, too!—and, instead, to present young children with developmentally appropriate learning activities.

But many preschool educators are unclear about the notion of developmentally appropriate practice. Should young children be limited to relatively simple and concrete forms of learning as is often the case in many preschool facilities? Is it developmentally appropriate for four-year-olds to learn some mathematics and reading? What kinds of activities will get them ready for school? What role should adults play in guiding the learning and development of preschool children? Until we have theory and evidence that help us answer questions about the nature of preschoolers' minds and about the ways in which they can be helped to learn, it will be very hard to develop appropriate preschool programs.

Psychological research conducted over the past twenty or thirty years can help illuminate some of these issues. Psychologists have made important discoveries about pre-schoolers' minds, about the deep questions preschoolers implicitly ask, and about the ways in which preschoolers attempt to construct an understanding of the world. As a result of this research, psychologists are now in a position to suggest a focus and goals for preschool education and can offer new insights into "developmentally appropriate" learning and teaching for preschoolers and into the tangled issue of school readiness. In this article, I focus on research dealing with preschoolers' mathematical thinking because it offers a fascinating view of preschoolers' minds and their intellectual motivation and suggests important lessons for preschool education. To convey the essence of this work, I describe in detail a few examples. Keep in mind, however, that these examples are entirely representative of preschoolers generally; they are not odd or unusual cases.

> It is a myth that young children have a short attention span for intellectual activities.

A CLINICAL INTERVIEW WITH ABDUL

Here is an interview with Abdul, recently turned four, an immigrant from Africa, a member of a low-income family. At the time I saw him, he was attending a local daycare center that did not devote much effort to mathematics education beyond simple counting. I asked him and other children in the center if they would like to have a turn "playing some games" with me. In "clinical interviews" like these, I give the child activities to engage in, games to play, materials to work with, and continually ask the child to describe how he or she is thinking and solving the various problems. The interview lasts anywhere from twenty to forty minutes. I end the interview sooner than that if the child does not like it. But that seldom is the case. Most children thoroughly enjoy these activities and often do not want to leave. After all, young children seldom receive so much individual attention from an adult who is interested in their thinking.

Abdul was no exception. He thoroughly enjoyed the various activities, stayed in the interview for some thirty to forty minutes, and in the end practically had to be dragged away so that other children could participate. It is a myth that young children have a short attention span for intellectual activities. If interested, four- and five-year-olds—and even some three-year-olds—can work at least thirty to forty minutes on challenging tasks. This is a general phenomenon: under the right conditions—and the right conditions usually are *not* the conditions of standard testing—young children are capable of an attention span much longer than that normally attributed to them.

I placed on the table five red checkers and asked Abdul to count them.

Interviewer (I): How many red ones are there?

Abdul counted very carefully, touching each checker as he counted it, and concluded very firmly that there were five altogether.

Abdul (A): Five!

I: Very good. Now let's make believe that you have five red apples.

A: [interrupts, eagerly exclaiming] I'll do it, I'll do it.

Abdul was extremely excited about all of the tasks and often wanted to get involved in a very active way, touching objects, moving them. He basically tried to take over the interviewer's role, so that it was necessary to calm him down a bit.

I: No, it's my turn. You have five red apples here, and you go to the store and you get some more. [I placed three more red checkers on the table, separate from the first group of five. Referring to the new group of three, I asked:] How many apples are here?

Abdul held up three fingers.

I: How many is that?

A: Three.

I: How many do you have altogether now?

Abdul carefully moved all of the checkers into one group containing two rows of four checkers each, like this:

● ● ● ●

● ● ● ●

He touched each checker, pair by pair, and counted it out loud. As he counted the fifth, he looked up to check my expression and in doing so skipped the sixth, so that he concluded that there were seven altogether.

Consider what has happened so far. First of all, Abdul showed a high degree of motivation in these apparently simple and perhaps dull counting tasks. Abdul's vivid interest in mathematical questions was evident; his excitement was palpable. The same cannot be said of many children in school. Abdul's behavior indicates that mathematical tasks can be "motivationally appropriate" for four-year-olds. A corollary is that it would be developmentally inappropriate to prevent young children from engaging in activities like these.

Most of us have been so turned off by many years of deadly schooling in mathematics—what the philosopher Arlo Guthrie calls "the boring method of education"[2]—that we forget how intrinsically fascinating basic mathematical questions are. From the little child's point of view, profound mysteries and puzzles are involved in such questions as, If I count these things this way—ball, pen, paper—and I get "three," what happens if I count them in another way—paper, pen, ball? I called the paper "three" the first time, but then I called the ball "three." How can they both be "three"? And what does "three" mean anyway? I call the ball "ball" and I also call it "three." Does "three" refer to the ball only or to the paper, pen, and ball? And if so, is this the same "three" that can also be used to describe a unicorn, Alexander the Great, and a popsicle? In the child's mind, these are questions worth careful thought and pleasurable engagement.

Second, Abdul's work also shows that he possessed an "everyday" concept (Vygotsky 1986) of addition as combining things (later he showed that he saw subtraction as taking things away). After all, combining—getting more—and taking away—or losing—are fundamental emotional events in children's lives. Is it not essential that they learn about these things, even if their parents are unaware of their doing so?

Abdul had *ideas* about addition and subtraction as well as techniques for calculation. He knew that adding involves combining sets, and he used counting to accomplish the result. At the outset, his idea of addition was sound, and so was his strategy. In fact, his strategy, placing objects in pairs, was elegant in the way it arranged objects in a manner highly convenient for counting. But although the spirit is willing, the flesh can be weak: he executed the strategy badly, skipping an object when he looked up at me. The resulting wrong answer, it is clear, does not provide an accurate measure of either his basic idea or his strategy for calculation. To understand children, we usually need to get beyond standard testing: we need to observe, to question in flexible ways, to interpret sensibly, as is possible in the clinical interview.

I saw that Abdul was wrong simply because he skipped an object. Instead of telling him that he was wrong or giving him the right answer, I asked him to try again.

I: OK, Abdul, do it again, more carefully.

At this point I thought that Abdul was about to go down a dangerous path. He undid the two by four arrangement of checkers and instead placed them in a circle. I was concerned with his strategy because a circle is a decidedly inelegant arrangement of objects for the purpose of counting. Unless he was able to remember where he started, he might not know where to stop counting. But Abdul proved my pessimism unwarranted. He counted all of the checkers once and only once, stopping at the right place and getting the correct answer, eight. This might be taken to show that what is the most rational approach for an adult may not necessarily be the most effective method for a child. Adults be humble: let children try it their (apparently inferior) way.

I: OK. Now Big Bird comes and takes away some apples. How many are left?

Abdul noted that two were taken away, counted those remaining, and correctly reported that six were left.

I: Now Big Bird brings *back* the two apples. How many are there now?

Abdul sighed deeply and began to count again the set of eight apples. Of course, knowing that if two apples were taken away from but then returned to a set (of any size), the adult would not have to count but would immediately *know* that the set must have what it started with, which in this case was eight. Once again Abdul counted accurately his not particularly well-arranged collection and concluded, as if it were a completely new result, that the number was eight.

In this episode, Abdul demonstrated some reasoning difficulties characteristic of young children. He failed to understand the inverse

relation between addition and subtraction. He did not see that if you
start with eight, take away two, and then return two, eight checkers
must remain. It is a logical necessity; you do not need to calculate to
get the answer—you just need to *think*. But young children generally
have difficulties with "reversibility" problems of this sort (Piaget
1952).

We have seen then, that despite evident limitations, Abdul, like
most other four-year-olds from all social classes and ethnic groups,
has some knowledge and skill in counting, addition, and subtraction,
as well as considerable interest in these topics. How does the child
develop notions like these? The child lives in an environment replete
with quantitative events and relations—my brother has more cookies
than I do, a clear inequality, or the daddy bear gets the largest bed,
the mommy bear the middle bed, and the baby bear the smallest, a
simple and morally appropriate "functional relation." In coping with
these situations, the child, aided by tools provided by the culture—
chiefly, a system for counting—*must* develop mathematical ideas. As
Vygotsky put it, ". . . children's learning begins long before they enter
school . . . children begin to study arithmetic in school, but long
beforehand they have had some experience with quantity—they have
had to deal with operations of division, addition, subtraction, and the
determination of size. Consequently, children have their own preschool arithmetic, which only myopic psychologists could ignore"
(Vygotsky 1978, 84). Vygotsky was right about the preschool arithmetic but wrong about who ignores it. Not only psychologists, but
parents and teachers often are unaware of the child's labors and
mostly do not provide help.

This example of preschool children's intellectual competence
and curiosity is significant and should not be ignored. As Montessori
put it, "Ah, before . . . dense and willful disregard of the life which is
growing within these children, we should hide our heads in shame
and cover our guilty faces with our hands!" (Montessori 1964, 27).

But I have shown you only one example. You may well ask, How
general are phenomena like these? We have conducted research
showing that this one little boy is not at all atypical. An everyday
mathematics, a system of knowledge not imposed by adult instruction, but at least partly constructed by the child, is extremely widespread. Our research has shown that before entering school, children
all over the world—schooled children and unschooled children,
children from literate societies and children from illiterate societies,
poor children and affluent children—develop concepts like these

(Ginsburg, Choi, Lopez, Netley, and Chi 1997). Indeed, our research, as well as investigations by many others (Ginsburg, Klein, and Starkey 1998), shows that key aspects of early everyday mathematics—like Abdul's concrete addition and subtraction—may well be universal.

WHAT DOES PLAY TELL US ABOUT CHILDREN'S MATHEMATICAL THINKING?

In attempting to understand young children's competence, we cannot rely on only one method. We must approach the issue from many directions. Clinical interviews show how children respond to adult questions. But what is the nature of children's *spontaneous* mathematical thinking? Do they think about addition and subtraction in their everyday lives? Are mathematical issues meaningful to their ordinary activities? What does "free play" reveal about their mathematical competence?

> **Do children think about addition and subtraction in their everyday lives? Are mathematical issues meaningful to their ordinary activities?**

To find out, I have spent considerable time in daycare centers in New York City. My students and I have made observations in the classrooms, we have conducted workshops and interviews with the parents, and we have played with the children, most of whom are from low-income African-American and Latino families. (And we have conducted interviews with these same children.) In the course of making observations in the classrooms, we noticed that in their everyday play, the children seemed to be dealing with "mathematical questions" in one way or another.

To investigate the issue carefully, we have been making videotapes of children's everyday activities and examining the mathematics imminent in them. Our technique is simple. After the children have become familiar with us and our equipment, we videotape individual children for a fifteen-minute period during free play. The target child, fitted with a cordless microphone, is taped whatever he or she does and wherever the activity takes place (except the bathroom) during the free play period, which in most cases is scheduled for the early morning. We have taped some ninety children in this way (including, for purposes of comparison, low-, middle- and upper-income children).

Here is an example involving Steven's counting.

"Let me see," Steven said as he carefully poured the small beads in his hand onto the table. "Oh, man—I got one hundred." Then he started counting the beads on the table. He picked out the beads one by one, and counted, "One, two, three . . ." When Steven reached the tenth bead, Barbara joined in, saying, "Ten, eleven, twelve . . ." However, Barbara was not actually counting the beads although she *said* the number words in sequence. They continued counting, reaching "Twenty-five, twenty-six . . ." Steven dropped the twenty-sixth bead, but ignored it and continued counting, picking out the next and saying "twenty-seven." Barbara kept pace, and they continued. Steven dropped the thirtieth bead. He paused for a second and said, "Wait! I made a mistake."

> Interestingly, they did not ask what he was doing or why he wanted to count the beads.

Notice that when he poured the beads on the table, Steven postulated a specific number of beads. Instead of saying "many" or "lots of," like many young children, he said "one hundred." He knew that a large number, whether or not it is exact, attaches to a rather large collection of beads. In this he was reasonably accurate; he did not say ten or twenty, which in fact would have been seriously wrong. So Steven began by offering a plausible estimate of a large collection.

His subsequent behavior suggests that he wanted to determine whether his estimate was correct: did he really have one hundred beads? He employed counting to answer the question. Not only did he have skill in counting, he clearly knew that counting tells how many. As he counted the beads, Steven made several mistakes because the beads were difficult to grab. Once or twice, he uttered a number word without picking up a bead; when he dropped the bead in his hand, he continued counting without replacing it. At first, he did not seem to care much about his mistakes. But when he dropped the thirtieth bead, he stopped counting. He seemed concerned at this point that his counting was not correct.

Steven poured the beads in his hands on the table and started to count them again. "One, two, three . . ." When he counted "three," Barbara picked out one bead, showed it to him, and said, "I have one." But Steven ignored her and continued to count. When he counted "five," Barbara joined him. When he counted "ten," Barbara again showed her beads to Steven, "I got, look . . ." But Steven again ignored her and continued counting. Barbara kept pace with him, uttering the same number words. When he counted "twelve," Barbara shouted meaningless words in his ear, as if she wanted to destroy his concentration. Steven ignored her again, and kept counting, "Nineteen, twenty [at twenty, he put out two beads], twenty-one . . ." When Steven counted up to forty-seven (almost entirely correctly), a girl asked him, "What do you count?" Again, he ignored her and kept on counting. After "forty-nine," Steven paused. As Barbara said "fifty," Steven followed her, "—ty, fifty-one, fifty-two . . ."

Steven's decision to count the beads all over again seemed to indicate that he was now really serious about the counting; he wanted his counting to be done right. He ignored Barbara's distractions and concentrated his attention on counting, which may have provided a sense of mastery. Interestingly, Barbara, who earlier interrupted his counting by shouting meaningless words in his ear, rescued him from being stuck at forty-nine. Her help allowed his counting to continue.

When they counted "fifty-two," Ruthie came to the table, picked out one bead, and joined their counting, "fifty-two, fifty-three . . ." Madonna also came to the table, tried to find a place, picked out one bead, and joined the counting, "fifty-six, fifty-seven . . ." The girls' counting sometimes violated the one-to-one correspondence rule; they sometimes selected several beads at once or sometimes did not select a single bead. After seventy-nine, Steven again paused. As the girls said, "eighty," Steven continued the counting, "eighty, eighty-one . . ." When they counted "eighty-five," the girls competed with one another to grab more beads. The plastic container was turned over, and the beads in the container dropped on the table and the floor and rolled in every direction. The girls grabbed the beads, trying to get more than one another. Through all of this disturbance Steven kept on counting, "eighty-six, eighty-seven . . . ninety-four."

Steven's counting turned into a social activity. Ruthie and Madonna came to the table in turn and spontaneously joined Steven's counting. Interestingly, they did not ask what he was doing or why he wanted to count the beads. They did not appear to enumerate the beads, although they correctly said the number words in sequence. Rather, they seemed to enjoy the repetitive behaviors of picking out the beads and saying the number words in a certain tune and rhythm. Steven did not care about them or what they were doing; he did not exchange a single word with them. But Steven used the help they gave him. He paused after seventy-nine, and as they said "eighty," he too said it and continued counting. For a while, the girls enjoyed picking out beads and saying the number words with Steven, but they soon became interested in having more beads than one another. Their fight over the beads led to chaos. Steven's persistence in counting was surprising. In spite of the girls' disturbance, he kept on counting. He made several mistakes, but this time did not correct them. He seemed to be determined to reach one hundred no matter what.

After he picked out the ninety-fourth bead, he found no more beads on the table. He bent over and picked out a bead from those on the floor, and continued counting, "ninety-five, ninety-six, and ninety-seven . . ." (inaudible after ninety-seven). After Madonna shouted "one hundred!" raising her arm, Steven, Barbara, and Ruthie joined in, saying "one hundred!" right after her. Then Steven concluded, "We all got one hundred."

Clearly, Steven wanted to reach one hundred. Interestingly, even though the girls did not know that Steven had one hundred in mind as the end point of his counting, they all stopped counting once they reached one hundred and gave a cheer. It was a special number for all of them, worth celebration.

Steven's example is instructive in several ways. He set himself a goal at the outset, namely to count to one hundred. Why this goal? Big numbers are challenging for little children—even though most state curriculum guidelines do not recommend counting this high and even though many early childhood educators do not believe children, especially poor children, can do it. A very popular children's book, *How Much Is a Million?* (Schwartz 1985), explores such issues as how long would it take if you wanted to count from one to one million. How long? The answer given is twenty-three days. Perhaps, too, Steven wanted to know what a large number of objects actually look like, which is a question fascinating even to jaded (or mathematically challenged) adults. Further, Steven knew what counting is for and used it with skill. He generally worked with great care, sometimes, but not always, repeating his count when he made a mistake. He was generally accurate but, more importantly, exerted effort and, despite major distractions, stayed focused on achieving his goal. Notice, too, that other children found his work fascinating, occasionally helped out, and joined the counting party. Intellectual work is a social event for young children; indeed, social interaction seems to stimulate intellectual activity.

Is Steven typical? Although our work on the topic is just beginning, I can report some preliminary results (Ginsburg, Inoue, and
Seo, in press). Mathematical activity appears
to be a fairly frequent occurrence in the low-
income children we studied, comprising
slightly less than half of children's play
(about 45%). In this group, the most frequently occurring mathematical activity
was concern with *patterns and shapes* (for
example, pattern/shape detection, prediction,
or creation—36%); and then *dynamics* (for
example, exploration of processes of change
or transformation—22%); *relations* (for example, magnitude evaluation or comparison—18%); *classification* (for example, sorting,
grouping, or categorization—13%); and *enumeration* (for example,
quantification or numerical judgment—11%). Interestingly enough,
we found "enumeration"—the topic most frequently investigated in
psychological research—relatively rarely occurring in children's play.
Instead, these preschool children engaged heavily in pattern analysis
and geometric thinking in their free play.

> Intellectual work is a
> social event for young
> children; indeed,
> social interaction
> seems to stimulate
> intellectual activity.

DESIGNING PRESCHOOL EDUCATION

We have seen that both interviews and naturalistic observation reveal
that preschoolers, including poor children, can engage in and do
engage in significant mathematical activities. Now, the question is
how these psychological insights can guide attempts to provide
preschoolers with a productive education. The research offers several
lessons.

One is that we should raise our expectations concerning what
preschoolers can do. At present, the expectations are low. The Agency
for Child Development aims at teaching children "relatively easy
skills and concepts."[3] Most American kindergarten texts expose children to numbers no higher than thirty-one, the largest number of
days that can appear on the calendar.[4] Even Big Bird and the Count
could stand to gain from some higher education.

As you have seen, the children are ready for more than the typical curriculum offers. Count to thirty-one? That's adult's play, not
child's play. Of course, ours is not the only evidence. We know that
young children can get deeply engaged in work with computers
(Shade 1997), often putting their parents' efforts to shame (Papert

1996). You might say that children have voted with their mice for a higher level of developmentally appropriate activity. We know that at Reggio Emilia, children can engage in meaningful projects in which the intensity of the intellectual effort surpasses the ten- or twenty-minute attention span normally attributed to four-year-olds (Raines 1997). So the first goal should be to give preschoolers exciting things to do.

Some might object that a curriculum of this type may be harmful. It might hurry children, put too much pressure on them, arouse anxiety, distort their emotional development. Of course any approach—from Bank Street to Montessori—executed badly can produce negative effects. But these need not occur. Implemented with sensitivity and skill, a challenging preschool curriculum should be a good deal of fun for preschoolers. It satisfies their intellectual needs. They enjoy learning, are eager to learn, and have not yet been taught that they are not capable of learning.

> You might say that children have voted with their mice for a higher level of developmentally appropriate activity.

Indeed, failing to provide preschoolers with challenging experiences is harmful: it deadens their curiosity and teaches them at an early age that schooling does not respond to their needs. A challenging curriculum is particularly important for poor, disadvantaged children. They need to excel in academic work as early as possible, because they are in for a rough time in school, and their early success may convince adults that there is no excuse for failing to educate these children.

Second, a developmentally appropriate curriculum—that is, interesting and challenging activities for young children—should respond, at least in part, to children's everyday interests, to their "personal curriculum." The research shows that in their free play preschool children implicitly "pose" important questions, like what combination of colors produces another. Of course, they do not ask these questions explicitly. Rather, their behavior suggests that they are interested in and struggling with a variety of intellectual problems. One approach to determining the content of the curriculum, then, is to attempt to discover preschoolers' implicit questions and then to develop activities that can help preschoolers explore the issues and learn something about them. Think of the origins of "curriculum" as the adult's attempt to help individual children explore, make explicit, formalize, and learn about issues in which they already have some interest. Later, this attempt can be offered to many children; then, it is "curriculum" in the formal sense.

Third, understanding children's minds helps us think more deeply about goals for preschool education.[5] Our research suggests two major goals for preschool education. First, it should help children engage in activities enabling them to elaborate on their everyday knowledge. After all, this everyday knowledge deals with interesting questions, and it is the child's own personal and valued possession. A second goal should be to help children understand the relations between their everyday knowledge and the ways in which the culture has come to systematize and formalize it. The personal knowledge is only a beginning: children need to learn how the questions they ask can be approached in a more organized, mature, and public fashion.

Fourth, how should we go about "teaching" this kind of curriculum? It is obvious that traditional, direct instruction—the "boring method"—is inappropriate for preschoolers. We certainly don't want them to engage in dull and disembodied workbook activities. But it also is clear that by itself free play is insufficient. We have seen that in the daycare center preschoolers can go only so far in their spontaneous investigations, as valuable as these can be. At some point, children require adult assistance to formalize ideas, to generalize them, to become conscious of them, and to communicate them.

What form of adult assistance should be used with preschoolers? It should certainly be sensitive to preschoolers' psychology—to their concerns, to their state of mind, to their motivations, to their modes of constructing the world. Beyond that, it is hard to say what form it should take. Experimentation is required, ideally in the kind of laboratory school John Dewey founded many years ago.

In brief, my argument is that the preschool curriculum should involve high expectations, it should draw on children's everyday interests, it should aim toward the integration of everyday and formal knowledge, and it should involve some form of adult assistance, not free play alone.

CONCLUSION

Children's informal mathematical knowledge takes many forms and is more complex and interesting than usually expected. Whether or not they are somewhat behind or ahead of their more advantaged peers, poor children are capable of engaging in exciting, challenging learning—learning that our research shows is developmentally appropriate. We need to meet preschoolers' intellectual needs by providing them with stimulating intellectual activities, based at least in part on their demonstrated interests, which seem to go far beyond what current state curricula and the early childhood education community seem to recognize as appropriate for preschoolers. We should accept the challenge of challenging early childhood educators to create challenging education for our young children.

NOTES

1. The research described in this paper was supported by a generous grant from the Spencer Foundation, Grant Number 199800041.

2. Listen to his hilarious spoof of education in the song "Inch by Inch" on the disk *Precious Friend,* with Pete Seeger, Warner Brothers 3644, 1982.

3. "The Agency for Child Development discourages programs from attempting to develop . . . skills within the narrow academic confines of having children orally recite 'their numbers and A, B, C' and having them complete paper-and-pencil worksheets. Instead, programs should sequentially develop these skills by using many varied and integrated activities and methods. Each day children should actively participate in a complementary variety of 'hands-on' activities which include: block scheduling, language development, arts, crafts, outdoor play, woodworking, music, manipulative toys, socio-dramatic play, field trips, cooking, sand and water play, and science exploration. The program gives children opportunities to acquire relatively easy skills and concepts and master them before being introduced to more advanced skills" (Agency for Child Development 1996, 1).

4. The official State of Texas guidelines for textbooks require teaching kindergartners the "use of numbers to describe how many objects are in a set (through 20)" (State of Texas 1997, Ch. 1, 1–2). To be fair, this is a minimum goal, but as is well known, many teachers will teach to it, making it the final goal.

5. This is of course an old idea. According to the father of child study, "All now agree that the mind can learn only what is related to other things learned before, and that we must start from the knowledge that the children really have and develop this as germs . . ." (Hall 1981, 154). Or as Dewey put it many years ago: "[Knowing] how the mind words in the construction of number, [the teacher] is prepared to help the child to think number . . ." (McLellan and Dewey 1895, 22). And of course we also want to help the preschool child to "think science" and "think reading" and think many other things. Doing this requires, as (Dewey 1976) proposed, that we determine how the child's ". . . experience already contains within itself elements—facts and truths—

of just the same sort as those entering into formulated study; and, what is of more importance, of how it contains within itself the attitudes, the motives, and the interests which have operated in developing and organizing the subject-matter to the plane which it now occupies. From the side of the studies, it is question of interpreting them as outgrowths of forces operating in the child's life, and of discovering the steps that intervene between the child's present experience and their richer maturity" (Dewey 1976, 277–278).

REFERENCES

Agency for Child Development. (1996). *Program assessment instrument.* New York: Author.

Bredekamp, S., and Copple, C. (Eds.). (1997). *Developmentally appropriate practice in early childhood programs.* (Revised ed.). Washington, DC: National Association for the Education of Young Children.

Dewey, J. (1976). The child and the curriculum. In J. A. Boydston (Ed.), *John Dewey: The middle works, 1899–1924, Volume 2: 1902–1903* (pp. 273–291). Carbondale, IL: Southern Illinois University Press.

Ginsburg, H. P., Y. E. Choi, L. S. Lopez, R. Netley, and C. Y. Chi. (1997). Happy birthday to you: Early mathematical thinking of Asian, South American, and U.S. children. In T. Nunes and P. Bryant (Eds.), *Learning and teaching mathematics: An international perspective* (pp. 163–207). East Sussex, England: Erlbaum (UK) Taylor and Francis.

Ginsburg, H. P., N. Inoue, and K. H. Seo. (in press). Preschoolers doing mathematics: Observations of everyday activities. In J. Copley (Ed.), *Mathematics in the early years.* Reston, VA: National Council of Teachers of Mathematics.

Ginsburg, H. P., A. Klein, and P. Starkey. (1998). The development of children's mathematical thinking: Connecting research with practice. In I. Sigel and A. Renninger (Eds.), *Handbook of child psychology: 5th ed., Vol. 4, Child psychology and practice* (pp. 401–476). New York: John Wiley and Sons.

Hall, G. S. (1891). The contents of children's minds on entering school. *Pedagogical Seminary* 1, 139–173.

McLellan, J. A., and J. Dewey. (1895). *The psychology of number and its applications to methods of teaching arithmetic.* New York: D. Appleton.

Montessori, M. (1964). *The Montessori method.* New York: Schocken Books.

Papert, S. (1996). *The connected family: Bridging the digital generation gap.* Atlanta, GA: Longstreet Press.

Piaget, J. (1952). *The child's conception of number* (C. Gattegno and F. M. Hodgson, Trans.). London: Routledge and Kegan Paul Ltd.

Raines, S. C. (1997). Developmental appropriateness: Curriculum revisited and challenged. In J. P. Isenberg and M. R. Jalongo (Eds.), *Major trends and issues in early childhood education: Challenges, controversies, and insights* (pp. 75–89). New York: Teachers College Press.

Schwartz, D. M. (1985). *How much is a million?* New York: Lothrop, Lee, and Shepard Books.

Shade, D. D. (1997). The role of computer technology in early childhood education. In J. P. Isenberg and M. R. Jalongo (Eds.), *Major trends and issues in early childhood education: Challenges, controversies, and insights* (pp. 90–103). New York: Teachers College Press.

State of Texas. (1997). *Texas essential knowledge and skills for mathematics.* Austin, TX: Author.

Vygotsky, L. S. (1978). *Mind in society: The development of higher psychological processes.* Cambridge, MA: Harvard University Press.

Vygotsky, L. S. (1986). *Thought and language* (A. Kozulin, Trans.). Cambridge, MA: The MIT Press.

Mediation of Cognitive Competencies for Students in Need

by Meir Ben-Hur

Keith, an average fifth-grade student, has just completed an exciting hands-on science unit investigating "planet Earth." It lasted
four months. Wanting to assess Keith's new understanding, his
teacher engages in a clinical interview with him.[1]

Teacher: Where is the sun after it sets?

Keith (pausing): I don't know . . .

Teacher (pointing to the student-made colorful globes with attached
labels hanging from the classroom ceiling and to students' pictures
and drawings on the walls): Is there anything in our classroom exhibit
that can help you think about this?

Keith (looking around): No . . . but I know it doesn't go into the
ocean.

Teacher: How do you know that?

Keith: Because it would splash the water.

Teacher: Oh. So where does it really go?

Keith (pausing): Maybe to China?

Teacher (relieved): And where is it when it sets in China?

Keith (troubled): I don't know . . .

Sound familiar? Have you ever wondered why it is that some student experiences—even rich, exciting, hands-on types of active learning—do not result in real learning of new concepts? Have you wondered how it happens that some students (perhaps as many as half) do not understand what they experience even in the most engaging classes?

WHY LEARNING NEEDS TO BE MEDIATED

The Piagetian constructivist school of developmental psychology, which views cognitive abilities as a product of the combination of the maturation of the central nervous system and earlier exposures, provides little help to our troubled teacher. She needs to find ways to facilitate the construction of concepts in mathematics, science, and other subjects for the half of her students who cannot build them on their own.

"Meaning" is not implicit in objects and events. Our concept of the world is, for the most part, not a product of our perception of the world. Rather, our perception is generally the product of our concept of the world. What we learn from our direct exposure to objects and events (direct learning) is strictly determined by our preconceived notions of these objects and events and by our ability to relate them to our previous learning. Our concepts, in turn, may be modified by those experiences that are incompatible with them. However, such modifications are unlikely to happen without some form of intervention or mediation. Remember, it took humans millions of years to change their idea that the Earth is flat, and they did not change their thinking until the interventions of maps and exploration provided evidence incompatible with their beliefs.

Keith's learning about planet Earth could not depend entirely upon his own ideas of planet Earth even in a hands-on, exciting, active-learning science class. His perceptions of the objects and events in his science class were entirely different from those his teacher expected.

Lev Vygotsky, a world-renowned social psychologist, argued that the origin of our concepts of the world must be found in our early learning of such things as language, culture, and religion.[2] This learning cannot happen without the help, or mediation, of such people as parents, caretakers, and siblings.

Reuven Feuerstein terms this form of learning Mediated Learning Experience (MLE), as opposed to Direct Learning Experience

(DLE). He argues that the "mediators" of our early learning interpose themselves between us and the world to help make our experiences meaningful. Furthermore, he argues that, in their deliberate attempts to change our concepts, mediators promote the development of our cognitive systems.

HOW MLE PROMOTES COGNITIVE DEVELOPMENT

In an attempt to produce mental models, modalities, and dispositions for our later experiences, mediated learning experiences transform our cognitive systems and facilitate our cognitive development. To "show us the meaning," mediators confront us with and draw our attention to selected stimuli. They teach us how to look at the world selectively, how to "see meaning." They schedule the appearance and disappearance of stimuli, they bring together stimuli that are separated by time and/or space, and they focus our attention on certain transformations in stimuli that we otherwise would overlook. In the process, they teach us how to focus and how to register the temporal and spatial properties of objects and events and the changes that occur in them. They teach us how to compare the same experiences using different criteria and how to sort relevant data from irrelevant data. They help us learn how to label our experiences, and they teach us how to group them by categories. Through MLEs, we learn how to learn and how to think. MLEs prepare us for future learning.

> **Have you wondered how it happens that some students do not understand what they experience even in the most engaging classes?**

Consider, for example, two groups of parents and children who visit a hands-on, exploratory science museum. In one group, a child skips eagerly from exhibit to exhibit, touching displays and occasionally pressing a button or listening to a recorded message. In the second group, the child and parents walk to each exhibit together. Then the parents direct the child's attention to specific features, they ask questions, they interpret displays, they search for causal relationships, and they eventually help the child formulate concepts about the exhibit. In the first group, there is no comparing of this new experience to what the child already knows, no new insights are gained, and no new learning takes place. In the second group, the parents provide an MLE, and the child learns and acquires meaning.

Children who have not received sufficient MLEs are not prepared to deal with the cognitive challenges confronting them as they enter school and are thus unable to benefit from the wealth of classroom experiences offered. Even when faced with hands-on, active-learning opportunities, they fail to find the meaning. They may enjoy creating the model planets, but they do not understand the related "whys." They fail to achieve academically, fall behind, and lose interest. These children often experience the world in a random, impulsive way and grasp it episodically. They cannot consider several sources of information simultaneously and do not compare their experiences. They do not form relationships between ideas or look for causes. They do not identify problems and are bored even in classes that teachers believe are challenging. They are children who do not feel a need to reason and draw inferences, children who have difficulties in making representations. Keith was one of these children and, as such, he benefited little from typical classroom experiences.

> They may enjoy creating the model planets, but they do not understand the related "whys."

WHY MLES MAY BE WITHHELD

Children may not receive mediated learning experiences as a result of certain biological, emotional, or social factors. Extensive research—such as studies on Down syndrome or emotionally disturbed children—has been done on biological and emotional factors. Indeed, the literature is replete with evidence of their importance in the cognitive development of children. Some of the research shows that even the consequences of biological and emotional conditions can be ameliorated with effective MLEs.

Feuerstein specifically directs our attention to social factors. He points to the social condition of many culturally different children as a determinant of their academic failure. He has observed that it is this population of children—those likely to be deprived of the benefit of a stable cultural context—who do not receive MLEs as a matter of their parents' choice. Because they do not see their own culture as necessary, or even appropriate, for the future of their children, many minority parents withhold MLEs from their children and delegate the responsibility for their cognitive development to the social institutions of the government. Cultural discontinuity, which turns into MLE deprivation, is indeed a growing social problem, as reported in

comparative studies with minority children. The population
of minority students with learning problems, including the gifted
underachievers, continues to grow.

Feuerstein's theory of MLE is tied to his belief that our cognitive
abilities are modifiable, that we can change our abilities from the
expected course of cognitive development. One of his fundamental
premises is that the structure of the intellect can be transformed to
enable one to learn better. Feuerstein argues that, regardless of age,
irrespective of the cause, and despite a poor level of functioning,
humans' cognitive abilities are malleable. This argument is well supported by research on the brain. If a child did not receive sufficient
MLEs as part of his or her early childhood experiences, MLEs in
the classroom can change the course of the child's early cognitive
development.

MLE IN THE CLASSROOM

Feuerstein's theory of MLE offers a refreshing outlook on education,
and many teachers find his humanistic approach exciting. However,
he warns against the misuse of his ideas. Good learning is not necessarily mediated, and, according to Feuerstein, mediation is not always
good teaching.

A teacher must first decide whether a student needs mediated
learning. If mediation is not needed, then it is useless and may even
be harmful. Mediation, by definition, replaces independent work. If a
student has formed an appropriate goal for his or her science observations (i.e., has formed a relevant hypothesis); can follow written
directions; can record, compare, and sort data; can write a report;
and can present findings, and if his or her learning requires only
these processes, then mediation is not needed. If the student cannot
perform any one, or more, of these functions, then mediation should
be offered to ameliorate the specific deficiency. Furthermore, mediation should be withheld as soon as the student achieves mastery.
Ultimately, all students should be able to benefit from all types of
learning opportunities, including direct learning experiences—such
as lectures, the Internet, and independent study—because they have
learned how to learn.

If you decide to offer MLE, you may want to follow Feuerstein's
guidelines for mediators. Feuerstein lists three characteristics that
define MLE and distinguish it from other teacher/student interactions.[3] None of these is sufficient by itself; rather, each provides a

necessary dimension for MLE. These characteristics are intentionality and reciprocity, transcendence, and meaning.

Intentionality and reciprocity. While children learn much of what they know and can do incidentally, mediation is not incidental teaching. In MLE the teacher interposes himself or herself intentionally and systematically between the children and the content of their experiences. At the same time, both the teacher and the children reciprocate with shared intentions. It is easy to apply this principle when a student initiates MLE—that is, when a student feels a need for the teacher's guidance. In such cases, a teacher intentionally addresses the existing need that engages the student in learning and responds to a child's need for mediation. The more challenging case for mediators is when a child does not feel the need for mediation. How can the teacher's imposed intentions achieve a reciprocal response?

Skillful mediators create *student-felt* needs by manipulating all the available classroom resources, including the content of instruction, the students' level of alertness, and the teacher's own behavior. The model of Feuerstein's Instrumental Enrichment (FIE) program helped me to understand this idea.

Let us first consider the choice of instructional content and material. The FIE program includes hundreds of problem-solving exercises—all using alternatives to the cultural content (ideas, values, beliefs, vocabulary, traditions, and so on) that is known to foster MLEs naturally in the childhood environment but that is often absent in the experiences of culturally deprived students. Teachers are always impressed by the students' excited responses to FIE tasks and by the power of the program to generate a felt need for mediation. FIE tasks challenge students appropriately both by their novelty (their unusual appearance and structure) and by their level of difficulty (not too easy, but progressively more difficult).

Teachers who have access to or are creative in developing and collecting alternative instructional contents usually know how to use variations to engage students. Such teachers may find or develop a variety of content for the mediation of specific abilities. For example, a teacher may want to mediate the sorting of data. If a student is not interested in sorting with one kind of content, the teacher may offer an alternative that does engage the student.

We also need to consider how a teacher's actions help to create student-felt needs for mediation. As teachers, we often behave in the classroom in unusual ways in order to keep students alert. We raise our voices, use exaggerated body movements, and ask direct questions of students who seem to be drifting off. Other teaching strategies, however, enhance the reciprocity in mediation. They focus on student expectations and intrinsic motivation. FIE teachers trained in MLE use questions to create a student-felt need for mediation. Questions are carefully chosen to be as challenging and rewarding as the FIE tasks are. This model can be applied throughout the curriculum.

> New learning experiences should always be built on past successful ones.

The choice of questions reflects the mediator's expectations of students. If the expectations are low, the questions are simple. If they are high, the questions are difficult. If the expectations are wrong, the instructional pace is too slow or too fast, or the questions are unchallenging, the mediation is likely to fail. Therefore, the choice of questions must be based on a fair assessment and analysis of the needs and abilities of the students. The analysis, assessment, and expectations of students must be dynamic, reflecting the changes sought by the MLE.

We often think about the choice of teacher questions in terms of levels, such as those represented by Bloom's taxonomy. When a teacher asks students "why" and "how" rather than "what," students need to generate ideas rather than reproduce and copy ideas. For example, a science teacher whose students completed a sorting procedure will ask the students to explain *how* they did the procedure rather than *what* the result of their work was.

New learning experiences should always be built on past successful ones, with a manageable progression between the two. When the challenge of the teacher's questions is manageable, students become intrinsically motivated to engage further in MLE. If the questions are too simple or too difficult, students disengage from the MLE.

The way we choose our questions is related to the time we allow students to think before they respond and to our reactions to their responses. Teachers often are impatient. The average pause or "wait time" after teachers ask a question in the classroom is two to three seconds. This impatience generally has three negative consequences. First, students may need more time to think a question through carefully. Premature student responses are likely to misguide teachers in forming subsequent questions. Second, short wait time reinforces students' impulsiveness. Third, when students don't respond during the short pause, teachers tend to become uncomfortable and replace the original question with another, lower-level question, thereby reducing the challenge to students, possibly below the optimal level. A mediator's (in this case a teacher's) patience, even an "exaggerated" pause, is critical to the learning experience.

The mediator's response to a student's answer must foster reciprocity in the interaction. Mediators may encourage and invite further elaboration and discussion or probe if initial responses are incomplete, unclear, or incorrect. At the same time, mediators should remain nonjudgmental in their comments. Examples of appropriate teacher responses are "Thank you for your answer," "Interesting answer," "Could you explain your thinking in a different way, so that all the students can understand?" and "Could you think of another answer?" Responses of this kind reflect the reciprocal nature of the interaction between mediator and learner, and they foster intrinsic motivation.

To summarize, teacher behaviors that foster reciprocity in an MLE include

- choosing content that students like to think about,
- changing stance, facial and body expressions, and level and inflection of voice,
- asking "why" and "how" questions rather than "what" questions,
- allowing sufficient wait time for student responses,
- responding to student reflections in a nonjudgmental manner,
- encouraging students to offer alternative ideas,
- revealing interest in student learning,
- listening carefully to students,
- showing readiness to spend more time for the benefit of a student's learning, and
- taking special interest in struggling learners.

Transcendence. While it may be an appropriate teaching goal, content knowledge by itself is not the mediator's concern. Content serves only as a means to reach the goals of MLEs. An MLE seeks changes in the way students learn and think. Such changes must transcend the content and context of the MLE. A teacher may use the science class to mediate the process and utility of sorting data by different criteria. However, the teacher's mediation must be aimed at the cognitive behavior and not at the specific data to which the process is applied. In fact, content may be a restrictive factor in an MLE.

Abstract as it may be, content always defines specific contextual, functional, or even conceptual boundaries. In order to ensure the transfer of learning to other content areas and contexts, mediators should attempt to *eliminate* the boundaries that intrinsically tie the target cognitive behavior in the learning experience to its content; that is, they must decontextualize the learning of cognitive behavior. To do this, mediators need to vary the content while focusing on the *same* target behavior. For example, if the mediator is focusing on representational thinking, then the classroom model for the rotation of Earth around the sun would be just one instance in which the students discuss the spatial configuration and relationships involved. The mediator would engage the students with other contents that model the same cognitive function. Thus a science teacher might ask students to model eclipses of the sun and the moon and to explain these conditions as observed from Earth, the moon, and the sun. When the students realize that the view differs depending on the point of reference, the teacher would ask them to think of other cases in which the outcome depends on the point of view.

> While it may be an appropriate teaching goal, content knowledge by itself is not the mediator's concern.

Typical examples of the transcendence principle can be found in mediated learning at home. As parents mediate the concept of organization, they choose different content areas and contexts. These may include the organization of toys, drawings, crayons, chairs, tools, the contents of a school bag, and so on. The organization of these objects will vary with the criteria applied. First, the items might be ordered by size or color, then grouped by function, and, eventually, by age or according to the different relationships between them.

The transcendent goal in these MLEs is to develop the child's need and ability to organize different objects and events by different criteria for different purposes. If the mediated learning of organization is limited to certain objects, certain criteria, and specific purposes, then the transfer or application of this learning will be limited. Similarly, parents use different content and contexts to mediate reflective behavior, comparative behavior, the concepts of space and time, the search for causal relationships, logic, communication skills, and so on. When parents mediate, they foster lifelong learning abilities.

If the goal of MLE is to foster independence and lifelong learning, then teachers, too, must focus on processes rather than content. Just think about the magnitude of change in the world since you were in grade school. If you are currently a teacher, then the amount of knowledge in the world has grown at least eightfold since you went to grade school; school curricula have been changed many times; work has changed radically; life has become vastly different. It is projected that in twenty years, knowledge will double every seventy-three days! Can you imagine how our lives will differ in twenty years? Mediated learning experiences must seek the development of learning and thinking abilities that will be useful with mostly unpredictable content.

> It is projected that in twenty years, knowledge will double every seventy-three days!

The key to teacher mediation is identifying appropriate transcendent goals. Current national and state standards for different academic fields call for the pursuit of such goals. For example, among the standards for science literacy established by the American Association for the Advancement of Science, the benchmarks for the use of patterns and relationships include measuring, estimating, seeing the shape of things, making graphs, comparing two groups of data, analyzing patterns, and so on.[4] These goals describe cognitive processes and dispositions rather than contents. While the content used to achieve these goals may vary, the transcending MLE goals are quite specific. The cognitive processes described by these goals are likely to be applicable even in the unforeseeable future.

Transcendent goals turn MLEs into deliberate and systematic, rather than incidental, experiences. Such goals provide the mediator with a context for structuring learning experiences. However, as indicated above, despite the implicit order in the learning experiences, students still might not make connections between current and previous learning and might not anticipate future learning experiences without the help of a mediator.

Mediators employ several practices to ensure that students understand how their learning is connected to transcending goals. First, mediators help students make a clear connection between a current learning experience and previous ones by asking them to review their past experiences, summarize a new experience, and compare both sets of experiences. Mediation of transcendent goals again takes the form of higher-level questions. Questions that elicit students' insights about "how" and "why" they perform the way they do help them to connect current and past experiences.

Second, mediators are always instrumental in bringing the learning outcomes to the level of the child's awareness. The typical questions "What was new today?" followed by "How did you change?" provide the vehicle for the production of this awareness of or insight into the learning outcomes.

Third, mediators help students relate current learning experiences to transcendent goals by asking questions that anticipate future uses, such as "What is it good for?" and "Where can it be used?" Student examples of such applications are meaningful because they illustrate the transcendence of the learning experience beyond the specific content. For example, if a child learns to organize his room and is asked to elaborate on the value of organization and to anticipate the future uses of this idea, the child might recognize that he needs to organize his school bag and that, when he is older, he will need to organize his tool box, and so on.

Teacher behaviors that model transcendence in an MLE include

- selecting a variety of instructional content in accordance with transcendent cognitive developmental goals,
- asking "why" and "how" questions rather than informative "what" questions,
- making a clear connection between a current learning experience and previous ones,
- discussing learning outcomes, and
- relating learning experiences and transcendent goals.

Meaning. The basic tenet of the theory of MLE is that mediation endows the learning experience with meaning. Meaningful learning may be considered the successful product of emotional and cognitive excitement. An MLE provides the student with the emotional excitement of learning and with the feeling of competence. An MLE also successfully targets the "whys" and "what fors" of the learning. Thus the learning experience simultaneously becomes a meaningful emotional experience and a meaningful cognitive one. Mediators do not expect their students to readily "see" this meaning in the learning experience. They guide the students through learning in the search for this meaning.

Much has been said about "making learning fun." I will not discuss this important idea here. Rather, it is my intention to elaborate the cognitive aspect of the mediation of meaning. In this article I am concerned with the common case of students who learn content and procedures and may have fun learning them but are still left without an understanding of why what they learned is important. Tricks, no less wonderful than magic, make such students absorb content and procedures whose meaning they don't understand. Unfortunately, in many cases, and certainly in the long term, even magic does not work, and meaningless learning stops. Students may graduate or drop out of school without ever appreciating the utility of mathematics, the beauty of art and literature, the purpose and process of scientific experiments, the importance of physical education, or the value of a healthy diet. These are the kinds of meanings mediators guide students to find in their learning experiences.

> **Tricks, no less wonderful than magic, make such students absorb content and procedures whose meaning they don't understand.**

Discovering how our theories apply to our observations—i.e., finding meaning—involves comparing experiences, grouping and regrouping them, considering when and where they occur, and examining relationships between them. Children are not the only ones who fail to do this. I remember an adult student in the FIE program who suddenly realized that his failure in school had to do with the fact that he did not know how to learn. One day he appeared extremely excited and instructed me to "look at this textbook!" I took the book from him, looked at the cover, scanned its contents, and struggled to find some intelligent comment to match his excitement as he exclaimed, "Look, I highlighted the whole book!" Indeed, his yellow marks covered the entire contents of the book. He said that he never knew that learning is not memorizing. Only now did he understand that to find meaning he needed to reorganize the information he read to fit his theories—or to adapt his theories of "why" and "how" things are or happen. Indeed, many students process their experiences this way only when a mediator guides them to do so. Experienced and independent learners do so automatically. They do it because they learned why and how to do it at some point in the past.

The mediation of meaning is essentially teaching how to learn. First, mediation makes it understood that learning has a target. By asking questions, the mediator helps the student anticipate a learning goal: "What are we looking for?" and "Why is it important?" Then the mediator makes sure that the student compares and classifies the new information or connects it with what has been previously learned, asking such questions as "How is it the same as before?" "What is new here?" and "How is it different?" Then the mediator helps the student construct new meaning, asking such questions as "What did you learn today?" "How did you find out?" "Why is it important?" and "Where can you use what you learned?" Eventually, the mediator will bring the process of learning itself into the student's conscious awareness: "What did you learn about learning [e.g., experimenting, thinking, and so on]?" and "Where will you use it?"

Teaching behaviors associated with the mediation of meaning are

- discussing learning goals with students,
- repeating concepts in their different applications,
- encouraging students to identify applications for what they learned,
- expecting students to transfer their learning across the curriculum,
- giving explicit value to a given experience,
- changing stance, facial and body expressions, and level and inflection of voice, and
- asking "why" and "how" questions, rather than "what" questions.

Throughout my career as an educator I have found that Feuerstein's theory of MLE, while "naturally appealing," is more a source of concern for educators than a source of relief. It is more demanding than it is comforting; it makes our expectations grow and our accomplishments shrink. Feuerstein's theory is hard to implement, for it requires the utmost in commitment, continuous learning, and systematic work. At the same time, I have learned that there is no alternative to hard work for enabling children to learn.

The reward for that hard work is well deserved. Keith is now 18 and will graduate from high school this year. The dialogue with Keith less than a decade ago was an important milestone in his teacher's career. She has since become a mediator and has helped many other students in Brooklyn, New York, develop appropriate science concepts. Together, a student and his teacher found out where the sun is before it rises.

NOTES

1. Madeleine Long and Meir Ben-Hur, "Informing Learning Through the Clinical Interview," *Arithmetic Teacher*, February 1991, pp. 44–47.

2. Lev Vygotsky, *Mind in Society* (Cambridge, Mass.: Harvard University Press, 1978).

3. Reuven Feuerstein, Rafi Feuerstein, and Yaron Schur, "Process as Content in Education of Exceptional Children," in Arthur L. Costa and Rosemarie M. Liebmann, eds., *Supporting the Spirit of Learning: When Process Is Content* (Thousand Oaks, Calif.: Corwin Press, 1997).

4. American Association for the Advance of Science, *Project 2061: The Nature of Mathematics, Grades 3–5* (New York: Oxford University Press, 1993).

Infusing Higher Order Thinking into Science and Language Arts

by Joyce VanTassel-Baska

How do we address the needs of our best learners in schools? This central question can be answered in several ways, all relating to the teaching of higher order thinking. Through the use of inquiry models that promote both convergent and divergent thinking, high-ability students may be best served.

VanTassel-Baska (1993a) examined research support for curriculum promoting higher order thinking:

> Studies of thinking have strongly contributed to understanding curriculum directions for the gifted. Expert-novice comparisons in various fields (Berliner 1985; Sommers 1980) have yielded differences favoring experts in metacognitive acts like planning and revising. A collection of research on expertise has revealed that the successful utilization of these skills may be content-specific. Rabinowitz and Glaser (1985) found that expert performance entailed a large knowledge base of domain-specific patterns, rapid recognition of situations in which these patterns apply, and the use of forward reasoning based on pattern manipulation to reach solutions.
>
> Further support for such domain-specific research comes out of studies that use general content-independent cognitive strategies and that find no clear benefits outside the specific domains in which they are taught (Pressley, Snyder, and Carigha-Bull 1987). Thus, research on transfer suggests that "thinking at its most effective [level] depends on specific context-bound skills and units of knowledge that have little application to other domains" (Perkins and Saloman 1989, 119).

From a paper based on a presentation at the Fourth International Teaching for Intelligence Conference, April 25, 1998, New York, NY. © 1998 by Joyce VanTassel-Baska. Reprinted with permission.

Teaching thinking skills to the gifted, then, or any learner, requires an integrated approach, with attention to several variables simultaneously. Curriculum for the gifted must always be concerned about multiple outcomes, in cognitive, affective, aesthetic, and social areas. Such curriculum can be deliberately designed in an integrated fashion to address all of these dimensions through an approach that recognizes the importance of three interrelated aspects: advanced content that honors the child's level of precocity in domain-specific areas, higher level thinking and problem-solving processes that honor the gifted child's ability to explore topics in greater depth resulting in substantive products, and the use of inter-disciplinary concepts, problems, and issues that honor the child's ability to make connections within and across domains of knowledge (VanTassel-Baska 1992).

> Teaching thinking skills to the gifted, then, or any learner, requires an integrated approach, with attention to several variables simulta-neously.

For the past eight years, with the support of special grants from the United States Department of Education, we at the Center for Gifted Education have been involved in the process of designing, field testing, and revising curriculum for gifted learners based on this conceptual model. Key aspects of curriculum development have included collaboration with experts in the content domains of science and language arts in the development process; review of existing curriculum materials based on validated criteria for what constitutes appropriate curriculum generally, what constitutes an exemplary curriculum in the subject areas, and what constitutes appropriate curriculum for gifted learners; the development of teacher training workshops on core strategies integrated into the units; and conducting three phases of research: on student learning gains, teacher implementation issues, and school change as a result of using the College of William and Mary curriculum units.

THE PROCESS OF CURRICULUM INFUSION

Several key features were part of the curriculum development process that appeared to make a difference with respect to the infusion of higher order thinking into the curriculum, the degree of acceptance in schools, and key aspects of classroom implementation (VanTassel-Baska, Gallagher, Bailey, and Sher 1993; VanTassel-Baska 1993b). These features included the following:

The importance of frameworks. Each of the curriculum projects has developed a set of goals and underlying objectives that provided the anchor point for curriculum development, implementation, and assessment. These frameworks, developed on the Integrated Curriculum Model (ICM) cited in earlier work (VanTassel-Baska 1992, 1994, 1995), served as a coherent structure for all phases of the work.

The curriculum, instruction, and assessment (CIA) relationship. The interplay of curriculum, instruction, and assessment is a critical understanding for the curriculum design enterprise, and it has become even more critical as teachers implement a new curriculum that they understand how these pieces fit together to enhance learning.

The collaborative nature of the development work. Our work was only possible because of the efforts of individuals with varying expertise and perspectives. The inclusion of a molecular biologist as a major player in the enterprise of developing science curriculum cannot be underestimated with respect to the integrity of the effort. Similar expertise in English and language arts was also available.

The alignment of national, state, and local standards. Part of the task in these projects is to show how one can serve high-end learners and address state and local concerns for curriculum mastery. Given that both projects were modeled on the National Standards work, the alignment tasks were very straightforward.

The linkage to other exemplary materials. We also have worked to link our materials to other exemplary materials found through the use of an extensive evaluation process (Johnson, Boyce, and VanTassel-Baska 1995). In science, we have aligned our work with several materials developed at Lawrence Hall of Science, including Great Explorations in Math and Science (GEMS), Full Option Science System (FOSS), and Insights. In language arts, we have established a relationship with the Junior Great Books Program, modeling our literature selections and questions after its approach.

Training on materials. Based on our preliminary work with these projects, we decided to develop a training model that was grounded in enhancing chances for strong implementation. Therefore, our training efforts modeled those employed by many National Science Foundation (NSF) projects, using materials as the basis for teaching strategies necessary for classroom use. Such an approach proved to be a critical component of our efforts. We have now conducted training in over thirty states and have implementation sites in twenty-two of them as a result. National training was also conducted at the College of William and Mary over a three-year period.

THE RESEARCH AGENDA

The research agenda for the project emerged out of the need to move beyond pilot efforts in teacher developer classrooms. Toward that end we began to look more closely at questions of impact. The overall model for the curriculum development effort linked to research may be found in Figure 1. Currently, the Center faculty, staff, and graduate students are engaged in a series of studies that are examining aspects of the implementation of the curriculum and its underlying pedagogy in schools. These studies may be clustered around the following categories:

Curriculum Effectiveness Studies

We are engaged in a series of curriculum effectiveness studies that are examining the curriculum impact by unit, by developmental level (primary, intermediate, and middle school), by classrooms over time (implementation of three or more units), and by teachers over time (three-year implementations). Moreover, the Center is also conducting replications of basic student impact studies at new sites (VanTassel-Baska, Hughes, Johnson, Boyce, and Hall 1997).

Classroom Implementation Studies

We also are interested in understanding how the curriculum works on a day-to-day basis at the classroom level. Thus, we are exploring teacher behaviors, use of specific strategies and embedded assessments (nonusable material, modifications, and extensions), and classroom interaction processes.

Special Population Studies

We also wish to understand the impact of the curriculum on special populations of students, especially disadvantaged and minority students. Two questions of interest are (1) how effective is the curriculum with disadvantaged and minority students? and (2) are the effects differential or comparable to those found with more advantaged populations? Comparison of student outcome effects also are of interest with other special populations as well. One dissertation study, for example, is focusing on the teaching of persuasive writing through the use of the Paul model with gifted, learning disabled, and average students (Hughes, in preparation).

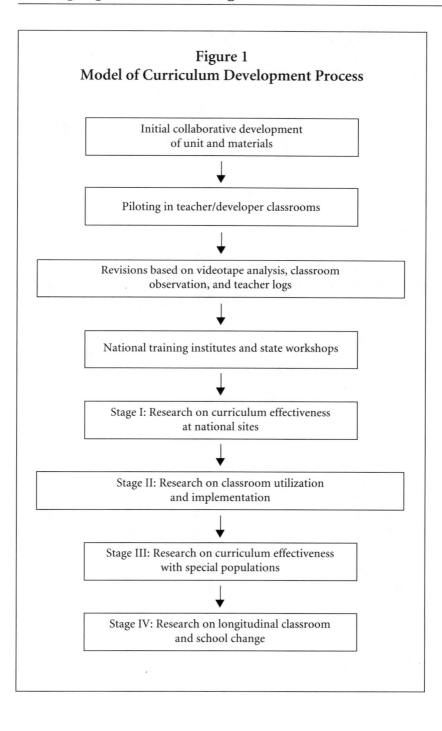

Figure 1
Model of Curriculum Development Process

Initial collaborative development
of unit and materials

↓

Piloting in teacher/developer classrooms

↓

Revisions based on videotape analysis, classroom
observation, and teacher logs

↓

National training institutes and state workshops

↓

Stage I: Research on curriculum effectiveness
at national sites

↓

Stage II: Research on classroom utilization
and implementation

↓

Stage III: Research on curriculum effectiveness
with special populations

↓

Stage IV: Research on longitudinal classroom
and school change

Classroom and School Studies of Change

Finally, we have an interest in studying how curriculum impacts on school change and reform. Consequently, we are studying teacher use of the units over three years and more to determine collective impacts on school and district use over time (VanTassel-Baska, Avery, Little, and Hughes, under review). We are specifically interested in how institutionalized the curriculum becomes in selected districts as judged by its presence in district policies, its classroom utility, and perceptions of it among relevant stakeholders, such as parents, students, and teachers.

NATURE OF PRELIMINARY FINDINGS

In the area of science we have found significant but modest gains for experimental groups on a pre/post measure of integrated science process skills (Fowler 1990). Content analysis of student responses across forty-five classrooms reveals students do not demonstrate gains in skills such as planning data collection, planning to control variables, interpreting data, and drawing conclusions. All of these skill areas require higher order thinking. Individual students, however, are showing strong improvement even in these areas.

The following example represents a pre-assessment for science learning in grade three. The prompt is the question "Are earthworms attracted to light?" The protocol is a 22-point scale judging initial layout, examination of data, and evaluation of results.

Student A pretest response:

> First, I would put some earthworms in a container. There would be lights and some dirt. I would put several different earthworms in it. If more earthworms liked the light, then that would be right. If more didn't like the light, then that would be right. I would try this with about seven groups and decide if they liked light.

The student in this pretest response reveals much about what he knows and doesn't know about the scientific design process. First, he demonstrates a narrative orientation to the prompt rather than a scientific one. He has an idea of "procedures" and is able to demonstrate a rudimentary manipulation of materials. He also has a sense about the setting of criterion levels for judging the results of experiments.

After twenty-five hours of instruction in a specially designed problem-based science curriculum unit, Student A's post-test response to the prompt "Are bees attracted to diet cola?" is as follows:

Materials: Diet cola, 3 large containers, 3 small containers, 6 bees

Hypothesis: If you give bees diet cola then they will be attracted to it

1. Gather 6 bees, diet cola, 3 large containers, 3 small containers.

2. Put 2 bees in each large container.

3. Pour 5 ml of diet cola in each small container.

4. Set the small container of diet cola in each large container that has bees in it.

5. Watch and observe to see if the bees are attracted to the diet cola.

6. You should record if the bees like diet cola on a chart like below.

Bee	If they are attracted to diet cola
1	
2	
3	
4	
5	
6	

In this post-test response, the same student is able to perform many more scientific research tasks well. He can delineate materials, provide clear and specific procedures, formulate a hypothesis, understand the need for a data table, demonstrate precision with respect to the experiment, and demonstrate understanding of repeated trials. His protocol score has risen from a 5 to a 14.

Has this student learned from the curriculum? Yes, in several interrelated science processes, yet he still does not evidence deep understanding of the role of interpretation of results linked to the original problem nor clear ways to judge results of the experiment.

Yet why is there such limited growth overall? Three hypotheses that are being explored include (1) that the curriculum may not be faithfully implemented, (2) that teachers teach what they know and therefore may not be focusing on the higher level science skills, and (3) that an integrated curriculum model may inhibit strong growth in any given area (VanTassel-Baska, Bass, Ries, Poland, and Avery 1998).

Teacher qualitative responses were overwhelmingly positive in respect to using the problem-based units of study, noting that students found the units highly motivating and interesting, a perspective shared by teachers as well. Evidence of significant learning based on problem-based learning (PBL), however, is yet to be documented (Boyce, VanTassel-Baska, Burruss, Sher, and Johnson 1997).

In the area of language arts, we have found significant and impressive gains in literature, persuasive writing, and linguistic competency for experimental classes using the curriculum (VanTassel-Baska, Johnson, Hughes, and Boyce 1996).

An example of a performance-based assessment task and the analysis of learning that has occurred in the area of language arts may also be examined. The prompt is "Should the poem 'Autobiographia Literaria' be required reading for students in your grade level?" The protocol focuses on the development of claim, data, warrant, and conclusion and has a 20-point scale.

The pre-assessment response for a student in grade 5 follows:

> In my opinion this poem has a good message because kids can relate to it. The first reason I say this is he writes about a child and his feelings, which can relate to children. Second this poem shows how much you can change in a lifetime, which teaches children. Finally this will help child who is feeling different know that he is not alone.

In a preliminary content analysis of this piece, we can note that the language fluency is low and relatively awkward; there is the presence of the fundamental structure of persuasive writing with an introduction, three reasons, but no conclusion; and there is sensitivity to literature in that the writer discerns the theme of loneliness that changes once the narrator has been exposed to poetry.

Let us now examine the post assessment after thirty hours of instruction in a College of William and Mary language arts curriculum unit.

The prompt reads "Should the poem 'Where the Rainbow Ends' be required reading for students in your grade level?" The same student's individual response reads:

> I really liked this poem "Where the Rainbow Ends" by Richard Rive. I think other kids my age would agree with me. I'm concerned about racism mainly because I'm Jewish and I know about the Holocaust. I totally agree with this poem. It's true that getting along together will be a part tune to learn.
>
> Most kids, no matter what their parents say, will play with whoever they like. I never ask my friends their religion, I just play with them. If these kids read this poem it will enforce positive beliefs that hopefully they will pass on to their children as well.

Because he uses the metaphor of music to explain a difficult idea, it makes it easier for kids to understand. The line "There is no white music and no black music" makes the idea that there is no difference between white and black people very clear.

It's important for fifth graders to read a poem by a black poet and then see that it is no different than one written by a white poet. This shows us that there is no white and black poetry—just poetry.

This is an excellent poem for a fifth grade class. We should read words by writers from all different ethnic groups, the metaphor makes his point clear to everyone, and since most kids don't discriminate Mr. Rive's poem makes you feel you are right to think that way.

The student demonstrates competency in several areas of the prompt. His language fluency is very strong, and he has cast a well-articulated response. The persuasive structure of his argument is also very strong in both basic areas and elaborative structure. He shows unusually heightened sensitivity to literature, apparent from his reference to the poem's central metaphor and the ability to articulate its relationship to the social realm. He also is sensitive to multicultural literature and its value. Moreover, he displays a recognition of the insidiousness of racism and its negative impact on society.

Has this student learned from the curriculum? Yes, we would argue, he has grown in several dimensions. He exhibits ideational fluency and elaboration (creativity), writing skills essential to high-level development (i.e., thesis, argument, conclusion), enhanced literary analysis and interpretation skills, and social understanding of similarities and differences among people. Specifically, his protocol score moves from a 10 to a 20.

Individual content analyses reveal different patterns of growth, however. Overall findings led to follow-up implementation studies and new questions. Why, for example, is there less growth in literature analysis and interpretation than writing for the majority of learners? Several hypotheses emerged around this question. One is that the curriculum units have a stronger emphasis on teaching the persuasive writing model directly than they do in teaching literary analysis. A second hypothesis is that the assessment of literary analysis and interpretation may not be taught to students as a rubric for self assessment as is the case for writing. A third hypothesis, also to be entertained, focuses on the possibility of uneven implementation of the units, with more emphasis placed on persuasive writing.

In schools, we have found extensive evidence of institutionalizing of the curriculum with many constituent groups voicing strong support for its impact. Teachers remarked that the units helped students look for the big picture instead of just memorizing a lot of isolated information and promoted teacher learning as well. Several administrators noted that teachers have learned to draw back and be coaches, letting kids hit or miss the mark. Regarding the language arts curriculum, teachers noted that after students have been exposed to more than one unit, they began to see improvements in habits of mind, writing and self-reflection skills, and the ability to work cooperatively in groups.

> "We get smarter as the units get harder."

Parents cited the benefits of the units' carryover into the home. One parent noted: "When my child hears a speaker, he starts to critique what is being said and how things are interrelated." Another parent related: "This notion of having three arguments has now permeated our life. We wanted to go bowling and my son kept saying 'elaborate'." Students agreed that the gifted materials keep their minds working, and one perceptive young man observed: "We get smarter as the units get harder."

IMPLICATIONS FOR PRACTICE

The benefit of using sound curriculum that has been well designed is a clear implication of all of our studies. Until the field is ready to critique existing materials and seek high quality, student learning will not be positively impacted. Variability in instructional technique also appears to be critical, particularly the use of inquiry—a central focus of all of the curriculum units in both science and language arts. The use of assessment as a direct vehicle for learning is also a strong implication from our work. It must be habitual, and rubrics need to be taught to students with well-defined criteria for guiding judgment. Monitoring implementation in the school context is also essential to curriculum success. Moreover, the role of the principal and how staff development needs are addressed impact greatly on positive effects.

In addition, there is a need for equal emphasis on the dynamics of curriculum, instruction, and assessment in the teaching and learning enterprise. Balanced emphasis on these dynamics may be the most vital force to yield the positive change in education so desperately sought by so many.

Key variables in the curriculum development cycle need to include equal attention to each part of the cycle. For curriculum, appropriate goals and outcomes are essential to begin the process, followed by activities that address those outcomes in a substantive manner. The curriculum must also be exemplary for the subject matter under study, demonstrated very well in the new national standards projects in all subject areas. It also should be designed according to high ability needs to ensure the level of challenge necessary.

Appropriate instructional emphasis requires the use of multiple types of strategies that simultaneously reflect classroom management of various groups, flexible use of differentiated materials, and the manipulation of core strategies. An emphasis on inquiry must be present to ensure the mental engagement of the learner. By the same token, a balance needs to be struck between direct instruction and facilitation. Use of higher level questions toward a focus or goal also is a critical component of instruction for high-end learners. Furthermore, effective use of individual, small group, and large group activities needs to be a basic part of effective teaching.

Assessment has to be viewed as integral to the teaching process, yielding important diagnostic information used to promote learning. Assessment should be frequent and ongoing, and include both performance-based and standardized measures. Most important as a teaching tool is the use of specific criteria for judgment of performance through which teachers can instill standards of excellence toward which students may aim.

While the curriculum, instruction, and assessment dynamic is important, it is also critical that school administrators see their role as instructional leaders, ensuring that a learning dynamic is taking place in an appropriate way. Thus, monitoring for classroom implementation is essential to the integrity of the process. The role of the principal as a visible instructional leader in classrooms puts the emphasis on student growth, where it belongs. In such a system, emergent staff development needs can be discerned through judging day-to-day practice. Teacher leaders can also act as catalysts in this process, engaging in peer coaching and other means to promote positive change.

Finally, it is important to specify what we mean by positive change for any learner and what our understanding of the gifted contributes to this oft used, but vague term. There are three essential components to judging positive change in a school context: enhanced learning for students, a climate of excellence, and learning-centered students, parents, and teachers. Until student learning is at the center of judgments made about any reform, it is a meaningless exercise in the technics of schooling. In respect to a climate of excellence, a school must provide visible symbols that learning matters. Lastly, learning-oriented stakeholders in the educational process are a necessary part of positive change. Teachers, parents, and students must collectively accept that the process of learning over a lifetime is a core value to be internalized.

> In respect to a climate of excellence, a school must provide visible symbols that learning matters.

Can appropriate curriculum become a reality in schools? The answer is a tentative "yes." We have 55 school districts on our national network of schools, using both the science and language arts units, and 100 districts using one or more units. Reports and ongoing work with these districts indicate a reawakening of a concern for coherence and quality in curriculum such that real learning for our best students has become a reality.

REFERENCES

Berliner, D. (1985). Presidential address to the American Educational Research Association. San Francisco, CA.

Boyce, L. N., J. VanTassel-Baska, J. D. Burruss, B. T. Sher, and D. T. Johnson. (1997). A problem-based curriculum: Parallel learning opportunities for students and teachers. *Journal for the Education of the Gifted* 20: 363–379.

Fowler, M. (1990). The diet cola test. *Science Scope* 13, 4: 32–34.

Hughes, C. (in preparation). A study of gifted, learning disabled, and average learners in the teaching of thinking through persuasive writing. Unpublished doctoral dissertation in preparation.

Johnson, D. T., L. N. Boyce, and J. VanTassel-Baska. (1995). Science curriculum review: Evaluating materials for high-ability learners. *Gifted Child Quarterly* 39: 36–43.

Perkins, D., and G. Saloman. (1989). Are cognitive research skills context bound? *Educational Researcher* 18, 1: 16–25.

Pressley, M., B. Snyder, and T. Carigha-Bull. (1987). How can good strategy use be taught to children? Evaluation of six alternative approaches. In S. M. Corner and J. D. Hagman (Eds.), *Transfer of learning* (pp. 81–120). New York: Academic.

Rabinowitz, M., and R. Glaser. (1985). Cognitive structure and process on highly competent performance. In E. D. Horowitz and M. O'Brien (Eds.), *The gifted and talented: Developmental perspectives* (pp. 75–98). Washington, DC: American Psychological Association.

Sommers, N. (1980). Revision strategies of student writers and experienced writers. *College Composition and Communications* 31: 378–387.

VanTassel-Baska, J. (1992). *Planning effective curriculum for the gifted.* Denver, CO: Love Publishing.

VanTassel-Baska, J. (1993a). Theory and research on curriculum development for the gifted. In K. A. Heller, F. J. Minks, and A. H. Passow (Eds.), *International handbook of research and development of giftedness and talent* (pp. 365–386). New York: Pergamon Press.

VanTassel-Baska, J. (1993b). The National Curriculum Development Projects for high ability learners: Key issues and findings. In N. Colangelo, S. G. Assouline, and D. L. Ambroson (Eds.), *Talent development* (vol. 2, pp. 19–38). Dayton, OH: Ohio Psychology Press.

VanTassel-Baska, J. (1994). *Comprehensive curriculum for gifted learners* (2nd ed.). Boston: Allyn and Bacon.

VanTassel-Baska, J. (1995). The development of talent through curriculum. *Roeper Review* 18: 98–102.

VanTassel-Baska, J., L. D. Avery, C. A. Little, and C. E. Hughes. (under review). Where the rubber meets the road: The impact of the William and Mary units on schools. Manuscript submitted for publication.

VanTassel-Baska, J., G. Bass, R. Ries, D. Poland, and L. Avery. (1998). A national pilot study of science curriculum effectiveness for high ability students. *Gifted Child Quarterly* 42: 200–211.

VanTassel-Baska, J., S. A. Gallagher, J. M. Bailey, and B. T. Sher. (1993). Scientific experimentation. *Gifted Child Today* 16, 5: 42–46.

VanTassel-Baska, J., C. E. Hughes, D. T. Johnson, L. N. Boyce, and D. R. Hall. (1997, April). Language arts curriculum effectiveness study: Results of a curriculum developed for high ability students. Presentation given at the annual meeting of the American Educational Education Association, Chicago, IL.

VanTassel-Baska, J., D. T. Johnson, C. E. Hughes, and L. N. Boyce. (1996). A study of language arts curriculum effectiveness with gifted learners. *Journal for the Education of the Gifted* 19: 461–480.

A Practical Approach for Developing the Gifts and Talents of All Students

by Joseph S. Renzulli

I f there is one thing upon which most leaders of educational reform agree, it is that remedial models for school improvement
have failed. Attempts to push up achievement test scores from
"the bottom" through highly prescriptive mastery learning models
have frustrated low-achieving students and dragged down the performance of average and high-achieving youngsters. An alternative to
what one student called the "drill-and-kill" approach is an enrich-
ment-based model that uses "high-end learning" strategies and accelerated content to improve the performance of all students.

The Schoolwide Enrichment Model (SEM) is a detailed blueprint for total school improvement that is flexible enough to allow
each school to develop its own unique program based on local
resources, student populations, school leadership dynamics, and faculty strengths and creativity. Although this research-supported model
is based on highly successful practices that have their origins in special programs for gifted and talented students, its major goal is to
promote both challenging and enjoyable high-end learning across the
full range of school types, levels, and demographic differences. It is
not intended to replace or minimize existing services to high-achieving students. Rather, its purpose is to integrate these services into
"a rising tide lifts all ships" approach to school improvement and to
expand the role of enrichment specialists by having these persons
infuse specific practices for high-end learning into the total school

From a paper based on a presentation at the Fourth International Teaching for
Intelligence Conference, April 25, 1998, New York, NY. © 1998 by Joseph S.
Renzulli. Reprinted with permission.

program. The Schoolwide Enrichment Model provides educators
with the means to

• Develop the talent potentials of young people by systematically assessing their strengths, providing enrichment opportunities,
resources, and services to develop their strengths, and using a flexible
approach to curricular differentiation and the use of school time.

• Improve the academic performance of all students in all areas
of the regular curriculum and to blend standard curriculum activities with meaningful enrichment learning.

• Promote continuous, reflective, growth-oriented professionalism of school personnel to such an extent that many faculty
members emerge as leaders in curriculum and staff development,
program planning, etc.

• Create a learning community that honors ethnic, gender, and
cultural diversity and that promotes mutual respect, democratic
principles, and the preservation of the earth's resources.

A CASE IN POINT

Two afternoons a week, twelve-year-old Kelvin goes to an enrichment cluster at the Noah Webster School in Hartford, Connecticut.
When he was selected for the program, Kelvin said, "It feels good, but
I was amazed. I was about to faint! I was super, super surprised." The
reason for Kelvin's amazement is that he never considered himself
to be a good student, at least not in the traditional way we usually
view students. And the program was not exactly the place where you
found kids like Kelvin, who lives in subsidized housing and whose
family manages to survive on a monthly welfare check and food
stamps.

But the program in which Kelvin is enrolled looks at talent
development in a different way. Based on a plan called the Schoolwide Enrichment Model, the program seeks to identify a broad range
of talent potentials in all students through the use of a strength
assessment guide called the Total Talent Portfolio. This guide helps
to focus attention on student interests and learning style preferences
as well as strengths in traditional subjects. These strengths serve as
building blocks for advanced achievement. Kelvin's strongest academic area is mathematics, and through a process called curriculum
compacting, he is now being provided with mathematics material
that is two grade levels above the level of math being covered in his
classroom.

Kelvin, who once described himself as a "mental dropout," now finds school a much more inviting place. He is hoping to enter the research he is doing on airplane wing design in his enrichment cluster into a state science fair competition. He is also thinking about a career in engineering, and the enrichment specialist at his school has helped him apply for a special summer program at the University of Connecticut that is designed to recruit and assist minorities into mathematical and engineering related professions. "School," says Kelvin, "is a place where you have must-dos and can-dos. I work harder on my must-dos so I can spend more time working on my can-dos."

> " . . . I work harder on my must-dos so I can spend more time working on my can-dos."

THE SECRET LABORATORY OF SCHOOL IMPROVEMENT

Kelvin represents one example of the ways in which numerous students are being given opportunities to develop talent potentials that too many schools have ignored for too many years. The type of program in which Kelvin is enrolled is not a radical departure from present school structures, but it is based on assumptions about learners and learning that are different from those that have guided public education for many years. We must consider new ways of solving problems than using the levels of consciousness that created them if there is to be any hope of turning around a public education system that is slowly but surely deteriorating into a massive warehouse of underachievement, unfulfilled expectations, and broken dreams. The factory model of schooling that gave rise to the clear and present danger facing our schools cannot be used to overcome the very problems that this model of schooling has created. And yet, as we examine reform initiatives, it is difficult to find plans and policies that are qualitatively different from the old top-down patterns of school organization or the traditional linear/sequential models of learning that have dominated almost all of the curriculum used in our schools. Transcending these previous levels of consciousness will not be an easy task. If there is any single, unifying characteristic of present-day schools, that characteristic is surely a resistance, if not an immunity, to change. The ponderous rhetoric about school improvement and the endless lists of noble goals need to be tempered with a gentle and evolutionary approach to change that school personnel can live with and grow with rather than be threatened by. If the traditional methods of schooling have failed to bring about substantial changes, we must look at different models that have shown promise of achieving the types of school improvement we so desperately have sought.

In many respects, special programs of almost any type have been the true laboratories of our nation's schools . . .

This article describes a plan that has demonstrated its effectiveness in bringing about significant changes in schooling. The plan, entitled the Schoolwide Enrichment Model, is a systematic set of specific strategies for increasing student effort, enjoyment, and performance and for integrating a broad range of advanced-level learning experiences and higher-order thinking skills into any curricular area, course of study, or pattern of school organization. The general approach of the SEM is one of infusing more effective practices into existing school structures rather than layering on additional things for schools to do. This research-supported plan is designed for general education, but it is based on a large number of instructional methods and curricular practices that had their origins in special programs for high-ability students.

In many respects, special programs of almost any type have been the true laboratories of our nation's schools because they have presented ideal opportunities for testing new ideas and experimenting with potential solutions to long-standing educational problems. Programs for high potential students have been an especially fertile place for experimentation because such programs usually are not encumbered by prescribed curriculum guides or traditional methods of instruction. It was within the context of these programs that the thinking skills movement first took hold in American education and the pioneering work of notable theorists such as Benjamin Bloom, Howard Gardner, and Robert Sternberg first gained the attention of the education community. Other developments that had their origins in special programs are currently being examined for general practice. These developments include a focus on concept rather than skill learning, the use of interdisciplinary curriculum and theme-based studies, student portfolios, performance assessment, cross-grade grouping, alternative scheduling patterns, and perhaps most important, opportunities for students to exchange traditional roles as lesson-learners and doers-of-exercises for more challenging and demanding roles that require hands-on learning, firsthand investigations and the *application* of knowledge and thinking skills to complex problems.

Research opportunities in a variety of special programs allowed researchers at the Neag Center for Gifted Education and Talent Development at the University of Connecticut to develop instructional procedures and programming alternatives that emphasize the need (1) to provide a broad range of advanced level enrichment experiences for *all* students and (2) to use the many and varied ways that students respond to these experiences as stepping-stones for relevant follow-up on the parts of individuals or small groups. This approach is not viewed as a new way to identify who is or is not "gifted." Rather, the process simply identifies how subsequent *opportunities, resources, and encouragement* can be provided to support continuous escalations of student involvement in both required and self-selected activities. This approach to the development of high levels of multiple potentials in young people is purposefully designed to sidestep the traditional practice of labeling some students "gifted" (and by implication, relegating all others to the category of not gifted). The term *gifted* is used in our lexicon only as an adjective, and even then, it is used in a developmental perspective. Thus, for example, we speak and write about *the development of gifted behaviors* in specific areas of learning and human expression rather than giftedness as a state of being. This orientation has allowed many students opportunities to develop high levels of creative and productive accomplishments that otherwise would have been denied through traditional special program models.

Practices that have been a mainstay of many special programs for "the gifted" are being absorbed into general education by reform models designed to upgrade the performance of all students. This integration of gifted program know-how is viewed as a favorable development for two reasons. First, the adoption of many special program practices is indicative of the viability and usefulness of both the know-how of special programs and the role enrichment specialists can and should play in total school improvement. It is no secret that compensatory education in the United States has largely been a failure. An overemphasis on remedial and mastery models has lowered the challenge level of the very population that programs such as Chapter I attempt to serve. Second, *all* students should have opportunities to develop higher-order thinking skills and to pursue more rigorous content and firsthand investigative activities than those typically found in today's "dumbed-down" textbooks. The ways in which students respond to enriched learning experiences should be used as a rationale for providing all students with advanced-level follow-up opportunities. This approach reflects a democratic ideal that accommodates the full range of individual differences in the entire student population, and it opens the door to programming models that develop the talent potentials of many at-risk students who traditionally have been excluded from anything but the most basic types of curricular experiences. But in order to operationalize this ideal, we need to "get serious" about the things we have learned during the past several years about both programming models and human potential.

The application of gifted program know-how into general education is supported by a wide variety of research on human abilities (Bloom 1985; Gardner 1983; Renzulli 1986; Sternberg 1984). This research clearly and unequivocally provides a justification for much broader conceptions of talent development. These conceptions argue against the restrictive student selection practices that guided identification procedures in the past. Laypersons and professionals at all levels have begun to question the efficacy of programs that rely on narrow definitions, IQ scores, and other cognitive ability measures as the primary method for identifying which students can benefit from differentiated services. Traditional identification procedures have restricted services to small numbers of high-scoring students and excluded large numbers of at-risk students whose potentials are manifested in other ways that will be described in a later section that describes an SEM component called the Total Talent Portfolio. Special services should be viewed as opportunities to develop "gifted behaviors" rather than merely finding and certifying them. In this regard, we should judiciously avoid saying that a young person is either "gifted" or "not gifted." It is difficult to gain support for talent development when we use statements such as "Elaine is a gifted third grader" as a rationale. These kinds of statements offend many people and raise the accusations of elitism that have plagued special programs. But note the difference in orientation when we focus on the behavioral characteristics that brought this student to our attention in the first place: "Elaine is a third grader who reads at the adult level and who has a fascination for biographies about women of scientific accomplishment." And note the logical and justifiable services provided for Elaine:

1. Under the guidance of her classroom teacher, Elaine was allowed to substitute more challenging books in her interest area for the third-grade reader. The schoolwide enrichment teaching specialist helped the classroom teacher locate these books, and they were purchased with funds from the enrichment program budget.

2. Elaine was allowed to leave the school two afternoons a month (usually on early dismissal days) to meet with a mentor who is a local journalist specializing in gender issues. The schoolwide enrichment teaching specialist arranged transportation with the help of the school's parent volunteer group.

3. During time made available through curriculum compacting in her strength areas (i.e., reading, language arts, and spelling), the schoolwide enrichment teaching specialist helped Elaine prepare a questionnaire and interview schedule to be used with local women scientists and women science faculty members at a nearby university.

Could even the staunchest anti-gifted proponent argue against the logic or the appropriateness of these services? When programs focus on developing the behavioral potential of individuals or small groups who share a common interest, it is no longer necessary to organize groups merely because they all happen to be "gifted third graders."

THE SCHOOLWIDE ENRICHMENT MODEL

The programming model that the researchers at the Neag Center for Gifted Education and Talent Development have advocated since the early 1970s has always argued for a behavioral definition of giftedness and a greater emphasis on applying gifted program know-how to larger segments of the school population. The model is currently being used in hundreds of school districts across the country, including major urban areas such as New York City, Detroit, St. Paul, San Antonio, and Fort Worth. The present reform initiatives in general education have created a more receptive atmosphere for more flexible approaches that challenge all students and, accordingly, we have organized the Schoolwide Enrichment Model so that it blends into school improvement activities currently taking place throughout the country. Space does not permit a detailed description of the full model; however, the following sections describe the school structures upon which the model is targeted and the three service-delivery components. A graphic representation of the model is presented in Figure 1.

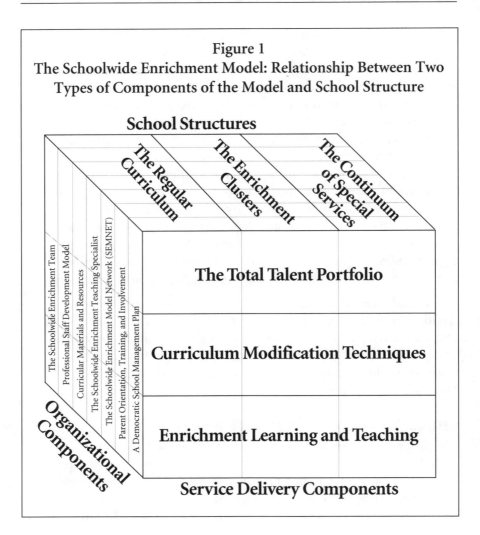

Figure 1
The Schoolwide Enrichment Model: Relationship Between Two Types of Components of the Model and School Structure

School Structures

1. *The Regular Curriculum*

The regular curriculum consists of everything that is a part of the predetermined goals, schedules, learning outcomes, and delivery systems of the school. The regular curriculum might be traditional, innovative, or in the process of transition, but its predominant feature is that authoritative forces (i.e., policy makers, school councils, textbook adoption committees, state regulators) have determined that the regular curriculum should be the "centerpiece" of student learning. Application of the SEM influences the regular curriculum in three ways. First, the challenge level of required material is differentiated through processes such as curriculum compacting, textbook content modification procedures, and group jumping strategies. Second, the systematic content intensification procedures used to replace eliminated content with selected, in-depth learning experiences increase the challenge level by introducing the broad underlying principles of a discipline. Third, the types of enrichment recommended in the Enrichment Triad Model (described below) are integrated selectively into the regular curriculum activities. Although the Neag Center researchers' goal in the SEM is to influence rather than replace the regular curriculum, the application of certain SEM components and the related staff development activities have resulted in substantial changes in both the content and the instructional processes of the entire regular curriculum.

2. The Enrichment Clusters

The enrichment clusters are nongraded groups of students who share common interests and who come together during specially designated time blocks to pursue these interests. Like extracurricular activities and programs such as 4H and Junior Achievement, the main rationale for participation in one or more clusters is that *students and teachers want to be there.* All teachers (including music, art, physical education, etc.) are involved in teaching the clusters, and teacher involvement in any particular cluster is based on the same type of interest assessment used for students. Community resource persons should also be invited to organize enrichment clusters. The model for learning used with enrichment clusters is based on an inductive approach to the pursuit of real-world problems rather than traditional, didactic modes of teaching. This approach, entitled enrichment learning and teaching, is purposefully designed to create a learning environment that places a premium on the development of higher-order thinking skills and the authentic application of these skills in creative and productive situations. The theory underlying this approach is based on the work of constructivist theorists such as Jean Piaget, Jerome Bruner, and John Dewey and applications of constructivist theory to classroom practice. Enrichment clusters are excellent vehicles for promoting cooperativeness within the context of real-world problem solving, and they also provide superlative opportunities for promoting self-concept. A major assumption underlying the use of enrichment clusters is that *every child is special if we create conditions in which that child can be a specialist within a speciality group.*

Enrichment clusters are organized around major disciplines, interdisciplinary themes, or cross-disciplinary topics (e.g., an electronic music group or a theatrical/television production group that includes actors, writers, technical specialists, costume designers, etc.). The clusters are modeled after the ways in which knowledge utilization, thinking skills, and interpersonal relations take place in the real world. Thus, all work is directed toward the production of a product or service. There are no lesson plans or unit plans. Rather, direction is provided by the following six key questions:

1. What do people with an interest in this area do?
2. What products do they create and/or what services do they provide?
3. What methods do they use to carry out their work?
4. What resources and materials are needed to produce high quality products and services?
5. How, and with whom, do they communicate the results of their work?
6. What steps need to be taken to have an impact on intended audiences?

The enrichment clusters are not intended to be the total program for talent development in a school, but they are major vehicles for stimulating interests and developing talent potentials across the entire school population. They are also vehicles for staff development in that they provide teachers an opportunity to participate in enrichment teaching and subsequently to analyze and compare this type of teaching with traditional methods of instruction. In this regard, the model promotes a spillover effect by encouraging teachers to become better talent scouts and talent developers and to apply enrichment techniques to regular classroom situations. Enrichment clusters are used by some schools on a one-half day per week basis and in other schools they meet daily. At the Webster Elementary School in St. Paul, Minnesota, for example, a broad array of interdisciplinary clusters is offered daily. At the Southeast School in Mansfield, Connecticut, enrichment clusters are offered two afternoons a month, and they are taught jointly by teachers, administrators, and parent volunteers. One of the most popular clusters is called Flight

School and was organized by the superintendent of schools, who is a licensed pilot.

3. *The Continuum of Special Services*

A broad range of special services is the third school structure targeted by the model. A diagram representing these services is presented in Figure 2. Although the enrichment clusters and the SEM-based modifications of the regular curriculum provide a broad range of services to meet individual needs, a program for total talent development still requires supplementary services that challenge young people who are capable of working at the highest levels of their special interest areas. These services, which ordinarily cannot be provided in enrichment clusters or the regular curriculum, typically include individual or small-group counseling, direct assistance in facilitating advanced-level work, arranging for mentorships with faculty members or community persons, and making other types of connections between students, their families, and out-of-school persons, resources, and agencies. For example, the schoolwide enrichment coordinator in the LaPorte, Indiana, School Corporation developed a Parent-Teacher Enrichment Guide of the city and surrounding area that includes information about a wide variety of enrichment opportunities for parents and teachers.

> **The model promotes a spillover effect by encouraging teachers to become better talent scouts and talent developers . . .**

Direct assistance also involves setting up and promoting student, faculty, and parental involvement in special programs such as Future Problem Solving, Odyssey of the Mind, the Model United Nations Program, and state and national essay, mathematics, and history contests. Another type of direct assistance consists of arranging out-of-school involvement for individual students in summer programs, on-campus courses, special schools, theatrical groups, scientific expeditions, and apprenticeships at places where advanced-level learning opportunities are available. Provision of these services is one of the responsibilities of the schoolwide enrichment teaching specialist or an enrichment team of teachers and parents who work together to provide options for advanced learning. A schoolwide enrichment teaching specialist in Barrington, Rhode Island, estimates she spends two days a week in a resource capacity to the faculties of two schools and three days providing direct services to students.

Figure 2
The Continuum of Services for Total Talent Development

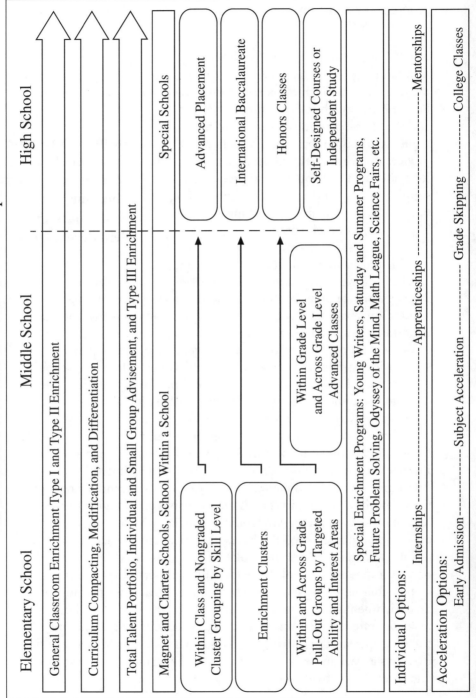

Service Delivery Components

1. The Total Talent Portfolio

The case study of Elaine presented earlier is an example of the ways in which the Schoolwide Enrichment Model targets specific learning characteristics that can serve as a basis for talent development. Our approach to targeting learning characteristics uses both traditional and performance-based assessments to compile information about three dimensions of the learner—abilities, interests, and learning styles. This information, which focuses on strengths rather than deficits, is compiled in a folder called the Total Talent Portfolio (see Figure 3) and is used to make decisions about talent development opportunities in regular classes, enrichment clusters, and in the continuum of special services. Two questions summarize the intent of the Total Talent Portfolio: What are the very best things we know and can record about a student's best work? and What are the best ways we can utilize this information to nurture the student's talent? This expanded approach to identifying talent potentials is essential if we are to make genuine efforts to include more underrepresented students in a plan for *total* talent development. This approach is also consistent with the more flexible conception of *developing* gifts and talents that has been a cornerstone of our work and our concerns for promoting more equity in special programs.

2. Curriculum Modification Techniques

SEM's second service-delivery component is a series of curriculum modification techniques designed to (1) adjust levels of required learning so all students are challenged, (2) increase the number of in-depth learning experiences, and (3) introduce various types of enrichment into regular curricular experiences. The procedures used to carry out curriculum modification are curriculum compacting, textbook analysis and surgical removal of repetitious material from textbooks, and a planned approach for introducing greater depth into regular curricular material.

Curriculum compacting (Reis and Renzulli 1992) is a systematic procedure for modifying or streamlining the regular curriculum in order to eliminate repetition of previously mastered material, upgrading the challenge level of the regular curriculum, and providing time for appropriate enrichment and/or acceleration activities. This process includes (1) defining the goals and outcomes of a particular unit or segment of instruction, (2) determining and

Figure 3
The Dimensions of the *Total Talent Portfolio*

Abilities	Interests	Style Preferences			
Maximum Performance Indicators	*Interest Areas*	*Instructional Styles Preferences*	*Learning Environment Preferences*	*Thinking Styles Preferences*	*Expression Style Preferences*
Tests • Standardized • Teacher-Made Course Grades Teacher Ratings Product Evaluation • Written • Oral • Visual • Musical • Constructed (Note differences between assigned and self-selected products) Level of Participation in Learning Activities Degree of Interaction with Others	Fine Arts Crafts Literary Historical Mathematical/Logical Physical Sciences Life Sciences Political/Judicial Athletic/Recreation Marketing/Business Drama/Dance Musical Performance Musical Composition Managerial/Business Photography Film/Video Computers Other (Specify) Ref: Renzulli 1997	Recitation & Drill Peer Tutoring Lecture Lecture/Discussion Discussion Guided Independent Study* Learning/Interest Center Simulation, Role Playing Dramatization, Guided Fantasy Learning Games Replicative Reports or Projects* Inestigative Reports or Projects* Unguided Independent Study* Internship* Apprenticeship* *With or without a mentor Ref: Renzulli & Smith 1978	Inter/Intra Personal • Self-Oriented • Peer-Oriented • Adult-Oriented • Combined Physical • Sound • Heat • Light • Design • Mobility • Time of Day • Food Intake • Seating Ref: Amabile & Gryskiewicz 1989; Dunn, Dunn, & Price 1978; Gardner 1983	Analytic (School Smart) Synthetic/Creative (Creative, Inventive) Practical/Contextual (Street Smart) Legislative Executive Judicial Ref: Sternberg 1984, 1988; Sternberg & Lubart 1992	Written Oral Manipulative Discussion Display Dramatization Artistic Graphic Commercial Service Ref: Kettle, Renzulli, & Rizza 1998; Renzulli & Reis 1985

documenting which students have already mastered most or all of a specified set of learning outcomes or who are capable of mastering them in less time than their peers, and (3) providing replacement activities for material already mastered through the use of instructional options that enable a more challenging and productive use of the student's time. These options include content acceleration, individual or group research projects, peer teaching, and involvement in non-classroom activities discussed in the section on the continuum of services. A key feature of these options is that students have some freedom to make decisions about the topic and the methods through which the topic will be pursued. Curriculum compacting might best be thought of as *organized common sense,* because it simply recommends the natural pattern that teachers ordinarily follow when individualizing instruction or teaching in the days before textbooks were "invented." Compacting also might be thought of as the "mirror image" of remedial procedures that have always been used in diagnostic/prescriptive models of teaching.

The second procedure for making adjustments in regular curricular material is the examination of textbooks in order to determine which parts can be economized upon through textbook analysis and "surgical" removal of repetitious drill and practice. The textbook *is* the curriculum in the overwhelming majority of today's classrooms; despite all of the rhetoric about school and curriculum reform, this situation is not likely to change in the near future. Until such time that high-quality textbooks are universally available, it is essential to deal with the curriculum situation as it currently exists. Although curriculum compacting is one procedure that can be used to get an unchallenging curriculum "off the backs" of students who are in need of curriculum modifications, the procedure is a form of "damage control." Therefore, we need to take a more proactive stance to overcome the well-documented low levels of American textbooks.

The procedures for carrying out the textbook analysis and surgical removal process are based on the argument that "less is better" when it comes to content selection, and it is necessary to make wise decisions when determining which material will be covered in greater depth. The first step in the process might best be described as "textbook triage." Each unit of instruction is examined by grade-level teams to determine which material is needless repetition of previously covered skills and concepts. When repetition is eliminated, teachers then decide which material is necessary for review and which material is important enough to cover in either a survey or an in-depth manner. What teachers teach is at the very heart of professional competency. The textbook analysis and surgical removal process offers teachers an opportunity to come together as a group of professionals around specific tasks within and across grade levels and subject areas to perform these important operations.

> **What teachers teach is at the very heart of professional competency.**

Adding more in-depth learning experiences is the third curriculum modification procedure. This approach is based on the work of Phenix (1964), who recommends that a focus on representative concepts and ideas is the best way to capture the essence of a topic or area of study. Representative ideas or concepts consist of themes, patterns, main features, sequences, organizing principles and structures, and the logic that defines an area of study. Representative ideas and concepts can also be used as the bases for interdisciplinary or multidisciplinary studies.

While the use of representative concepts allows teachers to capture the essence of an area of study, it also allows them to introduce economy into content selection. The vast amount of material within any given discipline prevents unlimited coverage of content; therefore, material must be selected so that it is both representative and maximally transferable. Excellent resources are available to assist in this process. Books such as the *Dictionary of the History of Ideas* (Weiner 1973) contain essays that cover every major discipline, and the emphasis of the essays is on interdisciplinary and cross-cultural relationships. The essays are cross-referenced to direct the reader to other articles containing similar ideas in other domains. Additional resources can be found in books such as *The Syntopicon: An Index to the Great Ideas* (Adler 1990), which lists concepts, ideas, and themes around which curriculum can be developed.

In-depth teaching also is concerned with the level of advancement or complexity of the material. First and foremost, the material must take into consideration the age, maturity, previous study, and background experiences of students. Beyond these considerations, three principles of content selection are recommended. First, curricular material should be selected so that it escalates along the hierarchy of knowledge dimensions: facts, conventions, trends and sequences, classifications and categories, criteria, principles and generalizations, and theories and structures. Second, movement toward the highest level, theories, and structures should involve continuous recycling to lower levels so that facts, trends, sequences, etc., can be understood in relation to a more integrated whole rather than as isolated bits of irrelevant information. Third, the cluster of diverse procedures surrounding the acquisition of knowledge, that dimension of learning commonly referred to as "process" or thinking skills, should itself be viewed as a form of content. These more enduring skills form the cognitive structures and problem-solving strategies that have the greatest transfer value.

A final characteristic of in-depth learning is a focus on methodology. This focus is designed to promote an understanding of, and appreciation for, the *application* of methods to the kinds of problems that are the essence of fields of knowledge. The goal of this emphasis on methodology is to cast the young person in the role of a firsthand inquirer rather than a mere learner of lessons, even if this role is carried out at a more junior level than that of the adult professional. This role encourages young learners to engage in the kinds of thinking, feeling, and doing that characterizes the work of the practicing professional because it automatically creates confrontations with knowledge necessary for active rather than passive learning.

3. Enrichment Learning and Teaching

The third service delivery component of the SEM is enrichment learning and teaching. Enrichment learning and teaching is based on the ideas of a small but influential number of philosophers, theorists, and researchers.[1] The work of these theorists, coupled with the Neag Center's research and program development activities, has given rise to the concept we call enrichment learning and teaching. The best way to define this concept is in terms of the following four principles:

1. Each learner is unique and, therefore, all learning experiences must be examined in ways that take into account the abilities, interests, and learning styles of the individual.

2. Learning is more effective when students enjoy what they are doing and, therefore, learning experiences should be constructed and assessed with as much concern for enjoyment as for other goals.

3. Learning is more meaningful and enjoyable when content (i.e., knowledge) and process (i.e., thinking skills, methods of inquiry) are learned within the context of a real and present problem and, therefore, attention should be given to opportunities to personalize student choice in problem selection, the relevance of the prob-

lem for individual students at the time the problem is being addressed, and authentic strategies for addressing the problem.

4. Some formal instruction may be used in enrichment learning and teaching, but a major goal of this approach to learning is to enhance knowledge and thinking skill acquisition that is gained through formal instruction with applications of knowledge and skills that result from students' own construction of meaning.

The ultimate goal of learning that is guided by these principles is to replace dependent and passive learning with independence and engaged learning. Although all but the most conservative educators will agree with these principles, much controversy exists about how these (or similar) principles might be applied in everyday school situations. A danger also exists that these principles might be viewed as yet another idealized list of glittering generalities that cannot be manifested easily in schools that are entrenched in the deductive model of learning. Developing a school program based on these principles is not an easy task. Over the years, however, the researchers at the Neag Center for Gifted Education and Talent Development have achieved a fair amount of success by gaining faculty, administrative, and parental consensus on a small number of easy-to-understand concepts and related services and by providing resources and training related to each concept and service delivery procedure. Numerous research studies (summarized in Renzulli and Reis 1994) and field tests in schools with widely varying demographics have been conducted. These studies and field tests have provided opportunities for the development of large amounts of practical know-how that are readily available for schools that would like to implement the SEM.

THE ENRICHMENT TRIAD MODEL

In order for enrichment learning and teaching to be systematically applied to the learning process, it must be organized in a way that makes sense to teachers and students. An organizational pattern called the Enrichment Triad Model (Renzulli 1977) is used for this purpose. The three types of enrichment in the model are depicted in Figure 4. Before discussing the role and function of each type of enrichment, it is necessary to discuss three considerations that relate to the model in general.

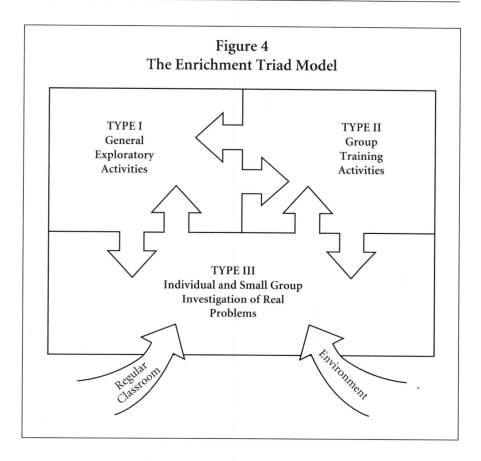

Figure 4
The Enrichment Triad Model

TYPE I
General
Exploratory
Activities

TYPE II
Group
Training
Activities

TYPE III
Individual and Small Group
Investigation of Real
Problems

Regular
Classroom

Environment

Learning in a Natural Way

The Enrichment Triad Model is based on the ways in which people learn in a natural environment rather than the artificially structured environment that characterizes most classrooms. Just as scientists "look to nature" when they attempt to solve particular types of problems, the process of learning is examined as it unfolds in the nonschool world. This process is elegant in its simplicity. External stimulation, internal curiosity, necessity, or combinations of these three starting points cause people to develop an interest in a topic, problem, or area of study. Humans are, by nature, curious, problem-solving beings, but in order for them to act upon a problem or interest with some degree of commitment and enthusiasm, the interest must be a sincere one and one in which they see a personal reason for taking action. Once the problem or interest is personalized, a need is created to gather information, resources, and strategies for acting upon the problem.

Problem solving in nature almost always results in a product or service that has a functional, artistic, or humanitarian value. The learning that takes place in real-problem situations is *collateral learning* that results from attacking the problem in order to produce a product or service. It was precisely this kind of natural problem-solving situation that gave rise to the Enrichment Triad Model. The only difference between the natural learning that takes place in real-life situations and the use of the triad model within the more structured world of the school is that the researchers at the Neag Center view products as vehicles through which a wide variety of more enduring and transferable processes can be developed. Learning that focuses on the interaction between product and process results in the kinds of learning experiences that enhance both the present and the future.

> "The unexamined lesson is not worth learning."

More Than a Sum of the Parts

A second general consideration about the Enrichment Triad Model is that the *interaction* between and among the three types of enrichment is as important as any type of enrichment or the collective sum of all three types. In other words, the arrows in Figure 4 are as important as the individual cells because they give the model dynamic properties that cannot be achieved if the three types of enrichment are pursued independently. A Type I experience, for example, may have value in and of itself, but it achieves maximum payoff if it leads to Type II or III experiences. In this regard, it is a good idea to view Types I and II enrichment as "identification situations" that may lead to Type III experiences, which are the most advanced type of enrichment in the model. As Figure 4 indicates, the regular curriculum and the environment in general (i.e., nonschool experiences) can also serve as pathways of entry into Type III activities. An identification situation is simply an experience that allows students and teachers an opportunity (1) to participate in an activity, (2) to analyze their interest in and reaction to the topic covered in the activity and the processes through which the activity was pursued, and (3) to make a purposeful decision about their interest in the topic and the diverse ways further involvement may be carried out. Types I and II are general forms of enrichment that are usually pursued with larger groups of students. Type III enrichment, on the other hand, is pursued only on a voluntary and self-selected basis.

The interactiveness of the three types of enrichment also includes what are sometimes called the "backward arrows" in Figure 4 (e.g., the arrows leading back from Type III to Type I, etc.). In many cases, the advanced work of students (i.e., Type III) can be used as Types I and II experiences for other students. Thus, for example, a group of students who carried out a comprehensive study on lunchroom waste can present its work to other groups for both awareness and instructional purposes, and for purposes of stimulating potential new interests on the parts of other students. In this regard, the model is designed to renew itself and to bring students "inside" the pedagogy of the school enterprise rather than viewing learning from a spectator's perspective.

Personal Knowledge

A third consideration about the Enrichment Triad Model in general is that it is designed to help students gain personal knowledge about their own abilities, interests, and learning styles. If, as Socrates said, "The unexamined life is not worth living," then we should also consider a corollary to this axiom about life in school: "The unexamined lesson is not worth learning." While it would be desirable to apply this corollary to all school experiences, the types of enrichment advocated in the triad model are excellent vehicles for examining preferences, tastes, and inclinations that will help students gain a greater understanding of themselves.

This corollary is operationalized in the model by recommending debriefings and post-learning analyses (sometimes called meta-learning) about both *what* has been learned and *how* a particular segment of learning has been pursued. Following exposure to a particular instructional style, a careful post-learning analysis should be conducted that focuses on the unique properties of the purposefully selected instructional technique. Students should be encouraged to discuss and record in personal journals their reactions to the instructional technique in terms of both efficiency in learning and the amount of pleasure they derive from the technique. The goal of the post-learning analysis is to help students understand more about themselves by understanding more about their preferences in a particular situation. Thus, the collective experiences in learning styles should provide (1) exposure to many styles, (2) an understanding of which styles are the most personally applicable to particular subjects, and (3) experience in how to blend styles in order to maximize both the effectiveness and satisfaction of learning.

In the sections that follow, a brief description of each component of the triad model is presented. It is helpful to keep in mind that the triad model is part of the service delivery component that is targeted on three school structures: the regular curriculum, the enrichment clusters, and the continuum of special services. In many ways, enrichment learning and teaching can be thought of as an overlay that can be applied to these three school structures.

Type I Enrichment: General Exploratory Experiences

Type I enrichment consists of general exploratory experiences that are designed to expose students to new and exciting topics, ideas, and fields of knowledge not ordinarily covered in the regular curriculum. This type of enrichment is carried out through a variety of procedures such as visiting speakers, demonstrations, mini visits, video presentations, interest centers, and the use of other audiovisual and technological materials. Type I enrichment and the debriefing that accompanies this type of enrichment represent an invitation to more advanced levels of involvement with the topic or area of interest.

Type II Enrichment: Group Training Activities

Type II enrichment consists of methods, materials, and instructional techniques designed to develop higher-level thinking processes, research and reference skills, and processes related to personal and social development. Type II enrichment is provided for all students within the regular curriculum, as well as students who are involved in enrichment clusters and self-selected, independent investigations. For example, science class students involved in determining water quality of a local river above and below the location of a major industrial park may need training in hypothesizing, data analysis, and research report writing. This training serves as motivation to participate in a self-selected independent investigation. A small group of students engaged in a real-world investigation related to oral history may need training on interview protocol, the use of tape recorder devices, and data analysis.

Type III Enrichment: Individual and Small-Group Investigations of Real Problems

Type III enrichment is the highest level of enrichment in which students can engage because they exchange their role from traditional lesson learner to firsthand inquirer. Type III enrichment is distinguished from other types of enrichment by five essential elements: (1) a personal frame of reference, (2) a focus on advanced-level knowledge, (3) a focus on methodology, (4) a sense of audience, and (5) authentic evaluation.

> **Most efforts to make major changes in schooling have failed.**

First, a Type III enrichment experience must be based on the interest of the individual or small group of students; students must "own" the real problem they will investigate. Second, this type of enrichment requires that students draw upon the roles and skills of practicing professionals. These skills include, for example, judging problem difficulty, apportioning time, and predicting outcomes. Third, Type III enrichment requires that students utilize authentic methodology. Students involved in a scientific investigation will employ the scientific method; students involved in video production will use the methodology of media experts in the field. A sense of audience is the fourth essential element in Type III enrichment. It is the real audience that encourages students to improve the quality of their product and develop new and effective ways of communicating their findings. Finally, Type III enrichment is characterized by authentic evaluation. Type III projects are products produced using the methodology of a field; by necessity, the products must be evaluated according to criteria provided by experts in the field and whether or not they have the desired impact on the intended audience.

SCHOOLWIDE ENRICHMENT AND EDUCATIONAL REFORM

Most efforts to make major changes in schooling have failed. Although there is endless speculation about why schools are so resistant to change, most theorists and policy makers have concluded that tinkering with single components of a complex system will give only the appearance of school improvement rather than the real and lasting change so desperately sought by educational leaders. Examples of single component tinkering are familiar to most educators. More rigorous curriculum standards, for example, without improved curricular materials and teachers able to use the materials effectively negate any potential value that new standards may have for improving academic performance. Similarly, single component tinkering designed to force change in classrooms (e.g., high-stakes testing) may create the illusion of improved achievement, but the reality is increased pressure on schools to expand the use of compensatory learning models that, so far, have contributed only to the "dumbing down" of curriculum and the lowering of academic standards. Teacher empowerment, school-based management, an extended school day and year, and revised teacher certification requirements are merely apparitions of change when state or central office regulations prescribe the curriculum by using tests that determine whether schools get high marks for better performance.

How, then, do we establish an effective change process—one that overcomes the long record of failed attempts? The leverage for meaningful change depends upon breaking two mind-sets: (1) that one person or single group knows the right answer and (2) that change is linear. The only reasonable solution is to develop a process whereby the adoption of policy and the adoption of practice proceed simultaneously. Policy makers and practitioners in schools need to collaborate during all phases of the change process by examining local capacity and motivation in conjunction with the desired changes. Thus, neither policy makers nor practitioners, by themselves, can reform schools; instead, both must come together to shape a vision and develop the procedures needed to realize and sustain that vision. Senge (1990) compares "visioneering" to the hologram, a three-dimensional image created by interacting light sources:

> When a group of people come to share a vision, . . . each sees his or her own picture. Each vision represents the whole image from a different point of view. When you add up the pieces of the hologram, the image does not change fundamentally, but rather becomes more intense, more lifelike, more real in the sense that people can truly imagine achieving it. The vision no longer rests on the shoulders of one person [or one group], but is shared and embodies the passion and commitment of all participants (Senge 1990, 312).

This article is based on my book *Schools for Talent Development,* which has been developed around a shared vision that my colleagues in the Neag Center for Gifted education and Talent Development and I have had for a number of years. This vision is also embraced by thousands of teachers and administrators with whom we have worked in academic programs and summer institutes that date back to the 1970s. *Simply stated, this vision is that schools are places for talent development.* Academic achievement is an important part of the vision and the model for school improvement described in *Schools for Talent Development;* however, we also believe a focus on talent development places the need for improved academic achievement into a larger perspective about the goals of education. The things that have made our nation great and our society one of the most productive in the world are manifestations of talent development at all levels of human productivity. From the creators and inventors of new ideas, products, and art forms, to the vast array of people who manufacture, advertise, and market the creations that improve and enrich our lives, there are levels of excellence and quality that contribute to our standard of living and way of life.

> **Single component tinkering designed to force change in classrooms may create the illusion of improved achievement.**

This vision of schools for talent development is based on the beliefs that *everyone* has an important role to play in societal improvement and that everyone's role can be enhanced if we provide all students with opportunities, resources, and encouragement to aspire to the highest level of talent development humanly possible. Rewarding lives are a function of ways we use individual potentials in productive ways. Accordingly, the SEM is a practical plan for making our vision of schools for talent development a reality. We are not naive about the politics, personalities, and financial issues that often supersede the pedagogical goals that are the focus of *Schools for Talent Development.* At the same time, we have seen this vision manifested in schools ranging from hard core urban areas and isolated and frequently poor rural areas to affluent suburbs and combinations thereof. We believe that the strategies described in this book provide the guidance for making any school a place for talent development.

There are no quick fixes or easy formulas for transforming schools into places where talent development is valued and vigorously pursued. Our experience has shown, however, that once the concept of talent development catches on, students, parents, teachers,

and administrators begin to view their school in a different way. Students become more excited and engaged in what they are learning;
parents find more opportunities to become involved in all aspects related to their children's learning, rather than "around the edges" activities; teachers begin to find and use a variety of resources that, until now, seldom found their way into classrooms; and administrators start to make decisions that affect learning rather than "tight ship" efficiency.

> Our schools are already dumping millions of functionally illiterate young people into the workforce.

Everyone has a stake in schools that provide all of our young people with a high-quality education. Parents benefit when their children lead happy and successful lives. Employers and colleges benefit when they have access to people who are competent, creative, and effective in the work they do and in higher educational pursuits. Political leaders benefit when good citizens and a productive population contribute to a healthy economy, a high quality of life, and respect for the values and institutions in a democracy. And professional educators at all levels benefit when the quality of schools for which they are responsible is effective enough to create respect for their work and generous financial support for the educational enterprise.

Everyone has a stake in good schools because schools create and recreate a successful modern society. Renewed and sustained economic growth and the well-being of all citizens means investing in high quality learning the same way that previous generations invested in machines and raw materials. Our schools are already dumping millions of functionally illiterate young people into the workforce; more and more colleges are teaching remedial courses based on material formerly taught in high school; and college graduates in almost all fields are experiencing difficulty entering career areas of choice.

Although everyone has a stake in good schools, America has been faced with a "school problem" that has resulted in declining confidence in schools and the people who work in them, drastic limitations in the amount of financial support for education, and general public apathy or dissatisfaction with the quality of education our young people are receiving. The parents of poor children have given up hope that education will enable their sons and daughters to break the bonds of poverty. And the middle class, perhaps for the first time in our nation's history, is exploring government-supported alternatives such as vouchers and tax credits for private schools, home schooling, charter schools, and summer and after-school programs that enhance admission to competitive colleges. A great deal has been written about America's "school problem," and studies, commissions, reports, and even a Governor's Summit Conference have been initiated to generate solutions to problems facing our schools. But the hundreds, if not thousands, of conferences, commissions, and meetings and the tons of reports, proclamations, and lists of goals have yielded minimal results, mainly because they generally focused on tinkering with traditional methods of schooling.

THREE KEY INGREDIENTS OF SCHOOL IMPROVEMENT

If the traditional methods of schooling have failed to bring about substantial changes, we must look to different models that show promise of achieving the types of school improvement we so desperately need. New models must focus their attention on three major dimensions of schooling—the act of learning, the use of time, and the change process itself.

The Act of Learning

School improvement must begin by placing the *act of learning* at the center of the change process. Organizational and administrative structures such as vouchers, site-based management, school choice, multiaged classes, parent involvement, and extended school days are important considerations, but they do not address *directly* the crucial question of how we can improve what happens in classrooms where teachers, students, and curriculum interact with one another. One of the things we have done in developing the SEM is to base all recommendations for school improvement on the learning process. It is beyond the scope of this summary to explain all components of the act of learning, but a figural representation of the learning process is depicted in Figure 5. The "Learner Circle" highlights important components students bring to the act of learning. Thus, when examining the learner we must take into consideration (1) the present achievement levels in each area of study, (2) the learner's interest in particular topics and the ways in which we can enhance present interests or develop new interests, and (3) the preferred styles of learning that will improve the learner's motivation to pursue the material being studied. Likewise, the teacher and learner dimensions have subcomponents that must be considered when we place the act of learning at the center of the school improvement process (Renzulli 1992).

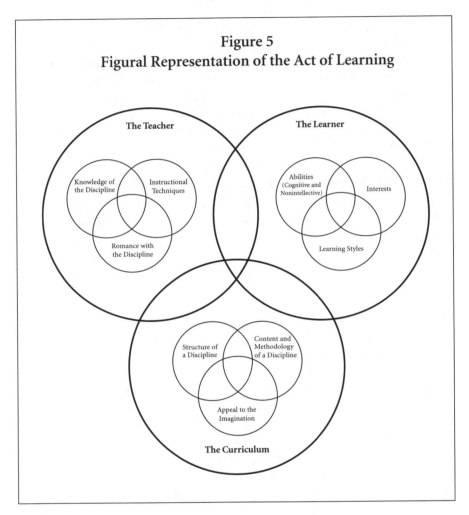

Figure 5
Figural Representation of the Act of Learning

The Teacher

The Learner

Knowledge of the Discipline

Instructional Techniques

Abilities (Cognitive and Nonintellective)

Interests

Romance with the Discipline

Learning Styles

Structure of a Discipline

Content and Methodology of a Discipline

Appeal to the Imagination

The Curriculum

The Use of Time

Although it would be interesting to speculate about why schools have changed so little over the centuries, at least part of the reason has been our unwillingness to examine critically the issue of school time. If the ways we currently use school time were producing remarkably positive or even adequate results, there might be an argument for maintaining the traditional schedule and calendar. But such is not the case.

A universal pattern of school organization that has emerged over the years has contributed to our inability to make even the smallest changes in the overall process of learning. This universal pattern is well known to educators and laypersons alike. The "major" subject matter areas (reading, mathematics, science, language arts, and social studies) are taught on a regular basis, five days per week. Other subjects, sometimes called "the specials," such as music, art, and physical education, are taught once or twice a week. So accustomed have we become to the rigidity of this schedule that even the slightest hint about possible variations is met with a storm of protest from administrators and teachers: "We don't have time *now* to cover the regular curriculum." "How will we fit in the specials?" "They keep adding new things [drug education, sex education, etc.] for us to cover." Our uncontested acceptance of the elementary and secondary school schedule causes us to lose sight of the fact that at the college level, where material is ordinarily more advanced and demanding, we routinely drop from a five-meetings-per-week schedule to a three-day- (and sometimes even two-day-) per-week schedule of class meetings. And our adherence to the "more time is better argument" fails to take into account research that shows quite the opposite. For example, international comparison studies report that eight of the eleven nations that surpass U.S. achievement levels in mathematics spend less time on math instruction than do American schools (Jaeger 1992). In the Schoolwide Enrichment Model, a number of alternative scheduling patterns are based on selectively "borrowing" one or two class meetings per month from the major subject areas. This approach guarantees that a designated time will be available each week for advanced-level enrichment clusters.

The Change Process

The approach to school improvement being recommended in the SEM is realistic because it focuses on those aspects of learning and development over which schools have the most influence, and, therefore, the highest probability of achieving success. Schools are being bombarded with proposals for change. These proposals range from total "systemic reform" to tinkering with bits and pieces of specific subjects and teaching methods. Oftentimes, the proposals are little more than lists of intended goals or outcomes, and limited direction is provided about how these outcomes can be achieved. Even less information is provided about the effectiveness of recommended practices in a broad range of field test sites. Worse yet are the mixed messages that policy makers and regulators are beaming at schools at an unprecedented rate, messages that often are incompatible with one another. One state, for example, mandated a core curriculum for students but then evaluated teachers on the basis of generic teaching skills that had nothing to do with the curriculum. Schools are encouraged to raise their standards, and advocates of site-based management encourage teachers to become more active in curriculum development. But these same schools are rated on the basis of test scores tied to lists of state-specified, outcome-based competencies. A recent study (Madaus 1992) showed that the most widely used tests measure low-level skills and knowledge and that teachers are under pressure to emphasize this kind of material because it shows up on the tests. The study also reported that teachers and administrators believed the tests forced them to compromise their ideals about good teaching. In another study, researchers asked a group of teachers how they would evaluate school reform initiatives in their schools. The group of teachers replied, "There's nothing but chaos. Our best strategy is to ignore them and close our doors and go about our business" (Olson 1992, 1).

The researchers at the Neag Center for Gifted Education and Talent Development believe that school improvement can be initiated and built upon through gentle and evolutionary strategies for change. These strategies must first and foremost concentrate on the act of learning as represented by the interactions that take place between and among learners, teachers, and the curriculum. In the early stages of the change process, these strategies should make minimal, but specific, suggestions for change in existing schedules, textbook usage, and curricular conventions. And these strategies should be based on practices that have already demonstrated favorable results in places where they have been used for reasonable periods of time and with groups from varying ethnic and economic backgrounds. We also believe that the individual school building is the unit of change for addressing school improvement and that effective and lasting change can only occur when it is initiated, nurtured, and monitored from within the school itself. Outside-of-school regulations and remedies have seldom changed the daily behaviors of students and teachers or dealt effectively with solutions to inside-of-school problems (Barth 1990). A simple but sincere waiver of top-down regulations, a plan that involves consensus and shared decision making on the parts of administrators, parents, and teachers and incentives for specific contributions to the change process are the starting points and the only "big decisions" policy makers need to make in order to initiate a gentle and evolutionary school improvement process.

Our goal in the Schoolwide Enrichment Model is not to replace existing school structures but rather to apply the strategies and services that define the model to improve the structures to which schools have already made a commitment. Thus, for example, if a school has adopted national standards or outcomes, whole language learning models, or site-based management, the purpose of SEM is to influence these structures in order to maximize their effectiveness. We view this process as an infusion rather than an add-on or replacement approach to school improvement. The main targets of the process are those factors that have a direct bearing on the act of learning. Evaluations of SEM programs (Olenchak and Renzulli 1989) have indicated that the model is systematic, inexpensive to implement, and practical in a common-sense sort of way that makes it appealing to both professionals and laypersons.

> "There's nothing but chaos. Our best strategy is to ignore them and close our doors and go about our business."

HOW TO START A SCHOOL IMPROVEMENT PROCESS

As is always the case with any change initiative, persons or small groups become interested in something they believe will be good for their school. It is our hope that persons reading this article and the book *Schools for Talent Development* will fulfill this role. If this happens, the following series of actions are recommended for using the material in this book.

The principal and representatives of groups in the nuclear family should form a steering committee. There are only three guidelines for the steering committee as it embarks on a process for *exploring* the plan presented in this book. (The word *exploring* is emphasized because consensus must be reached at each step of the process in order for the plan to work.) First, all steering committee members should be provided with information about the Schoolwide Enrichment Model so they are well informed and can engage in an intelligent discussion and debate about whether or not they are interested in the plan. All steering committee members should have equal rights and opportunities to express their opinions. If a majority decision is reached to recommend the plan to the school community at large, information should be made available to all faculty and parents. Older students (middle grade and above) should also be asked to participate in the discussions.

Second, the steering committee should arrange a series of discussion group meetings open to and inclusive of members of all subgroups in the school's nuclear family. In setting up the discussion groups, it is important to avoid separate parent groups, teacher groups, and administrator groups. Grouping by role is a classic error that has plagued understanding and communication in the school community, and it is the main contributor to the "us and them" mentality that pits one group against another. Printed information, key diagrams and charts, and the results of steering committee deliberations should be brought to the attention of the discussion groups. The discussion groups should elect a chairperson and recorder, they should remain intact for the duration of the examination process, and they should set a mutually acceptable schedule of meeting dates and times. The meetings should continue until everyone has had a chance to express his or her opinions, after which a vote should be taken as to whether or not to proceed with the plan. Voting results from each discussion group should be reported to the steering committee, and a report of all the votes should be issued to the nuclear school family. The report should also contain each group's suggestions and concerns. If at least two-thirds of the persons voting express an interest in going ahead with the plan, the steering committee should make arrangements to meet with the superintendent or appropriate central office personnel. Once again, descriptive material about the model should be provided, and the model characterized as a pilot or experimental venture. Assurances should be given that there is no intention to replace any of the programs or initiatives that the district has already adopted. The fastest way to get a polite but firm rejection from the central office is to threaten existing programs or policies to which decision makers already have made a commitment. It is worth repeating that the goal of the Neag Center researchers is to *infuse* exemplary learning and teaching opportunities into the existing school frameworks.

> The reality is that leadership for better schools can come only from people who are responsible for schools at the local level.

A third guideline is concerned with strategies for overcoming roadblocks that might occur during any of the above stages of the examination process. Any plan for school change is a lightning rod for naysayers, self-proclaimed experts, and those people reluctant to endorse almost anything involving thinking or doing something differently. This problem is an especially sticky one if these persons occupy positions of authority or informal status in the school community or if they are particularly adept at creating negative energy that is not easily overcome. Such persons, like all others, should have an opportunity to express their opinions in a democratic process. But in order for a majority opinion to be the deciding factor in determining whether or not the model is adopted, it may be necessary to pursue strategies that ensure majority rule.

What's in It for Me?

Although everyone has a stake in good schools, it would be naive to assume that already overburdened professionals or parents who have had a limited impact on school change historically will make a commitment to a new initiative that requires time, energy, and participation in activities that are a departure from the *status quo*. Each person examining the SEM should ask himself or herself: What's in it for me? What will I have to do? What will I have to give or give up? What will I get out of it? Policy makers and administrators should examine these questions with an eye toward the kinds of public support necessary for adequate, and perhaps even generous, financial commitments to public education. The tide of criticism that is constantly being directed toward our schools has taken its toll in the extent to which the public is willing to pay for public education and has resulted in low morale at all levels of the profession. Education is rapidly becoming a profession without an ego because of this criticism. Schools in other nations are constantly being held up to us as mirrors for pointing out our own inadequacies; hardly a month passes without someone writing yet another article or news story about the crisis in educational leadership. It would be nice to think that some magical force will "save us," but the reality is that leadership for better schools can come only from people who are responsible for schools at the local level.

More than any other group, teachers will have to ask themselves these hard questions. Almost every teacher has, or at one time had, an idea about what good teaching is all about. And yet, it is not an exaggeration to say that most teachers are dissatisfied with their work and with the regulations and regimentation imposed on their classrooms. A recent report on teachers' response patterns to classroom practices indicated that teachers who adapt to traditional practices

---

Schools do not need to be places to which so many of our young people dread going.

"... become cynical, frustrated, and burned out. So do their students, many of whom fail to meet expectations established for the classroom" (McLaughlin and Talbert 1993, 6). We still, however, must raise the questions: Are there benefits for teachers who are willing to take on the challenge of variations in traditional practice? Can we avoid the cynicism, frustration, and burnout that seems to be so pervasive in the profession? The SEM is designed to provide opportunities for a better "brand" of teaching through the application of more engaging teaching practices.

Finally, parents must examine the above questions with an eye toward the kind of education they want for their sons and daughters. The SEM is not intended to replace the schools' focus on traditional academic achievement, but it does emphasize the development of a broader spectrum of the multiple potentials of young people. Schools do not need to be places to which so many of our young people dread going, but in order to make schools more enjoyable places, parents must have an understanding of and commitment to an education that goes beyond the regimentation and drill that is designed only to "get the scores up." Schools are places for developing the broadest and richest experiences imaginable for young people.

WHY SHOULD SCHOOLS FOCUS ON TALENT DEVELOPMENT?

Many people view America's public education system as a failed public monopoly. Policy makers, parents, educational leaders, and the corporate and business community are expressing the lowest level of confidence in public education in our nation's history. Parents of economically disadvantaged youth have all but given up on expectations that schools can improve their children's future, and they have grown weary and suspicious of endless rhetoric and flavor-of-the-month reform initiatives that devour more and more of our limited dollars without producing any noticeable results. It doesn't take a rocket scientist, or even a person who knows little more than elementary arithmetic, to realize that the billions of federal and state dollars spent on remedial and compensatory education models have not produced achievement gains of any significance.

Lack of confidence in public education is also being expressed by middle-class parents who have watched the slow but steady decline of SAT scores at the top end of the achievement continuum. In an article entitled "The Other Crisis in Our Schools," Daniel Singal documented the effects of what happens when our brightest students get a "dumbed-down" education. "For the first time in the history of our country, the educational skills of one generation will not surpass, will not equal, will not even approach those of their parents. This failure will bring a lower sense of professional fulfillment for our youngsters as they pursue their careers, and will hamper their ability to stay competitive with European and Asian countries" (Singal 1991, 59). The middle class has become so disenchanted with the quality of public education that for the first time in history they are asking for *public* funds to pursue private educational alternatives.

Dr. Leon Lederman, the Nobel prize–winning physicist, recently said, "Once upon a time, America sheltered an Einstein, went to the moon, and gave the world the laser, electronic computer, nylons, television, and the cure for polio. Today we are in the process, albeit unwittingly, of abandoning this leadership role" (Hilts 1991, A16). Every school and classroom in this country has in it young people who are capable of continuing this remarkable tradition. But the tradition will not survive without a national resolve to invest in developing the talent potentials of *all* of our young people. Every school has within it students who possess the highest potential for advanced level learning, creative problem solving, and the motivation to pursue rigorous and rewarding work. As the United Negro College Fund aptly puts it, a mind is a terrible thing to waste. It's time to recognize that we have been wasting far too many minds.

NOTES

The work reported herein was supported under the Javits Act Program (Grant No. R206R00001) as administered by the Office of Educational Research and Improvement, U.S. Department of Education. The opinions expressed in this article do not reflect the position or policies of the Office of Educational Research and Improvement or the U.S. Department of Education.

1.   Although it is beyond the scope of this article to review the work of these eminent thinkers, the group includes William James, Alfred North Whitehead, John Dewey, Maria Montessori, Jean Piaget, Paul Torrance, Jerome Bruner, Philip Phenix, Howard Gardner, Robert Sternberg, and Albert Bandura.

REFERENCES

Adler, M. J. (Ed.). (1990). *The syntopicon: An index to the great ideas.* Chicago: Encyclopaedia Britannica.

Amabile, T. M., and N. Gryskiewicz. (1989). The creative environment scales: Work environment inventory. *Creative Research Journal* 2: 231–254.

Barth, R. S. (1990). *Improving schools from within.* San Francisco: Jossey-Bass.

Bloom, B. S. (Ed.). (1985). *Developing talent in young people.* New York: Ballantine Books.

Dunn, R., K. Dunn, and G. E. Price. (1978). *Learning style inventory.* Lawrence, KS: Price Learning Systems.

Gardner, H. (1983). *Frames of mind.* New York: Basic Books.

Hilts, P. (1991, January 6). Nobel physicist raises alarm on U.S. science. *New York Times,* A16.

Jaeger, R. M. (1992). *"World class" standards, choice, and privatization: Weak measurement serving presumptive policy.* Paper presented at the annual meeting of the American Educational Research Association, San Francisco, April 20–24, 1992.

Kettle K., J. S. Renzulli, and M. Rizza. (1998). Products of mind: Exploring student preferences for product development using my way . . . An expression style instrument. *Gifted Child Quarterly* 42: 48–61.

Madaus, G. F. (1992). *The influence of testing on teaching math and science in grades 4–12.* Boston College: Center for the Study of Testing, Evaluation, and Educational Policy.

McLaughlin, M. W., and J. E. Talbert. (1993). *Contexts that matter for teaching and learning.* Stanford, CA: Center for Research on the Context of Secondary School Teaching.

Olenchak, F. R., and J. S. Renzulli. (1989). The effectiveness of the Schoolwide Enrichment Model on selected aspects of elementary school change. *Gifted Child Quarterly* 32: 44–57.

Olson, L. (1992). Fed up with tinkering, reformers now touting "systemic" approach. *Education Week* 12, 1: 30.

Phenix, P. (1964). *Realms of meaning.* New York: McGraw-Hill.

Reis, S. M., and J. S. Renzulli. (1992). Using curriculum compacting to challenge the above-average. *Educational Leadership* 50, 2: 51–57.

Renzulli, J. S. (1977). *The Enrichment Triad Model.* Mansfield Center, CT: Creative Learning Press.

Renzulli, J. S. (1986). The three-ring conception of giftedness: A developmental model for creative productivity. In R. J. Sternberg and J. E. Davidson (Eds.), *Conceptions of giftedness* (pp. 332–357). New York: Cambridge University Press.

Renzulli, J. S. (1992). A general theory for the development of creative productivity through the pursuit of ideal acts of learning. *Gifted Child Quarterly* 36: 170–182.

Renzulli, J. S. (1994). Schools for talent development: A practical plan for total school improvement. Mansfield, CT: Creative Learning Press.

Renzulli, J. S., and S. M. Reis. (1985). *The school wide enrichment model: A comprehensive plan for educational excellence.* Mansfield Center, CT: Creative Learning Press.

Renzulli, J. S., and S. M. Reis. (1994). Research related to the Schoolwide Enrichment Model. *Gifted Child Quarterly* 38: 2–14.

Renzulli, J. S., and L. H. Smith. (1978). *The learning style inventory: A measure of student preference for instructional techniques.* Mansfield Center, CT: Creative Learning Press.

Senge, P. M. (1990). *The fifth discipline.* New York: Doubleday.

Singal, D. J. (1991, November). The other crisis in our schools. *The Atlantic* 268: 59–62.

Sternberg, R. J. (1984). Toward a triarchic theory of human intelligence. *Behavioral and Brain Sciences* 7, 2: 269–316.

Sternberg, R. J. (1988). Mental self-government: A theory of intellectual styles and their development. *Human Development* 31: 197–224.

Sternberg, R. J., and T. I. Lubart. (1992). An investment theory of creativity and its development. *Human Development* 34: 1–31.

Weiner, P. P. (Ed.). (1973). *Dictionary of the history of ideas.* New York: Scribner's Sons.

Creating the Climate and Conditions for Children to Learn

by James P. Comer

T hank you very much. I always start by saying I'm pleased to be here. This time, I'm really pleased to be here. I had back surgery ten days ago.

The first point I want to make is that I'm not really an expert on intelligence. As most of you know, my work has been in public schools, more with low-income schools, and while the findings apply to all, my interest started with, and continues to be, with what goes on in low-income schools.

My interest in factors that contribute to life success and the role of intelligence in all of this began in 1960 with an observation and with a question. I went back to my home town to become a general practitioner in medicine and I observed that my childhood friends were going on a downhill course in life. The question of what happened to them turned me away from my plan to become a general practitioner, and I began to pursue the question: Why were my friends going on a downhill course and how could we prevent it? The ability of my low-achieving friends and other observations made me suspicious of intelligence tests and of our concerns about the question of intelligence in the first place. So over the years I have been watchful, continually asking why we are paying so much attention to intelligence and intelligence tests instead of to how we create conditions to make the most of whatever a child has to offer. That is why I am pleased about this conference, where the emphasis is not on the test score but is on how we create the climate and the conditions that

From a paper based on a presentation at the Fourth International Teaching for Intelligence Conference, April 23, 1998, New York, NY. © 1998 by James P. Comer. Reprinted with permission.

make it possible for children to learn and to achieve at the highest level possible.

As a young psychiatrist, a couple of times I had brothers and sisters, once twins, in the same treatment. The one with the 20-points higher IQ test score performed less well than the one with the 20-points lower score. That raised a question for me about the efficacy of IQ tests to measure what really contributes to achievement. I grew up in a tough, low-income, steel mill town. As a teenager I would go out to the bars, to church and the barbershop, and I would listen to uneducated, low-achieving, by somebody's standards, people who were very creative, who were very smart, who were reflective and analytical and had great memory, and I realized these were bright people. Why didn't they do well in school and why didn't they do well on achievement tests?

> Creativity may be as important, maybe much more important, than whatever it is that we call and attempt to measure as intelligence.

I also remember early in my training a colleague, a white psychologist, told me of her experience in a Harlem hospital while testing a black youngster. He was testing in the retarded range. She took a break and as she went out of the room, she met a black colleague who had given a party for her. They embraced in the hallway, and clearly they were friends. The black youngster was watching. When the psychologist resumed testing after the break, this youngster scored in the above-average range. I began to think about the work of Ogbu[1] and many others who point out that there is about a 15-point IQ difference between groups who have been stigmatized and those who have not been stigmatized within the same society (e.g., the Baraku of Japan, the West Indians in Great Britain, the Maoris of New Zealand in favor of the nonstigmatized group.

Claude Steele,[2] a psychologist at the University of Michigan, observed that black students with the same ability level as white students were not achieving as well. The longer they stayed in college, the worse they did, increasing the disparity between people of the same ability level. He created a program in which students were randomly selected at the same ratio that they were represented at the college, but with overrepresentation of blacks and of non-black minorities. The only intervention given was a challenging calculus workshop and once-a-week meeting, a group discussion in which they talked about everything—all aspects of their lives. The students also all lived in the same wing of a large dormitory. They had this program for about ten weeks. Over a two-year period they absolutely wiped out the difference in achievement levels—the black youngsters did as well as the white youngsters.

So what is this business of intelligence all about? Why are we so committed to the IQ test, which is no more than a score based on something that we claim to be a measure of intelligence? There is serious question as to whether it really is. It seems to me that we really use the information to protect and promote privilege. Intelligence is reflected in the utilization of information to solve problems, general or specific, and to do that consistently. Creativity may be as important, maybe much more important, than whatever it is that we call and attempt to measure as intelligence.

I have always loved my daughter, but I particularly loved what she did and what she observed once when she was a senior in high school. She was on that honors track where they drove hard and fought to be at the top of the class. She decided to take a course they were offering called Outward Bound. One day she said to me, "Dad, how do you explain the fact that many of the kids who don't do well in school have the best answers about how you get out of a ditch without a shovel?" I was delighted by that observation and that concern, because there are too many Ph.D.s who haven't asked that question.

And so, the only thing we can say for certain about intelligence is that social and behavioral scientists, biological scientists, and all of us really have a lot to learn. In the meantime, we should be careful not to use intelligence as the absolute gatekeeping force in the way that we are beginning to use it. I believe there is a threshold[3] level of general intelligence that is needed in order to perform most tasks, and that most people have a high enough level to perform well in school. Swedish psychiatrists have shown that children can learn to read with IQs of 70 to 75. It doesn't take great intelligence.

But to perform adequately in school and in life, we really need to be motivated, flexible, to have social and emotional intelligence,[4] to have a culture that promotes learning, to have the opportunity structure that makes it possible for us to learn, and then most of all, to be lucky in one way or another. The expression of intelligence is an outgrowth of all these things, rather than the innate potential that we are born with. But I return to the question of what our preoccupation with the intelligence test and the achievement test scores is really all about.

Almost from the beginning, we have used intelligence in this country to justify the unfair distribution of opportunities and privileges. Because the system of slavery was so central to our economy and so contrary to our stated founding purposes and beliefs, we had to justify the system. Intelligence was used as a way of justifying it. As a result, deeply ingrained in much of our thinking in this society is this preoccupation with intelligence. We ignore that outcomes in life are determined only partially by your intelligence. Once you are above the threshold, it is your access to the political, economic, and social structure of the society that really determines your outcome.

Although we know that this is true, we still cling to the notion that it is intelligence that determines outcomes. Whether it is the media or the scholars, every five or ten years somebody comes out with a report that shows that blacks or some other group are not able, and we use that to justify the distribution of opportunities in our society. We do that in spite of the vast social and behavioral science literature that tells us that intelligence and achievement are greatly influenced by the quality of the child-rearing experience that we receive. I want to point out that I am talking here not only about the child-rearing that comes from mother and father, although they are most important. There is a child-rearing that takes place in the social network of mother and father, or mothers and family, that is important—a network of friends and kin and the institutions they are a part of. There is also child-rearing that takes place in schools and community organizations. We have the greatest opportunity in schools to promote child-rearing, and yet we ignore child-rearing in schools. We think of the schools as a place where we pass on information to children. That is only one part of what we do in schools. We should really be in the business of helping children grow.

What I would like to do briefly at this point is to cite some of the literature that talks about the importance of child-rearing. Then I want to tell you about my own child-rearing experience as a son of a "child of extreme poverty and abuse" and the way that education broke the cycle and permitted the development of an expression of the potential I had and that my brothers and sisters had. I'd like to show how that experience has led to my work in schools and how it suggested what must be done to make it possible for all children to achieve and to meet their highest potential and the greatest expression of their intelligence.

The key point that we pull from the literature on child-rearing is that the interaction between the parents and the child is critical.[5] Positive parent-child interaction allows bonding to occur, and it is bonding with the caretaker that prepares and enables the caretaker to lead the child along the developmental pathways. This makes learning at an increasing high level possible. The use of reasoning is important. The IQ of children whose parents use reasoning more than punishment is greater.[6] Parents who are attentive and responsive to the behaviors of their children produce children with higher IQs.[7] Warmth and appropriate use of limit setting is important. Positive interaction between parents is also important in improving IQs.[8] Where fathers are supportive of mothers and vice versa, decreasing the stress of the family, children have higher IQs.

> Almost from the beginning, we have used intelligence in this country to justify the unfair distribution of opportunities and privileges.

Depression among the parents lowers children's IQs.[9] In situations where verbal content is low and where the quality of the verbal content is poor, children's IQs tend to be depressed.[10] By high-quality verbal interaction, I mean that parents talk to their children about everything that is going on around them. By low-quality verbal interaction, I mean that parents use language mostly for control. Parents who organize the environment so that their children can take advantage of educational opportunities in it, where there are materials to play, produce children with higher IQs.[11] Parents who emphasize the importance of hard work and persistence at a task until they get good outcomes produce children with good academic achievement and higher IQs.[12] Parents who model what they want their children to do, rather than just talk at the children, produce better outcomes.[13]

Now I want to turn and talk about my own family because my family were low-income, working-class people. The point I want to make is that it is not the education of the parent alone that is critically important, it is how the parent carries out all of the other functions related to learning that I have mentioned and that researchers have found important. Some of you know my family story but I will tell it for the benefit of others, and for completeness.

My mother was born in rural Mississippi into extreme poverty. Her father was a sharecropper and a good man, but he was killed by lightning when she was six years of age. Because there were no support programs during that period, a cruel stepfather came into her life. He was abusive in every way, and he would not allow the children to go to school. My mother decided when she was about eight years of age that the way to a better life was through education. When she was sixteen, she ran away to a sister in East Chicago, Indiana, and tried to go to school. But she didn't get the support and had to drop out and become a domestic worker.

> Children also need protection—not only physical protection, but protection of their dreams and their ideas, and their hopes and their wishes.

She declared at that point that if she ever had children, she was going to make certain that all those children got a good education. Then she set out very, very, very carefully to find my father. She wanted to make certain that she didn't make the same mistake that her mother had made. My father had been married once before so she wasn't certain that he was the right one. So she insisted that he get a letter of recommendation from his ex–mother-in-law. It worked out okay—my mother, with no education at all, working as a domestic, and my father, with about a sixth-grade rural Alabama education, working as a steel mill laborer, eventually sent the five of us to college for a total of thirteen college degrees.

All of this took place in a social network of friend and kin and church that was supportive, protective, and promoting of our development. The three friends who I went off to elementary school with, and who were starting on a downhill course when I went back home to become a general practice physician, were in the same neighborhood, the same school. Their fathers worked in the same steel mills as my father, and yet they had a very different developmental experience. I realized that it was development that made the difference for me, and it is development that makes the difference for all of our children. One of my friends became an alcoholic and died early, one spent a good part of his life in jail, and the other had been in and out of mental institutions all of his life until he died recently.

I want to emphasize the point of development and go into some detail about my experience, my developmental experience. It is critically important in thinking about all children from all income groups, but very, very important in thinking about low-income children. Their parents, even when they want to do the right thing, even when they want to give their children the best experiences to succeed in school, very often have not had those experiences themselves and are not able to provide them to their children.

Let us think about my own experience. The first point is that we were very much wanted. My mother had a plan. She wanted to send her children to school and make certain that every one of them got a good education. My father shared the vision and fully supported the plan. We received enormous care, sometimes to the point of overprotection. But the latter was not harmful. I recall every Sunday evening, we four younger children would gather around my mother, two at her legs, one on her lap, one at her shoulder, and she would read us the funny papers. Now, my mother could just barely read, but that didn't matter. That wasn't the point. We were there to be close to her. When she finished reading the paper, one would ask her to read another cartoon, and then another cartoon, and then another, until she had read the paper all over again. The whole point was time and closeness. Also there was popcorn and malted milk on the front porch. We would sit and talk with our parents on the swing almost every summer evening.

We lived in a very predictable household. Every evening at the same time, my father came around the corner on his way home from work. The four of us would jump up and run down and all leap into his arms and grab his legs. On one occasion, I remember we were talking about the baseball glove that we were going to play with and how we were going to share it when my mother said, "But your father didn't say he was going to buy that glove." We said that he said he would think about it, and we knew from experience that when he says he'll think about it, that means he is going to do it. The reliability and predictability were terribly important.

Children also need protection—not only physical protection, but protection of their dreams and their ideas, and their hopes and their wishes. When I was a little boy of two years of age, I said I wanted to become a doctor. My parents bought me a doctor's kit for Christmas. I would fix the arm or the leg or whatever the problem was of anybody and everybody around. A neighbor came by and said, "Why are you encouraging him to be a doctor? We're poor people. You know he's not going to be a doctor." My mother said, "If you say that one more time you're going to have to leave this house!"

In fifth grade, a youngster moved into my school and said, "I know your mother." I was wondering how she knew my mother so I went home and asked her. My mother pointed out that she had worked for the girl's mother as a domestic years before. My mother saw that that bothered me a little bit because when you're in fifth grade you're very status conscious. My mother looked at me and said, "You're just as clean as she is, just as smart as she is, and you can do just as well as she can," and then gave me her no-nonsense look and said, "and you had better!" Protection.

Dinnertime was a very special time. We were always expected to be home at dinnertime and to be on time. Dinner was five o'clock. During dinner there was always discussion. In the process we were taught how to listen, and no one could take over the conversation. Sometimes we were helped to make a point. Thus, all of the rules and the skills of discussion were learned around the dinner table. Many of those discussions would spill over into the evening as informal debates. We had vigorous debates. The four younger children and sometimes my older sister would get into it. We would debate about everything. Those debates were very important. Sometimes it was not good to lose in our house because you'd get teased, and there was a rule that you couldn't fight—no matter how badly you lost a debate, you couldn't fight. And so, you might practice your argument, what you had to say, on the way home from school, because you didn't want to lose. The habit of thinking was well established.

On one occasion, my brother, who was usually on the conservative side of the argument, caught me arguing against public welfare. He was giving it to me about how I was cruel and that I lacked interest and so on. My mother, who usually stayed out of those discussions and just listened, said, "Jim, but what about the poor people?" I suggested that the government become an employer of last resort. She said, "Okay," and that was the end of her involvement. And so, my parents did not intrude but promoted thinking and the appreciation of fair and rational thinking.

The worst sin you could commit as a child in my family was of disrespect for my father. My father was a very religious man. But we had some questions about religion and we would ask them. My mother would try to stop us, but he wanted to hear those questions. There was no area where thinking, challenging, and raising questions was unacceptable when age appropriate. Values were caught more than taught. You can't just sit children down and tell them what they ought to value. They have to experience in an actual living and working environment values that are important.

We were Baptists. At the Baptist Young People's Training Union, my father was the moderator. When my brother correctly answered a question at the same time as another child, my father acknowledged the other child so as not to appear to favor his own. With my father, fairness was fairness, and that's what we learned. My mother would come to the steps where we were playing in the streets below. In those days, there were no grooves in the candy bars where they could break apart easily. She used a ruler to break the candy bar into four even parts so each of us got the same amount. So fairness was an important value that we learned.

> **Values were caught more than taught. You can't just sit children down and tell them what they ought to value.**

Social skills were also important. My mother said when you see trouble coming from one way, you go the other way. In other words, learn to read the environment and negotiate it wisely. We had many developmental experiences. When we were young children, my mother and father together took us to the lakefront and bundled us all up to go to see Franklin D. Roosevelt's caravan come through town. Anything and everything they thought was educational, they exposed us to. On one occasion, it got pretty close to being illegal. My mother worked at the polls, and as I was passing she invited me to come in. She took me into the voting area, which was probably illegal. I actually pulled a lever, which was illegal. But to this day, voting is important to me because of that involvement and that experience.

The issues related to race are very important because all children in our society are exposed to them in one way or another. They must understand and learn how to manage race-related issues so that they are not thrown by them when they are seven and eight years of age and begin to ask the question "Who am I?" The answer must be "You are somebody worthwhile, you need not be embarrassed about your roots, you are okay, you are very good." My mother and father never denied that there was a problem, but they taught us how to manage it. For example, my mother would always say that "if you think that your teacher is unfair, don't you bother with the teacher, tell me, and I will talk with the teacher." She did this on occasion and we would listen and learn.

In ninth grade I had a teacher who gave me a B and gave students who were one and two points ahead of me A's. She gave the next highest student, who was thirty points behind me, a B. I thought that was unfair. After talking with her for about half an hour, she said, "Well, you know, I just don't think you're capable of making A's." I understood what that meant, and that was the end of that discussion. I went back and worked very hard the next ten weeks. At the end of that time, I had the top score in the class. But instead of taking her my grade book, I waited until the end of the day. I had worked very hard the entire semester and I had all A's. I took the card to her and got my A. I learned how to manage that environment from living in a home where people managed the environment in a way that made bad matters better.

> All of those people wanted to succeed, but they were in an environment in which they couldn't succeed.

My mother wasn't operating off the top of her head. She had a child-rearing theory that said that the good times we have together make it possible for me and your father to chastise you when there are bad times, and for you to understand that chastising is in your best interest. The support and discipline that we received from our parents is what allowed us to go to school prepared to manage the school and the expectations of the school. All that I have described about my family meets the conditions that the researchers in child-rearing say produce improved IQ test scores and achievement.

I told my story because I know and you know that most of the low-income children that you deal with—black, white, Asian, and the like—are not receiving the kind of experiences that I'm talking about. And yet, some do. The underachievement that we observe among so many children is because they are not receiving the kinds of experiences that I had. But we can't give up on those children. We can't say they are underdeveloped and therefore they can't learn and that's too bad. The school is a developmental venue. It is a place along the developmental pathway where we can and must support the development of children. We can compensate for underdevelopment. And when we support the development of children, they will do well in school.

So let me turn now and tell you about our work in schools. The two initial schools in New Haven, and our continued work, have made a difference. I directed a team from the Yale Child Study Center that went into two elementary schools in New Haven, Connecticut, in 1968. What we did literally and simply was to recreate the community. We recreated a community that supported the rearing and development of children so that they could perform at a high level. The schools were 99 percent black, almost all poor, and had the worst achievement, worst attendance, and worst behavior in the city. They were thirty-second and thirty-third out of thirty-three schools in achievement on nationally standardized tests. By the time we left those schools, they were tied for the third and fourth highest levels of achievement in the city, a year above grade level in one school, and seven months above grade level in the other. They had the best attendance in the city, and there were no serious behavior problems.

What we found initially in those schools was chaos and apathy. When we go into such settings we have a tendency to blame. We blame the teacher, the union, the parents. We blame everyone involved. What we discovered was that teachers, the union, the parents, the custodian, and all of those people wanted to succeed, but they were in an environment in which they couldn't succeed. They couldn't succeed because the community of the past no longer existed to support the development of the children. The family support of the children was not there. I would say, as a way of stating it, that the kitchen table was gone. Families didn't sit around and organize their lives—think, reflect, and transmit values—like in the past.

The school remained a cognition factory where information was passed on. Some got it and others did not. The former were thought to be smart and the others not. That worked all right until the 1960s and 1970s because we could sweep everybody who was undereducated into an economy that did not require an education and they could take care of all their adult tasks and responsibilities and be okay. But that is no longer so. We were dealing with children who were underdeveloped, who needed to have experiences in which there was support for their development. Yet the staff, through no fault of their own, were not prepared to support the development of the children. What we did was create a community in school that supported development.

I am delighted that Mrs. Clinton is coming to mark our thirtieth anniversary next week. That is remarkable in that on the second day of our program I didn't think we were going to make it to the end of the week. We made it with twenty-nine years to spare.

What we did was put the kitchen table of the home into the school program. We begged those parents who came to throw us out to give us a chance. We created a governance and management team that was made up of parents, teachers, and administrators. They became the organizing, value-setting, skill-teaching mechanism within the program. That governance and management team developed a comprehensive school plan, staff development, assessment, and modification on an ongoing basis so that the school could keep changing and improving. There was a parents program that supported the program of the governance and management team. There was a school support team, we called it the mental health team at the time, that dealt with overall conditions in the school and made it a child-support place.

Most importantly, I think, was a change in the attitude and the climate and the way we understood and went about doing things. We developed three guiding principles. The first we called "no fault." We stopped pointing the finger of blame, and we asked, How do we solve this problem? In some ways, that's what I hear us doing and about to do now. We don't want to know the IQ score. We want to know what kind of conditions to create to make the most of what we have. That is the way the no-fault principle works; the emphasis is not on who is to blame but on how to solve the problem.

The second principle is consensus. Consensus means that decisions are made by common agreement rather than by voting. Decisions are based on what's good for the children, not what's good for the parents, teachers, or administrators, but what's good and necessary for the children to function well. The third principle is working in collaboration rather than paralyzing the principal on the one hand or the governance group being ignored on the other. Again, the three principles are no-fault, consensus, and collaboration.

Let me give you two examples of how it worked. We had a child who on a Friday was in rural North Carolina, a small, tight-knit, warm community, supported by his friends, his neighbors, and his family. An aunt from New Haven brought him to live with her. He was brought to King School on the following Monday. The principal took him directly to the classroom. The teacher had had three transfers the week before, and she was frustrated by all of this turnover and confusion. She nodded her head in frustration, and the youngster, eight years of age, looked at her and perceived rejection. Frightened, he panicked, kicked the teacher in the leg, and ran out.

We thought that was a fairly healthy response for an eight-year-old. But that's the kind of response that gets a child sent to the principal, punished, and sent back. Somebody laughs, he punches him in the mouth, he goes back to the principal, and it goes around and around and around, until he is labeled disturbed, and then he is sent off to somebody like me to have his head "fixed."

Creating the Climate and Conditions . . .

Our mental health team had a discussion with the staff. We asked them what it might be like to be eight years of age and have your entire support system removed and to find yourself in a strange place. Everybody began to think about that and about what could be done in the classroom to help with his transition. Suggestions included things like put up "Welcome, Johnnie" signs and assign him to some youngster who is very competent, capable, and well liked in the classroom to help him be accepted in that group. We called on the creativity of the teachers. We did not tell them what they had to do. We presented the problem and had them think about what they could do. Teachers come up with ideas very, very well.

> You don't take children and dump them into strange classrooms. You give them an orientation.

How do you change your school and make it a child-centered, friendly place for children? First, you don't take children and dump them into strange classrooms. You give them an orientation. You show them what they can do if they have a problem. You do whatever is reasonable and possible to help them make it in school. That is what happened with this transfer student and many more children. They made it because we began to think differently about children: how to support their functioning in that system and how that promotes their social development, behavior, and academic performance.

A second example: We had a child who for seven months did not look at or smile at the teacher. She had been traumatized by adults and didn't trust them. At the end of seven months, with a predictable, caring, responsible teacher, she finally looked up and smiled. The teacher was devastated, because in two more months she would have to pass that child on. She wouldn't be able to build on the positive relationship that was emerging. She went back to the teachers' lounge and expressed her concern. We held a mental health meeting, and we talked about the discontinuity in the lives of so many low-income children. (Many children across the socioeconomic spectrum now have discontinuity in their lives.) We talked about what we could do to promote continuity in the school. We worked out a program of keeping children with the same teacher for two years. Some children who made no academic gain the first year caught up to grade level or better. Some even made two years or more of academic gain in the second year. In short, all over the place, wherever there was a problem, we worked together as a school, as a team, to address the needs of the children. We modified the school to support the development and functioning of each child so that each child could make it in the school. In this way, we reduced many, many of the behavioral problems in that school. We went from forty-three major referrals of behavior problems in one school in the first year to three in the second.

> The teachers no longer believed that they were teaching people who were destined to become the dregs of the earth.

At that point, we began to think about children and how they learn and grow. We thought about how they grow along different developmental pathways—six that are critically important: physical, social-interactive, psycho-emotional, moral-ethical, linguistic, and intellectual-cognitive. We began to think about how all of our work supports development along those pathways, or doesn't.

We delayed deep involvement in this work until very recently. But we are picking it up again. We delayed because at that point people were still saying very loudly that low-income children can't learn, that what happened in school didn't matter. We felt it was very important to go out and create enough good schools where low-income children did learn rather than to go deeply into understanding the process. The fact that low-income children can learn has, and is, being established, and oddly enough, through an approach that I think is wrong. High stakes accountability—loss of job if test scores don't go up—does not get at the real problem. It forces us to teach to the test. But what is implicit in this approach is the expectation that children will be able to learn. But at any rate, providing evidence that low-income children can learn was our past concern and we didn't go deeply into integrating the developmental pathways into teaching and learning. We are now working on that.

Another approach we took in the past is very important. What we did was develop a program that would provide low-income children with the same kinds of experiences that middle-income children receive simply by growing up with their parents. We are renewing in a modified way this program that we called the Social Skills Curriculum for Inner City Children. We think of the school as a venue, along with the home and the parents, for the support and development of children. By systematically playing the role of a developmental venue, schools can overcome the underdevelopment of children.

Many low-income families have either never been connected to the mainstream or have been marginally involved. A good part of what we need to be doing in schools is to connect or reconnect low-income children to mainstream activities. Because of everything that we want adults to be able to do, we need to start having little children practice from the very beginning.

When we started work on the curriculum, we did not tell the parents "We want you to develop a social skills curriculum." What we asked was "What do you want for your children?" They wanted the same thing that every one of us in this room wants for our children. We then asked, "What kind of experiences would your children need to be able to carry out these activities?" Together, we thought about it and decided they would need activities in politics and government, business and economics, health and nutrition, spiritual and leisure time activities. Then we developed a program in each of these areas that allowed the integration of the basic academic skills, the social skills, and an appreciation of the arts.

When we started this social skills curriculum, there was a mayoral contest going on in the city. The children wrote letters inviting the candidates to come and speak to them, and sent thank-you notes after their visit. The parents took money from their activities and rented a bus, and with the teachers took the children through the town. They had discussions about the relationship of government to the conditions that they observed in the city. The children came back and wrote about it in language arts and social science classes.

The children put on a dance and drama program and hosted the event. They learned all the skills associated with being the hosts. These were all of the things that I learned at home with my parents and that most middle-income children learn at home with their parents. All of these activities created an excitement in the school. The teachers no longer believed that they were teaching people who were destined to become the dregs of the earth. They began to see bright, able young people. For example, a young man who stood up and spoke to an audience in an articulate way with great presence had not been a good student. Staff began to see the children in very different ways because the curriculum allowed more than a single way to perform.

An activity called "The Life and Times of Jackie Robinson" was developed as part of this project. The staff prepared to take the children to an exhibit in New York about Jackie Robinson. The academic program was centered around his life and times: what was going on in America at the time of Jackie Robinson and what his experience represented. Many such experiences turned those schools into very exciting places. We experienced the first significant jump in academic achievement after these schools turned into very exciting places.

We were not doing anything magical. We helped underdeveloped children from marginalized families catch up and began the process of connecting them to the mainstream society. We helped them and their teachers develop a future orientation. Their parents were involved in a way that avoided the conflict between their own family and social network, and mainstream institutions and culture. There is a natural conflict for children who grow up in low-income environments. We ask them to succeed in school and in the workplace in ways that their own parents had often not succeeded. But by having their parents involved in planning all of these activities and working through them, that gave students and staff the go-ahead signal.

I wish I could tell you that all of the schools we have worked with—almost 700 in 26 different states—just jumped up and performed in the same way as those two initial schools. Some have, but far too many have not performed in that way. I estimate that about a third have made significant improvement, a third have made some improvement, and a third have made no improvement. You cannot get the kind of improvement the country needs in environments where there is huge turnover, where people play political, economic, and social games of one kind or another, where there is a simple lack of sensitivity, where there is a deep-seated belief that these children cannot learn, where there is inadequate investment in teacher and administrative preparation.

One school in Virginia using our model went from twenty-fourth in achievement to first, ahead of the middle-income school. The central office was suspicious and they sent people out to retest the children. They did slightly better the second time than they did the first. Another school, thirty-fourth in New Jersey, went from thirty-fourth to first. They created a climate of trust and collaboration to the point where the teachers were really willing to take the math test that the children took. The teachers didn't do very well so the principal, previously a math supervisor, tutored the teachers. These low-income eighth-grade students soared to within 0.3 of a point of their affluent counterparts. This means that the children can.

The teachers, through no fault of their own, weren't adequately prepared. It wasn't their fault. It was the fault of our national education system. If we want a worldclass tennis team, wouldn't we make certain that the coaches know how to play and to teach tennis?

These conditions must change. We know that the children can learn. We know that school staffs start out eager and willing to learn and perform at a high level. We must arrive at a consensus and develop the political

> I am not convinced that everybody wants low-income children to achieve.

pressure to make the system change so that our children, all of our children, will have an opportunity to learn at the needed level. We must insist on the training, the selection, support, and the time to make these changes in the schools.

The new directions that we are going in—vouchers, charters, privatization, and all of those things—are really not the answer. Those models are basically economic and political. They are not developmental. But unless we pay attention to the development of children—train people and create programs that can support it—we're not going to improve our system of education.

Let me stop on that point. I am not convinced that everybody wants low-income children to achieve. We have a good idea what to do and how to do it, but we seem to lack the will. Therefore, in addition to creating ways to change schools, we've got to create the will to make certain that all our children achieve at a high level. The two schools that changed dramatically in 1996 and 1997 received limited news reports. There was a flurry of reports when they thought there might be cheating in one. When it was found out that the schools weren't cheating, the news interest ended. Unusually high achievement among low-income students would seem to deserve much inquiry.

Not only were the newspapers not interested, there has not been a researcher in asking questions about what went on in those schools. This suggests to me that the will is not there. We have got to work to create the will. All of us—not me, not the parents, but everybody in this room and everybody concerned about the future of this country—must do so because we cannot have a society where we have large numbers of people who are educated and doing well, and large numbers of people who are denied an education and who are not doing well. If we do that, all of us will pay, and there is no need for it.

We can create a country that will survive and thrive in the twenty-first century if we do the right thing.

Thank you very much.

NOTES

1.   Ogbu, J. (1986). The consequences of the American caste system. In U. Neisser (Ed.), *The school achievement of minority children: New perspectives* (pp. 19–56). Hillsdale, NJ: Erlbaum.

2.   Steele, C. M. (1997). A threat in the air. *American Psychologist* 52, 6: 613–629.

3.   Renzulli, J. (1986). The three ring conception of giftedness: A developmental model for creative productivity. In J. S. Renzulli and S. M. Reis (Eds.), *The triad reader* (pp. 2–19). Mansfield Center, CT: Creative Learning Press.

4.   Goldman, D. P. (1995). *Emotional intelligence: Why it can matter more than IQ.* New York: Bantam Books.

5.   Hart, B., and T. D. Risley. (1992). American parenting of language-learning children: Persisting differences in family-child interactions observed in natural home environments. *Developmental Psychology* 28, 6: 1096–1105.

6.   Mills, B. C., A. Stevens, and V. R. Weidner. (1989). Effects of maternal child-rearing practices on school readiness and achievement of young children. ERIC Document ED 329337.

7.   Beckwith, L., and A. Parmelee. (1986). EEG patterns of preterm infants, home environment, and later IQ. *Child Development* 57: 777–789.

8.   Pianta, R. C., and B. Egeland. (1994). Predictors of instability in children's mental test performance at 24, 48, and 96 months. *Intelligence* 18, 2: 145–163.

9.   Lyons-Ruth, K., D. Zoll, D. Connell, and H. Grunebaum. (1986). The depressed mother and her one-year-old infant: Environment, interaction, attachment and infant development. *New Directions for Child Development* 34: 61–82.

10. Hart, B., and T. R. Risley. (1992). American parenting of language-learning children: Persisting differences in family-child interactions observed in natural home environments. *Developmental Psychology* 28, 6: 1096–1105.

11. Gottfried, A. W. (1984). Home environment and early cognitive development integration, meta-analyses, and conclusions. In A. W. Gottfried (Ed.), *Home environment and early cognitive development: Longitudinal research* (pp. 329–342). San Diego, CA: Academic Press.

12. Olszewski, P., M. J. Kulieke, and T. Buescher. (1987). The influence of the environment on the development of talent: A literature review. *Journal for the Education of the Gifted* 11, 1: 6–28.

13. Ibid.

Authors

Richard Allington is Professor and Senior Research Scientist for the University of New York at Albany. He is the past president of the National Reading Conference and a member of the board of directors of the International Reading Association. Author of over 100 articles and several books, Dr. Allington currently directs a federally funded research project studying exemplary elementary school teachers.

John Barell is Professor of Curriculum and Teaching and Adjunct Professor of English Literature at Montclair State University. Past Director of the Association for Supervision and Curriculum Development (ASCD) Network on Teaching Thinking, he currently is conducting pilot experiences in field-based teacher education in the development of a Professional Development High School. He is continuing research on how to help students ask better questions in the classroom.

James Bellanca is internationally known as an expert in adult learning and motivation and is the president of SkyLight Training and Publishing Inc. A seasoned consultant, trainer, author, and professional development designer, Bellanca specializes in the practical applications of research-based teaching methods and school management techniques. He has authored and coauthored more than a dozen books and has developed training programs for site-based management. His works include *Active Learning Handbook for the Multiple Intelligences Classroom* and *Designing Professional Development for Change.*

Meir Ben-Hur is a consultant and facilitator trained in the practices of mediated learning and learning potential assessment. He has over twenty years of classroom teaching experience, ranging from teaching high school mathematics to college and university professorships. A recipient of Professor Reuven Feuerstein's training, he has worked as a trainer with Feuerstein all over the world.

John Brockman is a literary and software agent and science author. He founded The Reality Club, a group of scientists who contemplate intellectual issues, and is the president of Edge Foundation, Inc., which provides a Web site that is an interactive forum for the sharing and expression of ideas among scientists and others. He is the author and editor of nineteen books, including *By the Late John Brockman* and *The Third Culture: Beyond the Scientific Revolution.*

Kay Burke is the senior vice president of academics at SkyLight Training and Publishing Inc. She has presented over 600 keynote addresses, seminars, and courses throughout the United States, Canada, and Australia and trains educators in classroom management, authentic assessment, student portfolios, and professional portfolios. She is the author of numerous books, including *The Mindful School: How to Assess Authentic Learning* and *Designing Professional Portfolios for Change.*

James Comer has worked to bring inner city, low-income elementary schools from chaos to stability and academic and social achievement by creating the School Development Program. As Associate Dean of the Yale School of Medicine, he oversees student evaluation and progress and is an internationally recognized expert in child development. Dr. Comer is a noted author and columnist and serves as a consulting editor for *Parents* magazine. He is the recipient of some forty honorary degrees, numerous awards and honors, and has served as a consultant to the Children's Television Workshop, which produces programs such as *Sesame Street.*

Eric Cooper is Executive Director of the National Urban Alliance for Effective Education at Columbia University. He also is Adjunct Professor in the Education Administration Department of Teachers College, Columbia University. Prior to these positions, Dr. Cooper was Vice President for Inservice Training and Telecommunications in the Simon and Schuster Education Group. He has worked with the

College Board as the Associate Director of Program Development and has been an administrative assistant in the Office of Curriculum for Boston Public Schools. He has been a director of a treatment center for emotionally disturbed students, a teacher, a researcher, a counselor, and a Washington Fellow.

Arthur Costa is Emeritus Professor of Education at California State University, Sacramento, and Co-Director of the Institute for Intelligent Behavior in Berkeley, California. He has served as a classroom teacher, a curriculum consultant, an assistant superintendent for instruction, and as Director of Educational Programs for the National Aeronautics and Space Administration. He has made presentations and conducted workshops in all fifty states as well as Mexico, Central America, South America, Canada, Australia, New Zealand, Africa, Europe, Asia, and the Islands of the South Pacific. Active in many professional organizations, Dr. Costa served as the president of the California Association for Supervision and Curriculum Development and was the national president of the Association for Supervision and Curriculum Development from 1988 to 1989.

Linda Darling-Hammond is Charles E. Ducomman Professor in the Teaching and Teacher Education at Stanford, California. She also is Executive Director of the National Commission for Teaching and America's Future. She is actively engaged in research, teaching, and policy work on issues of school restructuring, teacher education reform, and the enhancement of educational equity.

Elliot Eisner is Professor of Education and Art at Stanford University. He was trained as a painter at the School of the Art Institute of Chicago and later studied design at Illinois Institute of Technology's Institute of Design. He works in three fields: arts education, curriculum studies, and educational evaluation. Professor Eisner's research interests focus on the development of aesthetic intelligence and on the use of critical methods from the arts for studying and improving educational practice. He has lectured on these topics throughout the world and is widely considered one of the leading scholars in arts education today.

Robin Fogarty, a leading proponent of the thoughtful classroom, trains teachers throughout the world in cognitive strategies and cooperative interaction. She has taught all levels from kindergarten to college, served as an administrator, and consulted with state departments and ministries of education in the United States, Russia, Canada, Australia, New Zealand, and the Netherlands. Dr. Fogarty is the author, coauthor, and editor of numerous publications in professional education.

Howard Gardner is the John H. and Elisabeth A. Hobbs Professor of Cognition and Education at the Harvard Graduate School of Education, Adjunct Professor of Neurology at the Boston University School of Medicine, and Co-Director of Harvard Project Zero. The recipient of many honors, including a MacArthur Prize Fellowship, Gardner is the author of eighteen books and several hundred articles.

Herbert Ginsburg is the Jacob H. Schiff Professor of Psychology and Education at Teachers College, Columbia University. For the past thirty years, he has conducted research on cognitive development, particularly the development of children's mathematical thinking, both within the United States and in various countries around the world. He has used the knowledge gained from research to develop several kinds of educational applications, including mathematics textbooks and video workshops designed to enhance teachers' understandings of children's learning of mathematics. He is now studying preschoolers' mathematical thinking.

John I. Goodlad is Professor Emeritus and Co-Director of the Center for Educational Renewal at the University of Washington and President of the Institute for Educational Inquiry in Seattle. The educational issues that most interest him are those he encountered early on, first as a pupil in schools, then as a teacher in a one-room school, and later as a teacher/inquirer in other schools, colleges, and universities.

Maxine Greene is Professor Emirata at Teachers College, Columbia University, where she has taught courses in aesthetics, educational philosophy, the arts and American education, and social philosophy. As the founder and director of the Center for Social Imagination, the Arts and Education, she has long served as a leader in the effort to infuse education with views of imaginative possibility.

Clifford Hill is Arthur I. Gates Professor of Language and Education at Columbia University, where he also chairs the Department of International and Transcultural Studies at Teacher College. In addition, he directs the Program in African Languages in the School of International and Public Affairs.

Jonathan Kozol moved in 1964 from Harvard Square to a poor black neighborhood of Boston and became a fourth grade teacher in the Boston public schools. He has devoted the subsequent three decades of his life to issues of education and social justice in America. He is the author of numerous books, including the award-winning *Death at an Early Age, Homeless Families in America,* and *Savage Inequalities.* His most recent book, *Amazing Grace: The Lives of Children and the Conscience of a Nation,* describes his visits to the South Bronx of New York, the poorest congressional district in America.

Daniel Levine is Professor of Education at the University of Nebraska at Omaha. He has worked in urban education for the past forty years. He has served on the boards of the National Urban Alliance for Effective Education and the Phi Delta Kappa Center for Effective Schools. He is the author of several textbooks and numerous articles on educational practice and research.

Rayna Levine recently retired as Principal of William Volker Applied Learning Magnet School, a nationally recognized Blue Ribbon school in Kansas City, Missouri. She has worked in urban education and public schools for more than twenty years as a teacher, a coordinator of instruction, a principal, and in central administration as Director of Elementary Schools. She has coauthored a text and several articles.

Valerie Hastings Moye is a consultant and staff member of SkyLight Training and Publishing's academic department. She is an educator whose professional training experience spans curriculum and instruction, assessment, and school restructuring. Moye has served as a teacher, assistant principal, central office administrator, adjunct professor, and staff member of the Center for Gifted Education, at the College of William and Mary. At the Virginia Department of Education, Valerie provided leadership, technical assistance, and professional development for school restructuring initiatives.

Barbara Z. Presseisen is Chief Education Officer and Vice President of Education of Nobel Learning Communities, Inc., a network of private schools across the United States. She has served as both a director and consultant for several educational organizations and has trained educators in critical thinking, Holocaust education, and reasoning in teaching history and social studies. Dr. Presseisen taught at Swathmore College and Temple University and is the author and editor of numerous publications and article on educational theory and practice.

Joseph Renzulli is Professor of Gifted Education and Talent Development at the Neag Center, University of Connecticut, where he also serves as Director of the National Research Center of Gifted and Talented. He has served on numerous editorial boards in the field of gifted education and has served as a senior research associate for the White House Task Force on Education for the Gifted and Talented.

Barak Rosenshine is Professor of Educational Psychology at University of Illinois at Urbana. His areas of research focus on effective classroom programs, teaching cognitive strategies, and pragmatic approaches to instruction.

Theodore Sizer is Director of the Coalition of Essential Schools at Brown University. He has worked extensively with secondary education to reshape the American high school so that academic success can be achieved by all students. The author of numerous seminal studies in education and history, Dr. Sizer served as Dean of Harvard's Graduate School of Education.

Robert Spillane is Regional Education Officer for Europe and the Newly Independent State of the former Soviet Union in the Office of Overseas Schools, U.S. Department of State. He was New York State Deputy and Superintendent of Boston schools from 1981 to 1985, and in Fairfax, Virginia, from 1985 to 1997. Dr. Spillane, often cited as an exemplary school administrator, developed an effective teacher evaluation program, initiated site-based management and accountability measures, and developed strong support for education in the larger business community.

Robert Sternberg is IBM Professor of Psychology and Education in the Department of Psychology at Yale University. Sternberg is the author of more than 650 publications. He has won numerous awards from various educational organizations and is Fellow of the American Academy of the Arts and Sciences, American Association for the Advancement of Sciences, American Psychological Association, and American Psychological Society.

Dorothy Strickland is State of New Jersey Professor of Reading at Rutgers University. A former classroom teacher, she is past president of the International Reading Association (IRA). She is active in the National Council of Teachers of English (NCTE) and the National Association for the Education of Young Children. She received IRA's Outstanding Teacher Educator of Reading Award and is the current president of the IRA Reading Hall of Fame. She received the 1994 NCTE Rewey Belle Inglis Award for Outstanding Women in the Teaching of English and the 1998 Outstanding Educator of Language Arts.

Joyce VanTassel-Baska is the Jody and Layton Smith Professor of Education and Director for the Center for Gifted Education at the College of William and Mary. Her research focuses on studies in curriculum and instructional interventions with gifted students and work on variables associated with the development of talent, especially for disadvantaged learners. She is the past president of CEC-TAG and is on the board of directors for the National Association for Gifted Children (NAGC). She is the author of eight books and over 200 articles and book chapters. She received the Distinguished Scholar Award from NAGC in 1997.

Acknowledgments

Grateful acknowlegment is made to the following authors and agents for their permission to reprint copyrighted materials.

SECTION 1

Theodore R. Sizer for "On the Habit of Informed Skepticism." © 1998 by Theodore R. Sizer. Reprinted with permission.

John I. Goodlad and Phi Delta Kappa for "Narratives of the Educative Surround." A portion of this article appeared in *Phi Delta Kappan*, May 1998, pp 670–671. © 1998 by John I. Goodlad. All rights reserved. Reprinted with permisssion.

Howard Gardner for "Truth, Beauty, and Goodness: Education for All Human Beings: John Brockman interviews Howard Gardner." Adapted from "Truth, Beauty, and Goodness: Education for All Human Beings, John Brockman interview Howard Gardner," which appeared on Edge Foundation's Third Culture web site at <http://www.edgeorg/3rd_culture/gardner/>, September 24, 1997. Reprinted with permission.

Maxine Greene for "Art, Imagination, and School Renewal." © 1998 by Maxine Greene. Reprinted with permission.

Robert J. Sternberg for "Schools Should Nurture Wisdom." © 1998 by Robert J. Sternberg. Reprinted with permission.

Dorothy S. Strickland for "Differentiating Instruction in the Classroom: Tapping into the Intelligence of Every Learner." © 1998 by Dorothy S. Strickland. Reprinted with permission.

Eric J. Cooper and Daniel U. Levine for "Teaching for Intelligence: Parameters for Change." © 1998 by Eric J. Cooper and Daniel U. Levine. Reprinted with permission.

Daniel U. Levine and Rayna F. Levine for "Considerations in Introducing Instructional Interventions." © 1998 by Daniel U. Levine and Rayna F. Levine. Reprinted with permission.

SECTION 4

Jonathan Kozol for "Working with Kids Like Mario." © 1998 by Jonathan Kozol. Reprinted with permission.

Herbert P. Ginsburg for "Challenging Preschool Education: Meeting the Intellectual Needs of All Children." © 1998 by Herbert P. Ginsburg. Reprinted with permission.

Joyce VanTassel-Baska for "Infusing Higher Order Thinking into Science and Language Arts." © 1998 by Joyce VanTassel-Baska. Reprinted with permission.

Joseph S. Renzulli for "A Practical Approach for Developing the Gifts and Talents of All Students." © 1998 by Joseph S. Renzulli. Reprinted with permission.

James P. Comer for "Creating the Climate and Conditions for Children to Learn." © 1998 by James P. Comer. Reprinted with permission.

Index

There are
one-story intellects,
two-story intellects, and three-story
intellects with skylights. All fact collectors, who
have no aim beyond their facts, are one-story men. Two-story men
compare, reason, generalize, using the labors of the fact collectors as
well as their own. Three-story men idealize, imagine,
predict—their best illumination comes from
above, through the skylight.

—Oliver Wendell

Holmes